Speculations on Speculation

Theories of Science Fiction

Edited by
James Gunn
Matthew Candelaria

THE SCARECROW PRESS, INC.
Lanham, Maryland • Toronto • Oxford
2005

SCARECROW PRESS, INC.

Published in the United States of America
by Scarecrow Press, Inc.
A wholly owned subsidiary of
The Rowman & Littlefield Publishing Group, Inc.
4501 Forbes Boulevard, Suite 200, Lanham, Maryland 20706
www.scarecrowpress.com

PO Box 317
Oxford
OX2 9RU, UK

British Library Cataloguing in Publication Information Available

Library of Congress Cataloging-in-Publication Data

Speculations on speculation : theories of science fiction / edited by James Gunn,
Matthew Candelaria.
    p. cm.
  Includes bibliographical references and index.
  ISBN 0-8108-4902-X (pbk. : alk. paper)
  1. Science fiction—History and criticism. I. Gunn, James E., 1923– II.
Candelaria, Matthew, 1973–
  PN3433.5.S64 2005
  809.3'8762—dc22

                                                              2004013012

∞™ The paper used in this publication meets the minimum requirements of
American National Standard for Information Sciences—Permanence of Paper
for Printed Library Materials, ANSI/NISO Z39.48-1992.
Manufactured in the United States of America.

~

Contents

~

Acknowledgments

Aldiss, Brian W., with David Wingrove. "Introduction" and "On the Origin of Species" in *Trillion Year Spree*. Brian W. Aldiss, 1973, 1986. Reprinted with permission from the author.

Berman, Judith. "Science Fiction without the Future." Judith Berman, 2001. Originally published in *The New York Review of Science Fiction*, May 2001. Reprinted with permission from the author.

Delany, Samuel. "Science Fiction and 'Literature'—or, The Conscience of the King." Author, 1979. "Some Presumptuous Approaches to Science Fiction" in *Starboard Wine*. Author, 1968. Reprinted with permission from the author and his agents Henry Morrison, Inc.

Greenland, Colin. "The 'Field' and the 'Wave': The History of *New Worlds*" from *The Entropy Exhibition*. Author, 1983. Reprinted with permission from the author.

Gunn, James. "Toward a Definition of Science Fiction."

———. "The Readers of Hard Science Fiction."

———. "Touchstones."

Hartwell, David. "The Golden Age of Science Fiction Is Twelve" in *Age of Wonders*. Author, 1984. Reprinted with permission from the author and his literary agent, Susan Ann Protter. All rights reserved.

Hartwell, David G., and Kathryn Cramer. "Space Opera Redefined" Authors, 2003. Reprinted with permission from the authors and their literary agent, Susan Ann Protter. All rights reserved.

Kelly, Jim. "Slipstream." Author, 2003. First appeared as "Slipstream" and "Genre" in *Isaac Asimov's Science Fiction Magazine*. Reprinted with permission from the author.

Ketterer, David. "The Apocalyptic Imagination, Science Fiction, and American Literature" from *New Worlds for Old*. Author, 1974. Reprinted with permission from the author and Doubleday Anchor Books.

Kincaid, Paul. "On the Origins of Genre." *Extrapolations* (Winter 2003). All rights reserved.

Le Guin, Ursula K. "Science Fiction and Mrs. Brown" from *The Language of the Night* © 1976 by Ursula K. Le Guin. First appeared in *Science Fiction at Large*. Reprinted by permission of the author and the author's agents, the Virginia Kidd Agency, Inc.

Malzberg, Barry. "The Number of the Beast," "I Could Have Been a Contender, Part One," "Some Notes toward the True and the Terrible," and "Wrong Rabbit" in *The Engines of the Night*. Author, 1982. Reprinted with permission from the author.

Panshin, Alexei and Cory. "Science Fiction and the Dimension of Myth."

Scholes, Robert. "The Roots of Science Fiction" and Afterword from *Structural Fabulation*. University of Notre Dame Press, 1975. Reprinted with permission from NDUP and the author.

Suvin, Darko. "Estrangement and Cognition" and "SF and the Genealogical Jungle" from *Metamorphoses of Science Fiction*. Yale University Press, 1979. Reprinted with permission from the author.

Swanwick, Michael. "A User's Guide to the Postmoderns." . First appeared in *Isaac Asimov's Science Fiction Magazine* (1986). Reprinted with permission from the author.

Wolfe, Gary K. "Coming to Terms."

~

Introduction

James Gunn

Defining science fiction is like measuring the properties of an electron: you may think you're measuring a solid object, but it's really a wispy cloud. Even its name leads to disputes. Jules Verne called what he wrote *voyages extraordinaires*, and H. G. Wells called it *scientific romance*. When Hugo Gernsback created the first true science-fiction magazine in 1926, he called what he intended to publish *scientifiction*, and he came up with the phrase "science fiction" only after he lost control of *Amazing Stories* in 1929 and created *Science Wonder Stories*. Robert A. Heinlein suggested that *speculative fiction* was a more appropriate designation. Abbreviations such as "sci-fi" (liked by the media but not by most fans, who use it to describe bad science-fiction movies) and "SF" (preferred by most readers) further complicate the issue.

SF's beginnings in the pulp magazines added to the confusion. While readers understood what the magazines offered, some of them put out a different mixture, combining SF with fantasy or science-fantasy or horror. And its origins in the pulp magazines made the issue seem petty, except to fans. Academic scrutiny was slow in developing, even though some scholars and teachers recognized that some science fiction was written with skill and intelligence and even, occasionally, grace. But what were writers writing, what were publishers publishing, and what were readers reading?

Some students of the genre, such as Samuel R. Delany, insist that, like poetry, science fiction is impossible to define. Others have pointed out that genre titles are booksellers' conveniences, telling them where to put books when they arrive—and equally, of course, book buyers' conveniences, telling them where to look for the books they want when they go shopping. But what are they looking for when they look for science fiction? My short definition: the literature of change. Brian W. Aldiss: hubris clobbered by nemesis. John W. Campbell: science fiction is what science-fiction editors publish. The fall-back position, epitomized by Damon Knight when he said, "Science fiction is what we mean when we point at it," is that we know it when we see it. And even if we can't define it to everyone's satisfaction, the effort helps us clarify our thinking about the genre. In lieu of a definition that everyone—or even a majority—can agree upon, this volume attempts to bring together a variety of views about science fiction by influential scholars and writers that will allow readers and students to think about the question and maybe come to their own conclusions.

The attempt to define science fiction, moreover, is like the attempt to measure electrons in another way: you can determine the location but you can't also determine the momentum—every attempt changes one or the other. From the evidence gathered in this volume, what is and isn't science fiction—and the way in which the consensus view has changed over the years—has been a fertile topic. As readers we make those distinctions, preferring one kind of narrative over another—science fiction over fantasy, for instance, and both over what fans call "mundane fiction"—and identify what we prefer by title and cover art or blurb, or, if necessary, by reading a few paragraphs, or, preferably, by having a publisher whose judgments we respect do the job for us by putting a label on the book. Sometimes when we aren't sure of our identification of the genre, we seek more books by an author we have enjoyed and move on tentatively to other authors and titles, and even genres until we at last recognize that we are fans of a particular kind of narrative. Amazon.com has tried to systematize this process by its listing of other titles under the heading: "Readers who purchase titles by this author also purchased titles by these authors. . . ." Computers may eventually do the job for us.

The difficulty with identifying science fiction—and proceeding from that to definition—is that science fiction isn't just one thing. It has no recognizable action, like the murder mystery, or recognizable milieu, like the western, or recognizable relationship, like the romance. It is about the future—except when it is about the past or the present. It can incorporate all the other genres: one can have a science-fiction detective story, a science-fiction western, a science-fiction romance, and, most commonly, a science-fiction adventure story. It is best characterized, as I point out in "The World View of Science Fiction," by an attitude, and even that is hard to define. It is the literature of change, the literature of anticipation, the literature of the human species, the literature of speculation, and more. And because it is the literature of change it is continually changing; if it remained constant, it would no longer be science fiction. For that reason some of the essays that follow are like snapshots. That's what science fiction looked like at that moment.

All that, of course, is what makes science fiction fascinating to read and to discuss. And because the people who have speculated about it are interesting—and even special—thinkers, they have written entertainingly about their speculations. I have tried these speculations out in two graduate seminars and I can testify to the fact that they produced vigorous discussion as well as disagreement. That's okay. Uncertainty is a way of life.

~

Before We Begin: Some Notes on Early SF Criticism

Matthew Candelaria

No anthology could hope to present all that has been meaningfully said about any given subject, let alone one as broad, controversial, and diverse as science fiction. However, this anthology assembles many of the most important voices of mature science-fiction criticism and, therefore, needs only the smallest of caveats.

What do I mean by "mature" science-fiction criticism? I do not mean to suggest a contrast with immature or childish criticism, and perhaps my point would be clearer if I called it "ripe" science-fiction criticism, which I would do, were it not for the fact that it sounds odd and carries a few unpleasant connotations. Nonetheless, if you will indulge the vegetable metaphor, I hope to make my meaning clear.

In order for a plant to produce fruit, it must go through a number of stages. First, there must be a seed, which sprouts into a seedling, and this seedling grows, producing a stem and leaves, perhaps even secondary growth, before producing a flower that then (in most plants) needs to be fertilized before the seed-bearing fruit can grow and ripen.

Science-fiction criticism has been around for almost as long as science fiction, and it has gone through a great deal of growth before finally producing its mature, ripe fruit. I won't belabor my metaphor by talking about which works were the seed and which the stem, leaves, etc., and which authors the busy little bees. Some people would find such a metaphorical flight to be amusing and illuminating (actually, I must confess to being one of them), and for them I reserve the pleasure of speculating at their leisure, but for most people it would seem silly and unnecessarily controversial. For us, the only thing that matters is the ripe fruit and what it says about the slight caveat needed for this anthology.

What represents ripeness in a genre? I submit that a genre is ripe when its practitioners rightly or wrongly cease to believe themselves isolated artists exploring heretofore unimagined ideas and begin believing that they are part of a coherent, continuous, and significant tradition of thought. Most people will believe that this happened for the genre of science fiction with the advent of Gernsback's *Amazing Stories*. Gernsback not only provided a forum for writers and fans interested in the newborn genre of scientifiction, he also put the genre in context with its literary antecedents and gave it a canon of recognizable founding masters. Through *Amazing Stories*, the genre became a ripe, if at times sour, fruit. The ripeness of a genre is a crucial concern, because it is only in a ripe genre that tropes, such as faster-than-light travel or galactic civilizations, can become conventions, building blocks toward more complex ideas. It is only in a ripe genre that ideological debates can take place. Unlike fruit, a genre does not begin to decay once it has grown ripe.

But when did this happen for the genre of science-fiction criticism? A comparison between two anthologies of essays will serve to demonstrate when this occurred. In 1953, *Modern Science Fiction: Its Meaning and Its Future*, edited by Reginald Bretnor, clearly presented itself as an originary text. Bretnor says the criticism that preceded his volume "is too widely scattered to be generally available, and too unorganized to present a comprehensive picture. Besides, much of it now is either obsolete or obsolescent" (ix). Therefore, he says, "it seemed better to me to start afresh" (x). He acknowledges that his "is not the first book to deal with science fiction," and cites Lloyd Arthur Eshbach's *Of Worlds Beyond*, and J. O. Bailey's *Pilgrims Through Space and Time*, but he still claims to be "the first general survey of science fiction against the background of the world today" (x). Furthermore, Bretnor takes care to stress that all the essays contained in his volume (with "one exception and a fraction"), are original. Bretnor saw no coherent body of science-fiction criticism from which to draw, and therefore sought to create one.

In contrast, editor Thomas D. Clareson begins the introduction to his 1971 anthology, *SF: The Other Side of Realism*, by citing the comments of Fred Pohl at the 1968 Modern Language Association's (MLA) Forum on Science Fiction. In fact, his entire introduction is dedicated to placing his volume in context with the criticism that had preceded it. And Clareson was in a great position to do that since he was at the time the editor of *Extrapolation*, the first journal devoted exclusively to science-fiction criticism. This placing of *The Other Side of Realism* signals that sometime during the interval from 1953 to 1971, science-fiction criticism ripened, and the caveat necessary for this anthology is that, for a number of reasons, we are not reproducing any of the key texts that helped this ripening take place.

Damon Knight's *In Search of Wonder* (1956) represents an important stage in the fruition of criticism. A collection of Knight's book reviews written from 1952 to 1955, this book may seem of dubious value for modern students of the genre because so much of the commentary is on very forgettable novels of the period, but in them Knight is making steps toward the first in-depth critical study of modern science fiction. The first essay of the collection puts forward the four critical principles under which Knight will operate throughout. His first principle is that "science fiction" is a misnomer, but, despite the existence of better labels, it is the one that he will use, and, rather than attempt to define the term precisely, readers should simply take it to mean what he points to when he says it (1). This practical solution is much referenced, but few accept it as the final word in defining the genre. His second principle is that criticism should not be written to promote books, which is the job of the "publisher's jacket blurb" (1). His third principle is that science fiction "is a field of literature worth taking seriously and that ordinary critical standards can be meaningfully applied to it" (1). As will be evident in the essays that follow, this is a controversial principle among science-fiction critics who often believe that science fiction should have either entirely or at least partially different standards from other literary "fields." His fourth principle is that negative reviews are far less detrimental to science fiction than the bad books about which they are written. By tearing apart the bad books, Knight sees himself as doing a service to the field, trying to make it live up to its complete potential. These are merely the introductory principles, and scattered throughout the reviews in this collection are a number of explicitly and implicitly stated opinions about the nature, function, and form of good science fiction. James Blish's *The Issue at Hand* (1964) and *More Issues at Hand* (1970) are also compilations of reviews that made a large impact at the time.

As in the formation of the genre proper, science fiction criticism's maturation was aided tremendously by the appearance of a periodical forum. *Extrapolation* was founded in 1959, originally printing papers presented at MLA's seminar on science fiction. In 1973, it also partnered itself with the Science Fiction Research Association. It continues to this day to print articles of serious criticism about science fiction. One of the greatest values of this critical organ is its lack of stringent editorial guidelines about subject matter, critical techniques, or approaches. Thus, it brings together a wide diversity of essays on many texts and from many different perspectives, making it distinct from the later *Science Fiction Studies* (1973), which publishes primarily "scholarly" texts and in its early days was criticized for taking a naively Marxist approach to the genre. Also during this time, the British journal *Foundation* (1972) appeared and remains to this day a unique critical voice, closer in form to *SFS* but in content more like *Extrapolation*.

Kingsley Amis' *New Maps of Hell* (1960) derives from a series of lectures he delivered at Princeton in the summer of 1959, and it retains from the lectures a charming conversational tone that makes it an entertaining read. Amis positions himself wisely, trying to appeal to people both within and without the science-fiction field. Through the story of his first encounter with science fiction at age twelve, he shows that he is not "that peculiarly irritating kind of person, the intellectual who takes a slumming holiday" (7) to discuss science fiction. He also assures his reader that he is not a member of the field proper that makes him free from its "discreditable provincialism of thought and . . . nervous or complacent reluctance to invoke ordinary critical standards" (8). In these lectures, Amis provides a brief history of the genre and some in-depth analysis of texts and themes as well as one of the clunkiest definitions of the genre ever forwarded: "Science fiction presents with verisimilitude the human effects of spectacular changes in our environment, changes either deliberately willed or involuntarily suffered"

(20). Amis never hesitates to invoke critical standards, never failing to let us know his attitude toward the texts under discussion and heaping a bit more scorn than praise. If we take the enduring nature of judgments to be a measure of their accuracy, then a great many of his evaluations are very good, such as, for example, his critical appraisal of Wells' work, dividing the earlier, more imaginative, and more successful work from the later utopias, which he says "give a soporific whiff of left-wing crankiness," although he, unlike some critics, would not exclude them from the science-fiction canon altogether. With its attention to the unconscious and sexuality, *New Maps of Hell* serves as an introduction to the 1960s as well as an introduction to science fiction, and it approaches the genre with a decidedly new wave slant.

H. Bruce Franklin's *Future Perfect* (1966) makes an interesting play to create science fiction as a significant category of literary production. His gambit has two main components: arguing for the special capacities of science fiction for representing some parts of the modern human experience, and arguing against the genrefication of science fiction. First, Franklin points out the co-development of science fiction and industrial society, and he claims that science fiction is uniquely suited to discussing the perils, problems, and promise that science and technology offer humanity. This part of Franklin's argument is almost universally accepted among science fiction critics, but his second part is not. Franklin argues that since it was not considered a separate category of literary production during the first century of its existence, and that most nineteenth-century writers wrote both science fiction and what is remembered as mainstream fiction, science fiction is not inherently a separate category of literary production. As part of this argument, Franklin reproduces and discusses the science-fiction production of a number of authors who are considered to be mainstream literary figures, including Hawthorne, Melville, and Twain. His basic argument is that "all fiction presumably seeks to represent some part of reality. . . . One may think of realistic fiction, historical fiction, science fiction, and fantasy as theoretically distinct strategies for describing what is real" (3). In this schema, "science fiction aims to represent what is real in terms of a credible hypothetical invention . . . extrapolated from . . . present reality" (3). This definition foretells schema like Darko Suvin's "cognitive estrangement" that seek to put science fiction in close relation to realistic fiction for purposes of making it equally worthy of serious consideration.

One final text worth noting here, which just barely squeaks in under the wire because its first chapter was published separately in 1971, is David Ketterer's *New Worlds for Old: The Apocalyptic Imagination, Science Fiction, and American Literature* (1974). This study makes two significant statements about the genre. Ketterer, like many critics, is unsatisfied with the inadequate label "science fiction," and though he continues to use the term, he subsumes the genre under the larger category of apocalyptic literature. According to his definition, "Apocalyptic literature is concerned with the creation of other worlds which exist, on the literal level, in a credible relationship (whether on the basis of rational extrapolation and analogy or of religious belief) with the 'real' world, thereby causing a metaphorical destruction of that 'real' world in the reader's head." Ketterer shows the spiritual dimensions of science fiction, exploring the development of science fiction within the Christian tradition. Ketterer stresses that the "New World" of science fiction seeks to supplant the current world, a statement very much in line with others in this anthology about the inherently subversive nature of science fiction. Ketterer's second major conclusion is that science fiction is one of, if not the central mode of American literature, and, at variance with critics like Delany and Gunn, he freely makes comparisons between science-fiction and non–science-fiction texts.

With the publication of these crucial texts, science-fiction criticism flourished from scattered pieces of unconnected notes, often repeating and restating one another, into a mature genre, and it is not coincidental that the Science Fiction Research Association was founded in 1970. It is the sad truth, however, that even this caveat needs a caveat. I have here highlighted what I believe to be the most important texts of modern science-fiction criticism during this period, but there are a few marginal texts that had I but world enough and time, I might also have included. First, there are the two pioneering books on the writing of science fiction: Eshbach's already-mentioned *Of Worlds Beyond* and L. Sprague de Camp's *Science Fiction Handbook*. Numerous surveys of fantastic voyages and utopias further reinforce the canon that some say anticipates modern science fiction, but in my opinion they are the last remnants of the flower, still hanging on, not the mature fruit of science-fiction criticism. A couple of single-author studies are worth noting as well. Bernard Bergonzi's *The Early H. G. Wells* (1961) is a valuable study of Wells' contribution to the origins of science fiction and is evidence of the genre's continued movement toward maturity, but I cannot help but feel that it and the spate of other Wells studies appearing at about the same time are also part of the clinging flower. However, Alexei Panshin's *Heinlein in Dimension* (1968) is a huge leap forward. Not only is it the first single-author study of a modern science-fiction writer—one whose craft flourished after the advent of the mature genre—but it approaches Heinlein's work with no more apology than anyone writing about a living, contemporary author would put forward. Panshin is not putting Heinlein's work on a pedestal, but through careful consideration and criticism of it, he proves that it, and comparable texts by other authors, rewards study and deserves attention.

Finally, it would be remiss of me to fail to mention the works of Sam Moskowitz during this period. *The Immortal Storm: A History of Science Fiction Fandom* (1954), *Explorers of the Infinite* (1963), and *Seekers of Tomorrow: Masters of Modern Science Fiction* (1966) are all valuable texts in their way. As the first text in the series suggests, these books are all written from the perspective of the science-fiction fan, and as such they are a little on the disorganized side, and, although they contain valuable information and insight, they lack the cohesion and seriousness of thought that characterizes the more mature works of SF criticism. *Seekers of Tomorrow*, for example, is primarily a collection of brief biographies and loose bibliographies of the major practitioners of the field from the 1930s to the 1960s interspersed with generous praise and occasional light criticism. In some ways, these texts, especially *The Immortal Storm*, come close to what Barry Malzberg called the "true unwritten history of science fiction," but for obvious reasons they fail to achieve that status.

The caveats all being made, let us sit in the shadow of the ripe fruit of science-fiction criticism and begin our speculations on speculation.

PART ONE

IDENTIFICATION

This section represents a kind of ruse. By calling it "Identification," we give the impression that the articles contained in it identify the subject at hand, science fiction. However, because that topic is the concern of this book as a whole, any such impression would be mistaken. In fact, most of the articles in this anthology address the difficulties in delimiting the field of science fiction. The very last article, Jim Kelly's "Slipstream," even goes so far as to demonstrate some of the benefits inherent in the uncertainties of definition, the desirbility of leaving room for play in our understanding.

Nonetheless, this section possesses a legitimate rationale. The essays here provide some of the most direct and useful definitions of the genre in the anthology. They raise many other issues, but all with an eye toward defining the genre and preparing readers for understanding the more detailed discussions to follow.

Darko Suvin's *Metamorphoses of Science Fiction* is probably the most rigorous and scholarly consideration of science fiction ever composed. In "Estrangement and Cognition," Suvin utilizes Russian formalism to argue very strongly for the existence of a non-naturalistic tradition in literature, dating from ancient times to the present. He explains the significance of this literary tradition and explores its premises and techniques.

Then, in a passage that is a surprising and singular pleasure to read, he places the label "science fiction" on this literary tradition. Like going through a long calculus derivation of a law that seems intuitively obvious, in Suvin's hands the passage contains the twin pleasures normally reserved for fiction: surprise and rightness. Drawing from a European critical tradition, Suvin puts forth a clear delineation of the field that he believes dismisses all significant uncertainties—a delineation that he will make even clearer in the selection in the next section.

Barry Malzberg's essay "The Number of the Beast" is the opposite of Suvin's in almost every way. Not only is Malzberg's prose flip and his tone exaggeratedly American, but he points again and again to the uncertainties in defining science fiction. He points to "the *Arrowsmith* problem," the difficulty of coming up with definitions of science fiction that include texts that readers know to be science fiction when they read them yet exclude texts that readers know are not. Ultimately, Malzberg defines science fiction through its attitude, an attitude that he sees as threatening to the mainstream middle-class populace. The subversive nature of science fiction is something on which Malzberg and Suvin are able to agree.

In contrast, James Gunn's title "Toward a Definition of Science Fiction" implies that his article presents only an initial rough sketch of a definition of the field. However, reading the article shows that when it was written he had been working toward a definition for better than thirty years. He goes through several of his earlier iterations and those of others to discuss some of the problems inherent in defining science fiction, and shows how his most recent version removes uncertainties and imprecision of the earlier ones, especially the significance of distinguishing between fantasy and science fiction, so commonly lumped together commercially, as fundamentally different literatures. He then goes on to show how crucial an understanding of the genre is to any appraisal of its worth, which will be explored in greater detail in the next section. Nonetheless, Gunn makes it clear through the title and tone of this piece that the definition of science fiction is an ongoing process, part of the "hard questions" crucial to the genre's existence.

The selection "Coming to Terms," from Gary K. Wolfe's *Critical Terms for Science Fiction and Fantasy*, highlights a number of important terms for joining the ongoing discussion of science fiction. Not all the terms contained in the selection are crucial to our discussion here, nor are all crucial terms defined here. Serious students are referred to Wolfe's landmark volume, in whose absence no science fiction library can be considered complete.

Finally, "On the Origins of Genre" by Paul Kincaid is a latecomer to this volume, and as such has certain advantages, including the ability to consider and include the definitions of earlier authors. Kincaid revisits Damon Knight's oft-quoted relativistic definition of science fiction in order to explore its subtlety—a subtlety that many critics neglect. Kincaid utilizes Wittgenstein's notion of "family resemblances" to avoid the questions of definition and origin, which he claims are hopelessly self-referential. Kincaid's argument is strong, but when he claims that there are "central" texts of science fiction, texts about which no argument about their SF status exists, he implies that there is a definition of science fiction, despite his argument against it. Even when we can only point at what we recognize, intuitively, to include the right stuff, we can still ask: what are we pointing at; what is the right stuff?

~

CHAPTER ONE

Toward a Definition
of Science Fiction

James Gunn

The most important, and most divisive, issue in science fiction is definition. I am brought back to it once more by an article in one of those fascinating developments in science fiction, the fanzine. The article "Science Fiction by the Numbers," written by Robert Sabella, was published in the winter 1985 issue of Richard Geis's *Science Fiction Review*.

My involvement with definition may have begun with my original discovery of science fiction and my realization that this literature was different from every other kind. I got deeper into the question when I wrote a master's thesis on modern science fiction in 1951 and even more involved when I started work on *Alternate Worlds* in 1970. My most pressing concerns, however, developed from my fifteen-year involvement in teaching science fiction and editing the anthology *The Road to Science Fiction* for my class. Much of my work in the field, as it turns out, has been the attempt to grope an understanding of what science fiction is, how it got to be that way, and how it differs from other kinds of literature.

The article in *Science Fiction Review* quoted my definition from *Alternate Worlds*, "a fantastic event of development considered rationally." That was an attempt to come up with a brief definition. But, as Mr. Sabella illustrates with his definition, brevity means lack of precision.

What my definition suggested was that fantasy and science fiction belong to the same general category of fiction—that is, the fictional world represented is not the world of the here and now or even the there and then but the fantastic world of unfamiliar events or developments. By "rational" the definition suggests (but does not explain) the difference between fantasy and science fiction.

A longer and more precise definition is attempted in my four-volume anthology, *The Road to Science Fiction*:

> Science fiction is the branch of literature that deals with the effects of change on people in the real world as it can be projected into the past, the future, or to distant places. It often concerns itself with scientific or technological change, and it usually involves matters whose importance is greater than the individual or the community; often civilization or the race itself is in danger.

But even this definition is not comprehensive, and I must confess to some waffling here with words like "often" and "usually." Perhaps for completeness the real definition requires the entire volume of *The Road to Science Fiction* with its examples. My semester-long course is actually a quest for definition that my students and I pursue by means of historical development, thematic analysis, comparison and contrast, and examples.

But let's have another go at what I consider to be the key critical question in the field. I remember an excellent debate between Damon Knight and me in my classroom in which Damon maintained there was no significant difference between fantasy and science fiction, and I insisted there was.

An immediate complication: do the words we use have the same meanings for us both? If Damon considers everything irrelevant except the fantastic element (or that part of the fiction that is contrary to things as we know them), then I never will convince him that there is a meaningful difference.

The problem of definition also is complicated by the fact that science fiction is not an ordinary kind of genre. Unlike the mystery, the western, the gothic, the love story, or the adventure story, to cite a few of the popular genres, science fiction has no typical action or place. Readers do not recognize it as they recognize other genres because of some critical event (such as a crime and its detection) or its setting (the mythical West during the period 1865–1900). As a consequence, science fiction can incorporate other genres: we can have a science-fiction mystery, a science-fiction western, a science-fiction gothic, a science-fiction love story, or most likely of all, a science-fiction adventure story.

The first step toward definition, then, must be the elimination of those aspects of the fiction that are not unique to science fiction—the aspects of the mystery, the western, the gothic, the love story, and the adventure story, or even those elements of traditional fiction that do not relate to the changed situation, such as sex or extraneous characterization—before we can begin to recognize what is left as being irreducibly science fiction. Sometimes, of course, nothing is left, and we may conclude that the piece in question was not science fiction at all. If there is something left, that something, I have observed, is change. Some significant element of the situation is different from the world with which we are familiar, and the characters cannot respond to the situation in customary ways, that is, without recognizing that a changed situation requires analysis and a different response. Or if the characters attempt to respond traditionally, without recognizing the need for a different response, they fail, or they fail for the rest of us, the human species.

It may be useful here to make a comparison with what was called "new wave" SF, which seemed like science fiction and was usually published in science-fiction magazines, but to many long-time science-fiction readers did not seem to have "the right stuff." In the usual "new wave" story the situation was different, but the characters responded to the situation in the traditional ways, or, if the new ways, in ways that were inappropriate or had no likelihood of coping with the situations. Thus, the characters in those stories usually failed to cope with their situations, but their failure was attributed to the catastrophic scope of their situations or its incomprehensibility or to universal defects in human nature, and not to individual lack of knowledge, wisdom, character, or effort.

The situations of traditional fiction are those of the everyday world, including the everyday world of history. The broad area of fantastic literature is characterized by situations in which a significant element is different from the everyday.

As a mid-term examination I give my students an opportunity to choose a brief definition among the following and write an essay upon it: Science fiction is a literature of (1) ideas; (2) change; (3) anticipation; (4) the human species. These are not particularly effective as definitions, though I think there is something to be said for (2) and (4), but they offer students the opportunity to develop and defend their own ideas. I bring it up now, however, because I may add another choice: (5) discontinuity.

Traditional fiction, it might be said, is the literature of continuity. Whatever the situation, it is continuous with everyday experience, and the decisions that must be made by the characters are decisions based upon prior experience, upon tradition. The moment characters in any kind of fiction encounter new situations or attempt new solutions to traditional situations, the story begins to feel like science fiction; science-fiction readers respond to them, and traditional critics reject them for a variety of reasons, but mostly because science fiction is the literature of discontinuity. Historical fiction that deals with moments of change, of discontinuity, often have appeals to readers similar to those of science fiction, which may explain why stories of prehistoric men, like those of Waterloo, London, Wells, and Golding, usually are considered science fiction.

One immediate objection might be raised to describing science fiction as the literature of discontinuity: perhaps the terms is appropriate to the "what if," speculative kind of story, in which the basis of the story is the element of the new and different. But what about the "if this goes on," extrapolative kind of story such as Pohl and Kornbluth's *The Space Merchants?* I would suggest that we only recognize the work as science fiction if the extrapolation produces a significant enough accumulation of change that it is, in actuality, discontinuous. If the extrapolation is minor, is not sufficiently discontinuous, such as *Seven Days in May*, for instance, or even *Dr. Strangelove*, then it doesn't feel quite like science fiction to us.

But we must then further differentiate science fiction and fantasy, which is also the literature of discontinuity, though often, to be sure, it is only discontinuous at certain moments or at certain periods of the day or night, and sometimes the discontinuity has alternative explanations. Mr. Sabella's suggestion, "A story is science fiction if it accepts *every* axiom of the real world plus one or more imaginary axioms," is on the right track, but I would like to approach it in another way.

The place I like to start is the reading experience, where, I believe, all criticism begins: First we read something and respond to it, and then we ask ourselves why we responded in that way. It seems to me that we read fantasy and science fiction differently—that is, we ask the text different kinds of questions. The kinds of questions we ask determine how we read it; if we ask the wrong kinds of questions, we will be unable to read the fiction properly. This, incidentally, is what we mean by "genre": our previous reading experience in literature with similar characteristics not only leads us to particular expectations about a particular piece when we encounter those characteristics but prepares us to ask the right questions, the questions to which it will respond.

Few of us analyze our generic experiences; we respond intuitively. And most readers respond intuitively (and differently) to fantasy and science fiction. If they do not they end up confused and sometimes disappointed because the fiction does not respond to their questions.

If the difference between fantastic literature and the literature of everyday experience lies in the changed situation, the difference between fantasy and science fiction lies in the fact that fantasy takes place in a world in which the rules of everyday experience do not apply, and science fiction in the world of everyday experience extended. That is, fantasy creates its own world and its own laws; science fiction accepts the real world and its laws. We could not live in the real world if we operated by the assumptions of the fantasy world; but the assumptions of the science-fiction world are compatible with our own. We can believe in the existence of aliens somewhere else in the universe, or that time machines or faster-than-light spaceships eventually may be developed, and still function without real-life problems; but if we behave in our everyday life as if werewolves, vampires, and doorways into other worlds exist, our lives will be difficult, even if we remain outside institutional walls.

When we read science fiction, we recognize that it applies to the real world, and we ask it real questions. The first one is: How did we get there from here? If the question is irrelevant or whimsical, then the fiction is fantasy. On the other hand, if we insist that the fantasy answer our real-world questions, we cannot read it. For instance, if we insist on knowing where the hole is located that Alice uses to get to Wonderland or how she can fall interminably without killing herself, or how one can get through a mirror into the world beyond, we cannot read *Alice in Wonderland* or *Through the Looking Glass*, and part of our experience in growing up is learning how to distinguish fantasy from reality. We all, as children, may have cherished the notion that, like Alice, we might one day find the mirror that we could pass through into a brighter, better, or more exciting world, but we learn not to act upon it.

As a consequence, a reader instinctively (and a critic analytically) looks for the author's instructions on how to read a work. Usually a writer offers them early (unless the writer's strategy depends on reader uncertainty, a risk that writers should assume only for a suitable payoff, and whose risk, and payoff, a critic should assess); most fantasies begin fantastically. When a character falls down a rabbit hole or passes through a mirror, the writer is telling the reader: Don't ask realistic questions.

In the science-fiction story, on the other hand, realistic questions are essential for full understanding and enjoyment; the reader is supposed to compare the fictional world to the real world and find it not only better or worse, or simply different, but be able to ascertain what made it better or worse or different. If the reader doesn't ask hard questions of *Mission of Gravity*, say, or *The Left Hand of Darkness*, and reads them instead as fantasy, the reader misses most of the significance of those novels. The point of those novels, substantially different in subject and theme, though both occur on alien planets, lies not only in their differences from our world and our society but their resemblances to our experiences. And part of the pleasure we derive from them and our ability to learn from them comes from our recognition that laws of nature and assumptions about behavior apply to us in the same way they apply to the characters in them.

Science fiction, then, is the literature of change. Change is its subject matter and its method. Fantasy might be defined as the literature of difference. Fantasy occurs in a world not congruent with ours or incongruent in some significant way. Science fiction occurs in the world of everyday experience extended into the unknown.

The fact that some element of a science-fiction story may violate existing scientific theories, the time machine, say, or the faster-than-light spaceship, does not necessarily control our decision about whether to read the work as fantasy or science fiction. What is not possible in our state of knowledge may be possible in a hundred years or a thousand or a million. The presence of a time machine or a faster-than-light spaceship does not make a work fantasy if we are supposed to consider them realistically, that is, if we are supposed to ask hard questions about them and their consequences. The reason authors like H. G. Wells in *The Time Machine* go to so much effort to make their time machines believable is to instruct the reader how to read their stories, to put them into the proper realistic frames of mind about the pasts or the futures they visit. A time machine could be used in a fantasy, of course, but if it is to be read as a fantasy the author should describe it in fanciful, that is, unrealistic, terms and warn the reader not to ask realistic questions.

Fantasy and science fiction belong to the same broad category of fiction that deals with events other than those that occur, or have occurred, in the everyday world. But they belong to distinctly different methods of looking at those worlds: fantasy is unrealistic; science fiction is realistic. Fantasy creates its own universe with its own laws; science fiction exists in our universe with its shared laws. Fantasy is a private vision that one accepts for the sake of vision; science fiction is a public vision that must meet every test of reality. The basis of fantasy is psychological truth; nothing else matters. The basis of science fiction is the real world. Does the story respond to hard questions? Nothing else matters.

The reason we should make a distinction between fantasy and science fiction is that we read them differently, and we misread them if we apply the reading protocols of one to the other. Borderline cases create the most serious difficulties. In my classes, I used to describe fantasy and science fiction as existing along a spectrum of explanation: the more explanation in a fantasy story the more like science fiction it seems; the more irrationalized assumptions in the science-fiction story, the more like fantasy it seems. And, I would say, when they met in the middle they were virtually indistinguishable, and we even call them, sometimes, "science fantasy."

I no longer find that satisfying. At that time, I think, I had not yet come to my realization that the science-fiction genre, because it has no characteristic action or place, is a kind of super-genre, capable of incorporating the others. Most of the difficult cases become easier to analyze if first the elements of other genres are peeled away. In the case of Edgar Rice Burrough's John Carter stories, for instance, we have a small residue of evolutionary notions and cultural criticism; in A. E. van Vogt's *Null-A* novels, we have a larger residue of ideas that we are supposed to consider in the light of the real world: the ability of a new system of logic to liberate the rational mind as well as to develop super powers, and the effect of these on political structures on Earth and Venus and later as they extend into the galaxy.

The critical decision as to whether these works, and others like them, are better read as science fiction or fantasy is controlled by our feelings about whether we get more out of the works by subjecting them to hard questions or to none. On this basis, I would suggest that the Burrough's John Carter novels will be destroyed by hard questions and are best read as fantasy, and that van Vogt's *Null-A* novels ask for intellectual scrutiny even though their adventure plots sometimes frustrate our attempts to make sense of them.

The differences between the literature of continuity and the literature of discontinuity, and in the literature of discontinuity between the literature of change and the literature of difference, are real and significant. Applying to one the critical standards appropriate to another comes from a failure to recognize those differences and results in misreading and misunderstanding. A case in point is James Thurber's "The Macbeth Murder Case," in which an inveterate murder mystery reader, trapped without his favorite reading material on an island resort, misreads Shakespeare. Examples could be multiplied.

Traditional critics, when they have condescended to consider science fiction, have found it inadequate when measured against traditional standards. Robert Scholes wrote in his introductions to the Oxford series of author studies, "as long as the dominant criteria are believed to hold for all fiction, science fiction will be found inferior: deficient in psychological depth, in verbal nuance, and in plausibility of event. What is needed is a criticism serious in its standards and its concern for literary value but willing to take seriously a literature based on ideas, types, and events beyond ordinary experience."

Science fiction's recent popularity has made it a more tempting target: Exposure is easier than explanation; ridicule is wittier than analysis. But science fiction and fantasy never will receive meaningful criticism until the qualities that make them special are understood, and an appropriate set of critical standards is developed for them.

CHAPTER TWO

∽

Coming to Terms

Gary K. Wolfe

One of the most common complaints about the scholarship of fantasy
and science fiction is that, as Everett Bleiler put it in his 1984 Pilgrim
Award acceptance speech, "Our terms have been muddled, imprecise,
and heretical in the derivational sense of the word." Critics often resort
to neologisms or specialized usages to talk about this literature, sometimes inventing whole new systems of literary classification. Fans and
writers sometimes complain about the gnomic nomenclature of the academics, while the academics themselves complain of the looseness of
the fans' favorite buzzwords. And since SF is a popular literature, the
critical vocabulary has come to include terms originally confined to the
publishing industry or the professional concerns of authors.

Few of these critical terms are defined in standard encyclopedic reference works about SF or fantasy, and fewer still are found in traditional
handbooks of literature. But if the field is ever to establish a coherent
critical vocabulary, scholars, fans, and writers each need to know what
the others are talking about.

> *Academic*: Used both as an adjective and a noun to describe the involve-
> ment of professional scholars and teachers in the criticism, history, theory,
> and teaching of science fiction. Such a meaning might seem obvious, but
> the term has gained a great many overtones, usually either disparaging or

defensive, and has come rather imprecisely to be contrasted both with "fan" or amateur scholarship in the field, and with the various "internal" works of history and criticism generated by science fiction and fantasy writers themselves. In this usage, the "academic" is often regarded as an outsider trained in traditional humanistic methodologies which are sometimes felt to be inadequate for science fiction; interestingly, the term is seldom applied to university scientists or even social scientists, suggesting that it refers not necessarily to the academic world per se, but specifically to inhabitants of English or history departments in universities.

Alternate History: A narrative premise claimed equally by science fiction and fantasy—namely, that time contains infinite branches and that universes may exist in which, for example, the Allies lost the Second World War (Philip K. Dick's *The Man in the High Castle* [1962]) or the Spanish Armada was victorious (Phyllis Eisenstein's *Shadow of Earth* [1979] or Keith Robert's *Pavane* [1962]). One of the earliest genre treatments of this theme, Murray Leinster's "Sidewise in Time" (1934), is clearly intended as science fiction. The theme has been present in the genre at least since 1926, although Darko Suvin has identified a number of "alternate histories" published as early as 1871. Suvin's definition, somewhat broader than the commonly accepted use of the term, relates the alternative history to utopian or satirical fiction, identifying it as "that form of SF in which an alternative locus (in space, time, etc.) that shares the material and causal verisimilitude of the writer's world is used to articulate different possible solutions of societal problems, those problems being of sufficient importance to require an alteration in the overall history of the narrated world." Another bibliography of such works, by Barton C. Hacker and Gordon B. Chamberlain, appeared in *Extrapolation*, 2.4 (Winter 1981).

Blurb: Promotional copy written on the dust covers of hard-bound books and on the front and back covers and front page of paperbacks. Although blurbs are most often written by promotional staff or freelance public relations writers, they often include quotations from reviews or specially solicited praise from fellow authors—to the extent that some well-known authors have reputations for excessive generosity in lending their names to the efforts of less well-known authors. Given the overall importance of marketing and packaging to the audience's perceptions of popular literature, blurbs can also be revealing clues to the changing attitudes toward genres such as science fiction or fantasy. One of the earliest science fiction anthologies, for example (Donald A. Wollheim's *The Pocket Book of Science Fiction*, 1943), featured a blurb that characterized the contents as belonging to "that realm of superscience where nonscientists try to anticipate science." Wollheim's later anthology *The Portable Novels of Science* (1945) avoided the term "science fiction" on the jacket cover by calling the contents "novels of scientific speculation," while an early Judith Merril anthology disguised the science fiction contents as "a different kind of mystery thrill" and a popular anthology by Orson Wells used the term "interplanetary stories." Similarly a 1944 fantasy anthology from Penguin disguised its contents as humor ("yarns based on delightful fantasy") despite the inclusion of such relatively grim tales as Jack London's "The Scarlet Plague." By the early 1950s, however, the paperback market for science fiction at least (fantasy would emerge later) became sufficiently strong that such evasive blurb copy was replaced by enthusiastic and frequent use of the term "science fiction" (except in the case of novels, such as Philip Wylie's *Tomorrow!* [1954], directed at a wider market) and this quickly led to complete lines of science fiction titles from Doubleday, Ballantine, and other publishers. (It is interesting to note, however, that after the success of Ray Bradbury's *The Martian Chronicles* [1950], which was labeled "Doubleday Science Fiction," his second book for Doubleday, *The Illustrated Man* [1951], was not identified as science fiction anywhere on the jacket.) As the market for science fiction grew and diversified, blurbs came more to reflect what was known of reader interest and consequently somewhat less hysterical; a common technique (still in use, although perhaps more in fantasy) was to compare the work with an acknowledged classic or a recent bestseller; reprints often became instant "classics" themselves. Although most serious readers claim not to be strongly influenced by blurbs, there is much to suggest that, along with cover design, they are crucial in capturing the casual reader and thus influencing sales figures, which in turn of course influence patterns of manuscript development and acquisition.

Cognitive Estrangement: Widely quoted term from Darko Suvin describing the defining characteristic of science fiction, which Suvin sees as estranged from the naturalistic world but cognitively connected to it. "Noncognitive estrangement," according to this scheme, would include myths, folktales, and fantasies that are neither naturalistic nor cognitively linked to the natural world. Suvin argues that the defining characteristics of science fiction are "estrangement" and "cognition," the latter referring to those elements of variability and detail drawn from the empirical environment which establish a link between the experienced world of the reader and the world of the work of fiction; a flying carpet would violate this principle of cognition.

Desire: A term sometimes used to describe the wish-fulfillment aspect of the appeal of fantasy and sometimes used (as by Rosemary Jackson) to characterize the nature of language in fantasy narratives, as opposed to the more representational language of conventional narratives. Leo Bersani's use of this term (in *A Future for Astyanix: Character and Desire in Literature,* 1976), suggests that it refers to a generalized yearning for something beyond the real, and thus might in part account for the structures of character and narrative found in fantasy. The term has been used of science fiction as well, notably in Eizykman's *Science fiction et capitalisme* (1974), again with the implication of subverting dominant social structures through idealization of the possible. Much contemporary use of the term derives from the work of French psychoanalyst Jacques Lacan, and in particular his discussions of desire in its relationships to fantasy and to the "other."

Extrapolation: Probably derived from "interpolation" and used by statisticians to refer to the process of predicting a value beyond a known series by detecting patterns within the series. Extended into the social and natural sciences, "extrapolation" has become one of the most common characteristics cited in discussions and definitions of science fiction, and even provided the title for the field's first academic journal, founded in 1959. Generally, it is used to mean the technique of basing imaginary worlds or situations on existing ones through cognitive or rational means; a "satire," therefore, may be based on an extrapolation but need not be, since the relationship of the world of the satire to our own might be purely metaphorical. An example of an extrapolative science fiction satire is Frederik Pohl and C. M. Kornbluth's *The Space Merchants* (1952), in which a future society dominated by advertising agencies is clearly an outgrowth of trends visible in the early 1950s.

The term is closely allied with Speculative Fiction, and one of its earliest important usages occurred in the Robert A. Heinlein essay in which he proposed the latter term: in the "speculative science fiction story," he wrote, "accepted science and established facts are extrapolated to produce a new situation, new framework for human action." Perhaps in part because of its scholarly sound, the term quickly gained popularity, and by

1955 Basil Davenport could report that extrapolation was "a word that is almost as great a favorite in discussions of science fiction as 'space-warp' is in science fiction itself; it may be defined as 'plotting the curve.'" While treating extrapolation as a defining characteristic of science fiction would seem to limit the genre to fiction of the future, critics have managed to adapt the word to include extrapolations about the past, about Alternate Worlds, and about other favorite themes. Other critics, however, have argued for distinctions between "extrapolative" and "non-extrapolative" kinds of science fiction narratives, while still others have expressed hope that the term might be banished altogether as restrictive and misleading.

Ghetto: A kind of literary backwater. Since at least the late 1940s, science fiction writers and editors have complained of the "ghettoization" of the genre by publishers, booksellers, and reviewers. "Ghetto" thus refers not only to the evolution of science fiction as a commercial book-selling category, but to a complex of critical and social attitudes that have come to influence factors as disparate as authors' contracts, book design, the placement of popular reviews, the teaching of the genre, and literary fellowships and awards. While other genre writers have also complained about "ghettoes" of westerns, mysteries, romance novels, and the like, science fiction writers have been perhaps the most vocal and possibly the best organized group in opposing this tendency.

Anthony Boucher argued that such literary ghettoes arose from four factors: the tendency of popular writers to specialize in a particular genre, the tendency of readers to buy fiction by category, the tendency of academics to increasingly separate popular from "serious" fiction, and the realization on the part of publishers that more predictable sales could be gained by segmenting audiences according to special interests. In fact, the latter factor is arguably the most significant in the historical evolution of the "ghetto" of science fiction, which for much of its history has been dominated by magazines (which have been sold by popular category since the nineteenth century), and that did not enjoy significant paperback publication until long after Robert de Graaf of Pocket Books had discovered the principle of shelving genre books together in order to increase their sales. Similarly, hardbound science fiction did not become widespread until after hardcover publishers had been forced into similar marketing techniques by the success of the "paperback revolution." In more recent years, the very success of science fiction has exacerbated the situation, as authors who have established track records of dependable sales within the genre often find it difficult to persuade publishers to market books in any other way; the most famous examples are Harlan Ellison's *contretemps* with a publisher who attempted to label as science fiction reprints of the author's early realistic and autobiographical writings, and Isaac Asimov's losing argument with a publisher who refused to label his 1972 novel *The Gods Themselves* as science fiction.

Hard Science Fiction (sometimes also "hardcore" science fiction): Science fiction in which the Ground Rules are known scientific principles, and in which speculation based on such principles constitutes a significant part of the work. Coined presumably on the model of "hard science" (the physical and biological, as opposed to social sciences), "hard science fiction" is ostensibly that "written around known scientific facts or at least not-unproven theories generated by 'real' scientists," according to Norman Spinrad. Thomas N. Scontia somewhat more narrowly defines it as a "closely reasoned technological story." Neither definition quite encompasses the breadth with which the term is actually used. However, in some cases it refers only to stories in which the setting is carefully worked out from known scientific principles (as in the work of Hal Clement or Larry Niven), in other cases to stories in which the plot hangs on such a principle, and in still other cases to almost any science fiction associated with such stories in time or place. In the latter sense, the term may become almost synonymous with science fiction of the Campbell Era. See also "Soft Science Fiction."

Heterotopia: Originally a medical and biological term referring to a displacement of an organ or an organism; thus, broadly, a "displacement." "Heterotopia" was suggested by Robert Plank in 1968 as a convenient term for works of fiction that invent "not only characters but also settings." Plank included science fiction, much fantasy, and utopian fiction under this term, which in this sense is obviously derivative of Utopia [151]. Although not widely adopted, the term was invoked in the subtitle of Samuel R. Delany's novel *Triton* (1976): "An Ambiguous Heterotopia."

Idiot Plot: Probably coined by James Blish but popularized through the reviews of Damon Knight, who defined it as a plot that "is kept in motion solely by virtue of the fact that everybody involved is an idiot." Specifically, he refers to stories in which characters act at the convenience of the author rather than through any perceivable motivation, and uses the term to attack fantastic works that seem based on the assumption that fantastic elements obviate the need for fictional credibility. Similar terms have been employed by other critics of popular fiction and film.

New Wave: Francoise Giroud's term (*nouvelle vague*) to describe a group of younger French film directors who emerged in the late 1950s has since been enthusiastically appropriated by promoters of almost any unconventional movement within a popular art form previously characterized by conventions or formulae. In science fiction, the term was introduced by Judith Merril in a 1966 essay for *The Magazine of Fantasy and Science Fiction* ("Books," 30, [January 1966]) to refer to the highly metaphorical and sometimes experimental fiction that began to appear in the English magazine *New Worlds* after Michael Moorcock assumed the editorship in 1964, and that was later popularized in the United States through Merril's own appallingly titled anthology *England Swings SF: Stories of Speculative Fiction* (Garden City: Doubleday, 1968). Although Harlan Ellison's anthology of original stories the preceding year (*Dangerous Visions*, Garden City: Doubleday, 1967) has sometimes been retroactively credited with unleashing the American version of the new wave, and though Ellison spoke of the book as "a revolution" of "new horizons, new forms, new styles, new challenges," Ellison himself has expressed chagrin at having been once labeled the "chief prophet" of the new wave in America (by *The New Yorker*: "The Talk of the Town: Evolution and Ideation," 16 September 1967). Similarly, many of the other writers associated with this movement, such as Brian Aldiss, J. G. Ballard, Thomas M. Disch, Samuel R. Delaney, and Robert Silverberg, have on frequent occasions expressed disdain for or confusion over the term. Nevertheless, writers associated with the new wave have been credited with introducing new narrative strategies into science fiction images as metaphor and with weakening the boundaries that had long separated science fiction from mainstream fiction.

Posthistory: Gene Wolfe's term for far future settings (such as in his own *Book of the New Sun* [1980–83]) in which artifacts from the present or near future constitute a kind of fragmentary or semilegendary history for the characters in that setting. The term is obviously modeled on "prehistory" in that it refers to a culture in which what we view as continuous historical process and documentation has been fragmented or obliterated; the technique is fairly common in works which have been characterized as medieval futurism.

Psychomyth: Term used by Ursula K. Le Guin to describe those of her stories which lack identifiable historical or science fictional referents, "more or less surrealistic tales, which share with fantasy the quality of taking place outside any history, outside of time, in that region of the living mind which—without invoking any consideration of immortality—seems to be without spatial or temporal limits at all."

Pulp: Originally a kind of cheap, acidic wood pulp paper, but now more often used to refer to the magazines published on such paper, which attained a collective circulation of nearly ten million per issue during the 1930s, according to Russel Nye (*The Unembarrassed Muse*, 1970). More broadly, the term came to characterize the fiction and illustrations published in those magazines, and finally to any fiction or illustrations making use of the pulp forms. The invention of the pulp magazine is generally credited to Frank Munsey, who in 1896 decided to convert his children's magazine *Golden Argosy* to a popular all-fiction magazine titled *Argosy*, and switched to cheap untrimmed wood-pulp paper in order to keep the price low. Pulp magazines are of particular importance to the history of American fantasy in that, beginning with *Weird Tales* in 1923, they provided a focal point, consolidated an audience, and began to establish conventions and formulas for several subgenres of fantasy, especially horror fiction and sword and sorcery. Science fiction pulps were equally successful, and many historians of the genre have dated its beginning as a self-conscious genre from the founding of *Amazing Stories* by Hugo Gernsback in 1926. Western, romance, detective, aviation, and war story pulps also flourished, but magazines devoted to other subgenres (such as *Oriental Tales*, begun in 1930) did not fare as well. John W. Campbell's *Unknown*, begun in 1939, did much to develop a modern popular genre of logical and often humorous fantasy parallel to science fiction, and such pulps as *Famous Fantastic Mysteries* and *The Avon Fantasy Reader* were instrumental in creating a younger audience for older lost-race fantasies and horror fiction. By the mid-1950s, most pulp magazines had been replaced by digest-size magazines, although critics and historians have since sometimes used the term to refer to any sensational formulaic fiction.

Sci-Fi: Neologism coined by science fiction fan Forrest J. Ackerman and that has become anathema to many science fiction writers and readers. Perhaps because of its widespread use in the popular media in what often seems a denigrating or stereotyping manner, "sci-fi" has, in effect, become science fiction's equivalent of "nigger." More recently, however, some writers and critics have begun to suggest that the term may in fact have a legitimate use in describing highly formulaic mass-audience entertainments and particular Hollywood movies. Isaac Asimov, for example, defines sci-fi as "trashy material sometimes confused, by ignorant people, with s.f.," and cites the film *Godzilla Meets Mothra* as an example. Damon Knight has suggested the term be used for "the crude, basic kind of s.f. that satisfies the appetite for pseudoscientific marvels without appealing to any other portion of the intellect" (he also suggests the term be pronounced "skiffy"). Somewhat less condemnatory, Elizabeth Anne Hull has suggested that films such as *Star Wars* might appropriately be termed sci-fi to distinguish them from the more complex (but still not clearly defined) fictions labeled SF. However, neither argument has gained much acceptance outside the science fiction community, and "sci-fi" remains in wide use as a popular media term for science fiction in general.

SF (S.F., S-F): Ambiguous abbreviation almost universally favored in the science-fiction community over the more journalistic sci-fi, but even less clearly defined. SF (or sf) is most often used as shorthand for science fiction, but has also been used for science fantasy, speculative fiction, or structural fabulation. Widely popularized even outside the science fiction community by Judith Merril in her series of "year's best" anthologies (1956–69), all of which used the SF rubric, the usage has since become so prevalent that Isaac Asimov has suggested that speculative fiction may have been coined as an attempt to retain the initials SF while abandoning the more restrictive use of "science" as a modifier. Some writers now prefer to use the term without specifying its particular meaning; if "sci-fi" is the "nigger" of the field, SF is its "Ms."

Shaggy God Story: Michael Moorcock's label for tales that seek to achieve a sense of wonder by mechanically adapting biblical tales and providing science fictional "explanations" for them—as, for example, the "surprise ending" that reveals two characters to be Adam and Eve.

Soft Science Fiction: Probably a back formation from hard science fiction and used sometimes to refer to science fiction based on so-called "soft" sciences (anthropology, sociology, etc.), and sometimes refer to science fiction in which there is little science or awareness of science at all. Chad Oliver might be an example of an author who falls under the former definition; Ray Bradbury an example of the latter.

Space Opera: A term borrowed from Fandom, where it was coined by Wilson Tucker in 1941 to refer to the "outworn spaceship yarn" of the sort that had been prevalent in the pulps during much of the 1930s. Sometimes called adventure science fiction or science adventure, space operas are generally fast-paced intergalactic adventures on a grand scale, most closely associated with E. E. Smith, Edmond Hamilton, and the early Jack Williamson. Often characterized as westerns in space or "straight fantasy in science fiction drag" (Norman Spinrad), space opera may be either an historical or a generic term; contemporary films such as *Star Wars* have been labeled space operas, as have more complex works such as Cecilia Holland's 1976 novel *Floating Worlds.*

Wonder: Frequently invoked in definitions of fantasy but seldom defined, as in C. N. Manlove's phrase "a fiction evoking wonder." The term is equally common in discussions of science fiction with its "sense of wonder," but it is quite possible the meaning there is somewhat different, relating to philosophical notions of the undiscovered universe and romantic notions of the sublime in the face of vastness. In fantasy, the term need not imply awe and terror in the face of the natural world, but rather suggests the desire and longing arising out of the promise of other worlds or states of being. In this sense, the term is perhaps related to *Sehnsucht.* Casey Fredericks has characterized the "wonder effect" as "presenting both a radical and a recognizable change on the known world." As for the science fictional "sense of wonder," Samuel R. Delany has suggested that the phrase gained currency through the criticism of Damon Knight, and may have been borrowed from W. H. Auden's 1939 poem "In Memory of Sigmund Freud" (which spoke of the "sense of wonder" offered by the night). It is equally possible, however, that the phrase had gained some currency before the Auden poem, perhaps through the use of "wonder" in the titles of pulp magazines as early as 1929.

CHAPTER THREE

~

Estrangement and Cognition[1]

Darko Suvin

1. Science Fiction as Fiction (Estrangement)

1.1. The importance of science fiction (SF) in our time is on the increase. First, there are strong indications that its popularity in the leading industrial nations (United States, USSR, United Kingdom, Japan) has risen sharply over the last 100 years, despite all the local and short-range fluctuations. SF has particularly affected such key strata or groups of modern society as college graduates, young writers, and the avant-garde of general readers appreciative of new sets of values. This is a significant cultural effect that goes beyond any merely quantitative census. Second, if one takes the minimal generic difference of the presence of a narrative novum (the dramatic personae and/or their context) significantly different from what is the norm in "naturalistic" or empiricist fiction, it will be found that SF has an interesting and close kinship with other literary subgenres that flourished at different times and places of literary history: the classical and medieval "fortunate island" story, the "fabulous voyage" story from antiquity on, the renaissance and baroque "utopia" and "planetary novel," the Enlightenment "state [political] novel," the modern "anticipation" and "anti-utopia." Moreover, although SF shares with myth, fantasy, fairytale, and pastoral an opposition to naturalistic or empiricist literary genres, it differs very significantly in approach and social function from such adjoining non-naturalistic or meta-empirical genres. Both these complementary aspects, the sociological and the methodological, are being vigorously debated by writers and critics in several countries, evidence of a lively interest in a genre that should undergo scholarly discussion, too.

In this chapter, I will argue for an understanding of SF as the *literature of cognitive estrangement*. This definition seems to possess the unique advantage of rendering justice to a literary tradition that is coherent through the ages and within itself, yet distinct from nonfictional utopianism, from naturalistic literature, and from other non-naturalistic fiction. It thus makes it possible to lay the basis for a coherent poetics of SF.

1.2. I want to begin by postulating a spectrum or spread of literary subject matter that extends from the ideal extreme of exact recreation of the author's empirical environment[2] to exclusive interest in a strange newness, a *novum*. From the eighteenth to the twentieth centuries, the literary mainstream of our civilization has been nearer to the first of these two extremes. However, at the beginnings of a literature, the concern with a domestication of the amazing is very strong. Early tale-tellers relate amazing voyages into the next valley, where they found dog-headed people and good rock salt that could be stolen or at the worst bartered for. Their stories are a syncretic travelogue and *voyage imaginaire*, a daydream and intelligence report. This implies a curiosity about the unknown beyond the next mountain range (sea, ocean, solar system), where the thrill of knowledge joined the thrill of adventure.

From Iambulus and Euhemerus through the classical utopia to Verne's island of Captain Nemo and Wells's island of Dr. Moreau, an island in the far-off ocean is the paradigm of the aesthetically most satisfying goal of the SF voyage. This is particularly true if we subsume under this the planetary island in the aether ocean—usually the moon—that we encounter from Lucian through Cyran to Swift's mini-Moon of Laputa, and on into the nineteenth century. Yet the parallel paradigm of the valley, "over the range" (the subtitle of Butler's SF novel *Erewhon*), which shuts it in as a wall, is perhaps as revealing. It recurs almost as frequently, from the earliest folktales about the sparkling valley of Terrestrial Paradise and the dark valley of the Dead, both already in *Gilgamesh*. Eden is the mythological localization of utopian longing, just as Wells's valley in "The Country of the

Blind" is still within the liberating tradition that contends that the world is not necessarily the way our present empirical valley happens to be, and whoever thinks his valley is the world is blind. Whether island or valley, whether in space or (from the industrial and bourgeois revolutions on) in time, the new framework is correlative to the new inhabitants. The aliens—utopians, monsters, or simply differing strangers—are a mirror to man just as the differing country is a mirror for his world. But the mirror is not only a reflecting one, it is also a transforming one—virgin womb and alchemical dynamo: the mirror is a crucible.

Thus it is not only the basic human and humanizing curiosity that gives birth to SF. Beyond an undirected inquisitiveness, which makes for a semantic game without clear referent, this genre has always been wedded to a hope of finding in the unknown the ideal environment, tribe, state, intelligence, or other aspect of the supreme good (or to a fear of and revulsion from its contrary). At all events, the *possibility* of other strange, covariant coordinate systems and semantic fields is assumed.

1.3. The approach to the imaginary locality, or localized daydream, practiced by the genre of SF is a supposedly factual one. Columbus's (technically or genologically nonfictional) letter on the Eden he glimpsed beyond the Orinoco mouth, and Swift's (technically nonfactual) voyage to Laputa, Balnibarbi, Glubbdubbdrib, Luggnagg, "and Japan" represent two extremes in the constant intermingling of imaginary and empirical possibilities. Thus SF takes off from a fictional ("literary") hypothesis and develops it with totalizing ("scientific") rigor—the specific difference between Columbus and Swift is smaller than their generic proximity. The effect of such factual reporting of fictions is one of confronting a set normative system—a Ptolemaic-type closed-world picture—with a point of view or look implying a new set of norms; in literary theory this is known as the attitude of *estrangement*. This concept was first developed on non-naturalistic texts by the Russian formalists ("ostranenie," Viktor Shklovsky) and most successfully underpinned by an anthropological and historical approach in the work of Bertolt Brecht, who wanted to write "plays for a scientific age." While working on a play about the prototypical scientist Galileo, he defined this attitude ("Verfremdungseffekt") in his *Short Organon for the Theatre*: "A representation which estranges is one which allows us to recognize its subject, but at the same time makes it seem unfamiliar."

And further: for somebody to see all normal happenings in a dubious light, "he would need to develop that detached eye with which the great Galileo observed a swinging chandelier. He was amazed by that pendulum motion as if he had not expected it and could not understand its occurring, and this enabled him to come at the rules by which it was governed." Thus, the look of estrangement is both cognitive and creative; and, as Brecht goes on to say, "One cannot simply exclaim that such an attitude pertains to science, but not to art. Why should not art, in its own way, try to serve the great social task of mastering Life?"[3] (Later, Brecht would note that it might be time to stop speaking in terms of masters and servants altogether.)

In SF the attitude of estrangement—used by Brecht in a different way, within a still predominantly "realistic" context—has grown into the *formal framework* of the genre.

2. Science Fiction as Cognition (Critique and Science)

2.1. The use of estrangement both as underlying attitude and dominant formal device is found also in the *myth*, a "timeless" and religious approach looking in its own way beneath (or above) the empiric surface. However, SF sees the norms of any age, including emphatically its own, as unique, changeable, and therefore subject to a *cognitive* view. The myth is diametrically opposed to the cognitive approach since it conceives human relations as fixed and supernaturally determined, emphatically denying Montaigne's "*la constance même n'est qu'un branle plus languissant.*" The myth absolutizes and even personifies apparently constant motifs from sluggish societies. Conversely, SF, which focuses on the variable and future-bearing elements from the empirical environment, is found predominantly in the great whirlpool periods of history, such as the sixteenth through seventeenth and nineteenth through twentieth centuries. Where the myth claims to explain once and for all the essence of phenomena, SF first posits them as problems and then explores where they lead; it sees the mythical static identity as an illusion, usually as fraud, at best only as a temporary realization of potentially limitless contingencies. It does not ask about "The Man" or "The World," but which man? In which kind of world? And why such a man in such a kind of world? As a literary genre, SF is fully as opposed to supernatural or metaphysical estrangement as it is to naturalism or empiricism.

2.2. *SF is, then, a literary genre whose necessary and sufficient conditions are the presence and interaction of estrangement and cognition, and whose main formal device is an imaginative framework alternative to the author's empirical environment.*

Estrangement differentiates SF from the "realistic" literary mainstream extending from the eighteenth century into the twentieth. Cognition differentiates it not only from myth, but also from the folk (fairy) tale and the fantasy. The *folktale* also doubts the laws of the author's empirical world, but it escapes out of its horizons and into a closed collateral world indifferent to cognitive possibilities. It does not use imagination as a means of understanding the tendencies latent in reality but as an end sufficient unto itself and cut off from the real contingencies. The stock folktale accessory, such as the flying carpet, evades the empirical law of physical gravity—as the hero evades social gravity—by imagining its opposite. This wish-fulfilling element is its strength and its weakness, for it never pretends that a carpet could be expected to fly—that a humble third son could be expected to become king—while there is gravity. It simply posits another world beside yours where some carpets do, magically, fly, and some paupers do, magically, become princes, and into which you cross purely by an act of faith and fancy. Anything is possible in a folktale, because a folktale is manifestly impossible. Furthermore, the lower-class genre of folktale was from the seventeenth to eighteenth century on transformed into the more compensatory, and often simplistic, *individualist fairytale*. Therefore, SF retrogressing into *fairytale* (for example, "space opera" with a hero-princess-monster triangle in astronautic costume) is committing creative suicide.

Even less congenial to SF is the *fantasy* (ghost, horror, gothic, weird) tale, a genre committed to the interposition of anti-cognitive laws into the empirical environment. Where the folktale is indifferent, the fantasy is inimical to the empirical world and its laws. The thesis could be defended that the fantasy is significant insofar as it is impure and fails to establish a superordinated maleficent world of its own, causing a grotesque tension between arbitrary supernatural phenomena and the empirical norms they infiltrate. Gogol's Nose is significant because it is walking down the Nevski Prospect, with a certain rank in the civil ser-vice, and so on; if the Nose were in a completely fantastic world—say H. P. Lovecraft's—it would be just another ghoulish thrill. When fan-tasy does not make for such a tension between the supernatural and the author's empirical environment, its monotonous reduction of all possi-ble horizons to Death makes of it just a subliterature of mystification. Commercial lumping of it into the same category as SF is thus a grave disservice and rampantly sociopathological phenomenon.

2.3.   The *pastoral*, on the other hand, is essentially closer to SF. Its imaginary framework of a world without money-economy, state appa-ratus, and depersonalizing urbanization allows it to isolate, as in a lab-oratory, two human motivations: erotics and power-hunger. This ap-proach relates to SF as alchemy does to chemistry and nuclear physics: an early try in the right direction with insufficient foundations. SF has much to learn from the pastoral tradition, primarily from its directly sensual relationships that do not manifest class alienation. This lesson has in fact often been absorbed, whenever SF has sounded the theme of the triumph of the humble (Restif, Morris, and others, up to Simak, Christopher, Yefremov, etc.). Unfortunately, the baroque pastoral abandoned this theme and jelled into a conventional sentimentality, discrediting the genre; but when pastoral escapes preciosity, its hope can fertilize the SF field as an antidote to pragmatism, commercialism, other-directedness, and technocracy.

2.4.   Claiming a Galilean estrangement for SF does not at all mean committing it to scientific vulgarization or even technological prog-nostication, which it was engaged in at various times (Verne, the United States in the 1920s and 1930s, USSR under Stalinism). The needful and meritorious task of popularization can be a useful element of SF works at a juvenile level. But even the *roman scientfique,* such as Verne's *From the Earth to the Moon*—or the surface level of Wells's *In-visible Man*—though a legitimate SF form, is a lower stage in its devel-opment. It is very popular with audiences just approaching SF, such as the juvenile, because it introduces into the old empirical context only *one* easily digestible new technological variable (moon missile or rays that lower the refractive index of organic matter).[4] The euphoria pro-voked by this approach is real but limited, better suited to the short story and a new audience. It evaporates much quicker as positivistic natural science loses prestige in the humanistic sphere after the world wars (compare Nemo's *Nautilus* as against the U.S. Navy's atomic submarine of the same name), and surges back with prestigious peacetime applications in new methodologies (astronautics, cybernetics). Even in Verne the "science novel" has a structure of transient estrangement, which is specific to murder mysteries, not to a mature SF.

2.5.   After such delimitations, it is perhaps possible at least to indicate some differentiations within the concept of "cognitiveness" or "cognition." As used here, this term implies not only a reflecting *of* but also *on* reality. It implies a creative approach tending toward a dynamic transformation rather than toward a static mirroring of the author's environment. Such typical SF methodology—from Lucian, More, Rabelais, Cyrano, and Swift to Wells, London, Zamyatin, and writers of the last decades—is a *critical* one, often satirical, combining a belief in the potentialities of reason with methodical doubt in the most significant cases. The kinship of this cognitive critique with the philosophical fundaments of modern science is evident.

3. The World of the Science Fiction Genre (Concept and Some Functions)

3.0.   As a full-fledged literary genre, SF has its own repertory of functions, conventions, and devices. Many of them are highly interesting and might prove very revealing for literary history and theory in general. I shall discuss some of these—such as the historically crucial shift of the locus of estrangement from space to time—in the chapters that follow. I shall not, however, attempt a systematic survey of such functions and devices, which would properly be the subject of another book, one that encompassed modern SF as well. I should only like to mention that all the estranging devices in SF are related to the cognition espoused, and that, together with the historical venerability of the genre's tradition, this seems to me a second, methodological reason for according SF much more importance than is usual in academe. However, it might here be possible to sketch some determining parameters of the genre.

3.1.   In a typology of literary genres for our cognitive age, one basic parameter would take into account the relationship of the world(s)

each genre presents and the "zero world" of empirically verifiable properties around the author (this being "zero" in the sense of a central reference point in a coordinate system, or of the control group in an experiment). Let us call this empirical world *naturalistic*. In it, and in the
corresponding "naturalistic" or "realistic" literature, ethics is in no significant relation to physics. Modern mainstream fiction is forbidden
the pathetic fallacy of earthquakes announcing the assassination of
rulers or drizzles accompanying the sadness of the heroine. It is the activity of the protagonists, interacting with other, physically equally unprivileged figures, that determines the outcome. However superior
technologically or sociologically one side in the conflict may be, any
predetermination as to its outcome is felt as an ideological imposition
and genological impurity: the basic rule of naturalistic literature is that
man's destiny is man.[5] On the contrary, in the non-naturalistic, *metaphysical* literary genres discussed in 2.1 and 2.2, circumstances around
the hero are neither passive nor neutral. In the folktale and the fantasy,
ethics coincides with (positive or negative) physics, in the tragic myth
it compensates the physics, in the "optimistic" myth it supplies the coincidence with a systematic framework.

The world of a work of SF is not a priori intentionally oriented toward its protagonists, either positively or negatively; the protagonists
may succeed or fail in their objectives, but nothing in the basic contract with the reader, in the physical laws of their worlds, guarantees either. SF thus shares with the dominant literature of our civilization a
mature approach analogous to that of modern science and philosophy,
as well as the omnitemporal horizons of such an approach—aspects
that will be discussed in the following chapters.

3.2. As a matter of historical record, SF has started from a pre-
scientific or protoscientific approach of debunking satire and naive
social critique and moved closer to the increasingly sophisticated
natural and human sciences. The natural sciences caught up and surpassed the literary imagination in the nineteenth century; the sciences dealing with human relationships might be argued to have
caught up with it in their highest theoretical achievements but have
certainly not done so in their alienated social practice. In the twentieth century SF has moved into the sphere of anthropological and
cosmological thought, becoming a diagnosis, a warning, a call to un-

derstanding and action, and—most important—a mapping of possible alternatives. This historical movement of SF can be envisaged as an enrichment of and shift from a basic direct model to an indirect model. What matters here is that the concept of a science fiction tradition or genre is a logical corollary of the recognition of SF as the literature of cognitive estrangement. It can be gleaned from my approach and examples that I think the literary genre that I am trying to define embraces the subgenres mentioned in 1.1, from Greek and earlier times until today (the Islands of the Blessed, utopias, fabulous voyages, planetary novels, *Staatsromane*, anticipations, and dystopias—as well as the Verne-type *romans scientifiques*, the Wellsian scientific romance variant, and the twentieth-century magazine- and anthology-based SF *sensu stricto*). If the argument of this chapter holds, the inner kinship of these subgenres is stronger than their obvious autonomous, differentiating features. Some historical discussion of these kinships and differences will be attempted later on in this book; here I want only to observe that the significant writers in this line were quite aware of their coherent tradition and explicitly testified to it (the axis Lucian-More-Fabelais–Cyrano-Swift-M. Shelley–Verne–Wells is a main example). Also, certain among the most perspicacious surveyors of aspects of the field, like Ernst Bloch, Lewis Mumford, or Northrop Frye, can be construed as assuming this unity.

3.3. The novelty of such a concept shows most distinctly when one attempts to find a name for the genre as it is here conceived. Ideally this name should clearly set it apart from (1) nonliterature; (2) the empiricist literary mainstream; (3) noncognitive estrangings such as fantasy; and furthermore (4) it should try to add as little as possible to the already prevailing confusion of tongues in this region. The academically most acceptable designation has been that of a literature of *utopian thought*. The concept is no doubt partly relevant but fails to meet the first criterion above; logically, such an approach was usually taught and considered within the scope of either the history of ideas or political and sociological theory. Although I would agree that literature (and especially this genre) is most intimately involved with life—indeed, that the destiny of humanity is its *telos*—I think one should quickly add that literature is also more than an ideational or sociological document. Since this is the rationale for any systematic literary study and scholarship, I may not need to belabor the point.

The only proper way of searching for a solution seems to require starting from the qualities defining the genre, since this would take care of the criteria 1 to 3 at least. Taking the kindred thesaurus concepts of *science* for cognition, and *fiction* for estrangement, I believe there is a sound reason for calling this whole new genre science fiction (*sensu lato*).

There are two main objections to such a solution. First, cognition is wider than science; I argued as much myself in 2.5. It is much less weighty, however, if one takes "science" in a sense closer to the German *Wissenschaft*, French *science*, or Russian *nauka*, which include not only natural but also all the cultural or historical sciences and even scholarship (cf. *Literaturwissenscaft, sciences humaines*). As a matter of fact, that is what science has been taken to stand for in the practice of SF: not only More or Zamyatin, but the writings of Americans such as Asimov, Heinein, Pohl, Dick, etc., would be completely impossible without sociological, psychological, historical, anthropological, and other parallels. Further, an element of convention enters into all names (compare "comparative literature"), but it has proved harmless as long as the name is handy, approximate enough, and above all applied to a clearly defined body of works. The second objection is that the use of "science fiction" confuses the whole genre with the twentieth-century SF from which the name was taken. Given the advantages of the only term at hand fulfilling the above criteria, I would argue that this is at worst a minor drawback; nobody has serious trouble in distinguishing between More's book, the country described in it, and the subgenre of utopia. The trouble begins with the variety of unrelated interdisciplinary and ideological interpretations foisted upon such a term; "science fiction" might perhaps escape the interdisciplinary part of that obstacle race. Furthermore, there are always advantages to acknowledging clearly one's methodological premises. As both Lukacs and Eliot would agree, any tradition is modified and reestablished by a sufficiently significant new development, from whose vantage point it can be reinterpreted. This is, I would maintain, the case with the mentioned *ci-devant* traditions, for example, of "utopian literature," in the age of science fiction. If that is accepted, the new name is no drawback at all, but simply an onomastic consummation.

4. For a Poetics of Science Fiction (Anticipation)

4.1. The above sketch should, no doubt, be supplemented by a sociological analysis of the "inner environment" of SF, exiled since the
beginning of the twentieth century into a reservation or ghetto that
was protective and is now constrictive, cutting off new developments
from healthy competition and the highest critical standards. Such a
sociological discussion would enable us to point out the important
differences between the highest reaches of the genre, glanced at here
in order to define functions and standards of SF, and its debilitating
average.[6]

4.2. If the whole above argument is found acceptable, it will be
possible to supplement it also by a survey of forms and subgenres.
Along with some that recur in an updated form—such as the utopia
and fabulous voyage—the anticipation, the superman story, the artificial intelligence story (robots, androids, and so on), time-travel, catastrophe, the meeting with aliens, and others, would have to be analyzed. The various forms and subgenres of SF could then be checked
for their relationships to other literary genres, to each other, and to
various sciences. For example, the utopias are—whatever else they
may be—clearly sociological fictions or social-science fiction,
whereas modern SF is analogous to modern polycentric cosmology,
uniting time and space in Einsteinian worlds with different but covariant dimensions and time scales. Significant modern SF, with
deeper and more lasting sources of enjoyment, also presupposes more
complex and wider cognitions: it discusses primarily the political,
psychological, and anthropological *use and effect of knowledge, of philosophy of science,* and the becoming of failure of new realities as a result of it. The consistency of extrapolation, precision of analogy, and
width of reference in such a cognitive discussion turn into aesthetic
factors. (That is why the "scientific novel" discussed in 2.3 is not
deemed completely satisfactory—it is aesthetically poor because it is
scientifically meager.) Once the elastic criteria of literary structuring
have been met, *a cognitive—in most cases strictly scientific—element becomes a measure of aesthetic quality, of the specific pleasure to be sought
in SF.* In other words, the cognitive nucleus of the plot codetermines
the fictional estrangement itself.

Notes

1. The first version of this essay emerged from a lecture given in spring 1968 in J. M. Holquist's seminar on fantastic literature in the Yale University Department of Slavic Languages and Literatures. I have derived much profit from discussions with him, with Jacques Ehrmann, my UMass colleague David Porter, and my McGill colleagues Irwin and Myrna Gopnik. The final version owes much to Stanislaw Lem's *Fantastyka i futurologia*, which considerably emboldened me in further pursuits within this protean field, even where I differed from some of Lem's emphases and conclusions.

2. A benefit of discussing the seemingly peripheral subject of "science fiction" is that one has to go back to first principles; one cannot really assume them as given. One must ask, for example, what is literature? Usually, when discussing literature one determines what it says (its subject matter) and how it says what it says (the approach to its themes). If we are talking about literature in the sense of significant works possessing certain minimal aesthetic qualities rather than in the sociological sense of everything that gets published at a certain time or in the ideological sense of all the writings on certain themes, this principle can more precisely be formulated as a double question. First epistemologically, what possibility for aesthetic qualities is offered by different thematic fields ("subjects")? The answer given by the aesthetics prevalent at the moment is: an absolutely equal possibility. With this answer is booted out of the field of aesthetics and into the lap of ideologists, who pick it up by our default and proceed to bungle it. Second, historically, how has such a possibility in fact been used? Once one begins with such considerations, one comes quickly up against the rather unclear concept of *realism* (not the prose literary movement in the nineteenth century but a metahistorical stylistic principle), since this genre is often pigeonholed as nonrealistic. I would not object but would heartily welcome such labels if one had first persuasively defined what is "real" and what is "reality." True, this genre raises basic philosophical issues, but it is perhaps not necessary to face them in an initial approach. Therefore, I shall here substitute for "reality" (whose existence independent of any observer or group of observers I do not at all doubt, in fact) the concept of "the author's empirical environment," which seems as immediately clear as any.

3. Viktor Shklovsky, "Iskusstvo kak priem," in *Sborniki po teorii poètich-eskogo iazyka*, 2 (Petrograd, 1917). In the translation "Art as Technique," in Lee T. Lemon and Marion J. Reis, eds. *Russian Formalist Criticism* (Lincoln, Neb., 1965), *ostranenie* is rendered somewhat clumsily as "defamiliarization." See also Victor Erlich's classical survey, *Russian Formalism* (The Hague, 1955).

Bertolt Brecht, "Kleines Organon für das Theater," in his *Gesammelte Werke*, 16 (Frankfurt, 1973), translated in John Willett, ed., *Brecht on Theatre* (New York, 1964). My quotations are from pp. 192 and 196 of this translation, but I have changed Mr. Willet's translation of *Verfremdung* as "alienation" into my "estrangement," since "alienation" evokes incorrect, indeed opposite connotations: estrangement was for Brecht an approach militating directly against social and cognitive alienation. See Ernst Bloch, "*Entgremdung, Verfremdung*: Alienation, Estrangement," in Erika Munk, ed., *Brecht* (New York, 1972).

4. Note the functional difference from the anti-gravity metal in Wells's *First Men in the Moon*, which is an introductory or "plausibility-validating" device and not the be-all of a much richer novel.

5. In such cases as certain novels by Hardy and plays by Ibsen, or some of the more doctrinaire works of the historical school of naturalism, where determinisms strongly stress circumstance at the expense of the main figures' activity, we have, underneath a surface appearance of "naturalism," an approach to tragic myth using a shamefaced validation for an unbelieving age. As contrary to Shakespeare or the romantics, in this case ethics follows physics in a supposedly causal chain (most often through biology). An analogous approach to fairytale is to be found in, say, the mimicry of "naturalism" in which Hollywood happy-end movies engage.

6. A first approach to the sociology of SF may be found in the special issue of Science-Fiction Studies, November 1977, edited and with an introduction by me.

~

CHAPTER FOUR

The Number of the Beast

Barry N. Malzberg

Well, what *is* it? Fifty experts—as the old Yiddish saying might have it—will produce fifty-one definitions. Still, we all try; here I am in Collier's *Encyclopedia*:

> Science fiction is that form of literature which deals with the effects of technological change in an imagined future, an alternative present or a reconceived history.

Workable and cautious, but it does not evade what could be called the *Arrowsmith* problem—Sinclair Lewis's novel, that is, which all of us science-fictioneers would instinctively agree is *not* of the genre, would probably fall into it under the terms of this definition. Certainly, technological (medical) change is an important aspect of this novel as are the effects of science upon the protagonist and his marriage. Clearly, my definition would also exclude some of the whimsical short stories of Robert Sheckley, whose bemused characters face the absurdities of a slightly disorienting metaphysics in the recognizable present: there is nothing technological about these stories, much less concern with technological change, and yet they appeared, most of them, in Horace Gold's *Galaxy* and fit indistinguishably into the format of that magazine. On the basis of this kind of work Sheckley was recognized in his early career as one of the most promising of the new writers. My definition would also exclude Randall Garrett's Darcy series whose novels and novelette depict an alternate present in which magic has assumed the role of science and modern science never found its way into being discovered. Change, to be sure, but not technological change: here is genre science fiction that deals with technological absence.

Shrug, consider the bar bill, try Theodore Sturgeon's 1940s dictum: a good science fiction story is one whose events would not have occurred without its scientific content. This is promising—among other things, it manages to summarize, for the decade, the essence of John W. Campbell's editorial vision in *Astounding* . . . but Anne McCaffrey's dragons could not fly in Sturgeon's science fiction and Sheckley's work, right through his great novel *Dimension of Miracles,* would not fit. Nor would the visions of J. W. Ballard and his descendants; if *The Terminal Beach* or *The Drowned World* are about anything, they are about a world in which science has failed and gone away . . . and yet the works of Ballard are considered central to any understanding of post-1960s science fiction.

James Tiptree's famous *The Women Men Don't See* has no science in it either, nor does Robert Silverberg's 1972 novel *Dying Inside,* generally regarded as one of the pivotal works of the decade. (It concerns a telepath, who has lived concealing his gift, slowly losing his powers in early middle age in contemporary New York.) Then, too, Sturgeon's definition would admit not only *Arrowsmith* but many novels *about* science— Morton Thompson's *Not as a Stranger,* Peter George's *Red Alert,* George P. Elliott's *David Knudsen.* Any definition so inclusive would obviously attenuate a category that, however ill-defined, is very clearly understood by its readers, writers, editors, and critics to be a distinct and limited (if not really limiting) form of literature.

Perhaps one throws up one's hands and dives back to the 1950s to Damon Knight's, "Science fiction is whatever we point to when we say 'this is science fiction.'" Lots of truth in that; whatever trouble we may have with definitions, there is a consensual feeling among those of us who pretend to understand the form: McCaffrey's *Dragonflight* belongs in the genre and *Arrowsmith* does not. Check the *Science Fiction Encyclopedia* and the bibliographies. Still, if Knight's path of implied least resistance is the way to go, I would prefer Frederik Pohl's useful, provocative and contained: "Science fiction is a way of thinking about things."

Science fiction, then, is a methodology and an approach.

Pohl is surely on the trail of something important here, and if one could define what that way of thinking about things *is*, one perhaps would come as close to a working definition of science fiction as will be needed to understand almost all of it. Let me have a try at this, noting my indebtedness to A. J. Budrys, who has prowled this corridor some, most notably in his introduction to John Varley's collection *The Persistence of Vision*.

Science fiction, at the center, holds that the encroachment of technological or social change will make the future different and that it will *feel* different to those within it. In a technologically altered culture, people will regard themselves and their lives in ways that we cannot apprehend. That is the base of the science fiction vision, but the more important part comes as corollary: the effects of a changed technology upon us will be more profound than change brought about by psychological or social pressure. What technological alteration, the gleaming or putrid knife of the future, is going to do will cut far deeper than the effects of adultery, divorce, clinical depression, rap groups, consciousness-raising, encounter sessions, or even the workings of that famous old law firm of Sack, Pillage, Loot & Burn. It will be *these* changes—those imposed extrinsically by force—that really matter; this is what the science fiction writer is saying, and in their inevitability and power they trivialize the close psychological interactions in which most of us transact our lives (or at least would like to).

Lasting, significant change, science fiction says, is uncontrollable and coming in uncontrollably; regardless of what we think or how we feel, we have lost control of our lives. When the aliens debark from their craft to deal with the colonization assignment, the saved and the unsaved, adulterous and chaste, psychoanalyzed and uncompensated will be caught in their terrible tracer beams and absorb the common fate. When the last layer of protective ozone is burned out by International Terror & Trade, discussion leaders, the born again and the members of the American Psychological Association will all go together.

This is what was being said, implicitly, in all of the crazy and convoluted stories of the 1930s and 1940s behind the funny covers; more sedately, and occasionally in hardcover, it is being said today. Because this vision is inimical to the middle class (which has been taught that increased self-realization is increased control), because it tends to trivialize if not actually mock the vision of the modern novel and drama (the shaping of experience is its explanation), genre science fiction has been in trouble in America from the outset. It has been perceived almost from the beginning as the enemy of the culture. Science fiction has had a hearing from those who control access to the broad reading audience at only a few points in its history (I suggest 1946, 1957, and 1972) and in every case has been swiftly repudiated. The successful media science fiction of the seventies (most, though not all of it, debased adventure stories with crude science-fictional props) has forced literary science fiction into juxtaposition with the culture. The increase in readership funneled in by "Star Trek" and *Star Wars* has indicated that publishers will not permit it this time to go away . . . but science fiction is hardly, at the outset of the decade of the 1980s, much more of a reputable and critically accepted genre than it was thirty years ago.

It is my assumption that it never will be. Science fiction is too threatening.

At the center, science fiction is a dangerous literature. It represents the beast born in the era of enlightenment to snarl at the heart of all intellectual and technological advances. As the technology becomes more sophisticated and intrusive, as our lives in the postindustrial twentieth came to be dominated in every way by technology, science fiction became more cunning in its template. We know not what we do; the engines can eat us up—this is what science fiction has been saying (among many other things) for a long time now. It may be preaching only to the converted, but the objective truth, the inner beast, will not go away—despite the hostility of the culture, the ineptitude of many of its practitioners, the loathing of most of its editors, the corruption of most of its readers—and so neither will science fiction. It, if no given writer, will persist; will run, with the engines, the full disastrous course.

CHAPTER FIVE

~

On the Origins of Genre

Paul Kincaid

There is no starting point for science fiction. There is no one novel that marks the beginning of the genre. We have all had a go at identifying the urtext, the source from which Heinlein and Ellison and Gibson and Ballard and Priest and Le Guin and a host of others flow. Brian Aldiss famously named *Frankenstein* by Mary Shelley, and his suggestion has been taken up by a number of later commentators. Other strong contenders include H. G. Wells, or Edgar Allen Poe, or Jules Verne. Gary Westfahl has nominated Hugo Gernsback as the true father of science fiction. Still others (including myself) have gone back to Thomas More's *Utopia*.

We are all wrong.

We have to be wrong, because there is no ancestral text that could possibly contain, even in nascent form, all that we have come to identify as science fiction.

What part of *Frankenstein*, for instance, as diluted as homeopathic medicine, is to be found in Philip K. Dick's *The Martian Timeslip*, or Gene Wolfe's *The Book of the New Sun*, or Octavia Butler's *Parable of the Talents*, or Isaac Asimov's *Foundation*? What, come to that, could possibly link these disparate texts, other than the fact that we have come to apply the name "science fiction" to all of them?

This inability to define science fiction is a problem we have long recognized. In his 1986 work, *Critical Terms for Science Fiction: A Glossary and Guide to Scholarship*, Gary K. Wolfe included thirty-three different definitions of science fiction, many of which overlapped to some degree or other, but all of which included contradictions. The critical test for any definition is that it includes everything we believe should be included within the term, and it excludes everything we believe should be omitted. Strictly applied, every single one of those definitions would admit to the genre works that we would prefer to exclude, or would omit works we feel belong in the genre. Even Darko Suvin's cognitive estrangement expressed thus: "SF in general—through its long history in different contexts—can be defined as 'a literary genre whose necessary and sufficient conditions are the presence and interaction of estrangement and cognition'" (4), which seems to have become the default definition of choice of most academic critics, is a prescriptive definition that works fine as long as we are comfortable with what it prescribes, but can lead to extraordinary convolutions as we try to show that certain favored texts really do conform to the idea of cognitive estrangement, and even more extraordinary convolutions to reveal that familiar non-SF texts don't.

Since Wolfe's *tour d'horizon*, science-fiction scholarship has expanded exponentially, and most commentators have felt the need to add a new way of defining what it is they are talking about. These vary from formulations that are so imprecise as to be virtually useless—Kim Stanley Robinson, in his Guest of Honor Speech at Readercon in 1997 said, "Science fiction is the history that we cannot know"—to those that attempt to touch every base, and end up tying themselves in knots in the process. The sixth edition of *The Oxford Companion to English Literature* (2000), says:

> The label "science fiction" suggests a hybrid form, not quite ordinary fiction, not quite science, yet partaking of both. Beneath this label, we find a variety of wares, some of which trail off from a hypothetical central point into utopianism or dystopianism, heroic fantasy, horror, and books on UFOs and the paranormal. Yet its statements are normally based either on a possible scientific advance, or on a natural or social change, or on a suspicion that the world is not as it is commonly represented. It fol-

lows that one of the unacknowledged pleasures of reading science fiction (or SF) is that it challenges readers to decide whether what they are reading is within the bounds of the possible. (906)

This is an interesting definition, clearly written by someone sympathetic to the genre, yet as a means of identifying what science fiction is—it is useless. "[N]ot quite ordinary fiction, not quite science, yet partaking of both": what does this mean? In what way is it not quite "ordinary fiction" (and what might that be)? To what degree is it "science"? By what proportions does it "partake of both"? The qualification "normally based" implies that a goodly portion of science fiction might not be based on any of the categories that follow. Yet these categories are hardly restricted to science fiction: "a suspicion that the world is not as it is commonly represented" has been the hallmark of conspiracy theories throughout history, without any suggestion that such theories are necessarily science fiction. And literature based on some form or notion of "social change" includes such key science-fictional texts as *Sense and Sensibility*, *The Road to Wigan Pier* and at least half the oeuvre of P. G. Wodehouse. I am being unduly harsh on what is, after all, an honorable attempt to apostrophize, briefly, the indefinable. But much the same criticisms could be leveled against any extant definition of science fiction, and it is only by looking at why these definitions fail that we can start to consider what it is that makes science fiction indefinable.

In brief: the more comprehensively a definition seeks to encompass science fiction, the more unsatisfactory it seems to those of us who know the genre. To which one response is that we simply ignore the question altogether. The Clute and Nicholls *Encyclopedia of Science Fiction* (1993) contains reference to just about every form of science fiction, but though there is an entry on "Definitions of SF," it doesn't actually include a definition of SF. The article, which covers much the same ground as the entry in Gary Wolfe's book, is a conspectus of the different and often incompatible definitions that have been proposed for the genre. But it does not arrive at a single, comprehensive overview of what science fiction is. Either there is no such single, comprehensive definition or, as when *The Oxford Companion to English Literature* concludes that science fiction "challenges readers to decide," we finally admit that science fiction is defined not by something intrinsic to the genre, but rather it is in the eye of the beholder. In other words, many of us end up echoing Damon Knight: science fiction is "what we point to when we say it." (Though it is worth remembering that what Damon Knight actually wrote in *In Search of Wonder* (1956) was: "The term 'science fiction' is a misnomer, . . . it will do us no particular harm if we remember that, like *The Saturday Evening Post*, it means what we point to when we say it." (1)) Knight's ostensive definition of science fiction has been so frequently misquoted and adapted—one brutalist variant is Norman Spinrad's (in *Modern Science Fiction*): "Science fiction is anything published as science fiction" (quoted in Wolfe, 110), which excludes *Frankenstein*, most of the works of H. G. Wells, and practically every contemporary science fiction novel, at least in Britain where publishers have mostly abandoned putting the descriptor "science fiction" on their books—that its subtlety and value is often missed. I will be trying to exploit that subtlety in this chapter.

The two questions are, of course, intimately connected. Where we find the starting point for science fiction inevitably affects how we define the genre, and vice versa. Thus Brian Aldiss's famous definition from *Billion Year Spree* (1973)—"Science fiction is the search for a definition of man and his status in the universe which will stand in our advanced but confused state of knowledge (science), and is characteristically cast in the Gothic or post-Gothic mould" (8)—cannily excludes anything that might precede his chosen urtext, *Frankenstein*. Alexei and Cory Panshin, in *The World Beyond the Hill* (1989), want to present science fiction as being centrally concerned with transcendence, so their definition, "Science fiction is a literature of the mythic imagination" (1), throws the net wide enough to include any of early man's attempts at myth-making, while excluding more recent science fictions that shade into social realism. Gary Westfahl wants to prove, in *The Mechanics of Wonder* (1998), that Hugo Gernsback was the true father of science fiction and so constructs a "description" of science fiction in which the community engendered by Gernsback through his magazines is a vital part of what makes the genre: "If we define a genre as consisting of a body of texts related by a shared understanding of that genre as recorded in contemporary commentary, then a true history of science fiction as a genre must begin in 1926, at the time when Gernsback defined science fiction" (8).

In the beginning is the definition. And what we conceive science fiction to be inevitably dictates how we identify its origin. What's more, where we place that starting point inevitably affects what we see as the history (and the prehistory) of the genre, which in turn changes our perception of what science fiction is. It is a mobius loop: the definition affects the perception of the historical starting point, which in turn affects the definition.

Except that just as we have no commonly agreed definition of the genre; we have no *primum mobile* that everyone can accept. Everyone is on a different mobius loop.

This is because, as I indicated in my opening statement, there is not one definition of science fiction but many; there is not one urtext but many. We choose whichever best suits our conceptions of science fiction, and change those choices (or devise new ones) as our conceptions change. In other words, whenever we talk about science fiction, we are effectively using a private language.

The amazing thing is that there is still enough overlap in our understanding of the terms for us to know, more or less and in most cases, what other people are talking about. The reason for this, I suggest, is best understood by taking a different approach to the linked questions of the definition and the starting point for the genre.

It is a neat and rational idea to imagine that we can look at science fiction, identify within it the various necessary elements that define the genre, and trace these back to find the earliest single instance in which these necessary lineaments are unequivocally combined. But reality is rarely so neat or so rational as this model might suggest. How do we identify which elements are necessary and which are sufficient to define the genre when, as I have noted, we cannot agree on a definition in the first place? Which combination of these elements has to be in place for that earliest instance to be unequivocal?

The truth is that this model could only work if science fiction was one thing, if every instance of the genre shared 99 percent of the same DNA. But if we take as the DNA of a genre the various story elements that we tend to hold up as identifiers of science fiction—for the sake of argument, these might include such disparate and often imprecise things as hardware, setting, theme, authorial intent, feel—it is possible for two stories to share none of the same DNA and yet have readers willing to identify them as science fiction: *The Time Machine* by H. G. Wells and *Pavane* by Keith Roberts, for instance. In Damon Knight's terms, we can confidently point to both these works, along with, for example, *Report on Probability A* by Brian Aldiss, *Counter-Clock World* by Philip K. Dick, *The Affirmation* by Christopher Priest, *The Female Man* by Joanna Russ, and proclaim: yes, that is science fiction. But we could point to nothing that makes every one of these science fiction at the same time and in the same way. And it is worth remembering that no story is wholly science fiction. Even stories like "Day Million" by Frederik Pohl or "Love Is the Plan, the Plan Is Death" by James Tiptree Jr.— works that seem comprehensively to occupy the science-fictionality of their worlds—will share something, be it use of language, characterization, satirical intent, or whatever, that still links it with non-science fiction works. So we cannot extract a unique, common thread that we could trace back to a unique, common origin.

Science fiction, in particular, and probably all genres in general, does not work that way. A genre does not emerge, entire and fully armed, from the body of literature. A better analogy might be evolution by means of natural selection. There is an inchoate mass of story, each individual writer struggling with each individual story to produce something that will succeed, that will sell, or will please an editor, or will please a reader, or will make a particular point, or will work in a formal experimental sense, or, more likely, that will do several or all of these and perhaps more besides. In order to do this they might use ideas or themes or settings picked up from other writers, or that are a reaction against those of other writers; they might distort something old and familiar or invent something entirely new; they might take bits and pieces from a dozen different sources and recombine them in a novel way or regard them from a novel perspective. The exact details of this evolutionary process need not concern us, but eventually enough writers will be producing work that is sufficiently similar for us to start recognizing patterns.

Once we have this identifiable pattern, and we have given a name to it (let us, for the sake of argument, call it "science fiction"), some people will work strictly within the pattern, others will deliberately avoid the pattern, still others will occupy a vague hinterland part in and part out of the pattern, while there will be yet more who cross the borders working within or without the pattern as the inspiration takes them. Yet none of them, even those working strictly within its boundaries, will replicate the pattern precisely in every instance. Were they to do so, they would be writing the same book; as long as writers are writing different books they will be in a constant process of taking different things from and adding different things to the pattern. The pattern, the genre, is hence in a state of constant flux.

Having already appropriated the phrase "private language" from Ludwig Wittgenstein's *Philosophical Investigations*, I now want to borrow another of his terms: "family resemblances." When he was looking at the way language is used, Wittgenstein had a problem with the word "sport." We use the word to identify a clearly understood set of activities, but what it is that identifies those activities as sport is not so clear. Some sports use a ball, but not all do. Some use some form of racket or bat, but many don't. Many involve strenuous physical exercise, but some (diving, snooker, target shooting) don't. Some require acute hand-eye coordination, many don't. Some demand brute strength but not grace, others demand grace but not brute strength, still others don't demand either. And so on. For every identifying characteristic, there are activities that we call sports that do not possess them (and there are activities that we do not call sports, certain games for instance, that may possess them). In other words, the more closely we look at what the word "sport" means, the fuzzier it becomes; but we are all quite clear in how we use the word, and we are confident when we say "X is a sport, but Y isn't" (we may disagree on particular instances—is synchronized swimming a sport?—but that doesn't affect our confidence in using the word). Wittgenstein's conclusion was that sports bear "family resemblances" to other sports. To simplify the process, we might recognize that a sport with characteristics A, B, C, and D bears a family resemblance to a sport with characteristics B, C, D, and E, and this in turn has a family resemblance to a third sport with characteristics C, D, E, and F, and so on. It is because we recognize this network of resemblances that we are able to use words like "sport" that stand for a wide variety of very different instances. It is also easy to see that we can trace this network of resemblances to discover a relationship between two sports that actually have no individual characteristics in common.

The analogy with science fiction is, I hope, obvious. Again, we have a term, "science fiction," which we use to apply to a wide variety of individual works and groups of works, some of which have no obvious characteristics in common with others. Again, we are confident, as Damon Knight implied, in using the term to say: "X is science fiction, but Y isn't" (and again, we may disagree over individual instances—is the film *Apollo 13* science fiction? Is the novel *Perdido Street Station* by China Miéville?—but that does not affect our confidence in using the term). Thus "science fiction" is as amenable to the idea of family resemblances as "sport" is, and I would suggest that it is a more productive way of looking at our use of the term than is any attempt at definition.

A definition attempts to fix the pattern that applies to science fiction, but the pattern, as I have shown, is in constant flux, and no definition has successfully managed to encompass all that it is, all that it has been, and all that it might be. Family resemblances are more flexible, since they allow us to keep pace with every change in the genre. A radical new work that takes science fiction in an unexpected direction would not require a redefinition; all that is required is that it bear a family resemblance to another work that we commonly agree is science fiction. (If the new work is so radical that we cannot agree that it bears any resemblance to any other work of science fiction, then perhaps we must concede that it is not science fiction; but such an instance would take us beyond the purview of this essay.) Thus, family resemblances recognize science fiction as a restless, dynamic form that might head out in multiple different directions from multiple different origins, and yet still be something that we can talk about sensibly under the one heading: science fiction.

If all that is required for us to call a work science fiction is that we recognize that it is a member of the same family as another work that we have already identified as science fiction, it might seem that we are simply pushing the question of definition back one stage. We cannot say that A is science fiction because it resembles B, which in turn resembles C, which resembles D, which in turn . . . etc. This is an endless regress that tells us nothing, and if all that family resemblances are doing is embarking on such a regress, it is as useless as any attempt to define the genre. But, in fact, all we need as a starting point is common agreement that something is science fiction. What makes it science fiction may, and probably will, vary from instance to instance, and is in fact irrelevant for our purposes here. It is not important why we agree that X is science fiction, it is only important that we agree. And there are many hundreds, indeed thousands, of works whose identity as science fiction is not problematic. We do not engage in heated arguments about whether *The War of the Worlds* or *The Moon Is a Harsh Mistress* or *I, Robot* is science fiction because such arguments would be fruitless. It is not in the heartland of science fiction that definitions, or family resemblances, are an issue, but on the borders, where science fiction is changing into something else, or something else is changing into science fiction.

Why certain works are unequivocally part of the heartland of science fiction may be historical accident; it may be as simple as certain editors (Hugo Gernsback, John W. Campbell) buying stories of a familiar type that were published in magazines labeled "science fiction." Whatever the precise details of the case, what has undeniably happened is that certain works with certain characteristics in common have been published so consistently under the label science fiction that they have come to be seen as representative of that label. Consequently, there are any number of works—"The Cold Equations" by Tom Godwin, "The Rose" by Charles Harness, *Fahrenheit 451* by Ray Bradbury—that, for most purposes and in most circumstances, we would not dream of labeling anything other than science fiction. We have no problem in identifying these and countless similar stories as science fiction, so much so that the question of what actually makes them science fiction never arises. As we move away from this heartland, however, the science-fictionality of individual works becomes less clear cut, less unquestioned. Is the *Canopus in Argos* sequence science fiction despite the fact that it was written by an author, Doris Lessing, not normally associated with the genre, and who has deliberately eschewed the term in favor of her own coinage, "space fiction"? Is *Perdido Street Station* science fiction despite the fact that it makes significant use of devices more commonly associated with genre fantasy or supernatural honor? Is *Frankenstein* science fiction despite the fact that it predates our commonly accepted use of the term by a century and its tropes have been most successfully taken up by the horror film?

It is precisely here where questions of our use of the term science fiction are most pertinent, that definitions of science fiction are generally least valuable. By establishing rigid formulations designed, of necessity, to encompass the heartland, they become questionable and often counterintuitive just where they are most needed, on the borderland. By tracing family resemblances, however, we have no problem with whether the name "science fiction" can be applied, even to works that actually cross the imprecise and ever-changing borders of the genre.

Moreover, it is rare for a work, even in the heartland of genre, to be all of one thing or all of another. A novel such as *The Caves of Steel* by Isaac Asimov, for instance, is clearly and unequivocally science fiction, but it also clearly and deliberately partakes of the detective story. It is a recognizable member of two different genre families. But there is no problem in saying that in respect of characteristics A, B, and C it resembles science fiction, and hence discussing it as a work of science fiction; that in respect of characteristics X, Y, and Z it resembles detective fiction, and hence discussing it as a work of detective fiction. Whether the science fiction aspects, or any other genre aspects, are done well or ill is beside the point; that they are there at all is what we recognize in a work. By the same token, in terms of the beauty or otherwise of the language employed or the characterization, or the scene setting, or any of countless other qualities, we might equally recognize a novel as a work of science fiction and at the same time more broadly as a work of fiction. Again, a novel like *Perdido Street Station*, which partakes of elements of, among others, science fiction, fantasy, and horror, can be included in the discussion of science fiction in relation to those elements that resemble science fiction, just as it can be included in the discussions of fantasy and horror in relation to those elements that resemble fantasy and horror.

What I am proposing is a development of Damon Knight's ostensive definition of science fiction. That is science fiction that we point to and say: it has family resemblances with what we agree is science fiction.

One thing to recognize, therefore, in this web of resemblances, is that one work might bear different resemblances to many other works. And any number of those resemblances might constitute what we would call science fiction. By thinking of science fiction as a network of such family resemblances, it is easier to see that science fiction is not one thing. Rather, it is any number of things—a future setting, a marvelous device, an ideal society, an alien creature, a twist in time, an interstellar journey, a satirical perspective, a particular approach to the matter of story, whatever we may be looking for when we look for science fiction, here more overt, here more subtle—that are braided together in an endless variety of combinations. A newcomer to the genre might find these combinations unsettling, hard to unravel, formulaic; but the more familiar we are with the genre, the more readily we can accept their variety, the more subtly we might interpret their combinations. So much so that at times we might identify a work as science fiction for no other reason than that "it feels like science fiction"; the furniture of a story, the obvious plot devices have become subsumed under our interpretation of authorial intent. What constitutes the warp and weft of science fiction, therefore, is endlessly subtle and intricate, made up at times of more things than we can readily identify. Which is why what makes science fiction is so hard to pin down, but what is science fiction is so easy to recognize.

What is more, the web of resemblances extends backward in time as well as forward. If we recognize a new work as science fiction because it resembles an earlier work of science fiction, so we can go back and recognize an historical work as science fiction because it resembles works we would later come to call science fiction. Supposing we accept Gary Westfahl's contention that science fiction only really began in 1926 when the term (or at least Gernsback's coinage, "scientifiction") was first applied to what we now recognize as genre SF; we can still identify certain works of the 1890s—*The Time Machine, The War of the Worlds, The Invisible Man*—as science fiction because they resemble so closely works that are clearly science fiction. Tracing the resemblances ever backwards will not lead to that original urtext, of course—there is no such a thing—but it does lead, rather, to a series of urtexts.

Science fiction, as I have described it, consists of a series of threads (themes, devices, approaches, ideas) that are braided together. This is cognate with David Seed's argument in *Anticipations* that science fiction, rather than being one genre, is actually a series of subgenres that have come together over time. But rather than thinking in terms of distinct subgenres, I want to suggest a series of strands, none of which would stand as a genre or even a subgenre in their own right but which, braided together in any of a possibly infinite number of combinations, make what we have come to recognize as science fiction. Any one of the threads might be removed from the braid and it would still be science fiction. The threads that make up the braid might be separated and then rewound to make two separate braids, both of which are science fiction. But there is not one single thread that can be removed and that in itself is science fiction. Similarly, there is probably no critical point at which we can say: this is the minimum number of threads required for us to call a work science fiction; or: these particular threads are the ones that must be included if the whole is to be called science fiction. Tracing family resemblances backward through the literature, therefore, is not going to lead us to the origins of science fiction; but it might lead us to the origins of some of the threads that constitute science fiction.

Thus, there are strands extant in contemporary science fiction that may have their origins in classical, or pre-classical, mythology. There are threads that may go back to identifiable individual works, to the satirical celestial journeys of Lucian of Samosata, for instance, to Thomas More's *Utopia*, to Mary Shelley's *Frankenstein*, to countless other works by Copernicus, by Cyrano de Bergerac, by Jules Verne or Edgar Allan Poe or H. G. Wells. Whether this necessarily makes any of these works the urtext of science fiction, or whether it makes them science fiction at all is open to debate, but they certainly resemble aspects of what we would come to call science fiction, they might be considered the starting point for threads that would come to constitute science fiction. Where the braid of these threads reaches the critical point at which it unequivocally becomes science fiction is impossible to say. All we can say is that science fiction starts here . . . and here . . . and here . . . and here. . . . Which of these particular starting points we choose, therefore, comes down not to a question of definition but of inclination.

Science fiction is what we point to when we say "science fiction," and where the genre begins historically and what constitutes that genre will vary as the direction in which we point varies. But because we can see the resemblances between works of science fiction, because we can identify the various threads that combine to form the whole, so we can talk sensibly about the genre and understand others when they do the same, and so we can draw an historical model for the genre in which the details may vary but the overall narrative tells a story we all understand.

Works Cited

Aldiss, Brian W. *Billion Year Spree: The History of Science Fiction.* London: Corgi, 1975.

Clute, John, and Peter Nicholls, eds. *The Encyclopedia of Science Fiction.* 2nd ed. London: Orbi, 1993.

Drabble, Margaret, ed. *The Oxford Companion to English Literature.* 6th ed. Oxford: Oxford University Press, 2000.

Knight, Damon. *In Search of Wonder.* 2nd ed. Chicago: Advent, 1971.

Panshin, Alexei and Cory. *The World Beyond the Hill.* Los Angeles: Jeremy P. Tarcher, 1989.

Seed, David, ed. *Anticipations: Essays on Early Science Fiction and Its Precursors.* Liverpool: Liverpool University Press, 1995.

Suvin, Darko. "Narrative Logic, Ideological Domination, and the Range of Science Fiction: A Hypothesis with a Historical Test." *Science Fiction Studies* 9, no. 26 (1982): 1–25.

Westfahl, Gary. *The Mechanics of Wonder.* Liverpool: Liverpool University Press, 1998.

Wittgenstein, Ludwig. *Philosophical Investigations.* Oxford: Blackwell, 1968.

Wolfe, Gary K. *Critical Terms for Science Fiction and Fantasy.* Westport, Connecticut: Greenwood, 1986.

PART TWO

LOCATION

No matter what definition of science fiction one has selected from the previous section (or cannibalized from the parts thereof), the simple fact remains that when we enter a bookstore, there will almost always be a section labeled "science fiction" or "science fiction and fantasy," to which we can wander if we are so inclined. More often than not, if there is no such section, it is because we have stumbled into one of those bookstores that abides by what Aldiss calls Generalization-22—all science fiction is rubbish—and therefore does not sell such stuff. And such divisions abound, not only in bookstores, but wherever media are circulated. Video stores, magazine stands, and calendar stores all have science fiction and/or fantasy sections and a TV guide will usually label a certain program with the dubious moniker "sci-fi," even if it gives no real description. Nor are these divisions wholly commercial ones, for they appear even where people are not trying to sell anything, such as nearly all public libraries (although research libraries utilizing the Library of Congress system interfile SF texts with the bulk of their national literatures).

These divisions exist for very pragmatic reasons that mainly boil down to the fact that "science fiction" as a label works very well as a marketing tool, a capitalist acknowledgment of Damon Knight's definition of the genre, but possibly capitalism, through the quirky, evolutionary genius of the marketplace, has labeled a real truth here, that science fiction is genuinely different from other types of literature and should remain separate. Or perhaps the division represents the marketing equivalent of the dodo: overdue for its own extinction. The essays in this section grapple with the very significant question of whether the genre belongs or should belong to the larger body of literature, or whether it should be considered a creature apart, a separate species, if you will.

Darko Suvin, in "SF and the Genological Jungle," continues his quest to separate what he calls "cognitive" and "non-cognitive" literary forms. This distinction is crucial for Suvin, who stresses again and again that true SF aspires to the cognitive category, rather than sinking into fantasy, which encourages readers to approach it non-cognitively. Some of his techniques are interesting, including the so-called test for his genological system, the addition of an additional dimension, time, which is in no way definable as a test, but rather is a carefully structured argument, rhetorically positioned as though it were a scientific experiment. Through this "test" Suvin seeks to keep science fiction separate but still pegged in value against "realistic" literature, almost the way the Soviet ruble was supposedly pegged against the dollar. Suvin is adamantly opposed to comparisons between science fiction and myth, arguing that science fiction is a subversive genre, while myth, like fantasy is a normative one. This contrast puts him at odds with critics such as David Ketterer and Cory and Alexei Panshin who seek to place science fiction under the aegis of myth.

In "The Readers of Hard Science Fiction," James Gunn gives a very clear rationale for the separation of science fiction from mainstream literature: its readers read differently, make different demands on the genre, and therefore any attempt to subsume science fiction under the mainstream would place the genre in an inferior position. Gunn, like Suvin, however, wants to separate the "cognitive" and "non-cognitive" forms of estranged literature, but he presents a better rationale for distinguishing them. Rather than looking simply at the works themselves and attempting to evaluate whether they contain the vital cognitive quality, Gunn argues that cognitive or "hard" science fiction is distinguished by the expectation that readers of the form will analyze it for its continuity with the world of naturalistic experience and fiction, whereas readers of "soft" science fiction will not make the analysis, while readers of fantasy assume that the world is discontinuous.

Similar to James Gunn, Samuel Delany in "Science Fiction and Literature" argues that the way science fiction is read is crucial to understanding the genre and its distinction from mainstream or "mundane" literature. First, he argues that because the world in which a science fiction story takes place is not a given, science fiction readers take a more active role in constructing the fictional world than readers of mundane literature. Science fiction also allows a greater range of expression because sentences that are meaningless, redundant, or "muzzily" metaphorical in mundane literature can be used literally, giving a good rationale for the boasts of John W. Campbell and others that mundane literature is a subset of science fiction. Delany gives further justification to this perspective on the two genres when he shows how reading mundane literature with a science-fiction mindset enriches the literature. Delany ends with the admonition that science-fiction writers should always aspire to the heights the genre is capable of, rather than allowing it to lapse into subliterature.

In "Science Fiction and Mrs. Brown," Ursula Le Guin provides a different rationale for science-fiction writers to aspire to great heights. Utilizing the Virginia Woolf essay "Mr. Bennet and Mrs. Brown" as a jumping-off place, Le Guin argues that real human characters are the central feature of all good literature, and that all the tropes of science fiction—universe-spanning civilizations, starships, and supermen—pale by comparison with genuine humanity. She does not, of course, advocate abandoning the tropes, but rather writing them into real novels centered on genuine humanity, and she gives several examples of ways this has been done successfully.

Brash and scrappy as always, Barry Malzberg tacks differently against this question in "I Could Have Been a Contender." Malzberg argues that Hugo Gernsback did the genre an invaluable favor when he separated it from mainstream literature and consigned it to its own subliterary ghetto. In doing so, Malzberg argues, Gernsback ensured that science fiction would have its own unique, separate, and spirited history. Malzberg argues that, far from being the inclusive genre others might imagine, it is a rigorous and limiting form, like the sonnet, and works within the form are all the more worthy of being called art because of these limitations.

~

CHAPTER SIX

SF and the Genological Jungle

Darko Suvin

> Thanks to the Greeks, we can distinguish tragedy from comedy in
> drama. . . . When we come to deal with such forms as the masque,
> opera, movie, ballet, puppet-play, mystery-play, morality, comme-
> dia dell'arte, and Zauberspiel, we find ourselves in the position of
> Renaissance doctors who refused to treat syphilis because Galen
> said nothing about it.
>
> —Northop Frye

1. A View from the Mountain: Taxonomy and a System

1.0.   As Northrop Frye has rightly remarked, "just as there is nothing
which the philosopher cannot consider philosophically, and nothing
which the historian cannot consider historically, so the critic should be
able to construct and dwell in a conceptual universe of his own."[1] For
the purposes of constructing the universe of this discussion, I take it (1)
that no field of studies and rational inquiry can be investigated unless
and until it is at least roughly delimited; (2) that there exist literary
genres, as socioaesthetic and not metaphysical entities; (3) that these
entities have an inner life and logic of their own, which do not exclude
but on the contrary presuppose a dialectical permeability to themes, attitudes, and paradigms from other literary genres, sciences, philosophy,

and everyday socioeconomic life; (4) that the genres pertinent to this discussion are naturalistic fiction, fantasy, myth, folk tale, pastoral, and science fiction. I am assuming that these four axioms will be justified by their cognitive yield, by the light that they might throw upon the field of inquiry. Should this assumption prove justified, it would go a long way toward indicating that the basic and possibly central task of SF theory and criticism at this historical moment is the construction of a heuristic model or models for "Science Fiction"—which is also the hypothesis of this chapter.

A heuristic model is a theoretical structure based on analogy, which does not claim to be transcendentally or illusionistically "real" in the sense of mystically representing a palpable material entity, but whose use is scientifically and scholarly permissible, desirable, and necessary because of its practical results. An example might be the construct according to which the molecules of a gas behave like minuscule elastic billiard balls in random motion. Though very little may be known or indeed knowable about what gas molecules are "really" like, both at the time this construct was promulgated and now it was certain beyond reasonable doubt that they were *not* elastic billiard balls of a microscopic size. Yet this heuristic model was among the decisive factors in the development of the whole discipline of thermodynamics. It had immense theoretical and practical consequences, among others a giant step forward in human understanding of natural and perhaps even social processes. It seems therefore unnecessary to reopen the debates of the medieval nominalists and realists about the "real" existence of entities such as SF or any other genre; such debates hinge on a pseudo-question. An acceptable heuristic model or set of models for a literary genre is as necessary for its understanding, for the setting up of standards pertaining to it, as the theory of ideal gases was for its time and discipline. In other words, however fragmented, laborious, or foolhardy this particular endeavor of mine might be, the critical community concerned with SF will have to solve a theory of the genre that can serve as a framework for its history and criticism. Anyway, poets—including the poets among SF writers—have often reminded us that what the positivist or philistine mentality considers foolhardy is, in Gorky's words, "the wisdom of life."

1.1. Conscious of the monsters and incubi lurking just beyond my path, and averting piously my eyes from the bleached bones of the pio-

neers fallen by its side, I proceed to recall my starting point, the iden-
tifications which I worked out for the aforementioned genres in the
preceding chapter. I brought forward some arguments for their delimi-
tation, which I shall here supply with further argumentation and subsume under the following taxnomic system:

Fiction is differentiated from other verbal structures by the presence
of a *fable, plot,* or *narrative,* through which the writer endeavors to illuminate human relations to other people and the universe. (At this point
the normal poetological distinctions of epic, dramatic, and lyric fiction
could ensue, based on the different stresses in the relationship of the
narrator and the characters or world of the fable, but such distinguishing does not fall within my scope in this book. I will assume it—as well
as certain other distinctions, such as that between verse and prose—as
given or at least as for practical purposes discernible in literary theory
from Aristotle to Brecht, Frye, and Barthes, and in the literary practice
which preceded the setting up of the theories. My presentation has in
mind at the moment epic prose—novels and stories—only, though for
all I know the resulting heuristic model or models might have a wider
scope.) Fiction, then, can be divided according to the manner in which
men's relationships to other men and their surroundings are illuminated.
If this is accomplished by endeavoring faithfully to reproduce empirical
textures and surfaces vouched for by human senses and common sense,
I propose to call it *naturalistic fiction.* If, on the contrary, an endeavor is
made to illuminate such relations by creating a radically or significantly
different formal framework—a different space/time location or central
figures for the fable, unverifiable by common sense—I propose to call it
estranged fiction. The normative trend of fiction after Boccaccio and
Shakespeare has been naturalistic in the above sense, though this does
not at all hold true for earlier stages of literature in our civilization nor
in other civilizations.

The world of naturalistic fiction has thus a straightforward relationship to the "zero world" of empirically verifiable properties around the
author. The ideal of *Tom Jones, The Red and the Black, Madame Bovary,
War and Peace, The Idiot, Huckleberry Finn,* or *Intruder in the Dust* is to
create a significant statement about the human condition by holding a
mirror to nature. In naturalistic fiction, as in the zero world, physics
stands in no significant relationship to ethics. It is the activity of the

protagonists, interacting with other equally unprivileged figures, that determines the course of narration and outcome of fable. In naturalistic fiction, the basic rule is that man's destiny is other humans and man-made institutions. In such a model, relating ethics to physics (Hollywoodian happy-end, say) signifies a descent into sentimentalism, into what is properly called sub-literature.

However, estranged fiction can quite legitimately postulate that circumstances around the hero—according to the basic "literary contract" making up a particular estranged genre—either *are* or *are not* passive and neutral. One, larger group of estranged literary genres, which embraces various kinds of myths and their later descendants—fantasy and folktale—is indeed defined by a contract inverse to that of naturalistic fiction: their world is actively oriented toward the hero. The folktale (*Märchen*, later fairy tale) world is oriented positively toward its protagonist; a folktale is defined by the hero's triumph: magic weapons and helpers are, with the necessary narrative retardations, at his beck and call. Inversely, the fantasy world is oriented negatively toward its protagonist; a fantasy is defined by the hero's horrible helplessness. Both fantasy and folktale derive from mythology: the folktale from the victorious-hero myth and the fantasy from the tragic myth. Thus, in the folktale and the fantasy, ethics coincides with physics—positive (hero-furthering) in the first case, and (hero-denying) in the second. In the tragic myth ethics compensates the physics; Oedipus, Osiris or Christ have to fail because of the empirical world they live in, but the failure is then ethically exalted and put to religious use, usually by postulating a metaphysical world beyond the empirical one in which the narrative finds its true, compensatory ending. Parallel to that, in the "optimistic" myth of Perseus, Saint George and other light-bearing heroes, ethics not only coincides with hero-furthering physics but also supplies a systematic cosmosociological framework to normalize the coincidence.

The literary genres in which physics is in some magical or religious way determined by ethics, instead of being neutral toward the hero or the total human population of the presented World, deny the autonomy of physics and can properly be called *metaphysical*. But not all estranged genres enter into such a contract with their reader. Notably, the pastoral and SF worlds offer no assurances as to the outcome of their protagonists' endeavors. (Phenomena such as the sentimentalized

Baroque pastoral or the "new maps of hell" of American SF represent particular, limited historical and ideological uses which do not necessarily flow out the basic contract of the genre but are superadded to it.) Together with some prefigurations in the pastoral, *SF is thus a metaempirical and non-naturalistic, that is, an estranged, literary genre which is not at the same time metaphysical.* On the contrary, SF shares with naturalistic literature, naturalistic science, and naturalistic or materialist philosophy a common sophisticated, dialectical, and cognitive *episteme*.

The genological system discussed above can be presented schematically by using the two parameters or binary oppositions of naturalistic/estranged, and cognitive/noncognitive:

	NATURALISTIC	ESTRANGED
COGNITIVE	"realistic" literature	SF (& pastoral)
NON COGNITIVE	sub-literature of "realism"	*metaphysical*: myth, folktale, fantasy

1.2.   In order to test the above taxonomy, let us introduce a new basic parameter of *time* and see whether the system can make sense of it. Naturalistic literature ranges through all empirical times. Though concentrating on the present, it has, parallel with the rise of historical sciences and dialectical philosophy, evolved the historical novel and drama, and it can even to some degree (admittedly not the same degree as non-naturalistic literature) deal with the future in the form of hopes, fears, premonitions, and dreams, as in the psychological novel beginning with, say, Stendhal and Dostoevsky. Carelessness about precise time location or restriction to a one-dimensional point-consciousness in the present—both of which do not critically question prevailing anthropological modes of behavior—is the mark of the subliterature of mainstream "realism," from Renaissance street-ballads to contemporary *kitsch*. The metaphysical genres shun historical time: myth is located above time, folktale in a conventional grammatical past which is really outside time, and fantasy in the hero's abnormally disturbed, historiosophically dislocated present into which irrupts a "black" timelessness of another extrahistorical time. Inversely, SF shares the omnitemporal horizons of naturalistic literature, ranging through all possible times.

though concentrating on the cognitively plausible futures and their spatial equivalents, it can deal with the present and the past as special cases of a possible historical sequence seen from an estranged point of view—since any empirical historical point or flow can be thought of as one realization among practically innumerable possibilities. The scheme from 1.1. *sub specie temporis* would thus look like this:

	HISTORICAL	ESTRANGED
PLURIDIMENSIONAL	"realistic" literature	SF
ONE DIMENSIONAL	sub-literature of "realism"	myth, folktale, fantasy

It is not surprising to anybody who has read Marx, Hegel, or Augustine of Hippo that *naturalistic* in the temporal sphere means historical. It is more interesting to note that temporal cognition is allied to a free movement back and forth in time. Myth in its timeless suffering or bliss, folktale in its world apart allied to the empirical world by a grammatical past, and fantasy as the present lifted out of time into black transcendency—all share the impossibility of such a humanizing movement. Out of their several shortcomings they have, as is known, made tremendous virtues; yet the limitations remain.

2. An Ecological Jungle Trip: Symbiosis, Parasitism, Mimicry, and Sundry

2.0.   So far my analysis has been conducted on a level which, no doubt, was abstracted from actual historical literary genres but one which endeavored to treat them as ideal types or pure heuristic models. In actuality, a particular work, literary opus, trend, or school is almost never entirely pure. Literary genres exist in historically precise and curious ecological units, interacting and intermixing, imitating and cannibalizing each other. To understand what one really has in mind when talking about SF, it is necessary to continue the analysis on the level of actual happenings in the noncanonic literature or paraliterature of this century. Only such a path, descending from the clear mountain sights and its wide horizons into the luxuriant and steamy jungle of literary genres, and supplementing an aerial survey with actual botanizing in the field, has a chance of leading to useful results.

2.1. The relationship of SF to naturalistic literature, usually to the species of *adventure-journey*, is by now relatively clear and can be dealt with briefly. It is a relationship of filiation, best evidenced in the work of Jules Verne: SF has historically had one of its roots in the compost heap of such juvenile or popular sub-literature, and in order to develop properly it has had to subsume and outgrow it the quicker the better for its generic affirmation. It found congenial or congeneric elements in the cognitive and marvelous bias of the *voyage extraordinaire* and its catalogues of wonders seen along Ulysses' or Captain Nemo's way. The sea haunts this filiation, the island story is its microparadigm or root situation, and locomotion the connecting thread of its narration. All the marvelous interstellar SF voyages and quests in Heinlein, Blish, Van Vogt, and a thousand others, the Nietzschean, Columbian, or Sindbadian poetry of navigation—*navigare necesse, vivere non necesse* belong here. Such voyaging is an honorable, though in retrospect one can scarcely fail to note that it is an initial (and for the reader initiatory), function of SF. It acts much in the way that a true long voyage does in the zero world, dialectically estranging the reader from familiar and usually contemptible shores, dissolving his umbilical connections with old and firm earth (or Earth), preparing him to accept the marvelous beyond seven seas or galaxies. When unduly prolonged, this adolescence of SF means arrested development. It should be kept in its proper humbly useful place in the ontogenetic development of the reader as well as in the phylogenetic development of the genre.

In close proximity to the didactic aspect of the journey is the *popular science* compost heap which can be found next to the adventure-journey heap in the early phylogenetic stages of SF from technologically developed countries. Verne used both, adding a dash of puzzle in the manner of Poe and a barrelful of Saint-Simonian romanticism. Unalloyed, or alloyed with the baser metal of subliterary conflict and sentiment, this leads no further than to a primitive technological or at best technocratic exterpolation, as evidenced in Bacon's *New Atlantis*, then in Gernsback and the "SF reservation" between the two world wars. A hybrid results that is neither good fiction nor interesting science; it is dislodged the first time the shapers of public and publishing opinion happened to read

Wells—or, indeed, a good straightforward essay of scientific popularization, which has from the time of Friedrich Engels and Thomas Huxley
been immeasurably more exciting and less reactionary than *Ralph 124C
41 +*. Of course, it usually takes those shapers a generation or two to acquire the necessary taste in reading. In the meantime, the Gernsbacks
keep SF alive at the cost of starving, stunting, and deforming it; comparing *The Iron Heel* with the output in the United States between the
World Wars, one strongly suspects the cost is too high.

2.2.   In 2.1 it was discussed how older paradigms of marvelous voyage, popular science essay, and individualist sub-literature (the Western
and the sentimental story) interfere with the formation of an autonomous SF paradigm or model if their grip is not loosened quickly.
Unfortunately, a majority of what is published as SF is still in that pre-
natal or, better, regression-to-womb stage: it is simply the Western or
some kindred sub-literary species masquerading its structures—generally
for venal and ideological reasons—under the eternals of SF: rockets, rayguns, monsters, or in the last dozen years their slightly more sophisticated equivalents. Usually the symbiosis of popular science and juvenile
adventure finds it impossible to mimic SF without regressing into their
homologue of the *fairy tale*, with its victorious hero, foiled villain,
damsel in distress, and quaint helpers or marvelous helping objects.
Such sub-Vernean or Gernsbackian SF does not change the fairy tale
structure but only the motivation of its devices: it pretends to example
away the supernatural by reassigning it to natural science and noble scientists (who are energetic and sentimental if young and in love with, ab-
sent-minded if old and fathers of, the eternal feminine). However, the
science is treated as a metaphysical and not physical, supernatural and
not natural activity, as gobbledygook instead of rational procedure.
From Ralph, Buck Rogers, and the post-Stapledonian supermen to Asimov's psychohistory (which has at least the advantage of identifying the
proper field of modern destiny, social relations), such metaphysical gobbledygook vitiates some of the best-known SF works. Neither cognitive
nor magical but shamefacedly passing off a juvenile idea of magic for
cognition, equating the photon rocket with the flying carpet and global
social destinies with the victory of the third son, such a mimicry is like
the newly fashionable pop wines: a hyping-up of the old grape juice into
the new wine. In the perfectly just world of taste and poetic creativity,
this procedure reaps the reward of hypocrisy: fairy tale readers rightly

prefer the classics, sophisticated SF readers disbelieve the fairy tale. Inversely, in the very imperfectly retributive world of social taste and commercial SF, such a procedure breeds generations of readers with juvenile taste, unable to develop the standards by which to judge SF (not to mention empirical human relations).

2.3.   The more ambitious reader and writer cannot for long be satisfied with such pap. Yet trying to find a fresh tack in the cruel world of instant obsolescence, SF often veers from Scylla to Charybdis. A further step down into pseudo-sophistication—correlative, no doubt, to a marked decadence of cultural taste in bourgeois society and its literary markets—is the parasitism of Gothic, horror, and weird *fantasy* upon SF. Such fantasy is characterized, as I have said, by the irruption of an anti-cognitive world into the world of empirical cognition. One can understand some readers' panic flight from a science which produces nuclear bombs, napalm, and nerve gases, from a reason which justifies class societies in mutual balances of terror, condemning two-thirds of the world to hunger and disease, and the remaining third—"hypocrite lecteur, mon semblable, mon frere"—to the boredom of a nine-to-five drudgery relieved by flashes of TV commercials. Maybe such readers ought to have an escapist enclave of sword-and-sorcery or Cthulhu cosmologies—I cannot say. But surely SF, built upon the premise that nature is neither a childishly wicked stepmother ("As flies to wanton boys are we to gods/They kill us for their sport") nor inscrutably alien to man—surely SF cannot allow its contract with the reader to be contaminated by the Great Pumpkin antics of fantasy. Even more perniciously than is the case with the bland fairy tale structure, the black ectoplasms of fantasy stifle SF completely. Its time shrinks to the point-consciousness of horror, gloom, and doom, its daydreams turn into an inchoate nightmare, and under the guise of cognition the ancient obscurantist enemy infiltrates its citadel. Fossilized fragments of reasoning are used to inculcate irrationality, and the social energy of readers is expended on Witches' Sabbaths instead of focusing it on the causes for our alienating, murderous, and stultifying existences: the power structures holding back the hominization of the sapiens, the true demonology of war and market breeding pride and prejudice. At its best, in Swift and Cyrano, in Jack London and the dystopian "new maps of hell," in Lucian and Wells, in the great utopians and Zamyatin, SF has with different degrees of precision, but with unerring precision of orientation, focused on these power structures, on such demonology. It is at its worst, at its most alienated and alienating, when it honors the parasitism and vampirism of fantasy.

2.4. There has also been a great deal of talk about affinities between SF and the *mythological tale*. Though also a story about supernatural events involving superhuman figures, as different from other metaphysical fiction (folktale and fantasy), the events and figures of this genre form a systematic whole, *a mythological edifice of tales whose norms are supposed to have supertemporally (timelessly or continuously) determined man's basic relations to man and nature*. Obviously, all religious systems are in this sense mythological. On the contrary, plays and stories are neither myth nor ritual but fictional literature, although myths and rituals may underlie their forms, plots, and sometimes their characters. For example, Murray has convincingly shown that the forms of Attic tragedy derive from Dionysian sacrificial rituals, and Cornford has done an analogous job for Attic comedy.[2] The Hellenic tragic characters derive primarily from Homer, but through him from other sacrificial rituals, which is why Homerian themes fitted so well into the mythic pattern of tragedy. Thus, *fiction can be formally or morphologically analogous to myth, but it is not itself myth*. It uses mythical morphemes for non-mythic and—except in folktale, fantasy, and subliterature—for anti-mythic ends. "Myth and literature are separate and autonomous entities, though any specific myth text can and should be considered as folk-literature."[3] However—and this is in itself highly important and largely justifies the attention that modern scholars have devoted to myth—bearing in mind the caveats and distinctions discussed earlier, it should be acknowledged that important aspects of literature (primarily, many basic and possibly most significant plots) are *mythomorphic*. What a writer like Faulkner or Kafka creates is not a myth but a personal fictional statement formally analogous to myth in a radically different and indeed incompatible cosmological or ideological context. In other words, a realistic parable such as *The Bear* or an SF parable such as *The Metamorphosis*, although it uses a mythological bestiary as well as the mythological pattern of trial and death with or without resurrection, is in its message and final impact very different from, often diametrically opposed to the religious myth expressing a collective static vision. Kafka and Faulkner are—they cannot but be—*historical* writers.

Obviously, SF will be as mythomorphic in some basic patterns as other fictional genres are. Beyond that, SF shares with myth the fictional estrangement, the "outer limits of desire" as Professor Frye aptly formulated it,[4] and its formal closeness to myth will extend beyond plots to many characters and situations. But all attempts to transplant the metaphysical orientation of mythology and religion into SF, in a crudely overt way as in C.S. Lewis, Van Vogt, or Zelazny, or in more covert ways in very many others, will result only in private pseudomyths, in fragmentary fantasies or fairy tales.[5] As I mentioned in my first chapter, myth absolutizes and even personifies apparently constant motifs from periods with sluggish social dynamics, and claims to explain the eternal essence of phenomena. On the contrary, SF claims to organize variable spatiotemporal, biological, social, and other characteristics and constellations into specific fictional worlds and figures. Mathematically speaking, myth is oriented toward constants and SF toward variables.

On a different level of fictional structuring, however, is the treatment of religious beliefs or mythic situations as historical material. When such mythic elements are—by transposition, as it were, into the demystifying key of SF—extracted from a mythological paradigm and fitted into an SF one, what results is perfectly legitimate, often first-class SF. As always, the critic will in any particular instance, have to rely on his literary tact and sense of measure to pierce this intricate double mimicry and parasitism, to decide with which type of interaction between SF and myth he is faced. To mention only two favorites of mine, Stapledon and Walter Miller, Jr., I believe that at a certain point (say in *The Flames*) Stapledon crosses the divide into pseudomyth, that is, into fantasy, and that Miller does the same at the resolution of *A Canticle for Leibowitz* with the character of Mrs. Grales. At such points the ideological attraction to myth as world view and not as formal pattern got the best of the SF writer.

3. To Greener Fields and Pastures New: The Extrapolative and Analogical Models of SF

3.0.   I would like now to try emerging from the jungle into the cultivated territory of selected SF, and analyze what look to be its two main species or models, the extrapolative and the analogical one.

3.1. SF written from, say, the period of the French Revolution on (though not necessarily in preceding epochs) has come to be considered as starting from certain cognitive hypotheses and ideas incarnated in the fictional framework and nucleus of the tale. This extrapolative model—of Mercier's *L'An 2440*, London's *Iron Heel*, Wells's *When the Sleeper Wakes* and *Men Like Gods*, Zamyatin's *We*, Stapledon's *Last and First Men*, Yefremov's *Andromeda*, Pohl and Kornbluth's *Space Merchants*, or Brunner's *The Jagged Orbit*—seems based on direct, temporal extrapolation and centered on sociological (that is, utopian and anti-utopian) modeling. This is where the great majority of the "new maps of hell" is taken to belong for which postwar SF is justly famous, in all its manifold combinations of sociotechnological scientific cognition and social oppression (global catastrophes, cybernetics, dictatorships).

Yet already in Wells's *Time Machine* and in Stapledon, this extrapolating transcended the sociological spectrum (from everyday practice through economics to erotics) and spilled into "billion-year" biology and cosmology. The ensuing radical estrangements can, no doubt, be *anticipated* in a chronological future, but they cannot, scientifically speaking, be *extrapolated*. By this token, futuristic anticipation reveals that extrapolating is a fictional device and ideological horizon rather than the basis for a cognitive model. It is thus dubious—as will be discussed further in chapter 4—that significant SF could be simply extrapolation. Nonetheless, whatever its ostensible location (future, "fourth dimension," other planets, alternate universes), the self-understanding of much SF—as shown in the historical section of this book—was uneasily futurological. Being written in a historical epoch dominated by anticipatory expectations, this SF demanded to be judged by the "scientific" import of the tale's premises and the consistency with which such premises (usually one or very few in number) were narratively developed to their logical end, to a "scientifically valid" conclusion.

SF could thus be used as a handmaiden of futurological foresight in technology, ecology, sociology, and so on. Whereas this may at times have been a legitimate secondary function the genre could be made to bear, any forgetfulness of its strict secondariness leads to confusion and indeed danger. Ontologically, art is not pragmatic truth nor is fiction fact. To expect from SF more than a stimulus for independent thinking, more than a system of stylized narrative devices understandable only in their mutual relationships within a fictional whole and not as isolated realities, leads insensibly to the demand for scientific accuracy in the extrapolated *realia*. Editors and publishers of such "hard" persuasion, from U.S. pulp magazines to the Soviet Agitprop, have been inclined to depress the handmaiden of SF into the slavery of the reigning theology of the day (technocratic, psionic, utopian, catastrophic, or whatever). Yet this fundamentally subversive genre languishes in straitjackets more quickly than most others, responding with atrophy, escapism, or both. Laying no claim to prophecies except for its statistically probable share, SF should not be treated as a prophet: it should neither be enthroned when apparently successful nor beheaded when apparently unsuccessful. As Plato found out in the court of Dionysius and Hythloday at Cardinal Morton's, SF figures better devote themselves to their own literary republics, which, to be sure, lead back but in their own way—to the Republic of Man. SF is finally concerned with the tensions between *Civitas Dei* and *Civitas Terrena*, and it cannot be uncritically committed to any momentary city.

3.2. The analogic model of SF is based on analogy rather than extrapolation. Its figures may but do not have to be anthropomorphic or its localities geomorphic. The objects, figures, and up to a point the relationships from which this indirectly modeled world starts can be quite fantastic (in the sense of empirically unverifiable) as long as they are logically, philosophically, and mutually consistent. The analytic model can thus comprehend the extrapolative one, but it is not bound to the extrapolative horizon.

The lowest form of analogic modeling is that in which an extrapolation backwards is in fact a crude analogy to the past of the Earth, from geological through biological to ethnological and historical. The worlds more or less openly modeled on the Carboniferous Age, on tribal prehistory, on barbaric and feudal empires—in fact modeled on handbooks of geology and anthropology, on Spengler's *Decline of the West* and Dumas *père's Three Musketeers*—are unfortunately abundant in the foothills of SF. Some of this may be useful adolescent leisure reading, which one should not begrudge; however, the uneasy coexistence of such worlds with a superscience, which is supposed to provide an SF alibi, largely or wholly destroys the story's cognitive credibility. The E.R. Burroughs-to-Asimov space opera, cropping up in almost all

U.S. writers right down to Samuel Delany, belongs to the uneasy territory between inferior SF and non-SF—to forms that, as I argued earlier,
mimic SF scenery but are modeled on the structures of the Western and
other avatars of fairy tale and fantasy.

The purest form of analogic modeling would be the analogy to a
mathematical model, such as the fairly primary one explicated in Abbott's *Flatland*, as well as the ontological analogies found in a compressed overview form in some stories by Borges and Lem. A somewhat
more humane narration with a suffering protagonist is to be found in,
say, Capek's *Krakatit* or Le Guin's *Left Hand of Darkness*, and even more
clearly in Kafka's *Metamorphosis* or *In the Penal Colony* and Lem's *Solaris*. Such highly sophisticated philosophico-anthropological analogies
are today perhaps the most significant region of SF, indistinguishable in
quality from other superior contemporary writing. Situated between
Borges and the upper reaches into which shade the best utopias, anti-
utopias, and satires, this semantic field is a modern variant of the
"conte philosophique" of the eighteenth century. Similar to Swift,
Voltaire, or Diderot, these *modern parables* fuse new visions of the world
with an applicability—usually satirical and grotesque—to the shortcomings of our workaday world. Departing from the older rationalism,
a modern parable must be open-ended by analogy to modern cosmology, epistemology, and philosophy of science.[6]

The analogic model of SF falls, however, clearly within cognitive
horizons insofar as its conclusions or import is concerned. The cognition gained may not be immediately applicable, it may be simply the
enabling of the mind to receive new wavelengths, but it eventually
contributes to the understanding of the most mundane matters. This is
testified by the works of Kafka and Twain, Rosny and Anatole France,
as well as of the best of Wells and the "SF reservation" writers.

4. The Jungle Explorer: Medicine Man or Darwinist

4.0.   Thus far I have not explicitly referred to the theory and practice
of SF criticism, since it is impossible to discuss an intellectual activity
before its field has been determined. The field of SF criticism is SF, and
this truism becomes significant when we pause to consider how little
agreement there is about the basic parameters of SF. Having discussed

them, in the remainder of this chapter I would like to essay some remarks on SF criticism. They will have to be as disjointed, tentative, and unsystematic as that criticism, since the basic lesson one can draw from the history of literary criticism is that it is difficult for criticism to be more significant than the works it criticizes.

4.1.   Beyond the necessary but subsidiary critical activity of reviewing and chronicling, it seems that the most fashionable critical approach to SF is that of *mythical analysis*. In order to comment upon it, I shall have to try to disentangle the main meanings of this protean and tantalizing term.

Few writers considering myth in the last third of a century have failed to lament the divergent and indeed incompatible meanings given to this term in different professional and ideological fields of discourse. Though everyone—including myself—has to try to group these meanings for purposes of an overview, it is sometimes difficult to escape the conclusion of a philologist that there are as many interpretations of myth as there are critics. In ethnology "myth" is indistinguishable from "legend" or "folklore." Cultural historians "employ 'myth' with the quite separate meaning of a popularly accepted cluster of images."[7] The term can also be loosely used to mean "tale, fantasy, mass delusion, popular belief and illusion, and plain lie"; an essay as early as 1947 reduced this confusion of tongues to the absurd by adopting the title of "The Modern Myth of the Modern Myth."[8] But, cutting a long story short, it seems to me that the literary theoretician has presently to deal with three principal views of the field: that of Cassirer and his followers, that of literary scholars who consider all literature to be some kind of myth—a view most ably and influentially formulated by Northrop Frye—and that of a third group which would insist, as I argued earlier (see note 2), that literary artifacts are not myths and yet that many of them are significantly marked by genetic and morphological connections with myths.

4.1.1.   Cassirer treats myth as a kind of symbolic vision correlative to the mythopoeic mode of consciousness, "mythopoeia" meaning the world view and forms of expression characteristic of a hypothetical early stage of culture "when language is still largely ritualistic and prelogical in character." In this view, myth "is simply a basic way of envisaging experience and carries no necessary connotation of storytelling."[9] Rather, all creative, poetic, metaphoric thinking is "mythical." To this it must be briefly objected that metaphor is feasible only when some cognitively defined terms with fixed meanings are available as points of comparison, and that as far as literature is concerned poetic metaphor and language begin exactly where mythology ends. In the best mythical fashion, if poetry springs from the mother-soil of mythology, it does so only by spurning or destroying its parents. Finally, if everything (including science, philosophy, the arts, and all other aspects and motives of social practice) is myth or mythopoeia, if in myth, as Cassirer says, "everything may be turned into everything,"[10] then this term loses all usefulness for distinguishing literature from anything else, let alone for any distinctions within literature itself. Historically hypothetical, philosophically idealistic, and aesthetically useless, Cassirer's hypothesis for all its influences in the American cultural climate after World War II (for example, Susanne Langer) cannot contribute to our present needs.

4.1.2. At the opposite extreme—but *les extrêmes se rejoignent*—is the position which preserves the autonomy of literary studies but affirms that myth is story and any story is myth. It possesses a heroic paradigm in Frye's *Anatomy of Criticism*. Though mentioning the secondary sense of myth as "untruth,"[11] and of "myth in the narrower and more technical sense" as stories about "divine or quasi-divine beings and powers,"[12] and then discussing a mythical *phase* or context of literary art which is primarily concerned with "poetry as the focus of a community,"[13] Frye concentrates on a Cassirerian "mythical *view* of literature" which leads "to the conception of an order of nature as a whole being imitated by a corresponding order of words."[14] This is based on his belief, explicated in the section subtitled "Theory of Myths," that "in myth we see the structural principles of literature isolated."[15] If structural principles are to mean isolatable formal narrative patterns, this is acceptable as a basis of discussion subject to historical verification. However, if they are also meant to subsume the motivation of a literary work, what the *Theory of Literature* calls "the inner structure of psychological, social, or philosophical theory of why men behave as they do—some theory of causation, ultimately,"[16] then I do not see how myth can contain the structural principles of all literature or be the "total creative act" which could account for all basic components of the final impact or message of all literary modes and genres.

In other words, among many brilliant insights in *Anatomy of Criticism* there is one about mythical patterns not only being formally analogous to basic patterns in other literary modes—which one would a priori expect in the imaginative products of the same human species—but also being more clearly identifiable in supernatural stories "at the limits of desire"[17] than in stories cluttered with surface naturalism. However, there is an essential difference between this and treating the fourfold seasonal mythos of Spring, Summer, Autumn, and Winter as the basic organization of all literature and indeed all verbal structures imaginable, including science and history.[18] Here the formal similarity has been left behind, and literature has (by way of a semantically redefined mythos) been identified to myth *tout court*, since original meaning of superhuman story has not been abandoned.[19] Unfortunately, this is the most easily vulgarized and therefore possibly the best-known part of Frye's book. Logically, literature and verbal structures in general are finally reduced to a central unifying myth, adumbrated in Milton and Dante but fully manifest in the Bible, which is a "definitive" myth.[20] All writing, one might therefore expect, has in the past aspired to and will in the future be confined to variations on smaller or larger bits of the Christian myth of salvation. Obviously such a conclusion will finally be shared only by those who acknowledge the hegemony of a cyclical theory of history and a closed cosmology—that is, by anti-utopians. Therefore, this brilliant work can persuade us that much literature is morphologically informed by patterns which we might perhaps call mythical. However, "mythical" then proves to be simply shorthand for "basic narrative patterns which are seen at their clearest in some myths."

4.1.3. For, when we have rendered unto myth what is of the myth, we must recognize that finally, for a cognitive pursuit such as literary theory and criticism, myth as an instrument is fairly limited. Philosophically, myth is an evasion of precise distinctions and of full intellectual commitment: a myth is not true or false but believable or unbelievable, vital or dead. On its own grounds it is irrefutable, for as soon as it is queried as to its truth it is not treated as myth but as historical cognition or formal hypothesis. In other words, it seems to me that Frye has rendered a signal service to poetics by his formal hypothesis, but I find myself unpersuaded by his historical premises and his semantical gliding between myth as a historical genre, mythos as a formal para-digm, and both of them as a "structural principle or attitude."[21] I am un-able to accept the conclusion that "in literary criticism, myth ulti-mately means *mythos,* a structural organizing principle of literary form,"[22] which does not differentiate between the formal and structural functions of myth.

As distinct from Cassirer and the Cassirerian aspect of Frye, it seems to me that myth cannot constitute a useful theory of history in general and artistic or literary history in particular. Myth is parascientific and some-times prescientific in its interpretations of nature and society. Although some among its numerous configurations are statistically bound to become precursors of scientific ones, it is essentially an insufficiently critical hu-man experience which, for all its ideological and artistic uses, cannot be dignified as anything more than a first significant step on the human way to a cognition of reality. Speaking of the myth's "unity of feeling," Cassirer rightly concludes that its pragmatic function is to promote social solidar-ity through feelings of cosmic sympathy at the time of social crisis.[23] Myth embodies and sanctions authoritarian social norms and the basic institu-tions that determine the life of each member of a certain collective au-thority-structure. It is intrinsically—whatever its surface innovations in this age where every new car fashion is "revolutionary"—a conservative force, a guarantee of the status quo (say of the mass existence of private cars). In the forceful words of David Bidney:

> To my mind, contemporary philosophers and theologians, as well as stu-dents of literature in general, who speak of the indispensable myth in the name of philosophy and religion, and anthropologists and sociologists who cynically approve of myth because of its pragmatic social function, are undermining faith in their own disciplines and are contributing un-wittingly to the very degradation of man and his culture which they oth-erwise seriously deplore. Myth must be taken seriously as a cultural force but it must be taken seriously precisely in order that it may be gradually superseded in the interests of the advancement of truth and the growth of human intelligence. Normative, critical, and scientific thought pro-vides the only self-correcting means of combating the diffusion of myth, but it may do so only on condition that we retain a firm and uncompro-mising faith in the integrity of reason and in the transcultural validity of the scientific enterprise.[24]

Thus, the literary scholar and critic, building his autonomous and yet rational conceptual world, must honor myth, in the Frygian "narrow sense" of stories about superhuman beings, as both occasionally fetching folk poetry and a reservoir of literary forms. At the same time, the critic—and in particular the critic of SF—must, I believe, abandon the belief that he has done much more than his formal homework when he has identified Yefemov's *Andromeda* as containing the myth of Perseus or Delany's *Einstein Intersection* and Verne's *Chateau des Carpates* as containing the myth of Orpheus. He is still left face to face with the basic questions of his trade, namely, is the myth or mytheme transmuted (1) into valid fiction; (2) into valid science fiction? "Mythical analysis" as a self-sufficient critical method collapses at this point, as an ideology it remains a contributing factor to the Babylonian confusion of tongues, a particularly lethal quicksand region on the path to SF.

4.2.   Finally, it might be possible to sketch the basic premises of a significant criticism, history, and theory of this literary genre. From Edgar Allan Poe to Damon Knight and Stanislaw Lem, including some notable work on the other subgenres from the utopias to Wells and some general approaches to literature by people awake to methodological interest, much spadework has been done. If one may speculate on some fundamental features or indeed axioms of such criticism, the *first* might be that the genre has to be and can be evaluated proceeding from its heights down, applying the standards gained by the analysis of its masterpieces. We find in SF, as we do in most other genres of fiction, that 80 to 90 percent of the works in it are sheer confectionery. However, contrary to subliterature, the criteria for the insufficiency of most SF are to be found in the genre itself. This makes SF in principle, if not yet in practice, equivalent to any other "major" literary genre. The *second* axiom of SF criticism might be to demand of SF a level of cognition higher than that of its average reader: the strange novelty is its *raison d'être*. As a minimum, we must demand from SF that it be wiser than the world it speaks to.

In other words, this is an educational literature, hopefully less deadening than most compulsory education in our split national and class societies, but irreversibly shaped by the pathos of preaching the good word of human curiosity, fear, and hope. Significant SF denies thus the "two-cultures gap" more efficiently than any other literary genre I know of. Even more importantly, it demands from the author and reader, teacher and critic, not merely specialized, quantified positivistic knowledge *(scientia)* but a social imagination whose quality of wisdom *(sapientia)* testifies to the maturity of his critical and creative thought. It demands—to conclude the botanical marvelous voyage of this chapter—that the critic be a Darwinist and not a medicine-man.

Notes

[au: need publishers]

1. Northrop Frye, *Anatomy of Criticism* (New York, 1966), p. 12.

2. Gilbert Murray, "Hamlet and Orestes," in his *The Classical Tradition of Poetry* (New York, 1968), and "Excursus on the Ritual Forms preserved in Greek Tragedy," in Jane Ellen Harrison, *Epilegomena to the Study of Greek Religion—Themis* (New York, 1966); F. M. Cornford, *The Origin of Attic Comedy* (Gloucester, Mass., 1966). See also other anthropological works by the Cambridge School that, as far as literary studies are concerned, culminate in George Thomson's elegant *Aeschylus and Athens* (New York, 1968).

3. Stanley Edgar Hyman, "The Ritual View of Myth and the Mythic," in Thomas A. Sebeok, ed., *Myth* (Bloomington, 1970), p. 151.

4. Frye, p. 136

5. See Harry Levin, "Some Meanings of Myth," in Henry A. Murray, ed., *Myth and Mythmaking* (Boston, 1969), pp. 111–12.

6. I have attempted to analyze some representative examples of such modern SF parables in chapters 10 and 12 of this book, *à propos* of Wells's *Time Machine* and Capek's *War With the Newts*, in my afterword to Stanislaw Lem, *Solaris* (New York, 1971 and 1976), enlarged into a parallel to US and Russian examples in "Stanislaw Lem und das mitteleuropäische soziale Bewusstsein der Science-Fiction," in Werner Berthel, ed., *Insel Almanach auf das Jahr 1976—Stanislaw Lem* (Frankfurt, 1976); and in essays on Philip K. Dick and Ursula K. Le Guin, reprinted in Mullen and Suvin, eds. (see Bibliography 1).

7. Richard M. Dorson, "Theories of Myth and the Folklorist," in Murray, ed., p. 84.

8. First quotation from Hyman, in Sebeok, ed., p. 153; see also, for a psychologist's attack on loose definitions of myth, Henry A. Murray, "The Possible Nature of a 'Mythology' to Come," in Murray, ed., p. 303. The Second quotation is the title of Donald A. Stauffer's essay in *English Institute Essays 1947* (New York, 1948).

9. P[hilip] Wheelwright], "Myth," in Alex Preminger, ed., *Encyclopedia of Poetry and Poetics* (Princeton, 1965), pp. 538–39; see Ernst Cassiere, *An Essay on Man* (New Haven, 1962) and *The Philosophy of Symbolic Forms*, vol. 2 (New Haven, 1955)

10. Cassierer, *Essay*, p. 81.

11. Frye, p. 75.

12. Frye, p. 116; see also, on "the mythical or theogonic mode," pp. 120, 33–36, et passim.

13. Frye, p. 99; see the whole section, pp. 95–99.

14. Frye, p. 118.

15. Frye, p. 136.

16. René Wellek and Austin Warren, *Theory of Literature* (Harmondsworth, 1973), p. 207 et passim.

17. Frye, p. 134.

18. Frye, p. 341 et passim.

19. Frye: redefining *mythos*, pp. 134–40 and 158 ff.; retaining the meaning of super-human tale, e.g., p. 317.

20. Frye, pp. 120–121; also p. 315, 325 et passim.

21. Frye, p. 310.

22. Frye, p. 341.

23. Cassirer, *Essay*, pp. 79–84.

24. David Bidney, "Myth, Symbolism, and Truth," in Sebeok, ed., p. 23.

~

CHAPTER SEVEN

The Readers of
Hard Science Fiction

James Gunn

Criticism developed to deal with mainstream literature has difficulty dealing with science fiction. One reason is put forward by Robert Scholes in the introduction to the Oxford University Press series of one-author studies: "As long as the dominant criteria are believed to hold for *all* fiction, science fiction will be found inferior: deficient in psychological depth, in verbal nuance, and in plausibility of event. What is needed is a criticism serious in its standards and its concern for literary value but willing to take seriously a literature based on ideas, types, and events beyond ordinary experience."

Another reason may be that most traditional criticism (there is, to be sure, "reader response" criticism) looks at the artist and science fiction looks at the reader. Traditional criticism holds that it is the reader's responsibility to understand, science fiction, by and large, that it is the author's responsibility to make the reader understand. I would like to consider here the readers of hard science fiction, why they read it and what serious critical standards can be suggested for it, but first I must deal with some problems of definition.

From the point of view of the science-fiction magazines, where contemporary science fiction was born and nurtured, fiction is an emotional experience for the reader induced by the author's persuading the reader to invest concern in the plight of a character, to care about what happens to him or her, and to obtain a release of concern, identified as pleasure, when the character resolves his situation. Satisfaction is produced when the situation of a story is resolved in a way that the reader has not foreseen but recognizes as appropriate, even inevitable. This view does not insist that readers cannot look for and obtain other rewards—as indeed they do in science fiction and in hard science fiction—but that the fictional response is basic. Science fiction obtains its unique fictional response by dealing with characters whose situation has been created by change, and usually scientific or technological change. The reader's involvement is dependent upon his intellectual recognition of the change, and his emotional satisfaction is dependent upon the character's rational response to the situation, or upon the reader's recognition of the character's failure because the obstacles are too great, because the character did not know enough to achieve the correct response, or because the character's response was irrational. Mary Shelley's *Frankenstein*, for instance, seems more like a gothic novel than science fiction because the experienced science fiction reader keeps wanting the tormented scientist to behave rationally, and he doesn't even behave like a scientist when he shrinks in revulsion from his creation; instead, it is the monster who behaves rationally when he asks about the responsibility of the creator to his creature.

The insistence that emotion derives from the intellectual in science fiction often confuses the discussion, as if the heart and the mind actually were the location of the humors attributed to them rather than part of a gestalt. An emotional response often is irrational, but a rational response is not always dispassionate. As an example we need only think of Archimedes shouting, "Eureka!" and leaping from his bath to streak the streets of Syracuse.

The difficulty of defining science fiction is basic. Every critic has tried his hand at one or several definitions. Damon Knight finally gave up and said, "Science fiction is what I mean when I point at it," but even this criterion is subject to questions about the difference between the kinds of fiction pointed at.

I've tried a few definitions myself, and I think the problem is that science fiction, unlike other genres, has no characteristic action or location; instead it is more like an attitude toward experience, an attitude that can be applied to almost any subject. We might compare the attitude of the mainstream author that man is a fallen creature placed on earth to refine his soul (or find salvation) through misery and despair to the attitude of the hard science-fiction author that man is here to understand the universe and discover his place in it. The first attitude makes suffering the central fact of the human experience and uses the mind only to find acceptance; the second insists that understanding is central and that not only is misery not inevitable but that understanding can change human behavior. The late John W. Campbell used to say that science fiction encompassed mainstream literature, because science fiction covered everything from the origin of the universe to its end, and the mainstream covered only a small range and a tiny space within that longer and larger literature. Although this is mostly intellectual goading on Campbell's part, nevertheless, it makes the point that almost anything can be written as science fiction—and often is. It is hospitable to all the other genres: one can have a science fiction western, for instance, or a science fiction detective story or love story or gothic or sports story, or a fantasy, or even a mainstream story of character. Most common, of course, is the science-fiction adventure story. Much of the confusion about science fiction is created by this fact. Readers who view science fiction as escape are usually attracted by a non-science-fiction element, the adventure, say, or the wish-fulfillment fairy tale, like that of *Star Wars*. If one removes the elements of the other genres, what one has left is the irreducible quality that makes the work science fiction. Sometimes, of course, nothing is left, and we conclude that the piece wasn't really science fiction after all.

The irreducible quality is change. In science fiction the situation in which the characters find themselves is significantly different from the here and now; nevertheless, the events, though they can be considered fantastic because of the significantly different situation, take place in a universe that is recognizably our own.

The only example I wish to present here is "The Cold Equations," Tom Godwin's influential story. In *The Road to Science Fiction* I call it a touchstone story because if readers don't understand it they don't understand science fiction. The intellectual point made by the story is that sentimentality divorced from knowledge and rationality is deadly. "The Cold Equations" could have been told only as science fiction, not because the point of the story is science fiction but because every other situation retains an element of hope for rescue. In a contemporary lifeboat story or a story about wagon trains crossing the plains, the sacrifice of an innocent stowaway to save the lives of the remainder brings up images of the Donner party: the point of those stories would be the survivors' lack of faith and their love of life above honor. Science fiction gave Godwin an unparalleled opportunity to purify the situation in such a way that there was no hope left for last-minute salvation, no possible sight of land or rescue ship, no company of soldiers to ride over the hill. The girl is to blame for her own predicament, her innocence is irrelevant, the universe doesn't care about her motives, and the others would be as guilty as she if they compounded her fatal mistake by dying with her. The reader who does not understand this has not read the story correctly. The intellectual perception that the girl must die produces the emotional response the reader gets from the story. Perhaps the point of the story is science-fictional after all; where else would such a point be made; by what other audience would it be understood? And considered satisfying?

Still we are not yet to our discussion of hard science fiction, although "The Cold Equations" is one example of the form. First we must contrast the reader's reaction to science fiction with his reaction to fantasy. On the basis of the fact that everything in science fiction is fantastic, Damon Knight has denied that a difference between science fiction and fantasy exists. Other writers, such as Brian Aldiss, refuse to use such science-fiction conventions as faster-than-light travel because they are impossible and thus elements of fantasy rather than science fiction. Where we must begin in differentiating between science fiction and fantasy is with the reader's response.

Because science fiction takes place in a universe recognizably our own, when we read science fiction we are continually comparing the events of the story to reality. That is why plausibility ranks so high in the qualities necessary to science fiction, and why H. G. Wells, in his famous advice to science-fiction writers, though he speaks of tricking the reader, stresses the need for a "plausible assumption." "Possibility" is another key word. John Campbell made use of it when he called for a science-fiction story that was "interesting and good and possible," but a fantasy story that was "interesting and good." "Possibility," of course, suggests subjectivity: one reader's possibility may be another reader's ridiculous fantasy. By "possibility," however, I mean that which is presented plausibly and which the reader is supposed to accept as real for scientific reasons, not as a willing suspension of disbelief. Faster-than-light travel, for instance, may be considered "possible" if we assume that Einstein's theory, like Newton's, was only an approximation, or that ways have been found around the limitation of the speed of light. Where it is used only as a convenience, as a way of getting on with the story, readers accept it as a convention rationalized in earlier stories.

Plausibility and possibility lead the reader to question the text: "How did we get there from here? What does that mean? Did it come about through human decision? Was that decision good or bad? Are people responding to the changes around them rationally or emotionally? What is the right course of action for them? What does that mean?" All of these questions are intellectual, comparisons of the changed environment of the story with the environment of the here and now and judgments about the relationships of people to environment and proper responses to it. The science-fiction story demands that we ask these questions and make these judgments.

So-called science-fiction stories and novels that do not tell us how we got there from here seem much more like fantasy, for fantasy does not tell us these things—or, if it tells us, does so only by a wave of the wand that changes a closet into the portal to another world or a rabbit hole into a passageway to wonderland. Our reaction to that, as readers, is to accept if we wish, but not to question. At its best, fantasy leads us to psychological insights; at its least, to mindless adventure.

Which brings us—finally—to hard science fiction. By hard science fiction we mean that science fiction in which the story turns around a change in the environment that can be understood only scientifically and generally through what are known as the hard sciences, usually the laboratory sciences such as chemistry, physics, and biology, and the observational sciences such as astronomy, geology, and geography. Mathematics and computers are two of the tools used by all the hard sciences. These sciences are considered hard because they deal with objective data, and predictions can be made from these data that are verifiable. The soft sciences—the behavioral and social sciences—are considered soft because their data are at least partially subjective and because they deal with theories and general statements rather than predictions on whose truth the validity of the theories must rest. But the soft sciences can become the substance of hard science fiction if the story revolves around them and if the story imagines a situation in which the soft sciences have become hard sciences.

John Campbell, the long-time editor of *Astounding/Analog* who did more than anyone else to give meaning to hard science fiction, wrote in the 1947 symposium *Of Worlds Beyond*:

> To be science fiction, not fantasy, an honest effort at prophetic extrapolation of the known must be made. Ghosts can enter science fiction—if they're logically explained, but not if they are simply the ghosts of fantasy. Prophetic extrapolation can derive from a number of different sources, and apply in a number of fields. Sociology, psychology, and Parapsychology are, today, not true sciences; therefore instead of forecasting future results of applications of sociological science of today, we must forecast the *development* of a *science* of sociology. From there the story can take off.

Implicit in the scientific method is the provisionality of all truths, the questionability of all facts, the falsifiability of all theories. In fact, a test suggested to distinguish between scientific theories and nonscientific theories, such as creationism, is that scientific theories are falsifiable, that is, can be proved wrong. So the hard sciences are not truly hard in the sense that their current interpretations of data are final, and one science-fictional technique, similar to assuming that some soft science has been turned into a hard science, is to assume that new discoveries and theories have turned current hard sciences, at least partially, into soft sciences.

Norman Spinrad believes that there are discernible differences between stories based on the hard sciences and those on what he calls the "rubber sciences." There is, he says in his article in *The Craft of Science Fiction*, a hard science fiction "feel": "a sense of hard black vacuum and cold pinpoint stars, a universe filled with hard-edged metallic artifacts and a reality whose rules are all of a piece, fixed, seamless, and invariant." Its "hard-edged, materialistic, deterministic reality," he says, "admits of no fuzziness in locus, no blank spots, no indeterminacy, no multiplexity—more Newtonian than Einsteinian." But when the soft sciences are treated as hard sciences, rather than material for what Spinrad calls "visionary science fiction," the universe in which the fiction takes place is rational and ruled by law, not arbitrary. And it should be pointed out that Einstein rejected indeterminacy with his "God does not play dice with the universe."

We might make one last comparison: that of hard science fiction with "new wave" speculation fiction. All new wave fiction was not the same, any more than all hard science fiction, but new wave fiction characteristically was anti-science, even anti-science fiction. The events encountered in the fiction that represented the heart of the new wave, J. G. Ballard's catastrophe fiction, for instance (though much of it, to be sure, appeared before Michael Moorcock took over as editor of *New Worlds*), discouraged reader curiosity: the catastrophes clearly were arbitrary—they had no discernible cause and the characters either knew this or were incurious, and the reader's intellectual desire to know how we got there from here was deflected in a manner similar to that of fantasy.

What hard science fiction worked upon, then, was the same motivation that produced science: the desire of the reader to understand the universe, and himself and the human species in relationship to that universe. Hard science fiction, like science, took as its first premise that the universe could be understood by an organized application of observation and thought. The use of accepted scientific theory or, where necessary, the theory that, in a rational manner, superseded accepted theory focused the reader's attention on rational explanation. Often the fiction dealt with rational people moving into the unknown, most commonly by spaceflight and the future; once having reached the unknown, the characters do not simply experience it but try to understand it. The reader of hard science fiction embarks on a voyage of discovery not unlike that of Charles Darwin aboard the *Beagle*. In fact, one collection of stories, in which A. E. van Vogt made hard sciences out of education and history in order to shape adventure stories and fairy tales into hard science fiction, is called *The Voyage of the Space Beagle*. To observe what the impact would be without the sciences, without the search for explanations, one need only view the film *Alien*—all terror and no effort to understand, no rational behavior.

Ultimately the attempt to deal rationally with change, whether it is change created by people or change encountered during exploration into the unknown or change that comes to humanity out of the un-known, produces a reader not only prepared for change and prepared to deal with it rationally, but one who reads science fiction about aliens or alien environment realizing that it is really larking about the influence of environment on people.

Mission of Gravity, Hal Clement's masterpiece, is considered one of the hardest of hard science-fiction novels. Its scene is an alien world whose gravity at the poles is five hundred times what it is on earth, but, because of the equatorial bulge, only two or three times earth's gravity at the equator. Its dominant race has evolved from caterpillar-like crea-tures, built low to the ground and with many legs in order to cope with gravity, but inside they are a great deal like humans The reason for this is not only that the reader will care about the Mesklinites but will un-derstand their problems, when, at the equator, they must conquer the normal fears and precautions that their polar environment has bred into them. If the reader reads the novel correctly, he asks himself at the end how gravity—a physical fact he has seldom considered—has cre-ated in him uninspected responses, including fears and prejudices.

On a different level but in an almost identical process, Ursula K. Le Guin's The Left Hand of Darkness explores the influence of bilateral sex on human history, politics, psychology, social status, myth, and many other aspects of existence by studying alien androgyny on an alien world. This makes hard science fiction seem cerebral, and it is, but it also can work as fiction, and the standard of critical judgment is how well the message of the work is matched by the means: a good hard science-fiction piece is one in which the story is completely integrated with the idea. The Left Hand of Darkness, though it displays a bit of what I call the idiot plot (that is, the events of the novel would not have happened if the major characters had displayed normal levels of intelligence), proceeds through a journey of discovery in which Genly Ai is continually educated in the facts of Gethenian sex (and, by con-trast, his own) until he at last accepts Estraven as a person. Using this criterion, it seems to me that Le Guin's The Dispossessed is a lesser novel; as a utopia, ambiguous or otherwise, it does not present politics as a hard science but as an exploration of a wish. What Theodore Stur-geon calls "if only" stories (an addition to the conventional wisdom that divides science fiction into "if this goes on" stories and "what if" stories) tend to develop through the less convincing strategies of lecture and parable.

Ringworld displays another way in which hard science fiction can be softened. Larry Niven is considered a leading hard science-fiction author, and *Ringworld* one of his finest achievements of this type. In fact, it has often been described as a novel that might have been written by Hal Clement. What is "hard" about it is a concept of staggering scope: a world or worlds that have been fashioned into a gigantic ring spinning around its sun; on its great surface thousands of races and different civilizations can live out their lives with no knowledge of each other. This is the image that defines and sustains the novel (a concept derived from the speculations of astronomer Freeman Dyson), but the novel turns vaguely disappointing when Niven chooses to explore only a tiny fraction of the Ringworld and plays the ring for adventure rather than making the magnificent artifact the heart of his work. A sequel written much later, *Ringworld Engineers*, to be sure, answers a number of the questions left open at the end of the first novel without exploring the Ringworld image much more significantly.

On the other hand, Bob Shaw's *Orbitsville*, which also was based on Dyson's speculations about advanced civilizations converting planetary matter into a sphere about a sun and utilizing all that star's energy and all the converted planet's area as living space was not as spectacularly popular as *Ringworld* but kept the concept of the Dyson sphere at the center of the novel. Shaw's world turns out to be an alien construct intended to consume the time and energy of ambitious space-faring creatures and delay their further expansion into the galaxy.

Perhaps the best way of illustrating the differences between hardcore science fiction and other kinds is to look at some classic examples. Van Vogt's most famous early novels, *Slan* and *The World of Null-A*, seemed at the heart of the hard science-fiction magazine *Astounding* when they were first published in its pages; probably because they treated not soft sciences but even softer concepts like telepathy, telekinesis, teleportation, general semantics, and the entire bundle of concepts collectively known as superman as if they were hard sciences. But even then they read more like myths. Some critics call them power fantasies, but this seems pejorative, and I prefer to call them fairy tales—fairy tales of science such as Tennyson referred to in "Locksley Hall." And Van Vogt's stories had all the innate power of fairy tales to structure the dreams of its readers—witness the fans who built a Slan Shack in the 1940s as an early experiment in communal living.

To compare another famous pair of books, Isaac Asimov's *I, Robot* seems consistently more "hard" than his *The Foundation Trilogy*. *I, Robot* projects the development of a robot industry and its social and technological consequences, as well as the problems of dealing with individual robots due to conflicts between the famous three laws of robotics. *The Foundation Trilogy*, on the other hand, does speculate about the creation of a science of general social prediction, psychohistory, but—important as psychohistory is in preserving civilization—psychohistory is not truly central, and, in fact, becomes virtually irrelevant throughout the second half of the *Trilogy*. What is central is the concept of the Foundation, which halfway through the series becomes Foundations in the plural. And even though the Second Foundation makes an exact science out of psychology, the uses of that science remain more mysterious than rational. The heart of the stories, moreover, is the struggle of determined men against great difficulties—the greatest of these being the fall of a galactic empire and the shortening of thirty thousand years of dark ages to a thousand. Asimov has described the series as adventure stories, and so they are, even if the adventure is almost totally cerebral.

The Caves of Steel is Asimov's best example of a novel in which the theme of environment is central and in which fiction and theme are skillfully integrated. *The Gods Themselves*, however, is Asimov's best-developed "hard" novel, in which he used his knowledge of chemistry and of scientists to speculate about the kinds of universes that might have developed where the "strong force" in the atomic nucleus had different values.

All John Brunner's ecological novels—*Stand on Zanzibar, The Jagged Orbit, The Sheep Look Up*, and *The Shockwave Rider*—are hard science fiction in that each is clearly extrapolative from present to future conditions and in each of them science plays a central part in trying to cope with the conditions. Robert Silverberg has written a number of hard science-fiction works, but his *Dying Inside*, in which telepathy was used as a metaphor rather than an exploration, was a mainstream novel that was unappreciated and probably misunderstood by science-fiction readers—and probably by mainstream critics as well.

Religion can be the subject of hard science fiction, as in James Blish's A *Case of Conscience*, which considers with great rigor the efforts of a Jesuit priest to deal with the fact of an alien race born without sin. C. S. Lewis's *Perelandra* trilogy, however, as a retelling of Christian beliefs rather than a critical consideration of them, does not come close.

Another soft science turned into a hard science is linguistics in Jack Vance's *The Languages of Pao* and Samuel R. Delaney's *Babel-17*. Vance's novel is "harder" because of its more rigorous and more central use of linguistics. In another well-known Delany novel, *The Einstein Intersection*, the initial reactions of the science-fiction reader is bewilderment because he never learns "how we got there from here." The novel is more profitably read as fantasy.

Often, of course, novels are mixtures of hard and soft. *Dune*, for instance' leaves readers with conflicting reactions because the ecology is hard, the anthropology and the psychic abilities are soft, and the structure is palace intrigue. This may be the reason for its success, and that of its sequels—readers attracted by the structure can enhance their enjoyment with richness of other kinds.

If the writer wishes to make a point in what he or she writes, a point that the reader is intended to consider rationally and perhaps be convinced of its merits, the writer might well consider the potential of science fiction, particularly hard science fiction. If the writer wishes to describe behavior or analyze character, either non-judgmentally or in terms of social or religious morality, then the writer does better to couch the fiction as fantasy or mainstream literature and stay away from science fiction. That is why science fiction, at least of the hard variety, is primarily didactic; rational consideration of how we got there from here and how we can cope with the process or the end result is necessarily judgmental.

Writing hard science fiction has its difficulties. The major one is knowing the science, at least enough to know what questions to ask or what sources to search, and how to place the information into some reasonable context of how science works. Even if the writer's only desire, as it often is, is to make the science sound plausible, research is usually essential, although too much knowledge of a science can be inhibiting to the imagination.

A related problem is how to explain the science to the reader, and to explain it in such a way as to enhance, not distract from, the story's narrative flow. Sometimes this problem is solved with epigraphs, sometimes with discussions between the characters or with descriptions or explanations worked into the action. Brunner, in *Stand on Zanzibar*, accomplishes this expository purpose in a variety of ways but partially through chapters of fragmented clues; Le Guin, in *The Left Hand of Darkness*, inserts entire chapters of anthropological reports or accounts of myths and Gethenian stories.

Authors whose works are truly hard also run into the problem of readers who spend long hours trying to catch the authors in a scientific or logical inaccuracy, like the general criticism of Ringworld (the artifact) for basic instability, or the even more embarrassing criticism that the author made the sun come up in the wrong direction. The committed "hard" author, however, enjoys the game, and like Niven, admitting his errors in the foreword to *Ringworld Engineers*, turns it to his own didactic advantage.

It may be instructive about the reader's response to hard science fiction to ask this question: what reader ever worried about these kinds of questions concerning a fantasy or mainstream work? On the other hand, writers who deal in turning soft sciences hard, like the fantasy writer, are limited largely by psychological plausibility.

Recent developments have created what seems to me an ideal mixture of fiction and science at this moment. In a pair of introductory essays in *The Road to Science Fiction* #4 entitled "Fiction and Science" and "Science and Fiction," I held up two stories as illustrations of what I have been trying to describe. One author approached his subject—a solar nova (or solar flare) from the viewpoint of the mainstream writer seeking metaphor, but the science seemed accurate and the human relationships were revealed and made meaningful by the science. The other author approached his subject from the viewpoint of science; he made his science believably human and his protagonist made sense of his scientific decisions by connecting them with human exercises. The first story was Ed Bryant's "Particle Theory," and the second was Gregory Benford's "Exposures." Benford also provided an instructive blend in his award-winning novel, *Timescape*, where his scientists had human problems but seemed like real scientists doing science.

Hard science fiction does not have to mean an ignorance of literary values, nor do literary critics have to remain invincibly ignorant of science and its influence on our lives. At its best, hard science fiction brings together the two cultures in a way achieved by no other dialogue, no other art.

~

CHAPTER EIGHT

Science Fiction and "Literature"— or, The Conscience of the King

Samuel R. Delany

Delivered at Minicon, 1979

At Oxford in 1892 the French poet Mallarmé delivered a lecture that began with the now famous line, *"On à touché au vers"*: someone has been tampering with poetry. Today, some 80 years later, I had thought of beginning, "Someone has been tampering with science fiction." But if I did, I would have to make some distinctions between 1892 and 1979 right off. For one thing, in 1892 the person who was doing (by far!) the most tampering was Mallarmé himself—along with a few poets who were comparatively closely associated with him (they came for coffee every Tuesday evening). The tampering I'm talking of is not coming from within science fiction. When I read writers who are just my juniors, in length of time published if not in age (John Varley, James Tiptree, Jr., Michael Bishop, Vonda McIntyre, Jean Mark Gawron, Suzy McKee Charnas, or Joseph Haldeman, to name the most random few), though of course I see local disagreements, a whole variety of different approaches to the world between them and me, between each of them and each other, I don't sense any violent rupture between these newer writers and those writers who are my immediate contemporaries (Disch, Le Guin, Niven, Russ, Zelazny, to name another random few).

Also, though most of us within the field no doubt feel the new wave controversy of a decade or so ago is far too frequently exhumed. There's at least one point about it that is all too seldom made and might well vanish if someone doesn't record it. Again, there were obviously a variety of local differences. But even the term *new wave* (first used for science fiction in 1966), which was applied to me often enough by 1968, gained its currency mainly in the mouths of a number of writers who apparently took a great deal of pleasure in standing up on platforms and saying, "Well, I guess I'm an Old Wave writer." I can honestly say I never seriously referred to myself as a "new wave writer" and the number of times I did jokingly could be counted on one hand; and I think the same would probably go for the other writers who, from time to time, got lumbered with the term. Consider: The writer whom I personally heard say, most often and from the most platforms, "Well I guess I'm an Old Wave writer," was Frederik Pohl, who was back then my most supportive editor at the now defunct magazines *If* and *Worlds of Tomorrow*. Today he is my most supportive editor at Bantam Books. Does this allow for differences? Yes. But it doesn't speak of rupture.

The tampering I'm talking about does produce a sense of rupture. Though there is much disagreement among writers of all generations about whether this rupture is a good or a bad thing, we all sense it. It is the tampering that comes from academia, from critics who have become "interested" in science fiction.

Mallarmé came from Paris to Oxford to defend his own tampering and that of his fellow poets. I have barely recovered from a term as research fellow at the Center for Twentieth Century Studies at the University of Wisconsin (research topic: contemporary science fiction) and have limped back to the fold here . . . to *defend* academic tampering.

"*On à touché au vers?*" Well, to paraphrase Yale critic Paul de Man, "*On a touche au critique.*" People have also been tampering with academic criticism recently. Myself, I've been tampering with SF criticism for all I'm worth. But the only way to launch a good defense of anything is first to separate out what's definitely bad; when something doesn't work and leads nowhere, covering it up doesn't do anyone any good. We have to locate why this tampering is experienced as rupture and as encounter—and I don't mean simple xenophobia. Having had a chance to teach science fiction at two universities in the last few years, as well as a chance to write my share of criticism and survey the present academic response to science fiction, I'm in a particularly good position to experience the rupture aspect—and yes, it is an experience!

In 1975, when I was organizing a scholarly symposium on science fiction at the University of Buffalo, SUNY, I was extremely excited to have in attendance an exemplary Joyce scholar and literary theoretician who was about to publish a book on science fiction with a polysyllabic title from a highly respected university press. The day the symposium began, advance copies of the book arrived. I made a breakfast appointment with this very affable gentleman to discuss his book with him the next day—and stayed up till four o'clock in the morning reading the book twice and filling the margins with notes and comments. Over scrambled eggs and toast, I gave him my notes: they ranged from proofreading errors to corrections of dates to respectful differences on matters of opinion. But at one point I referred to something he had said about the use of matter transmission in science fiction, using Niven's *Ringworld* for his example. His idea had to do with "matter transmission as a metaphor for telekinesis" and what he felt telekinesis meant to people. "I'm just curious," I said, "why, if you wanted to make a point about telekinesis, you didn't refer, say, to Alfred Bester's *The Stars My Destination*, where the idea is dealt with directly and in very much the manner that you outline. Do you think, perhaps, the book has received too much attention? Or perhaps it's not as good as people are always going on as if it were?"

And this gentleman, who had been writing so eloquently about Le Guin's themes and Sturgeon's prose, looked at me with perfect ingenuousness and asked: "Bester? *The Stars My Destination?* Is this a book or an author I should have heard of before?"

This is totally disorienting; it throws the whole discussion onto the level of surrealism. Someone who writes a book on a topic, about whom you can say "They don't know the field," is usually someone who gets dates wrong, forgets small facts, comes to wrong-headed opinions. Perhaps there are a number of important works they haven't read recently enough or closely enough and therefore are relying too heavily on what another writer had to say about them. But imagine asking someone who has just written a book on twentieth-century poetry why T. S. Eliot or *The Waste Land* weren't mentioned, only to get the perfectly serious answer, "T. S. Eliot? *The Waste Land?* Is this a poem or a poet I should have heard of before?"

This is rupture.

And it is a rupture that a graduate degree generally precludes from the field of literary studies.

This particular critic, I'm happy to report, over the following two years did a lot of homework and wrote a much better book on science fiction with a much less polysyllabic title, which was published by a different university press.

But the experience of rupture remains.

Then there was the academic critic who had discovered Michael Moorcock's delightful *Warlord of the Air* and claimed, in a chapter on science fiction in his book on the fantastic, that Mr. Moorcock had, out of sheer original genius, invented an entirely new subgenre of science fiction, which he dubbed "the historical alternative story." He went on to say that, although he suspected there would be a lot of argument among regular SF fans about whether Moorcock's brand-new SF twist should be accepted or not, he felt this new form really should be included in the overall genre of science fiction . . . just as if Dick's *The Man in the High Castle* had never been written, nor been presented its much deserved Hugo Award for best SF novel of its year—not to mention his complete ignorance of all the other parallel-world stories ("historical alternative" indeed!) from Ward Moore's *Bring the Jubilee* to Hilary Bailey's "The Fall of Frenchy Steiner" and Joanna Russ's *The Female Man!* This same academic, comparing the reader response to Sturgeon's *More Than Human* and Clarke's *Childhood's End* (two novels published in 1953), though noting that both books were good felt Sturgeon's was the better; he then went on to locate internal reasons in both novels to explain why the Clarke had outsold the Sturgeon! Does anyone remember that about 10 years ago there was a very successful movie called *2001: A Space Odyssey*, which catapulted Clarke into a multimillion-dollar ad campaign, from which time the numerous reprints of all his books by and large date? If you compare the first 14 years of both books, you find that both were reprinted six times; and according to people who were then at Ballantine Books, the paperback publisher of both novels, the Sturgeon marginally outsold the Clarke! So much for internal reasons.

Perhaps the most awkward ignorance I've encountered in an academic concerned what academics themselves have done in science fiction: on the organizing end of another SF symposium, I recently received an abstract of a paper to be presented that opened with the blanket statement that nobody ever took science fiction seriously before 1973! The first time I was ever invited to address the Modern Language Association on science fiction was in 1967. But the Continuing Seminar on Science Fiction of the Modern Language Association was founded in 1958—indeed, it is the second-oldest continuing seminar in that august organization that includes thousands of college professors!

I experience all of these as rupture. They represent simple ignorance. They are bad criticism. The healthiest response I can think of to start with is a good, hearty laugh. But we can't stop with laughter, because there is so much ignorance. One of the things laughter allows us to do is get back far enough to see that there is a pattern of it. The rupture we experience—that I experience—is not a rupture that comes from the critics' abuse of specific texts. After all, I've been reading SF book reviews in the magazines for going on 25 years, and I've certainly developed enough calluses to badly thought-out appraisals of individual SF books by now.

The rupture I experience is a rupture with my own knowledge of the history of SF writing. The working assumption of most academic critics (an assumption that certainly, yes, distorts what they have to say of specific texts) is that somehow the history of science fiction began precisely at the moment they began to read it—or, as frequently, in the nebulous yesterday of 16th- and 17th-century utopias. For both notions accomplish the same thing: they obviate the real lives, the real development, and finally the real productions of real SF writers, a goodly number of whom are still alive, if not kicking. This is why the best histories of science fiction remain the commentaries of Merril and Asimov in their various anthologies, the collected reviews of Knight in *In Search of Wonder*, of Blish in *The Issue at Hand* and *More Issues at Hand*, and of the Panshins in *SF in Dimension;* for the rest one must go digging through back issues of old SF magazines for reviews by Merril, Budrys, del Rey, and Miller. Frequently wrong, frequently brilliant, wrong or right they were *responding* to what was happening in the field; and their criticism, in conjunction with the texts, is the only way to find what was happening, whether as ambiance or as dates and occurrences. And this is equally why something like Aldiss' *Billion Year Spree*, entertaining as parts of it are, is basically useless as a history of science fiction—for it covers desultory writing from Mary Shelley's *Frankenstein* to the first use of the term *science fiction* in 1929, then careens through all that legitimately bears the SF label itself in a handful of pages that, once it passes the Second World War, becomes mere listing.

Then what do we do with this debacle of historical ignorance; what do we do with the rupture?

I'll start by telling you the very first time I sensed it—because, oddly, back then it did *not* come from an academic. It came from directly within the SF precincts. In 1966 I attended my first World Science Fiction Convention (the 24th annual), the Tricon, with somewhat over 3,000 attendees, held over Labor Day weekend in Cleveland. All the talk among the professional writers that year was of one New York editor at a major publishing house who had just upped his company's output of hardcover science fiction from two novels a year, which it had been for the last 10 years, to 24 (!) novels a year (which, incidentally, it has been for the last 12 years). All we pros, young and old, talked of this man in reverent tones as a great gentleman, practically a scholar, seriously committed to the field and deeply concerned with the development of the genre. That weekend Roger Zelazny's *This Immortal* tied with Frank Herbert's *Dune* for the Hugo. Indeed, that weekend was the first time I met Zelazny in person. (Back then, because our last names shared five letters, we were frequently mistaken for one another by readers.) Over dinner with Roger and his wife in the hotel's rather ornate restaurant—it had a transparent plastic bridge over a luminous fishpond—he mentioned that *This Immortal* had, months ago, been submitted to this fabled editor, who'd bounced it. Well, certainly there was nothing remarkable there. But back in New York, a week later, the will of the gods conspired so that this very editor called up and invited *me* to lunch! And that is how it came to pass, during a lull in the conversation after the first very dry martini and before the fillet of sole, that I casually remarked: "I was just in Cleveland last week, and Zelazny's *This Immortal* tied with *Dune* for the Hugo. You may have missed out on something there: Zelazny tells me he submitted it to you and you bounced it."

And the great man, shining hope of the genre, committed to and concerned about the development of the field, looked at me across the rim of his martini glass and, with a slight frown, inquired: "The Hugo award? Now what's that?"

This was my first encounter with that complete dissociation with what I had taken to be the real world: the SF editor of a major publishing house, who himself edited 24 SF novels a year, did not in 1966 know what the Hugo award was! It was precisely this feeling that returned, only a few years later, when I began to encounter what, with only a little overpoliteness, one might call "certain academic blind spots."

The point, of course, is that such rupture as we experience it at the hands of academics is not new. We've experienced it before in the hands of editors and publishers who really *do* have their hands on our economic jugular veins. And we've survived it, survived it very well! In 1951 there were some 15 texts published that could reasonably be called SF novels—including the serials in magazines and the first volume of Isaac Asimov's *Foundation* series, a compilation of stories written since 1942. Last year over 14% of *all* original fiction published in the United States was science fiction. (That's just shy of 500 books.) And so my anecdote about my 1966 editor is finally just curve-fixing to show how sharply the slope has been rising. No, the imposition of a rupture with our own history is not new to us.

You simply cannot break off one history from a phenomenon, however, without replacing it by another—even if you replace it with nothing more than the equally historical assumption that the phenomenon you have just stripped of its past *has* no significant history. We've talked a lot about rupture and only in passing about encounter. The encounter, of course, is between the new history that has been stuck on the original phenomenon and the phenomenon itself—in this case science fiction. Now here's a little leap. But follow it carefully, because it tells a lot about where we're shortly going to go. To say that a phenomenon has *no* significant history at all is a way of allowing yourself to treat it *as if* its history were exactly the same as that of some other phenomenon you are already acquainted with. I don't mean the same in its dates and occurrences, but rather the same in its values, processes, ways of understanding it and responding to it. To say that a phenomenon *does* have a significant history is to say that its history is *different* from the history of something else: that's what makes it significant. To assume that something—like science fiction—has no *significant* history in the past is to assume that its history-to-come will be no different from the last phenomenon whose history you've been studying. (Again, I don't mean identical dates and happenings, but in values and responses to ways the phenomenon can be meaningful.) And the historical phenomenon most literary critics have been studying hardest is, of course, literature.

After we have passed the sense of rupture, here is where we locate the sense of encounter. And it's the growing number of feet of shelf space in bookstores, the growing number of readers who turn to science fiction, the growing number of hours that readers are devoting to science fiction, and the growing number of courses given on science fiction in the country's high schools and universities (over 500 at last count) that give this encounter its interest and urgency.

What we have to remember, before all our images of growing amounts of shelf space, growing numbers of readers, all with their economic implications and insinuations, is that the battle is *not* between texts.

If I hold a copy of, say, Clement's *Mission of Gravity* in one hand and Salinger's *Catcher in the Rye* in the other, there's no encounter. Even if I read one right after the other, there still is no real encounter between the stories themselves. The encounter comes after both texts are read, in the whole space of values, judgments, ways of response, which responses (and reading itself is basically a *response* to a text) are more pleasurable, which are more useful; and it's only when we reach the question "Which text is more available?" that the whole economic situation which lurks behind our initial set of images for this encounter intrudes on and contours this encounter—rather than being (according to the capitalist ideal anyway) simply an economic response to the encounter itself.

For the purposes of the rest of this essay (and the rest of this book), then, we must think of literature and science fiction not as two different sets of labeled texts, but as two different sets of values, two different ways of response, two different ways of making texts make sense, two different ways of reading—or what one academic tradition would call two different discourses (and the meaning of *discourse* here is not simply explanation, but rather a range of understanding that involves certain characteristic utterances: the larger process that allows explanations to be and be a part of). The encounter, then, is between two discourses, science fiction and literature, and it is won or lost through pleasure and use. The encounter could be hugely influenced by economic availability; but since availability of both discourses seems assured (the one, literature, wide; the other, science fiction, growing), we can discount that for the present.

A number of times I have written extensively about the way the discourse (the way of understanding, the way of responding, the way of reading) called science fiction differs from the discourse called literature, particularly that bulk of literature we SF readers call mundane fiction (from *mundus*, meaning the world; stories that take place on the Earth in the present or past. Any other connotations? Well, turnabout is fair play). There are clear and sharp differences right down to the way we read individual sentences.

Then her world exploded.

If such a string of words appeared in a mundane fiction text, more than likely we would respond to it as an emotionally muzzy metaphor about the inner aspects of some incident in a female character's life. In an SF text, however, we must retain the margin to read these words as meaning that a planet, belonging to a woman, blew up.

He turned on his left side.

The discourse of mundane fiction more or less constrains us to read such a string of words as referring to some kind of masculine, insomniac tossings. SF discourse retains the greater margin to read such words as meaning that a male threw a switch activating the circuitry of his sinistral flank.

And there are many other sentences with a perfectly clear and literal meaning in science fiction that if written within the discourse of mundane fiction (e.g., *The door dilated,* from Heinlein's novel *Beyond This Horizon* [1948]) would simply be meaningless or, at best, extremely awkward.

Consider: There is no sentence I can think of that could theoretically appear in a text of mundane fiction that could not also be worked into some text of science fiction—whereas there are many, many sentences in science fiction that would be hard or impossible to work into a text of mundane fiction. SF discourse gives many sentences clear and literal meanings, sentences that in mundane fiction would be meaningless or at any rate very muzzily metaphorical. Just at the level of lucid and literal sentences, then, which is the larger way of response, the wider range of understanding? Which offers the greater range of readings for possible sentences? The point should be made here, lest I be misunderstood, that greater statistical range does not necessarily mean higher aesthetic accomplishment. Within the precincts of literature, Racine's plays use only about 3,000 different words while Shakespeare's use approximately 10,000—and Joyce's novel *Ulysses* uses over 30,000. The relative number of words available and, by extension, the relative number of sentences only suggest why writers of varying temperaments might be attracted to one field or the other.

More recently I have been exploring the way we actually organize the information from SF texts, exploring the organization principles of SF discourse. Because in the discourse of mundane fiction the world is a given, we use each sentence in a mundane fiction text as part of a sort of hunt-and-peck game: All right, what part of the world must I summon up in my imagination to pay attention to (and, equally, what other parts—especially as sentences build up—had I best not pay attention to at all) if I want this story to hang together? In science fiction the world of the story is not a given, but rather a construct that changes from story to story. To read an SF text, we have to indulge a much more fluid and speculative kind of game. With each sentence we have to ask what in the world of the tale would have to be different from our world for such a sentence to be uttered—and thus, as the sentences build up, we build up a world in specific dialogue, in a specific tension, with our present concept of the real.

Again, to take a string of words that, alone, might lend itself to either discourse, here is a sentence from Pohl and Kornbluth's *The Space Merchants*: "I rubbed depilatory soap over my face and rinsed it with the trickle from the fresh water tap."

If this were mundane fiction, because the world in mundane fiction is a given world, we would read the adjective "fresh" (in the real world, of course, the vast majority of water faucets are fresh water faucets) as either an unnecessary writerly redundancy (and therefore an auctorial failing) or some comment on the consciousness of the character: perhaps he is abnormally aware of the water's freshness for some subjective reason. Similarly, the trickle we would read either as support for, or contrast with, this particular subjective state. But though hints of this reading are of course there, in the SF text where it actually occurs this sentence is telling us much, much more. In the world of *The Space Merchants*, because of the overpopulation, apartments have both fresh water *and* salt water taps—and the second half of this sentence is one of the more important phrases from which we learn this. The trickle tells us specifically that the fresh water supply in this particular building is low, even though it's a luxury apartment complex. Yes, states of mind are suggested about the character by this sentence in context; but in SF discourse we must retain the margin to take such information and build a world specifically different from, and in dialogue with, our own.

With readers who have difficulty negotiating the specific rhetoric of the SF text, I've found that their problems center on the numberless rhetorical figures SF writers use to suggest, imply, or sometimes vividly draw the differences between the stories' world and ours. Unless the nature of the world of the story is completely spelled out for them in solid, expository paragraphs, they simply can't take the hints, the suggestions, the little throwaways with which inventive SF writers get this dialogue going in the minds of those readers comfortable with the discourse. They can't form these hints and throwaways into any vision of a different world. But then, where would they have had the opportunity to learn? Certainly not in contemporary mundane fiction. And yes, with practice most of them got a *lot* better at it.

I find science fiction's literalization of the language and its wealth of clear and lucid sentences simply and sensually pleasurable. I find the dialogue it sets up with the real world (a dialogue that mundane fiction simply cannot indulge) both pleasurable and useful—if only because it keeps the possibility of dialogue alive. But if we really want to explore the encounter between values that, finally, *is* the encounter between literature and science fiction, we have to go into the values of literature as well.

The French scholar Michel Foucault is one of the most radical and fascinating thinkers to tackle this problem. In an essay called "What Is an Author?" he notes that many of the values of literary discourse are tied up in the very concept of the "author" of a work. The author (or, as he sometimes calls it, the "author-function") becomes the focus for some of literature's most central values. In this essay he writes:

> It seems . . . that the manner in which literary criticism once defined the author—or rather constructed the author, beginning with existing texts and discourses—is directly derived from the manner in which Christian tradition authenticated (or rejected) the [religious] texts, at its disposal. In order to "rediscover" an author in a work, modern literary criticism uses ways similar to those that Christian religious commentary employed when trying to prove the values of a text by its author's saintliness. In *De Viribus illustribus*, Saint Jerome explains that bearing the same name is not sufficient to identify legitimately authors of more than one work: different individuals could have had the same name, or one man could have, illegitimately, borrowed another's patronymic. How then can one attribute several discourses to one and the same author? How can one use the author-function to determine if one is dealing with one or several individuals? Saint Jerome proposes four criteria: (1) if among several books attributed to an author one is inferior to the others, it must be withdrawn from the list of the author's works (the author is therefore defined as a unified level of value); (2) the same should be done if certain texts contradict the doctrine expounded in the author's other works (the author is then defined as a field of conceptual or theoretical unity); (3) one must also exclude works that are written in a different style, containing words and expressions not ordinarily found in the writer's production (the author is here conceived of as a stylistic unity); (4) finally, one must consider as interpolated those texts which quote people or mention events subsequent to the author's death (the author is here seen as a historical unity and the crossroads of a limited number of events).
>
> *Modern literary criticism, even when—as is now customary—it does not concern itself with authentification, still defines the author no differently . . . (using the author's biography, the determination of his individual perspective, the analysis of his social position, and the revelation of his basic design): the author is . . . the principle of a certain unity of writing—all differences having to be resolved, at least in part, by the principles of evolution, maturation, or influence.*

This is from a revised version of the lecture *What Is an Author*, given in 1969 at the Societe Française de Philosophie, which will soon appear in an anthology *Textual Strategies* (Cornell University Press; Ithaca, 1979), edited by Josue Y. Harari. (I have very modestly revised the translation at a few points. The unrevised version of this lecture may be found in *Language, Counter-Memory, Practice,* by Michael Foucault, edited by Donald F. Bouchard, Ithaca, New York, Cornell University Press, 1977.)

Clustered around the literary concept of "author," then, we find this quartet of literary values: unity of value, theoretical unity, stylistic unity, historical unity. It is a little sobering to consider that a discipline like literary criticism fell out of the dogmatic religious enterprise. But these values are certainly among its controlling parameters. One of the last major battles in the history of the English novel was the furor over whether or not D. H. Lawrence was to be accepted as a Great Author or consigned to the category of interesting crackpot. The critic R. F. Leavis, in his book on Lawrence that pretty much settled the question (*D. H. Lawrence: Novelist* [1955]), sets out to prove Lawrence's greatness, right in chapter one, by showing the "unity" of Lawrence's works.

And I have seen at least one master's thesis written about my own science fiction that set out to show me an author worthy of serious consideration, by demonstrating the "unity" in my own works.

At this point we have to ask: Are these unities part of SF discourse? Should they be applied to science fiction?

I've already talked about the way, sentence by sentence, science fiction can differ from mundane fiction. I've talked as well about the way science fiction organizes this sentential information—not only into a story but also into a world—differently from the way mundane fiction organizes its information. I also feel that if we look for this quartet of literary unities—valuative, theoretical, stylistic, and historical—in SF discourse, whether clustered around the "author" or not, we will find absolutely diametric values.

Working backwards through them:

One must consider as unauthentic "those texts that quote people or mention events subsequent to the author's death." Well, that certainly lets science fiction out of the historical-unity game! Science fiction's very commitment to its future vision means that the SF writer is always quoting people and mentioning events subsequent to the writer's death! So this basic image of historical unity is denied at the outset. But it's not the image we are concerned with so much as the value as an operative function—and the historical value science fiction seems to operate by, more than any other, is one of historical plurality, a value diametric to the unitary value of literature. This is reflected not only in the diverging historical views within the production of a single writer (nothing stops me from writing three SF stories, all set in New York City in 2001, one in an overpopulated world, one in a depopulated world, and one in a world whose population has managed to stabilize at, say, two and a half billion: they would simply be three different "historical" extrapolations), but also the parallel universe tales set in the pasts that so astonished the academic about whom I wrote earlier.

This is possibly the place to point out that the author, or author-function, simply plays a very different role in SF discourse from the one it plays in the discourse of literature. I doubt I have ever called myself an "SF author"; the term would simply feel too uncomfortable in my mouth. When someone asks me my profession, I say I'm an SF writer. Again, I think most other SF writers feel the same. By and large SF readers tend to be much more concerned with stories than with writers. But this leads us to the next value, the value of unity of style.

Science fiction's origins in the pulps and its persistence as a generally popular writing category simply mitigate against the sort of stylistic unity that literature privileges both in the productions of single writers and, certainly, in the production of the whole field. SF writers are always adopting different styles for different stories; and evolution, maturation, or even influence are just not operative factors: the stories, and the various levels of the readers, demand them. For a good long time now science fiction has been responding to readers of all levels: someone who loves the simplistic thrust of a Ferry Rhodan book is probably not going to love the techno social recomplications of a John Varley or the logicolinguistic invention of a Jean Mark Gawron (although I know of at least one mathematics professor who reads all three avidly). The point, however, is that all three are science fiction. But because of the range of markets, the range of readers, there is simply very little chance of stylistic unity as we find it in the literary concept of author-function. If anything, there seems to be a highly valued ideal of stylistic plurality—especially since the science fiction of the 1960s.

And what about theoretical unity? The other side of science fiction's commitment to historical plurality is an equal commitment to theoretical plurality. What has most confounded the folks searching for definitions of science fiction relating to scientific subject matter is the number of SF stories that clearly contradict known science—all the stories with faster-than-light travel, for example. Then, of course, there are all the undeniably SF stories about magic (e.g., Cogswell's "Wall Around the World," Blish's *Black Easter*). To say, "Well, in these tales magic is treated in a 'scientific way,'" only confuses the question: currently the existence of magic runs counter to scientific theory, and that's all there is to it. Then there are all the stories about ESP, which, if not exactly contradicted by prevailing theory, are certainly rendered highly dubious by it. Mumbling about "exceptions that prove the rule," whatever that means, simply doesn't cover the case. The concept of theoretical plurality, as an operative value, does. For there to be such a value, science fiction, across its range, must deal with conflicting theories. This value does not have to fix itself to the "author" function in science fiction: not every writer feels it necessary to choose opposing theoretical constructs from tale to tale—although many of the best have. I would venture, however, that every SF writer aware that her/his own work is theoretically consistent with itself is also aware of one or more SF writers with whom that theory conflicts, whether the theory be political, sociological, or scientific. And there's your value of theoretical plurality.

Finally there is unity of value itself. As history and theory, whether unitary or plural, form two sides of a single coin, so style and value, whether unitary or plural, form two sides of another (and here, of course, style means a little more than merely the way one uses words: there are styles of thinking, styles of perception). The same factors that ensure that science fiction will not exhibit any unity of style in the literary sense, but rather a plurality of styles both within the production of single writers and throughout the field's range, also ensure that science fiction actively strives for a plurality of value (i.e., worth). Once a text is adjudged "literature," we can say it partakes of a certain (admittedly vague and almost impossible to define) value, a value that, however vague, consists of a juxtaposition of theoretical, stylistic, and historical elements. This value— the text's literary value—mitigates for the text's preservation, its study, its reproduction. But once more, this is *not* the case with science fiction. Having adjudged a text science fiction, we have made no unitary statement, however vague or at whatever level of suggestion or implication, about its value. I suspect this is because, again, innate to the discourse of science fiction is the concept of value plurality.

It may be well to point out here exactly what I have done so that no one is tempted to overvalue *this* exploration. I have simply taken the list of values Foucault has recovered from the literary concept of "author" and let them guide me through a range of science fiction—whereupon I found some values that pretty much oppose the literary ones. I have not necessarily discovered the *most* important values of science fiction. *They* may lie completely elsewhere. The ones I've found are highlighted only when held up against the literary.

So . . . do I feel that science fiction will, or should, be taken over by literature in the current encounter? I sincerely hope it is not. And the only way I feel it can be taken over is for very bad academic criticism—the kind that strips science fiction of its history; that ignores it as a discourse, as a particular way of reading and responding to texts; and that obscures its values of historical, theoretical, stylistic, and valuative plurality—to swamp what I feel is a responsible academic approach, of which I offer my own preceding argument as a modest example.

This brings us to what may well be the most important battlefield in the encounter. Around every text there is a space for interpretation. There is no way to abolish the interpretive space from around the text: it comes into existence as soon as we recognize that words have meanings, most more than one each. Most of us who have a strong sense of that space have it through the interpretive use it has been put to in literary criticism.

Take a sentence from a very entertaining book by the poet John Ciardi, *How Does a Poem Mean:* "A poem is a machine for making choices." Does this mean a poem is a machine to decide between A and B? Or does it mean a poem is a machine for generating situations in which some choice is involved? In other words, is *making choices* to be taken idiomatically (make a choice: choose A or B) or literally (make—that is, create—a choice situation). Having unpacked these two possible meanings from our text, there are several possible ways to relate them, and which one we choose depends on whether our basic discursive values are unitary or plural.

I can say: Let it mean either *one you* want; choose which *one you* prefer. (Liberal as it is, it's still unitary.)

Or I can say: Logically, you can't decide between A and B *until* you've generated the choice situation. Therefore, it must mean generate a choice situation first, then make it. (Here, we've made a logical hierarchy out of the two meanings, which is tantamount to reducing it to a single argument. We're still unitary here.)

If I'm feeling very inventive I can say: first one must choose whether or not to interpret the poetic text, and only after one has made this choice is there the possibility of the text generating a choice situation; so it must mean first choose, then generate. (I've just reversed the hierarchy, but it's still unitary.)

And the other thing I can say is: To read the sentence "A poem is a machine for making choices," we have to read it first one way *or* the other. But the moment we have, the suggestion of the other meaning rises up to obliterate the former in our minds, and the meaning plays back and forth between the two; so that the joy, the wit, the delight of the text comes from that play between *both* meanings, which prevents it from totalizing into any unitary or hierarchical form.

Here we have followed plural values, in an attempt to capture something of the experience of reading the line in the first place—the same experience that got us started on our various unitary interpretations.

Locating the play in the interpretive space, rather than positing a unitary or hierarchical explanation, is something that some of the most intriguing academics have been working with. Some names? Jacques Derrida, Shoshana Felman, Paul de Man, Barbara Johnson. It can be done in a number of ways: In the song from Shakespeare's play *Cymbeline* we find the lines

> Golden lads and girls all must
> As chimney sweepers come to dust.

It seems a clear (if double) statement about the inevitable death of (or the necessity of work for) even the young and beautiful as well as the dirty and grubby. Some time in the 1930s, however, a scholar traveling in Warwickshire, the county of Shakespeare's birth, discovered that the local term for the flowers we call dandelions was *golden boys*, and that when the pale fuzz was blown off the dandelions' heads the farmers then called them *chimney sweepers*. Apparently, these local terms are several hundred years old. Read the two lines again. They haven't *lost* any of their meaning. But a range of play has been introduced with the recovery of the local Warwickshire dialect. If one wants to be "literary" about things, one can hierarchize *all* the meanings into a logical, unitary order to turn them into a single, coherent essay. Indeed, as we have seen before, we can turn them into several different coherent essays and then (if you want) begin all over again, hierarchizing *them*. I would hazard that Shakespeare's delight in the line, as well as the delight of his audience, was in the simple play of plural meanings that we now have, knowing both the literal and dialectal interpretation of the terms.

What does this little diversion have to do with science fiction? Well, when Roger Zelazny, in *This Immortal,* writes of a biologist breeding poisonous fleas (called *slishi)* to kill off an invasion of spiderbats on the Monterey coast, "When the spiderbats return to Capistrano, the slishi will be waiting," he is basically initiating the same sort of play as Shakespeare. But to perceive the play one must know that there was once an extremely sentimental old lyric, "When the Swallows Return to Capistrano." Zelazny's line puts that sentiment in play with the grim literalness, and the result is amusing and entertaining; and, though highly suggestive, it does not really lend itself to a unitary, single interpretation.

(If we may add play to play: it seems that the play's the thing . . . !)

Here's another way that historical awareness can indicate the play in both a "literary" writer like Shakespeare and an SF writer like . . . Isaac Asimov!

We know from historical research that Shakespeare's plays were performed with elaborate costumes—and no scenery at all (if you don't believe me, check Asimov's two-volume *Asimov's Guide to Shakespeare).* This is why the characters spend so much time describing where they are in ways that, if a cowboy in your latest Western movie did it, ("Well, here I am in this dark wood full of elms and sycamore, as the light dims and the pinecones cast long shadows over the dead leaves around my boots"), would make the audience howl. To know this today allows us to read these parts of the dramas in a context that lets them do their jobs again; it lets us respond to the many subtle ways descriptions of locations are worked in—rather like the little throwaway bits that give you the world of an SF story—even in the midst of dialogue. They no longer seem grey, awkward, and superfluous. We are no longer left giggling at best, or simply scratching our heads at worst. I think a good giggle may be the better way to start because it is a *response* to the text. And the person who can't giggle at all is simply unresponsive to *our* current movie and theater conventions of realistic scenery; that's a little less forgivable than not knowing Shakespeare's theatrical conventions. Moreover, without the giggle, you miss out on the historical play that time has overlaid on Shakespeare's texts.

Where did Asimov go in all this?

Here's a bit of history that time and again I've found helpful in teaching people the "Foundation" stories. The first story we read today in *Foundation* (the last actually written) was written in 1951; it begins in a spaceport. Most of the students at the class where I taught the stories had come to the college by plane. One of the facts I found helpful for the students in trying to visualize the story is this:

In 1951 air travel was much less a part of people's lives than today. There was *no* commercial jet travel. Asimov had never ridden on a plane at this time, nor probably visited an airport more than a time or two at most. If you want to visualize Asimov's spaceport, don't start with your own experience at Kennedy, O'Hare, or L.A. International. Instead, just before you read the story, go back and visualize a major train station. Grand Central Station in New York City, Union Station in Los Angeles, Victoria Station in London, or Gare de l'oest in Paris. Does this mean Asimov's spaceport is a train station? Of course not! But if you use a train station as your basic imaginative material, the whole story will be more vivid, things will seem to make more sense, and you will see much more in your mind's eye when you read it. (And for what it's worth, well after I started using this little pedagogic prod, Dr. A. heard about it and complimented me on my insight.)

Notice that all this information, when written into the interpretive space around the text (whether it is Shakespeare's text, Asimov's, or Zelazny's), results in the text's becoming more vivid. *More* things can go on in the text. The information is not used to constrain the text to a single, unified meaning. Rather, in each case it releases meanings that then come into the play of meanings that is the text. (Think of *play* not so much as children's fun or adult competition, but as the give in a gear or a steering wheel that has play in its movement; although all those other meanings represent points about which the play—in the word *play*—moves, as does the idea of theatrical play as well.) Notice this is *not* the same as saying "The text can mean anything you want," with its implication, "Choose whichever *one* you prefer," which gets us back to the unitary.

This seems to me to be, with both literary texts *and* SF texts, the proper use of the interpretive space that lies about them both. An awful lot of SF readers, however, confuse the existence of that interpretive space with the values the interpretations most often written into that space have, most often, supported: those literary values that are unitary or authoritarian. The response of these readers (frequently our older readers), no doubt impelled by the best of intentions and a suspicion that unitary values are inappropriate to a writing field so clearly a pluralistic enterprise, is simply to deny all existence to the interpretive space around the SF text. The usual way of accomplishing this is for these readers to assume a conscientiously philistine approach—which is what they intuitively feel is opposed to a "literary" approach. "First of all," they say, "science fiction is merely entertainment." But can't you hear, King behind this statement, an appeal not to the notion of a plurality of values but to a single value, "entertainment value," meant to totalize the whole field? This is simply the mirror image of the statement "Literary texts have literary value." The good ones presumably have more of it, the bad ones less, but all literary texts have some. This, presumably, is why they are literature in the first place. "SF texts have entertainment value." The good ones, again, have more, the bad ones less.

The values are different, but both are unitary.

Whenever I encounter that particular phrase, "Science fiction is entertainment," I like to insert a little verbal play into the interpretive space around it. *Entertain* has two meanings in English: one can entertain friends, an audience, oneself. But one can also entertain ideas (trivial or profound), notions (pleasant or sad), and fancies (pretty or ugly).

If science fiction is "entertainment" in both senses, then its values must generate from the play between them.

But of course the significance of "Science fiction is merely entertainment" is not just as a single pronouncement that ends there. It is part of a whole philistine reader-view, and is associated with a whole galaxy of pronouncements. Anyone who has been around science fiction for any length of time will recognize that they all go together:

"I like an SF story that's told in good, simple language with none of your fancy writing or experimentation, with a nice, clear beginning, middle, and end."

But haven't we encountered, on the level of values, something very like this? Of course. It's nothing but an appeal for a unity of style.

"I like an SF story that sticks to good, hard science that we can all understand if we just know our general physics and chemistry."

But on the value level, we should recognize this one too: it's the call for theoretical unity, loud and clear.

"I guess I just wish they would write SF stories the way they did back in the 1960s/1950s/1940s. . . ;" (You can choose your decade; there're adherents to all of them today.) You guessed it: it's the cry for historical unity.

Paradoxically, it is just this most philistine of reader reactions that, despite its good intentions, most strongly encourages the appropriation of science fiction by literature—because it writes in that space an interpretation of science fiction (and the philistine interpretation of science fiction is no *less* an interpretation of science fiction than the notion of science fiction with no significant history is a historical notion) that, through a process finally not too far from bad academic criticism, has very little awareness of the structure of SF discourse, either as a historically sensitive process (although the philistine may be aware of the history and able to spot academic bloopers with the best) or as a present reality, in which each contemporary writer is inserting her or his play into the plurality—valuative, theoretical, stylistic, and historical—around which our SF discourse is organized. For we are not talking about complexity, or even quality, of interpretation, but about the values a whole range of interpretations, good and bad, simple and complex, reinforce. And the philistine view is right there, with all its authoritarian vigor, at the center of the literary enterprise—even though it may well be the play of pluralities that the person expressing that view is actually responding to in any given SF text that delights.

What this essay has been on the verge of proposing, as some of you by now no doubt have suspected, is nothing less than the appropriation of literature by science fiction. This has been suggested, with varying degrees of play, by various writers at various times in the past. But it is just what gives the phenomenon its aspect of encounter that also, today, makes that a possible outcome. Again, I must remind you, I do not mean an economically encouraged encounter between texts—texts labeled "science fiction" driving texts labeled "literature" off the shelves of the stores and out of the hands of the readers. Even the rise of science fiction from practically zero percent to 15% of American fiction production in 25 years or the rise from zero to about 500 SF classes does not seriously threaten the production of texts of the sort we call mundane fiction or poetry. There are too many other economic pressures, pressures from universities and journalistic pressures, that would bring the process to a grinding halt at 50/50 if not well before. I am still talking about the encounter between discourses, between responses, between ways of reading texts, ways of using the interpretive space around them.

There are many people who read only literature.

There are many people who read only science fiction.

But there are also people who have moved from one to the other. The label "silly kid's stuff," so long applied to science fiction, was there to suggest that the natural and healthy movement over the period of maturation was from science fiction to literature, with its concomitant suggestion that any movement in the other direction implies mental softening. But of course there *are* many people who have recently moved in the other direction—another expression of the encounter.

I talked to one such man not long ago. A historian specializing in the beginnings of the 19th century, he had been a great reader of literature, but had found, over a period of five or six years, that he was reading more and more science fiction until, for the last two years, other than his journals and nonfiction he read nothing else. "I was really afraid to go back and read a 'serious' novel," he told me. "I didn't know what would happen. Finally, in fear and trembling, I picked up Jane Austen's *Pride and Prejudice*, always one of my favorites, just to see what happened when I did. . . . Do you know something? I thoroughly enjoyed it, more than I ever had before. But I realized something. Before, I used to read novels to tell me how the world really was at the time they were written. This time, I read the book asking myself what kind of world would have had to exist for Austen's story to have taken place—which, incidentally, is completely different from the world as it actually was back then. I know. It's my period."

As far as I can tell, this man has started to read Austen as if her novels were science fiction. There had been an encounter. And on some very deep level, part of the discourse of science fiction has triumphed over the discourse of literature—without, I suspect, any significant rupture for literature.

I think I have made it fairly clear by now: I believe that reading science fiction as if it were literature is a waste of time. I suspect that reading literature as if it were "literature" is also pretty much a waste of time. The discourse of science fiction gives us a way to construct worlds in clear and consistent dialogue with the world that is, alas, the case. Literature's unitary priorities do not. And in a world where an "alas" must be inserted into such a description of it, the dialectical freedom of science fiction has to be privileged.

It is possible that, on the level of values, reading literature as if it were science fiction may be the only hope for literature—if, while we're doing it, we don't commit the same sort of historical ruptures that we in science fiction have already suffered at the hands of both editors and uninformed academics. And we must read—and write—science fiction as if it were *really* science fiction, and not just a philistine hack job purveying the same unitary values as literature but in their most debased form.

~

CHAPTER NINE

Science Fiction and Mrs. Brown

Ursula K. Le Guin

Just about fifty years ago, a woman named Virgina Woolf sat down in a carriage in the train going from Richmond to Waterloo, across from another woman, whose name we don't know. Mrs. Woolf didn't know it either; she called her Mrs. Brown.

> She was one of those clean, threadbare old ladies whose extreme tidiness— everything buttoned, fastened, tied together, mended, and brushed up— suggests more extreme poverty than rags and dirt. There was something pinched about her—a look of suffering, of apprehension, and, in addition, she was extremely small. Her feet, in their clean little boots, scarcely touched the floor. I felt that she had nobody to support her; that she had to make up her mind for herself; that, having been deserted, or left a widow, years ago, she had led an anxious, harried life, bringing up an only son, perhaps, who, as likely as not, was by this time beginning to go to the bad ("Mr. Bennett and Mrs. Brown").

Mrs. Woolf, who was an inveterate snooper, listened to the fragmentary conversation between the old lady and the man traveling with her—dull comments, snatches of incomprehensible business. Then all of a sudden Mrs. Brown said, "Can you tell me if an oak tree dies when the leaves have been eaten for two years in succession by caterpillars?"

She spoke quite brightly, and rather precisely, in a cultivated, inquisitive voice. And while her companion was replying at length, about plagues of insects at his brother's farm in Kent, Mrs. Brown took out a little white handkerchief and began to cry, very quietly, which annoyed the man. And then he got off at Clapham Junction; and then she got off at Waterloo. "I watched her disappear, carrying her bag, into the vast blazing station," says Mrs. Woolf. "She looked very small, very tenacious, at once very frail and very heroic." And I have never seen her again.

This Mrs. Brown, says Virginia Woolf, is the subject matter of the novel. She appears to the novelist, inside a railway carriage or inside the mind, and she says, "Catch me if you can!"

> I believe that all novels begin with an old lady in the corner opposite. I believe that all novels, that is to say, deal with character, and that it is to express character—not to preach doctrines, sing songs, or celebrate the glories of the British Empire, that the form of the novel, so clumsy, verbose, and undramatic, so rich, elastic, and alive, has been evolved. . . . The great novelists have brought us to see whatever they wish us to see through some character. Otherwise they would not be novelists, but poets, historians, or pamphleteers. *(ibid.)*

I accept this definition. I don't know if it is a critically fashionable one at the moment, and really don't care; it may seem banal to critics who love to talk about epiphanies, apocalypses, and other dim religious polysyllables, but to a novelist—this novelist, at any rate—it is simply, and profoundly, and in one syllable, true.

It was true in 1865, when Mrs. Brown was named Sarah Gamp; it was true in 1925, when Mrs. Brown was named Leopold Bloom: it is true in 1975. Mrs. Brown's name in England today is Rose, in Margaret Drabble's *The Needle's Eye;* Silvia, in Angus Wilson's *Late Call.* She is Leni, in Heinrich Boll's *Group-Portrait with Lady.* She has found her way to Australia, where her name is Voss, or Laura. She has never left Russia, where her name is of course Natasha or Anna or Raskolnikov, but also Yury Zhivago, and Ivan Denisovitch. Mrs. Brown turns up in India, in Africa, in South America, wherever novels are written. For as Mrs. Woolf said "Mrs. Brown is eternal. Mrs. Brown is human nature. Mrs. Brown; changes only on the surface; it is the novelists who get in and out. There she sits."

There she sits. And what I am curious about is this: Can the writer of science fiction sit down across from her? Is it possible? Have we any hope of catching Mrs. Brown, or are we trapped for good inside our great, gleaming spaceships hurtling out across the galaxy, antiseptic vehicles moving faster than the Richmond-Waterloo train, faster than the speed of light, ships capable of containing heroic captains in black and silver uniforms, and second officers with peculiar ears, and mad scientists with nubile daughters, ships capable of blasting other, inimical ships into smithereens with their apocalyptic, holocaustic rayguns, and of bringing loads of colonists from Earth to unknown worlds inhabited by incredibly sinister or beautiful forms of alien life, ships capable of anything, absolutely anything, except one thing: they cannot contain Mrs. Brown. She simply doesn't fit. It's funny, the idea of Mrs. Brown in a spaceship. She's much too small to visit a Galactic empire or to orbit a neutron star. "Her feet, in their clean little boots, scarcely touched the floor." Or is that quite it? Could it be that Mrs. Brown is actually, in some way, too large for the spaceship? That she is, you might say, too *round* for it—so that when she steps into it, somehow it all shrinks to a shiny tin gadget, and the heroic captains turn to cardboard, and the sinister and beautiful aliens suddenly appear to be, most strangely, not alien at all, but mere elements of Mrs. Brown herself, lifelong and familial, though startling, inhabitants of Mrs. Brown's unconscious mind?

So that's my first question: Can Mrs. Brown and science fiction ever sit down together in the same railway carriage, or spaceship?' Or to put it plainly, Can a science fiction writer write a novel? And then there will be a second question: Is it advisable, is it desirable, that this should come to pass? But I will come back to that later on.

I suspect that Virginia Woolf would have answered my first question with a characteristically subtle and apparently tentative but quietly decisive no. But in 1923 when she wrote the essay "Mr. Bennett and Mrs. Brown" she really could not have answered it, for there was very little science fiction available to her eye and judgment. H. G. Wells's scientific romances were a quarter-century old; he had put them behind him and was busy writing Utopias—Utopias of which Virginia Woolf said, very decisively indeed, "There are no Mrs. Browns in Utopia." And she was absolutely right.

But even as she said it, a book was being published in England, and another was being written in America; very strange books; written under strange circumstances, which prevented their receiving much critical notice or general attention. The one printed in England was written by a Russian, Zamyatin, in Russian, though it was not, and has never been, published in Russia. It has existed for fifty years only in foreign editions and in translation—in exile. Its author died in exile. The pattern is not wholly unfamiliar, now. As for the other book, it was not written for publication at all, and was published only after the death of the author, Austin Tappan Wright, in 1942.

A simple test to detect the presence or absence of Mrs. Brown in a work of fiction is this: A month or so after reading the book, can you remember her name? It's silly, But it works pretty well. For instance, almost anybody who reads *Pride and Prejudice* will remember the names Elizabeth and Darcy, probably for very much longer than a month. But anyone who has read one of Mr. Norman Mailer's works of fiction need not apologize if he can't remember a single name from it—except one, of course: that of Norman Mailer. Because Mr. Mailer's books aren't about Mrs. Brown, they're about Mr. Mailer. He is a marvelous writer, but not a novelist. Very few Americans are. You see, it does work, roughly. But the first use I want to make of it on science fiction is an acid test, and I admit I failed it. I could remember only two of the three main characters' names. The women are O, and I-330 and there's that wonderful minor character named S; but what's the name of the narrator, the central character? Oh, damn. I had to look at my copy of the book. D-503, of course, that's it. That's him. I will never forget him, poor soul; but I did forget his number. I plead the fact that I sometimes forget the telephone number we have had for sixteen years. I am very poor at mathematics. But I have sat facing D-503, not in a railway carriage to be sure, but in a great glass-walled, glass-floored, glass-roofed, super-Utopian building; have suffered with him; escaped with him; been recaptured and dragged back to Utopia, and lobotomized, with him; and I will not forget it. Nor the book's name, *We*, nor its author's name, Yevgeny Zamyatin, the author of the first science fiction novel.

We is a dystopia that contains a hidden or implied Utopia; a subtle, brilliant, and powerful book; emotionally stunning, and technically, in its use of the metaphorical range of science fiction, still far in advance of most books written since. Austin Tappan Wright's novel *Islandia is* quite another kettle of fish. It is old-fashioned. It does not look forward; neither does it look back. It looks sideways. It does not offer a Utopia, but merely an alternative. And the alternative seems, on the surface of' it, an, escapist one, a mere daydream. A lifelong daydream. A book written by a successful lawyer, secretly, for his private solace and delight; a child's imaginary country, maps and all, carried on for thirty years, a huge manuscript, whole volumes on the geology of the continent of Islandia, its history, its institutions . . . and also a story. A narrative, with characters. The author's daughter extracted the story, Knopf published it, and a few people found it. And since then there have always been a few people who find it, and who treasure it. It is not a great book perhaps, but a singularly durable one, and a durably singular one. There is nothing else in all literature like *Islandia.* It is a life work; Wright put himself into it totally. It is a genuinely alternative society, worked out thoroughly, pragmatically, and humanely. And it is a novel. It is full of real people. There is plenty of room in Islandia for Mrs. Brown. That, in fact, is the point of it. I think that Wright saw a world, his America, his century, becoming psychotic, depersonalized, unlivable, and so he created a nonexistent continent, geology and weather and rivers and cities and houses and weaving-looms and fireplaces and politicians and farmers and housewives and manners and misunderstandings and love affairs and all, for human beings to inhabit. And thus he rendered questionable Virginia Woolf's statement, "There are no Mrs. Browns in Utopia." I think it possible she might have been quite pleased to know it.

But meanwhile, while Austin Tappan Wright is scribbling happily in his study, and Zamyatin is silent in exile in Paris, the 1930s are upon us, and science fiction is getting underway. The first rockets leave the launching pad. Decades of thrilling adventures ensue. Evil Venusians are thwarted. Scientists' nubile daughters are rescued, squeaking. Galactic empires rise and fall. Planets are bought and sold. Robots receive the Tablets of the Three Laws from Mount Sinai. Marvelous hardware is invented. Humanity grows old, destroys itself, redeems itself, replaces itself, transcends itself, reverts to bestiality, becomes God. The stars go out. The stars blink on again, like neon signs. Awful and wonderful tales are told—truly wonderful, some of them; some of them really awful. But in none of the spaceships, on none of the planets, in none of the delightful, frightening, imaginative, crazy, clever stories are there any people. There is Humanity, and After, as in Stapledon. There is Inhumanity, and After, as in Orwell and Huxley. There are captains and troopers, and aliens and maidens and scientists, and emperors and robots and monsters—all signs, all symbols, statements, effigies, allegories, everything between the Stereotype and the Archetype. But not Mrs. Brown. Name me a name. There are no names. The names don't matter. The names are mere labels—Gagarin, Glenn—symbols, heroic labels, names of astronauts. The humanity of the astronaut is a liability, a weakness, irrelevant to his mission. As astronaut, he is not a being he is an act. It is the act that counts. We are in the age of Science, where nothing *is*. None of the scientists, none of the philosophers, can say what anything or anyone is. They can only say, accurately, beautifully, what it does. The age of Technology; of Behaviorism; the age of the Act.

And then?

Well, then, as the century nears its midpoint and the Act seems to be heading ever more inevitably toward a tragic dénouement there comes along the most improbable Mrs. Brown we have seen, and coming from the most improbable direction. It must be some kind of sign and portent. If any field of literature has no, can have no Mrs. Browns in it, it is fantasy—straight fantasy, the modern descendant of folktale, fairy tale, and myth. These genres deal with archetypes, not with characters. The very essence of Elfland is that Mrs. Brown can't get there— not unless she is changed, changed utterly, into an old mad witch, or a fair young princess, or a loathely Worm.

But who is this character, then, who really looks very like Mrs. Brown, except that he has furry feet; a short, thin, tired-looking fellow, wearing a gold ring on a chain around his neck, and heading rather disconsolately eastward, on foot? I think you know his name.

Actually, I will not argue hard in defense of Frodo Baggins as a genuine, fully developed, novelistic character; as I say, his importance to my theme here is rather as a sign and portent. If you put Frodo together into one piece with Sam, and with Gollum, and with Sméagol—and they fit together into one piece—you get, indeed, a complex and fascinating character. But, as traditional myths and folktales break the complex conscious daylight personality down into its archetypal unconscious dreamtime components, Mrs. Brown becoming a princess, a toad, a worm, a witch, a child—so Tolkien in his wisdom broke Frodo into four: Frodo, Sam, Sméagol, and Gollum; perhaps five, counting Bilbo. Gollum is probably the best character in the book because he got two of the components, Sméagol and Gollum, or as Sam calls them, Slinker and Stinker. Frodo himself is only a quarter or a fifth of himself. Yet even so he is something new to fantasy: a vulnerable, limited, rather unpredictable hero, who finally fails at his own quest—fails it at the very end of it, and has to have it accomplished for him by is mortal enemy, Gollum, who is, however, his kinsman, his brother, in fact himself. . . . And who then goes home to the Shire, very much as Mrs. Brown would do if she only had the chance; but then he has to go on, leave home, make the voyage out, in fact die—something fantasy heroes never do, and allegories are incapable of doing.

I shall never cease to wonder at the critics who find Tolkien a "simple" writer. What marvelously simple minds they must have!

So now we have got a kind of primitive version of Mrs. Brown into fantasy, the ancient kingdom of which science fiction is a modern province. There she stands, quite steady on her furry feet. And we have met her twice in the borderlands of Utopia. But there haven't been any Utopias written for decades; the genre seems to have turned inside out, becoming purely satirical and admonitory. And what about science fiction proper? As we come into the sixties and seventies and a new kind of writer is writing science fiction, and science fiction is even being printed on a new kind of paper which doesn't get yellow and crumbly at the edges quite so fast, and as the real rockets really take off and land on the real moon and thus leave science fiction free to stop describing the future and to start imagining it—do we now find any more room in the spaceship for Mrs. Brown?

I am not sure.

I am going to have to talk about myself and my own work for a while here; but before I do so—and so that I don't seem to be setting myself up as a kind of stout Cortez silent upon a peak in Disneyland, sole discoverer of uncharted seas—let me mention a couple of names.

Mrs. Thea Cadence.

Mr. Nobusuke Tagomi.

Do those names mean anything to you? They do to me; a good deal. They are the names of two of the first Mrs. Browns I met in modern science fiction.

Mr. Tagomi turns up in Philip K. Dick's *Man in the High Castle*. Thea is the protagonist of D. G. Compton's *Synthajoy*.

They are not unique; they're rare birds still in science fiction but not unique. I just picked those two because I like them. I like them as people. They are people. Characters. Round, solid, knobby. Human beings, with angles and protuberances to them, hard parts and soft parts, depths and heights.

They also stand for a great deal of course. They are exemplars, teaching aids if you like; they express something the authors wanted urgently to say as clearly as possible. Something about human beings under stress, under peculiarly modern forms of moral pressure.

If the authors wanted to speak clearly why didn't they write an essay, a documentary, a philosophical or sociological or psychological study?

Because they are both novelists. Real novelists. They write science fiction, I imagine, because what they have to say can be said using the tools of science fiction and the craftsman knows his tools. And still, they are novelists because while using the great range of imagery available to science fiction, they say what it is they have to say through a character—not a mouthpiece but a fully realized secondary creation. The character is primary. And what used to be the entire object of science fiction—the invention of miraculous gadgets, the relation of alternate histories, and so on—is now used subjectively, as a metaphor, as a means for exploring and explaining what goes on inside Mrs. Brown, or Thea, or Tagomi. The writers' interest is no longer really in the gadget, or the size of the universe, or the laws of robotics, or the destiny of social classes, or anything describable in quantitative, or mechanical, or objective terms. They are not interested in what things do, but in how things are. Their subject is the subject, that which cannot be other than subject: ourselves. Human beings.

But these are human beings who live in the universe as seen by modern science, and in the world as transformed by modern technology. That is where science fiction still remains distinct from the rest of fiction. The presence of science and technology is essential in both of these books. It is the given. Only, as I say, the speculations and facts, the idea of relativity, the idea of a machine to reproduce emotions, are not used as ends in themselves, but as metaphors. Metaphors for what? For what is not given; an X; an X that the writers are pursuing. The elusive individual, upon whom all the givens act, but who simply is. The person, the human psyche, life, Mrs. Brown, "the spirit we live by." Catch me if you can! And I think they caught her. She's there. Thea, shrewd and tragic in her madhouse, Mr. Tagomi, shrewd and tragic in his business office, both of them trying, in a half-conscious, muddled agony, to reach freedom, both failing or succeeding depending on how you look at it, "very small, and very tenacious, at once very frail and very heroic. . . ."

Welcome aboard the spaceship, Mrs. Brown.

Angus Wilson (whose book *The Old Men at the Zoo* is quite definable as science fiction, by the way, although I doubt he'd much like to have it *categorized* as science fiction) has described, in *The Wild Garden*, the way a novel first came to him.

> In my original conception of *Hemlock and After* . . . I saw Mrs. Curry, obese, sweet, and menacing, certain in her hysteric sense of power that she can destroy a good man, Bernard Sands; and because my vision is primarily ironic, I saw Bernard painfully thin, bitter, inward-turning. . . . A momentary powerful visual picture of a fat woman and a thin man. The whole of the rest of the novel, for good or bad, is simply an extension needed, as I thought, to communicate this very visual ironic picture to others . . .
>
> The novels, in fact, *are* those moments of vision. No didactic, sociological, psychological, or technical elaboration can alter that significance for the novelist himself. Like any other artist's, the novelist's statement is a concentrated vision . . . but unlike the others he has chosen the most difficult of all forms, one that makes its own discipline as it goes along. We can never hope for perfection . . . that other arts can achieve. But any serious novelist who . . . does not announce this vision as his central impulse is either playing down to some imaginary "plain chap" audience or has forgotten his original true inspiration in the polemics of moral, social, or formal purpose. Everyone says as a commonplace that a novel is an extended metaphor, but too few, perhaps, insist that the metaphor is everything, the extension only the means of expression.

That is splendid, and splendidly continues the Virgina Woolf quotations with which I started. It moves me very much, because it states my own experience very nearly. A book does not come to me as an idea, or a plot, or an event, or a society, or a message; it comes to me as a person. A person seen, seen at a certain distance, usually in a landscape. The place is there, the person is there. I didn't invent him, I didn't make her up: he or she is there. And my business is to get there too.

Once, like Mr. Wilson, I saw two of them. As my vision is not ironic, but romantic, they were small figures, remote, in a tremendous waste landscape of ice and snow. They were pulling a sledge or something over the ice, hauling together. That is all I saw. I didn't know who they were. I didn't even know what sex they were (I must say I was surprised when I found out). But that is how my novel *The Left Hand of Darkness* began, and when I think of the book, it is still that vision I see. All the rest of it, with all its strange rearrangements of human gender and its imagery of betrayal, loneliness, and cold, is my effort to catch up, to get nearer, to get there, where I had seen those two figures on the snow, isolated and together.

The origin of my book *The Dispossessed* was equally clear, but it got very muddled before it ever came clear again. It too began with a person, seen much closer this time, and with intense vividness: a man, this time; a scientist, a physicist in fact; I saw the face more clearly than usual, a thin face, large clear eyes, and large ears—these, I think, may have come from a childhood memory of Robert Oppenheimer as a young man. But more vivid than any visual detail was the personality, which was most attractive—attractive, I mean, as a flame to a moth. There, there he is, I have got to get there this time. . . .

My first effort to catch him was a short story. I should have known he was much too big for a short story. It's a writer's business to develop an infallible sense for the proper size and length of a work; the beauty of the novella and novel is essentially architectural, the beauty of proportion. It was a really terrible story, one of the worst I have written in thirty years of malpractice. This scientist was escaping from a sort of prison-camp planet, a stellar Gulag, and he gets to the rich comfortable spoiled sister planet, and finally can't stand it despite a love affair there, and so re-escapes and goes back to the Gulag, sadly but nobly. Nobly but feeblemindedly. Oh, it was a stupid story. All the metaphors were mixed. I hadn't got anywhere near him. I'd missed him by so far, in fact, that I hadn't damaged him at all. There he stood, quite untouched. Catch me if you can!

All right. All right, what's-your-name. What is your name, by the way? Shevek, he told me promptly. All right, Shevek. So who are you? His answer was less certain this time. I think, he said, that I am a citizen of Utopia.

Very well. That sounded reasonable. There was something so decent about him, he was so intelligent and yet so disarmingly naive, that he might well come from a better place than this. But where? The better place; no place. What did I know about Utopia? Scraps of More, fragments of Wells, Hudson, Morris. Nothing. It took me years of reading and pondering and muddling, and much assistance from Engels, Marx, Godwin, Goldman, Goodman, and above all Shelley and Kropotkin, before I could begin to see where he came from, and could see the landscape about him—and yes, in a way it was a prison camp, but what a difference!—and the other people, the people whom his eyes saw; and the place, the other place, to which he was going, and from which I now knew, as he had always known, *why* he must return.

Thus in the process of trying to find out who and what Shevek was, I found out a great deal else, and thought as hard as I was capable of thinking, about society, about my world, and about myself. I would not have found out or been able to communicate any of this if I had not been doggedly pursuing, through all byways and side roads, the elusive Mrs. Brown.

The book that resulted is a Utopia, of sorts; it is didactic, therefore satirical, and idealistic. It is a thematic novel, in Angus Wilson's definition, in that it does not entirely manage to "disseminate the moral proposition so completely in a mass of living experience that it is never directly sensed as you read but only apprehended at the end as a result of the life you have shared in the book. This," Mr. Wilson goes on, "is the real challenge and triumph of the novel" (*The Wild Garden*). I did not fully meet that challenge or achieve that triumph. The moral proposition of *The Dispossessed* is sometimes fully embodied, sometimes not. The sound of axes being ground is occasionally audible. Yet I do believe that it is, basically, a novel, because at the heart of it you will not find an idea, or an inspirational message, or even a stone ax, but something much frailer and obscurer and more complex: a person. I have been strengthened in this belief by noticing that almost every reviewer, however carried away he gets in supporting or attacking or explaining the book's themes and ideas, somewhere in the discussion has mentioned its protagonist by name. There he is!—there, if only for a moment. If I had to invent two entire worlds to get to him, two worlds and all their woes, it was worth it. If I could give the readers one glimpse of what I saw: Shevek, Mrs. Brown, the other, a soul, a human soul, "the spirit we live by. . . ."

I suppose I have answered my second question before I got around to asking it. It was, if you remember, Should a book of science fiction be a novel? If it is possible, all the same is it advisable or desirable that the science-fiction writer be also a novelist of character?

I have already said yes. I have already admitted that this, to me, is the whole point. That no other form of prose, to me, is a patch on the novel. That if we can't catch Mrs. Brown, if only for a moment, then all the beautiful faster-than-light ships, all the irony and imagination and knowledge and invention are in vain; we might as well write tracts or comic books, for we will never be real artists.

So then let me play my own enemy for a little, and try to argue the other side: the antinovel, or postnovel, point of view, which says that science fictioneers will never be novelists, and a good thing too.

From this point of view, the novel, the novel of character, is dead—as dead as the heroic couplet, and for the same reason: the times have changed. Such writers as Wilson and Drabble are mere epigones, draining the last dregs of an emptied cask; such writers as Bhattacharya and Garcia Márquez flourish only because their countries are marginal to the place of origin of the novel, which was late in arriving at the periphery and correspondingly late in dying there. The novel is dead; and the task, the hope, of a new form such as science fiction is not to continue the novel, or to revitalize it, but to replace it.

There is, really, no Mrs. Brown anymore. There are only classes, masses, statistics, body counts, subscription lists, insurance risks, consumers, randomly selected samples, and victims. Or, if somewhere beyond all the quantification some hint of quality remains, some wisp of Mrs. Brown, she is not to be reached any longer with any of the traditional tools of fiction. No one can catch her. She has been too profoundly changed by our life, and too rapidly changed. Mrs. Brown herself has attained the speed of light, and become invisible to our finest telescopes. What is "human nature" now, who dares talk about it seriously, in 1975? Has it any recognizable relation to what was called "human nature" in the novel a century ago, which we now see as one tiny, limited fragment of the vast range of human variety and potentiality? The subject matter of the novel was the conscious, articulate portion of the minds of certain Europeans and North Americans, mostly white, mostly Christian, mostly middle class, mostly quite unaffected by science and, though affected by technology, totally uninterested in it; a handful of natives intensely interesting to the ethnologist because of their elaborate developments of manners, and their extraordinary absorption in interpersonal relationships. They thought their nature was human nature; but we don't; we can't. They thought themselves a norm; we have no norm. Through technology, which lets us travel and converse, and through such sciences as anthropology and psychology, we have learned too much about the complexity and variety of human behavior and the even vaster complexity of the human mind, conscious and unconscious; we have learned, that is, that we really know almost nothing at all. Nothing solid is left, nothing to take hold of.

For an example of solidity, look at Mrs. Sarah Gamp. There she is. Everything about her is almost appallingly solid. She represents a definite, established social stratum, though I, an ignorant American, won't try to specify it exactly. She is English; she is white; she is Christian—at least, she would say she's Christian. She is a product of urbanization and the Industrial Revolution, but her traditions are much older than that, and you would find her ancestors hanging harpylike about the bedsides of Ovid and Orestes. She is fixed in history, and in custom, and in her own self-opinion. She knows who she is and she knows what she wants. What she wants is a bottle to be placed handy on the mantelpiece, to which she "may place her lips from time to time when so disposed."

Now what is a modern, 1975 equivalent to Mrs. Gamp? Let me, to avoid odious comparisons, simply invent one. She would be younger than Mrs. Gamp, most likely. She might not bathe any oftener. If she was a Christian, she might be a Jesus freak, but more probably she would be on some kind of vague occultist trip, or into astrology. She would probably be better clothed, fed, and housed than Mrs. Gamp, and would take for granted some luxuries Mrs. Gamp had never heard of—automobiles, bottled shampoo, television in the sickroom, penicillin, and so forth. She would, however, have very much less certainty as to her place in society: she might be quite unable to say either who she is or what she wants. She would almost certainly not have a bottle handy. She would have a needle handy. Her addiction would not be funny; as Mrs. Gamp's, in its outrageous hypocrisy, is. It would be too visibly, drastically disastrous to be funny. She would be too far out of touch with daily reality, too incompetent, even to function as badly as Mrs. Gamp does as a night nurse. And her involvement with criminality would not be, like Mrs. Gamp's, a desperate grasping at respectability, or at least at the hope of unlimited gin. Her involvement with the criminal and the violent would be passive, helpless, pointless. Indeed, wherever Mrs. Gamp is most revoltingly indomitable, I see this modern version of her as most passive. It is very hard to loathe her, to laugh at her, or to love her—as we do Mrs. Gamp; or at least Dickens did, and I do. She doesn't amount to enough. She is a drifter, a pawn, a fragment, jagged bits of a person never annealed, never grown to a whole. Is there enough of her, indeed, to enter a novel as a real character, enough to paint a portrait of? Isn't she, aren't we all, too battered, too changed and changeable, too whirled about, future-shocked, relativized, and inconstant, ever to sit still for a painted portrait, ever to stay still long enough that the slow, clumsy art of the novelist can catch up with us?

Click, the camera-eye—a moment, not a person, not a portrait, only a single moment implying nothing before or after, no continuity, click. And the whirr of the movie camera, catching the moment as it dissolves into the next, unrelated moment. These are our arts. The technological arts, dependent upon an incredible refinement of machinery and a vast expense of mechanical energy, expression of a technological age. There is poetry, still, but there is no more Mrs. Brown. There are snapshots of a woman at various moments. There are moving pictures of a woman in various places with various other persons. They do not add up to anything so solid, so fixed, so Victorian or medieval as a "character" or even a personality. They are moments; moods; the poetry of flux; fragments of the fragmented, of the changing of the changed.

Do we not see this foreshadowed in the art of Virginia Woolf herself?

And what is science fiction at its best but just such a "new tool" as Mrs. Woolf avowedly sought for fifty years ago, a crazy, protean, left-handed monkey wrench, which can be put to any use the craftsman has in mind—satire, extrapolation, prediction, absurdity, exactitude, exaggeration, warning, message-carrying, tale-telling, whatever you like, an infinitely expandable metaphor exactly suited to our expanding universe, a broken mirror, broken into numberless fragments, any one of which is capable of reflecting, for a moment, the left eye and the nose of the reader, and also the farthest stars shining in the depths of the remotest galaxy?

If science fiction is this, or is capable of being this, a true metaphor to our strange times, then surely it is rather stupid and reactionary to try to enclose it in the old limits of an old art—like trying to turn a nuclear reactor into a steam engine. Why should anyone try to patch up this marvelously smashed mirror so that it can reflect poor old Mrs. Brown—who may not even be among us anymore? Do we care, in fact, if she's alive or dead?

Well, yes. Speaking strictly for myself—yes. I do care. If Mrs. Brown is dead, you can take your galaxies and roll them up into a ball and throw them into the trashcan, for all I care. What good are all the objects in the universe, if there is no subject? It isn't that mankind is all that important. I don't think that Man is the measure of all things, or even of very many things. I don't think Man is the end or culmination of anything, and certainly not the center of anything. What we are, who we are, and where we are going, I do not know, nor do I believe anybody who says he knows, except, possibly, Beethoven, in the last movement of the last symphony.[1] All I know is that we are here, and that we are aware of the fact, and that it behooves us to be aware—to pay heed. For we are not objects. That is essential. We are subjects, and whoever among us treats us as objects is acting inhumanly, wrongly, against nature And with us, nature, the great Object, its tirelessly burning suns, its turning galaxies and planets, its rocks, seas, fish and ferns and fir trees and little furry animals, all have become, also, subjects. As we are part of them, so they are part of us. Bone of our bone, flesh of our flesh. We are their consciousness. If we stop looking, the world goes blind. If we cease to speak and listen, the world goes deaf and dumb. If we stop thinking, there is no thought. If we destroy ourselves, we destroy consciousness.

And all this, the seeing, hearing, speaking, thinking, feeling—all this we do one by one. The great mystics have gone deeper than community and sensed identity, the identity of all; but we ordinary souls cannot do that, or only for a moment, maybe one moment in a lifetime. One by one we live, soul by soul. The person, the single person. Community is the best we can hope for, and community for most people means *touch*: the touch of your hand against the other's hand, the job done together, the sledge hauled together, the dance danced together, the child conceived together. We have only one body apiece, and two hands. We can form a circle, but we cannot *be* a circle. The circle, the true society, is formed of single bodies and single souls. If not, it is not formed at all. Only a mechanical, insensate imitation of true society, true community, is made up out of objectified, quantified, persons—a social class, a nation-state, an army, a corporation, a power bloc. There is no more hope in that direction. We have followed it to the end. I really see no hope anywhere except in Mrs. Brown.

Most of us these days could do with a little hope; and I am inclined to think that you as readers have a right to ask—not to demand, never to demand, but to ask—for some hope from our arts. We really cannot ask for it from science. Science isn't in the hope business, and never was. When it offers us something affirmative, it's a mere spin-off, a secondary application; meanwhile science proceeds on its true course, which is toward an ever closer imitation of nature, an ever completer objectivity. The freer science is to proceed thus toward the inevitable, the freer it leaves art in its own domain of subjectivity, where it can play, in its own way, and if it has the courage, with nature, and with science itself, our surrogate nature.

In Stanislaw Lem's *The Invincible,* the protagonist Rohan and others of the crew of the starship *Invincible* face a hostile and enigmatic world. They gradually develop an elegant explanation of the nature of that world, a literally mechanical explanation; but the explanation isn't the point of the book. It's not a mystery story. The book's theme is moral, and its climax is an extremely difficult ethical choice made by an individual. Neither reward nor punishment ensues. All that we and Rohan have learned is something about himself, and something about what is, and what is not, invincible. In Lem's *Solaris,* the protagonist takes on a world that cannot be understood objectively at all. A large part of the book is Lem's delighted, Borgesian send-up of the efforts of scientists to explain the planet Solaris, which resists and confounds them all, and yet which participates in the very deepest psychic motivations and troubles of the protagonist Kelvin, so that in the end, if he has not understood Solaris, yet Solaris seems in a way to have understood him. The dazzlingly rich, inventive, and complex metaphors of these novels serve to express, or symbolize, or illuminate the mind and emotions of late-twentieth-century man[2] as exactly and as powerfully as the slums of London, the Court of Chancery, the Circumlocution office, and Mrs. Gamp's bottle served Dickens to illuminate the characters and destinies of his contemporaries.

In the essay with which I began, Virginia Woolf was criticizing the school of Arnold Bennett because, as she saw it, such writers, had substituted the external, the objective—houses, occupations, rents, income, possessions, mannerisms, etc.—for the subject, in whom they were really no longer interested. They had deserted novel-writing for sociology. The modern "psychological novel" is a similar case, usually being not a portrait of a person, but a case study. "Socialist realism" is another example of the same flight from subjectivity. And most science fiction has shown the same tendency. It may rise from a yearning for the seemingly godlike detachment of the scientist, but what it results in is an evasion of the artist's obligation to reproduce—indirectly, for it cannot be reproduced directly—a vision. Science fiction has mostly settled for a pseudo-objective listing of marvels and wonders and horrors that illuminate nothing beyond themselves and are without real moral resonance: daydreams, wishful thinking, and nightmares. The invention is superb, but self-enclosed and sterile. And the more eccentric and childish side of science fiction fandom, the defensive, fanatic in-groups, both feed upon and nourish this kind of triviality, which is harmless in itself, but which degrades taste, by keeping publishers' standards, and readers' and critics' expectations, very low. It's as if they wanted us all to play poker without betting. But the real game is played for real stakes. It's a pity that this trivial image is perpetuated, when the work of people from Zamyatin to Lem has shown that when science fiction uses its limitless range of symbol and metaphor novelistically, with the subject at the center, it can show us who we are, and where we are, and what choices face us, with unsurpassed clarity, and with a great and troubling beauty.

The beauty of fiction is always troubling, I suppose. It cannot offer transcendence, the peace that passes understanding, as poetry and music can, nor can it offer pure tragedy. It's too muddled. Its essence is muddle. Yet the novel, fiction concerned with individuals, in its stubborn assertion of human personality and human' morality, does seem even now to affirm the existence of hope. Despite the best efforts of talented antinovelists, it continues to avoid the clean and gleaming sterility of despair. It is muddled, elastic, inventive, adaptable.

It needs to be adaptable. These are bad times, and what is art to do in a bad time? Art never fed anyone—often not even the artist. Half the world is hungry, and art feeds only the spirit, on an immaterial food. Words, words, words. I may well live to eat my words.

But till then, here is what I think: I think art remains centrally important in any age, the best or the worst, because it doesn't lie. The hope it offers is not a false hope. And I think the novel is an important art, because it talks about what we live by, other than bread. And I think science fiction is—well, no, not important, yet still worth talking about, because it is a promise of continued life for the imagination, a good tool, an enlargement of consciousness, a possible glimpse, against a vast dark background, of the very frail, very heroic figure of Mrs. Brown.

Mrs. Brown Twenty Years Later[3]

On the launch pad.

MRS. BROWN: Oh dear, oh dear. I suppose I'm making some kind of quite dreadful mistake. I really don't know how to run this, I think. Look here, my feet don't even reach the pedals. How fast does it go, I wonder?

PROF. X: Mrs. Brown! Get out of there at once, Mrs. Brown! You have no business there. Leave that wretched machine alone and get back into the railway carriage where you belong. Your duty is to liter—achoo!

MRS. BROWN: God bless you, professor. I just thought it might be nice to see how it worked.

MR. XX: Hey! You! Get out of there! And don't get back into that train either. You got no business traveling. Stay home with the goddamned kids where you belong. Goddamned castrating feminist!

MRS. BROWN: Oh dear. Language. How they do hop about. I wish they wouldn't shout so. I wonder if this shuts the door.

CAPT. Z: Lady! Listen! Open the door! Please, lady! You don't know what you're doing. Let me in! I'll take over. It's a man's job. You're too tender and delicate for a job like this. You're squashy, lady, and it's hard, lady! The equations are cold! Only men of steel and characters of cardboard belong aboard the *Genre*. No! NO! Don't touch that!

Mrs. BROWN: Oh, my goodness. Oh, my. Look at that! How they do whiz by.

A long period of silence.

Mrs. BROWN: The silence of these infinite spaces terrifies me. Goodness, did I say that? No, I believe I read it somewhere. But how very quiet it is. The stars are very pretty. But it would be nice if there were someone to talk to. I never did find out if the oak tree is going to die because its leaves were eaten for two years in succession by caterpillars. And it's a very pretty oak. But a long way away by now, I imagine. And twenty years ago, or is it seventy? Just think!

I know Professor X thinks I don't understand anything about spacetime, but I do think about it, in my own way. (*Hums "Long Ago and Far Away" as she recalibrates the megathorium input nodes.*) This goes here, I expect; and this goes there; yes, that looks very nice, and the humming thing sounds better now.

I hope the Captain doesn't feel too badly about my taking his ship. I certainly will return it. After a while. What a very rude man that was. The one with the language. The way young people swear nowadays is a pity. Not that he was all that young. Quite an old dinosaur actually. But young people are always a pity, poor things, to think how many of them will get old, and all of them die, it makes one quite sad to think about.

All the same it would be nice to have some company, even if one didn't speak. Like that curious-looking woman in the railway carriage when I was coming here, so pretty. No, not exactly pretty, I should almost have said she was quite beautiful, but a bit odd, somehow. Unusual. And how she did watch me! Every time I looked at her she was watching me, not staring, but it seemed she was seeing everything. Not quite ladylike, although she did look quite the lady. Such beautiful, sad eyes. Yes, really beautiful. I should have liked to have spoken to her. But George was there. And I was so upset. It wouldn't have done to speak to a complete stranger. I wonder what she would have said?

Oh, dear, that little red light is blinking again. Oh, shaw! Where *did* I put the captain's manual? This is very bad. They say when you begin talking to yourself you're in a bad way, but when there's nobody else for parsecs and parsecs. . . . Oh, I see. That must be the gravitonometer, and if I just push this . . . . Yes. Now. There we are. For goodness sakes! I do believe I'm landing on a planet!

ALIEN: Bfrdz skwf grztmn? Skwf?

MRS. BROWN: I'm so sorry, I don't speak Welsh.

ALIEN: Grksnzztt vgljust your Wfgzxmatic Translator.

MRS. BROWN: Oh. I see. Like this?

ALIEN: Yes. Very good. You come out now? You relate to me?

MRS. BROWN: Well I really don't know. What is likely to happen if I relate to you?

ALIEN: We will have relationship thus making story.

MRS. BROWN: What kind of relationship?

ALIEN: Any kind relationship. Skwf!

MRS. BROWN: I suppose it is expected of me. After coming all this way. But you do realize that I only have two arms? And that I'm British?

ALIEN: That OK. You got gender? You got religion? You got ideas? You got teeth? You engineer? You dance? We make story together. Skwf! Skwf! Science fiction story! Skwf!

MRS. BROWN: Very well. I'm coming out now. How do you do? I am Mrs. Brown. I wonder if you happen to know anything about oak trees?

ALIEN: Hey, Esmiss Esbrown, you better put on helmet, atmosphere different here.

MRS. BROWN: My dear man—no, certainly not that—my dear friend, I can breathe any air. Now, please, do not take me to your leader.

Exeunt, conversing. Behind them the Genre *towers, brilliant in the light of the green sun.*

Notes

1. Note (1989). Or Schubert, in the Great Symphony, but he isn't saying at all what Beethoven said.

2. Note (1989). I let "man" continue here to stand for "humanity," because Lem, infact, writes only about men. The women in *Solaris* are mental constructs of the characters, and many Lem novels contain no women at all.

3. By Ursula Le Guin for the forum at the ICA, 8 February, 1995.

∽

CHAPTER TEN

I Could Have Been a Contender. . . .

Barry Malzberg

Revisionist canon now holds that science fiction would have had a different—and superior—history if Hugo Gernsback, by creating *Amazing Stories* in 1926, had not ghettoized the genre, reduced it on the spot to a small asylum plastered with murals of ravening aliens carrying off screaming women in wondrous machines from a burning city and thus made it impossible for serious critics, to say nothing of serious writers, to have anything to do with it. After all, in the early part of the century novels of the speculative and fantastic were part of the literature; the Munsey magazines ran futuristic adventure serials all the time, and Hawthorne and Melville were writing fantasies or absurdist speculation without any damage to their literary credibility.

It simply could have gone on that way, the revisionists suggest; science fiction would not have been thrown into a charnel house that it would spend four decades trying to escape, seeking that respectability and acceptance it had possessed before Gernsback defined it and made it live by its worst examples and most debased audience.

The argument has a certain winsome charm—I believed it myself when I was but a wee lad, and some of our best or better minds hold to it right now—but is flawed. At the risk of aligning myself with Hugo Gernsback, a venal and small-minded magazine publisher whose reprehensible practices, long since detailed, were contemptible to his contributors, partners, and employees, I think that he did us a great service and that were it not for Gernsback, science fiction as we understand it would not exist. We would have—as we do—the works of fabulation in the general literature—Coover, Barthelme, Barth, and DeLillo—but of the category that gave More Than Human, The Demolished Man, Foundation and Empire, Dying Inside, The Dispossessed and Rogue Moon we would have nothing, and hence these works would not exist. It is possible that some of these writers, who were inspired to write science fiction by a childhood of reading, would never have published at all.

"Science fiction builds on science fiction," Asimov said once, and that truth is at the center of the form. Before Gernsback gave it a name (he called it "scientifiction," but close enough; Ackerman a few years later cast out a syllable), the literature did not exist; before he gave it a medium of exclusivity, its dim antecedents were scattered through the range of popular and restricted writing without order, overlap, or sequence. It was the creation of a label and a medium that gave the genre its exclusivity and a place in which it could begin that dialogue, and it was the evolution of magazine science fiction—slowly over the first decade, more rapidly after the ascension of Campbell—that became synonymous with the evolution of the field.

Only the rigor and discipline of the delimited can create art. Musicologists considering Bach, who worked within desperately restrictive format, will concur as will those considering the sonata form. The sonnet and the eight-bar chorus of almost all popular song and operetta give similar testimony. It was the very restraint with which science fiction was cloaked from the outset that gave the genre its discipline and force. Without the specialized format of the magazines, where science-fiction writers and readers could dwell, exchange, observe one another's practices, and build upon one another's insight, the genre could not have developed.

The first-generation science fiction writers—those whom Gernsback, Harry Bates, and F. Orlin Tremaine brought into Amazing and Astounding after their small stock of recycled Wells and Verne had been used—worked under the most generalized influence and without canon: their work showed it. The second generation—those identified with Campbell—was composed of people who had grown up reading the early science fiction and were prepared to build upon it. The third generation, coming in the 1950s, was composed of writers who had correspondingly more sources and possibilities (and also a larger stock of ideas already proved unworkable or exhausted) and the increasing subtlety and complexity of the form through their years testifies once again to, as it were, the influence of influence . . . upon influence.

Science fiction, as John W. Campbell once pointed out expansively, may indeed outdo all of the so-called mainstream because it gathers in *all* of time and space . . . but science fiction as it has evolved is an extraordinarily rigorous and delimiting medium. Like the canon and the fugue, the sonnet and the sonata, like haiku, it has its rules, and the control of those rules is absolute. Extrapolative elements, cultural interface, characteriological attempt to resolve the conflicts between the two: *this* is science fiction.

The fact pervades all the decades after about 1935: no one could publish science fiction unless exposed to a great deal of it; virtually everyone who has ever sold a story has a sophisticated reader's background in the form, usually acquired just before or around adolescence. At the underside, this has led to parochialism, incestuousness, and the preciosity of decadence (and there has been too much). In the end it may even be these qualities that finish science fiction off, make its most sophisticated and advanced examples increasingly inaccessible to the larger reading audience. But whatever happens to science fiction, it would not exist at all if it had not been given a name and a medium and for this, if we are not led to praise Gernsback, we must entomb him with honor. He was a crook, old Hugo, but he made all of us crooks possible.

PART THREE

DERIVATIONS

One of the most important controversies in the theory of science fiction, as an astute reader will have gathered by now, is whether science fiction is a new literature or an old one. Those who wish to argue that science fiction is new can make a relatively easy argument, saying either that science itself is relatively new, and that science fiction cannot possibly predate science, or going so far as to point out that the term "science fiction" was not coined until 1929, and therefore using the term to describe anything prior to that is a regrettable mistake.

On the other hand, those who wish to make a credible argument for a science fiction that predates either of these benchmarks have to work a little harder. Naive attempts to lump together fantastic voyages dating from Gilgamesh forward are unconvincing. What is necessary is an exploration of themes and traditions that bind over the ages and across paradigms caused by the Enlightenment, the Industrial Revolution, and the postulation of Darwinian evolution, among other, major fractures in Western thought and culture.

In this selection from *Trillion Year Spree*, Brian Aldiss convincingly makes both arguments, that science fiction is something new, but with strong ties to older literary productions. He does this through his powerful two-part definition of science fiction: "Science fiction is the search for a definition of mankind and his status in the universe which will stand in our advanced but confused state of knowledge (science), and is characteristically cast in the Gothic or post Gothic mode." Utilizing this definition and a host of historical detail, Aldiss shows how Mary Shelley did what Wells claimed for himself, transforming the "fantastic element" of literature from magic to science. Shelley's cultural surroundings brought her in contact not only with the new ideas of science, but also with the Gothic tradition, and through the fusing of these two influences gave birth to science fiction.

While Aldiss marshals a horde of texts and specific details in his argument, Robert Scholes, in "The Roots of Science Fiction," cites very few titles and almost no dates whatsoever. It is as though he is trying to peer past individual texts toward the eternal forms of which they are mere shadows, a style of argumentation ideally suited to the "science fiction is old" perspective. There is a significant resonance between Scholes' structural fabulation and Suvin's cognitive estrangement that comes from their common roots in Russian Formalism, but there are a number of important differences. First, Suvin sees different genres as having sharp lines, easily separable into their different categories, while Scholes sees no such hard-and-fast lines. Second, Scholes is much more forgiving to the "lesser forms" of literature, which he sees as fulfilling our "psychological need for narration," an argument that I find hard to dispute.

In a similar move, Alexei and Cory Panshin in "Science Fiction and the Dimension of Myth," explore the way that science fiction is a manifestation of the "characteristic human activity" of mythmaking. Utilizing the mythography of Joseph Campbell, they show how science fiction represents an exploration of "The World Beyond the Hill." Through parallels between a number of science fiction texts and world mythologies, the Panshins legitimate the feeling many of us have: reading science fiction can be an almost religious experience.

~

CHAPTER ELEVEN

Introduction to *Trillion Year Spree*

Brian W. Aldiss with David Wingrove

Someday my father would stop writing science fiction, and write
something a whole lot of people wanted to read instead.

—Kurt Vonnegut: *Galapagos*

You are standing on a vast flat plain. Something appears on the horizon and moves rapidly towards you. It is a shaly hillside on which a cave
is evident, its mouth fortified. It whirls by.

Something else is approaching. A series of objects moves towards
you. A village on stilts wading into a lake. A small brown city with mud
walls. A pyramid, encrusted with bronze. A ziggurat. Immense fortifications from the Aztec culture. The palisades of ancient Zimbabwe.
The intricate temples of the East, Angkor Wat, Borabadur. Chinese
mausoleums.

The monstrous structures loom up and pass, throwing their shadows
briefly over the plain. Monuments to life, to death, to conquest. And
to piety—the gothic cathedrals of Europe drift past.

Tombs, towers, universities.

Something else, moving with great noise and gasps of smoke. Nearer
and nearer it comes, at first laboring, a cumbersome shape with a high
smoke stack. Refining itself as it approaches, writhing through metal

147

metamorphoses. Now it is sleek and streamlined, rushing forth on metal rails, its carriages trailing snake-like behind it. As it hurtles by, there is a hint in its mutating shape of the rocket ships that lie in its future.

Why is this machine different from all the other shapes, as it roars out of the industrial revolution towards us?

Because it has the power to move itself. Because it is the first thing on land ever to move faster than a cheetah, a stag, a galloping horse.

Because it brings us into a world of timetables, where we have to conform to a thing's convenience, not it to ours. Because the timetables induce us to look ahead to the material world stretching like the endless plain before us.

Because it emerges from the eighteenth century vibrating with technological change.

Science fiction is one of the major literary success areas of the second half of the twentieth century. It is now largely—in emphasis and in fact—an American art form, coinciding with a time of great technological evolution and with the rise of the United States to superpower status.

The origins and inspirations for science fiction lie outside the United States, though within the period of the Industrial Revolution. As we might expect. Only in an epoch when a power source more reliable than ocean currents or the wind, faster than the horse, has been developed, can we expect to find a literature that will concern itself with problems of power, either literal or metaphorical. Such problems lie at the heart of SF, the fiction of a technological age.

Nowadays, everyone knows of SF and thinks he or she knows what it is. Not everyone reads, not everyone approves. But every age gets the art it deserves.

Good SF does not necessarily traffic in reality; but it makes reality clearer to us.

This is the story of science fiction, told from its humble beginnings right up to the present day. It is a wonderful and fascinating story, even to those who are not necessarily aficionados. When Cinderella finally makes it to the ball, everyone is pleased. (Except those ugly sisters.)

But what is science fiction? Read on.

This book has grown out of *Billion Year Spree*, which was published in 1973. Since then, science fiction has gone forth and multiplied to a remarkable extent. What was once virtually a secret movement has become part of the cultural wallpaper. This new book chronicles and makes sense of that dramatic growth while discussing the milestones along the way.

Anyone even remotely connected with the science-fiction field knows that great advances are taking place. But are such alterations tokens of a wider general acceptance or of a dismal decline in standards? Indecision, an awareness of crisis, is in the air. We hope to clarify the situation, whether or not all our arguments are found immediately acceptable.

All discussion of science fiction involves generalization. The time has never existed when "science fiction" was a homogeneous commodity—regurgitated, it might be, by some vast alien mass mind. True, attempts have been made from various points of the literary compass to impose uniformity—by Michel Butor, by John W. Campbell, by fandom. Most writers evade such stereotypes. Yet still the trademark "science fiction" carries much weight with friends and foes alike.

At any time, there are only individuals working under a common banner, though some individuals are more individual than others. Some would like to get out from under the banner. Others would like to get further in. Many march with overweening pride under the banner.

Those who subscribe most ardently to a set of common derived conventions will produce the most clearly defined generic fiction. Those who are most independent will produce work that—obviously enough—pays least heed to the restrictions of formula and will transcend it.

To defy or meet expectations? Both are well-recognized literary ploys.

The difficulty—the infinitude of SF—lies in the obdurate fact that it is both formulaic and something more than a genre. It is a mode that easily falls back into genre.[1] The model is flexible, changing with the times. New designs are forever produced. SF can be conventional and innovative at one and the same time.

The science fiction field flourishes best when both kinds of writer, the iconoclast and the iconolater, exist in tension, one set distrusting the other. But there is rarely close agreement even between members of the same set. Some writers do not feel themselves to be members of either set, and reject categorization.

This point requires stressing at a time when some publishers have set up clearly defined SF lines. Others publish only SF. The perils of such monoculture are twofold: generic (generally action) SF will get published while less flamboyant work is rejected; and a boom-or-bust situation, an unpleasant symptom of SF publishing, will be perpetuated.

SF cannot exist without divergent opinions. The material with which it deals is itself controversial. Shall we increase technology until the whole surface of the planet is covered by concrete and steel? Is all religion an aberration? Is war inevitable? Will artificial intelligence take over our governance, and is that desirable? Do we need to conquer space? How would utopia come about? What of our immortal souls?

Of course, the ability to generalize is a vital instrument of reason. Without the ability to deal in generalities, we should have no laws. If this book did not trade in generalities, we should have no book. We talk of the Thirties, for instance, as if those years had a unique flavor, like raspberries or mangoes. We all know this was not the case. It still remains convenient to point to "the Thirties" or "the Sixties", sure of a general understanding.

There is an argument that says that SF has no history, and that the story in this book is another generalization, and a false one. That E. E. Smith has no place in a book with Lucian of Samosata, or A. E. van Vogt with Jonathan Swift. That no evolution such as is described ever took place. That the pulp magazines are entirely irrelevant to the writings of Aldous Huxley or George Orwell.

This argument, put forward by the Disintegrators, is ingenious—too ingenious. It is an argument that pays attention to the aims of the writer. A history of science fiction, however, must pay attention to the interests of the reader. And to the reader of science fiction, Thomas More's Utopia is as interesting as Burroughs's Barsoom, or 1984 as 2010. C. S. Lewis is as rewarding as Robert Heinlein. In this volume, we are entirely on the side of the reader. Definite generic interplays exist.

One generalization we shall be unable to abolish. That is the generalization that says that all science fiction is rubbish. Generalization-22.

Generalization-22 is not solely the creation of the hostile outside world. It has been fostered in part by the SF world, which has insisted for several generations that its kind of reading is Different. And not just Different but Better. Such defensive boasting is counterproductive.

The illogic is apparent: this latest dismal SF novel by X (once so brilliant when we were young) is not better than Y, the new Argentinean novelist's first book. But maybe, just maybe, the next brilliant SF novel by Z may be even better than Y's second novel. Literary judgment has to deal with individual cases, not with a cattle market.

The sooner this truth is acknowledged within the SF field, the sooner we shall convert the heathen and make Generalization-22 obsolete. One of the unreasonable hopes of this book is that it may convert the odd heathen here and there. The heathen always have their own viewpoint.

For many, science fiction has become an environment. It contains all they wish from life. Yet an SF story or novel consists of words, like any other kind of book. And generally a recognizable form of words—a particular kind of narrative guarantees much of SF's interest. Yet the form, which is an inheritance of the gothic, is often ignored. The gothic was a type of romance developed in the late eighteenth century, relying on suspense and mystery and containing a number—a limited number—of startling props. A word more about that.

The rise of industrialization fostered the growth of large manufacturing towns and the spread of cities. People were obliged to live among strangers to make their living. Church bells were replaced by the more exacting railway timetable.

The effects of these unprecedented changes—culminating in our day in an *umwelt* of continual change—was far-reaching. The human psyche was not immune to them.

The fiction that evolved to accommodate this situation—a middle class fiction, somewhere between romance and realism, as it was between science and myth—was the gothic fantasy. Backward-looking and nostalgic at first, it developed rapidly during the nineteenth century to confront more closely the conditions that nurtured it.[2] The archetypal figures of cruel father and seducing monk were transformed into those of scientist and alien.

Designed as pure entertainment, as "escapism," the gothic proved to have remarkable strengths when it traded on current fears, hopes, and obsessions. It could venture where the solid realistic social novel could not go. Although the social novel is seen as the dominant literary form of the nineteenth century, its doppelganger, the gothic, kept in silent step with it, from *Frankenstein* at the century's beginning to *Dracula* at its end. Indeed, the archetypal figures who emerged from those novels are now familiar all over the world; Oliver Twist, Madame Bovary, and Anna Karenina enjoy a more tenuous existence beyond their respective volumes than do Frankenstein and Count Dracula.

Such a thing as pure genre does not exist. The gothic is by no means homogeneous. It can incorporate and reinforce itself by the qualities of Romance and of a partial Realism. Quest novels, which enjoy such popularity in the 1980s, are clearly a blend of gothic fantasy and veins of storytelling far more ancient. But impurity, adaptation, invention, even imitation, are of the essence of storytelling. Listeners and readers require novelty; they also require the touchstone of familiarity.

One strong gothic theme is that of descent from a "natural world" to inferno or incarceration, where the protagonist goes, willingly or otherwise, in search of a secret, an identity, or a relationship. This volume embraces many stories with such motifs, from famous exercises such as Jules Verne's adventures at the center of the earth to Frankenstein's descent into charnel houses, Dracula's descent to his earth-coffins, or the journey to Trantor, in effect a total underground planet, to the metaphysical search for his father undertaken by the less-known hero of *Land Under England*.

This reluctant protagonist developed from the distressed maidens of Mrs Radcliffe into modern figures. The vital role emerged, via the refinements of Poe, Wilkie Collins, and Conan Doyle, into the modern detective or private eye. Along the way, the role divided, to become also the scientist, the inventor, the space traveler.

The need to find a secret, an identity, a relationship, accompanied the questing traveller to other worlds or futures. Industrialization had assisted many sciences, including geology and astronomy. A new comprehension of the dynamism of the natural world (once regarded as a static stage for a theological drama) was incorporated in Charles Darwin's theory of evolution, one of the great gloomy interventions of the nineteenth century that still colors our intellectual discourse. Evolution provided an essential viewpoint powering the new subspecies of gothic, science fiction. Here, it seemed, was a key to the most puzzling, most impressive question of identity of all—the identity of mankind. A mere brute in clothes, a degenerate ape, a culmination of eon-long processes, a godling?

And evolution also provided a clue in that dark search for a relationship. In the struggle for survival, who are our friends? Is the alien always to be feared? Should we not regard ourselves as some kind of alien? Shall we become utopians and live in peace?

Many questions to be dramatized, treated deeply or frivolously. Along with the changed questions went elements practically unchanged since Ann Radcliffe's day: the climate, the effects of the light, the desolate scenery. No longer, in fifteenth century Italy, perhaps . . . but on a planet just as remote from us. In that remoteness lies another marked feature of science fiction, alienation. Both the Industrial Revolution and evolution have brought a marked sense of isolation to humanity in general: isolation from one another—and from Nature, so often seen in science fiction as an enemy to be conquered, as if we were no longer ourselves a part of the natural world.

Trillion Year Spree is a very much revised, altered, and enlarged version of the 1970s book. It includes and attempts to digest all that has been happening in the science-fiction field over the last two decades.

What has not altered in that time are my convictions. True, I have changed my opinions of this or that; how could it be otherwise? But my basic convictions have merely strengthened over the intervening years. I refer to certain ideas that, tentatively proposed before, roused anger, shock, vituperation, threats of violence, and occasional acceptance, in my readers.

Of course I understand that bosoms can scarcely be expected to remain tranquil in companies where SF is supported, is idolized, is a way of life. Any deviation from an established order of ritual must be challenged. Equally, one must stand by one's beliefs.

Foremost among these beliefs is a certainty about the origins of SF. Of course, it is in a way a Stone Age truth to say that SF began with Mary Shelley's *Frankenstein* (1818). The more we know, the less certain we can be about origins; the date of the Renaissance becomes less clear decade by decade as research goes on.

Nevertheless, bearing in mind that no genre is pure, *Frankenstein* is more than a merely convenient place at which to begin the story. Behind it lie other traditions like broken skeletons, classical myth, a continent full of *Märchen* tales. But Mary Shelley's novel betokens an inescapably new perception of mankind's capabilities. Moreover,

Frankenstein is marvelously good and inexhaustible in its interest. Not a negligible point.

Were there women writers before Mary Shelley? Research into this subject is carried out in all the world's universities. One name at least emerges, that of the lively Margaret Cavendish, impoverished Duchess of Newcastle, whose *The Description of a New World, Called the Blazing World* was published in 1666. The absence of Margaret Cavendish and Mary Shelley from standard literary histories reminds us that science fiction is not the only thing against which learned men have harbored baseless prejudices.

Before I wrote, almost no one paid any attention to that old pre-Victorian novel of Mary Shelley's. Having seen travesties of the theme on film and television, they believed they knew what they did not. The situation has remarkably improved since then. (After writing the history, I wrote a novel, *Frankenstein Unbound*, designed to draw attention to its great original.)

Like all discoveries, this one was prompted by more than circumstantial evidence. It was born of a wish to refute certain nonsensical claims previously put forward, which did a mode of writing I much enjoyed no honor.

My belief in SF has not diminished over the intervening years, and remains strong at a time when true science fiction appears under threat, swamped by an avalanche of imitations and wish-fantasies in the United States and, in England, the virtual disappearance of young science fiction writers, thanks to the chill climate of discouragement that there prevails.

For all its tragic flaws, its absurd pretensions, its monstrous freights of nonsense, the platonic ideal of science fiction remains alive, as the literature most suited to our progressing and doom-threatened century, the literature most free to take aboard new perspectives, new manifestations of the *zeitgeist*.

Critics expected the gothic to go away. It never has. Born pseudonymously from the mind of Horace Walpole, fourth Earl of Orford, it proved to have all the adaptability of a living species. Critics expected SF to go away. It never has. It is the urban literature and will, we hope, exist as long as there are cities, in whatever form.

Both the thesis that *Frankenstein* marked a beginning and that SF was a gothic offshoot were so unacceptable that *Billion Year Spree* scarcely received any reviews in those journals in which its appearance should have been instantly greeted; indeed, had it not been for the vigilant intervention of my old friend and ally, Harry Harrison, those reviews would have been even sparser.

It is hard to recognize now the confusion that existed then. Before my book appeared, there was no accepted idea of when SF began. Some critics claimed it all started in a semi-juvenile pulp magazine in the twenties, others that Homer wrote science fiction. Ludicrously enough, these were often the same critics. Yet to have no understanding of this matter is to have no understanding of the function and nature of SF.

The new synthesis I developed was embodied in my definition of science fiction. Of course that definition has been challenged, and rightly. Of course I have wanted to improve it. And rightly. And I have done so by one word.

The definition defines both function and mode, which together comprise SF's nature. The pretensions of the first part of the definition are defused by the limitations of the second. The gothic is, after all, a mode of entertainment, generally ranked below what we may call for convenience the modern novel. My definition is the only one to link content and form, which are inseparable.

Here perhaps I should add parenthetically that neither I nor my collaborator, David Wingrove, have any aversion to the modern novel; we do not adopt the philistine stance of so many commentators, in praising SF at the expense of the modern novel, with which we are tolerably familiar.

We take SF seriously, and would be crazy not to; but we do not forget that it is in the main a commercial genre, and treated as such even by some of its most honored practitioners. Our title acknowledges as much. A trillion years is no laughing matter; a spree is.

Part of the problem of seeing SF in true perspective lies in the difficulty of judgment on attendant on the early SF magazines, notably Hugo Gernsback's. Most of the opprobrium first visited *Billion Year Spree* centered round my comments on Gernsback and his magazines.

Yet no convincing argument was put forward to make me retract what I said. One has merely to consult the texts.

Those readers who enjoyed such magazines as *Amazing Stories* and *Wonder Stories* in their youth—often their extreme youth—naturally retain fond memories of those pages and those days. Nostalgia, however, provides no sound basis for literary judgment. The covers of those old magazines retain a weird specialized attraction; but the reading matter between the covers is, almost without exception, unutterably poor. This situation did not improve until about 1938 and a small miracle.

If we do not perceive this, if we believe that these pathetic tales, in which the namby-pamby has intercourse with the sensational, represent some kind of a Golden Age, then we can have no engagement with contemporary SF, at least in its higher reaches. Appreciation is not omnivorous.

It is an old-fashioned idea, yet not entirely false, that we read to develop our understanding and aesthetic appreciation. That is part of our pleasure. Reading, like the taking of lovers, rarely begins in exalted taste. Cultivation is important. If we remain loyal to the reading of our childhood, it is a false loyalty, a puppy-love. Uncle Hugo has his place in sub-literature, perhaps an honoured place. But we must set his works aside with a sigh, to see clearly how greatly SF has evolved and sophisticated itself since then.

As much needs saying, though it is obvious enough. A lot rests on that obvious truth, for what follows from it provides the whole *raison d'être* of this chapter. Our chronicle has a thesis, never insisted upon: that the best SF being written today is an improvement on the crude SF of the early magazines; that it has acquired many skills and graces, possibly at the expense of new ideas; that we are now in a Modern Period of SF, the birth of which may be dated roughly from the first publication of *Dune* in 1963–4, which period actually exhibits many of the same traits as does the modern novel, in terms of amplification and sophistication at the expense of innovation; that there remains much to be admired, as well as much to be deplored; that recent achievements are real, and to be praised. Our perspective is a positive and forward-looking one, as we hope will be acknowledged.

An argument has been advanced recently that says that it is impossible to write a history of science fiction. That SF consists merely of the worst. That such writers as Gore Vidal in *Messiah,* or Olaf Stapledon in *Last and First Men,* or Doris Lessing in her *Canopus in Argus* series, knew nothing of the continuity of science fiction, of its traditions, or of its rules (which means in fact a few prescriptions laid down by a small clique of, in the main, non-writers); and in consequence cannot be said to be a part of science fiction at all.

This is a fallacy. If we can imagine that a playwright like Eugene O'Neill, or a poet like Thomas Hardy, or a novelist like Gabriel Garcia Marquez, knew nothing of the history of the drama, poetry, or the novel, the fact would in no way lessen the contributions those writers made to their chosen medium, or to the influence they had on those who followed them.

There is no such entity as science fiction. We have only the work of many men and women which, for convenience, we can group together under the label "science fiction." Many dislike that label; many glory in it.

Throughout the book, as previously, we allow only the abbreviation "SF." That down-market appellation "sci-fi," sometimes heard on the lips of the would-be trendy in the media and elsewhere, is purposely avoided. We bow to the fact that much of what passes for science fiction these days is nearer fantasy. SF can, after all, be imagined to stand for science fantasy, as it can for speculative fiction (for those who are attached to that term).

Billion Year Spree concluded with a prediction concerning the future rise of SF as study and an SF academia. The prediction has been fulfilled beyond my expectations. There was then almost no body of SF scholarship; nor was there more than the smallest student body. Now SF is a recognized discipline in universities and colleges across the United States. Such associations exist as the SFRA, the Science Fiction Research Association, which was amiable and perceptive enough to bestow on me a Pilgrim Award, mainly for the earlier edition of this book, and the IAFA, the International Association for the Fantastic in the Arts—which has kindly presented me with its first Distinguished Scholarship Award—to which two societies the most eminent SF scholars belong.

Following this development, publishers have sprung up who publish nothing but SF criticism. Not all criticism is of the first rank, as is to be anticipated of such a youthful discipline, but we may have every expectation that it will improve, strengthening its present rather remote relationship with real English and becoming more adventurous in its subject matter. Journals like *Fantasy Review* do much to raise the quality of discussion.

Trillion Year Spree is devised for the enjoyment of the reader, that reader whom Dr. Johnson and Virginia Woolf rejoiced to call "the common reader"; nor has anything changed in that respect. But we move with the times. More rigour has now been shown. The book is designed to serve in schools where SF is on the curriculum. It provides, as no other volume does, a synoptic grasp of the whole field, with as much neutrality and freedom from favoritism or prejudice as its authors can contrive between them.

Yet it remains, in some aspects, a personal book. I have excluded all discussion in the text of my own writing, whether fact or fiction; yet the book is imbued—or so I hope—with the intuitions gained from many years as a writer of science fiction (and not only science fiction). My hope is that it may prove of some value to my fellow writers, so hostile to it the first time around, and to beginner writers.

Perhaps I have not always shown what some may regard as proper reverence. I am too familiar with it for that: my first SF story was written when I was eight.

Nor are these aspirations mine alone. The extensive work and research involved in the compilation of this book would never have been undertaken, let alone completed, without the assistance of my staunch ally, David Wingrove. Indeed, more than assistance. Perfect collaboration.

Appreciation is not omnivorous. I felt I could not bring the same fresh eye to the books, films, and events of the startling last fifteen years as I did to previous ones. A more eager and energetic—a younger—presence was required.

David and I met many years ago. As a fan, he surveyed me first through field-glasses from a neighboring property, the way one spots rare old birds of a migratory nature. There has been nothing migratory about our friendship since, which dates from the moment he set down his field-glasses and came up our drive. *Billion Year Spree* was one of the first SF books he read, so he makes a particularly appropriate partner in the enterprise. I played a minor part in two of David's critical works, *The Science Fiction Source Book*, and *The SF Film Source Book*, as well as forming the main dish in the Brian Griffin and David Wingrove *Apertures: A Study of the Writings of Brian W. Aldiss*. It has been a pleasure to work with him in collaboration. His enthusiasm and cheerfulness have never failed.

Our opinions are not always identical. If they were, it would be useless for us to work together. Many of the judgements are his, not mine. For a lot of readers, David will have written the more interesting part of the book. We have modified but rarely altered each other's opinions. We have rewritten each other's texts to such an extent that it is now hard to determine who exactly said what.

A word to critics who dislike science fiction. The over-productivity of science fiction writers is a byword. There is a lot of it about, and it is popular. For some, that is enough to condemn it without further enquiry. The question upon which all literary criticism runs on the rocks is this: if it is good, can it be popular; if it is popular, can it be good?[3]

We take the reasonable point of view that science fiction gives pleasure to many people; our task is to compare the varying degrees of pleasure. We find SF (some of it) immensely readable and enriching.

Conversations with many friends have greatly helped in forming critical opinions. Special thanks must go to Michael Collings, Patrick Edington, and Charles N. Brown. Also to Dr. Robert Collins of Florida Atlantic University, whose influence has been greater—and more benign—than he probably realizes. The title, *Billion Year Spree*, was first mentioned in print in 1964. Much has happened since then. Friends change, publishers change, the world changes. But I am happy to acknowledge now, as I did then, the help of my wife Margaret as we sailed these endless seas of paper. She it was who aided us through successive drafts, and poured the whole enterprise through the word processor into its present form.

Notes

1. Although SF is better described as a mode rather than a genre, the term genre has stuck, and so is often used in these pages where the term mode might have been more accurate but more obtrusive. For an excellent investigation of popular genres other than science fiction, see John G. Cawelti, *Adventure, Mystery, and Romance: Formula Stories as Art and Popular Culture*, Chicago, 1976.

Although Cawelti does not discuss SF, his comments often throw light on its virtues and problems, as for instance here:

> When I began my study of popular genres, I assumed that popular literature was simply an inferior form of high art; that is, I viewed it as art for lowbrows or middlebrows, or as Abraham Kaplan puts it, as an immature form of art. As my thinking on this subject has developed, I have come increasingly to feel that it is important to stress that there are different kinds of artistry rather than a single standard in terms of which all fictional creations should be judged. Our age places a particularly high value on innovation and originality, to the extent that we tend to judge our most strikingly inventive writers and artists as the most significant creators of the age. But an examination of formulaic art also suggests that there is an artistry based on convention and standardization whose significance is not simply a reflection of the inferior training and lower imaginative capacity of a mass audience. Each conventional formula has a wide range of artistic potential, and it has come to seem mistaken to automatically relegate a work to an inferior artistic status on the ground that it is a detective story or a western. (Final chapter.)

2. A recent volume on the gothic in fiction is William Patrick Day, *In the Circles of Fear and Desire: A Study of Gothic Fantasy*, Chicago, 1985. Day makes clear the relationship between imagination and reality of which other commentators often seem unaware:

> At the heart of the novels intended to provide escape and entertainment, nineteenth-century readers came face to face with the very thing from which they were trying to escape. The great power of the gothic stems from its capacity to transform these fears into pleasure. (Introduction)

Cannot as much be said for the latest manifestation of the gothic, the science fiction mode?

3. This question of virtue versus popularity has bedeviled many writers, in all kinds of writing, over which intense snobberies are generated. Bram Stoker, author of *Dracula* and other supernatural novels, is one example. An anonymous critic reviewing new editions of several of Stoker's novels in *The Times Literary Supplement* (December 8, 1966) has this to say on the vexed question of sales versus sainthood:

> The trouble, it is usually said, is that whatever his gifts as an inventor of spine-chilling situations, he does not "write well." The phrase is used, generally, as though its meaning were self-evident. But any such assumption would be optimistic. It is a sign, perhaps, as much as anything, that we remain slaves of the intentional fallacy in literature, pathetically ready to accept writers according to

their ambitions rather than their achievements. We will suppose, for instance, that George Moore must in some mysterious way be a better writer than Bram Stoker, even if Stoker is still read and Moore on the whole is not, because Moore spent a lot of time and energy carrying on about his dedication to high art while Stoker churned out bestsellers in the spare moments of an otherwise busy life. Moore, in his later books, writes with extreme care and self-conscious artistry, but the result is unreadable; Stoker, whatever else may be said of him, is still intensely readable. So which, in the final analysis, writes better?

~

CHAPTER TWELVE

On the Origin of Species: Mary Shelley

Brian W. Aldiss with David Wingrove

The mirrors of the gigantic shadows which futurity casts upon the present. . . .

—Percy Bysshe Shelley, *The Defence of Poetry*

"The stars shone at intervals, as the clouds passed from over them, the dark pines rose before me, and every here and there a broken tree lay on the ground; it was a scene of wonderful solemnity, and stirred strange thoughts within me." Thus Victor Frankenstein, after an encounter with the creature he has created out of dismembered corpses, while he tries to decide whether or not to build it a mate.

The shattered scenery, the sense of desolation, the speaker's dilemma—ghastly but hardly the sort of quandary one regularly meets—are all characteristic of a broad range of science fiction. As for Victor's strange thoughts, science fiction is a veritable forest of them.

That forest has reached such proportions that a new formal exploration is necessary. The present authors hope to drive a new motorway through the heart of the forest. Without marking every tree, we will provide a contour map of the whole science-fiction landscape.

To emerge from the undergrowth of our metaphor, this volume investigates the considerable corpus of writing that, with other media, has come to be regarded as science fiction in order to illuminate what is obscure, and to increase the enjoyment of what is already enjoyable.

We attend to three matters. We look at the dream world of the gothic novel, from which science fiction springs; we identify the author whose work marks her out as the first science fiction writer; and we investigate the brilliant context—literary, scientific, and social—from which she drew life and inspiration.

As a preliminary, we need a definition of science fiction.

Many definitions have been hammered out. Most of them fail because they have regard only to content, not form. The following may sound slightly pretentious for a genre that has its strong fun side, but we can modify it as we go along.

Science fiction is the search for a definition of mankind and his status in the universe which will stand in our advanced but confused state of knowledge (science), and is characteristically cast in the gothic or post-gothic mode.

The final word of our definition is chosen with deliberation. Science fiction is one mode of writing among several. It is often tamed to generic writing and generic expectations for commercial reasons. A wider potential remains.

There's a corollary to our definition. The more power above the ordinary that the protagonist enjoys, the closer the fiction will approach to hardcore science fiction. Conversely, the more ordinary and fallible the protagonist, the further from hardcore. It is often impossible to separate science fiction from science fantasy, or either from fantasy, since both modes are part of fantasy in a general sense. Nevertheless, one admires the boldness of Miriam Allen deFord's dictum, "Science fiction deals with improbable possibilities, fantasy with plausible impossibilities" (in her Foreword to *Elsewhere, Elsewhen, Elsehow*).

My shorter definition of SF may also be mentioned, since it has found its way into a modern dictionary of quotations. This is—*Hubris clobbered by nemesis*. By which count, ordinary fiction would be hubris clobbered by mimesis.

One etymological dictionary offers such definitions of fantasy as "mental apprehension," "delusive imagination," and "baseless supposition"—terms which serve well enough to describe certain types of science fiction. H. G. Wells pointed to a similarity between the two genres when he said of his early stories, "Hitherto, except in exploration fantasies, the fantastic element was brought in by magic. Frankenstein even, used some jiggery-pokery magic to animate his artificial monster.* There was trouble about the thing's soul. But by the end of last century it had become difficult to squeeze even a momentary belief out of magic any longer. It occurred to me that instead of the usual interview with the devil or a magician, an ingenious use of scientific patter might with advantage be substituted . . . I simply brought the fetish stuff up to date, and made it as near actual theory as possible."[1]

Thus science assimilates fantasy. Fantasy is almost as avid in assimilating science; in 1705, Daniel Defoe wrote *The Consolidator: or, Memoirs of Sundry Transactions from the World in the Moon* featuring a machine that would convey a man to the Moon, which was inspired by popular expositions of Newton's celestial mechanics. In its wider sense, fantasy clearly embraces all science fiction. But fantasy in a narrower sense, as opposed to science fiction, generally implies a fiction leaning more towards myth or the mythopoeic than towards an assumed realism. (The distinction is clear if we compare Ray Bradbury's Mars with the painstakingly delineated Mars of Rex Gordon's *No Man Friday* or Frederik Pohl's *Man Plus*; Bradbury's Mars stands as an analogy, Gordon's as a Defoe-like essay in definition and Pohl's as a projection of ongoing NASA activity).

We must understand that the science fiction search for that "definition of mankind" is often playful. And what the definition does not do is determine whether the end product is good, bad, sheer nonsense, or holy writ (as Heinlein's *Stranger in a Strange Land* was taken as holy writ). Definitions are to assist, not overpower, thinking.

The definition takes for granted that the most tried and true way of indicating man's status is to show him confronted by crisis, whether of his own making (overpopulation), or of science's (new destructive virus), or of nature's (another Ice Age). And that there are forms of fiction which may appear to fulfill the definition but nevertheless are not science fiction—generally because they are ur-science fiction (existing before the genre was originated), from Dante's great imaginary worlds of *Inferno*, *Purgatorio*, and *Paradiso* onwards—or because they transcend the gothic format, as do *Moby-Dick*, Thomas Hardy's novels, John

---

* This is not the case at all; Wells's memory was at fault.

Cowyer Powys's *A Glastonbury Romance*, the plays of Samuel Beckett, Thomas Pynchon's writings, and so forth.

If this all sounds somewhat all-embracing, nevertheless this volume errs on the side of exclusiveness. Our preference is for that elusive creature, "real SF," which has set itself apart from other modes of literature by embracing technological imagery, and by perceiving its characters as statistics.

Having fought the good fight to define SF, we have to admit defeat in distinguishing between SF and fantasy. Fantasy's eel-like versatility as a descriptive term is well known. Other critics have had the same problem: "We often find ourselves wondering if we can really distinguish between, say, science fiction and fantasy"[2] remarks one scholar.

This book, however, makes it clear that we can recognize SF fairly easily, although it is rarely found in a pure isolated state. Just like oxygen.

It so happens that the most ancient forms of literature are often recognizably kin to science fiction; voyages of discovery, mythical adventures, fantastic beasts, and symbolic happenings are part of a grand tradition in storytelling which the realistic novel of society has only recently rejected. Thus, the *Epic of Gilgamesh*, with the world destroyed by flood, the Hindu mythology, the *Odyssey*, *Beowulf*, the Bible—and practically everything down to *Mickey Mouse Weekly*—have been claimed at one time or another by science fiction fans with colonialist ambitions.

The phrase in my definition about "advanced knowledge" takes care of that bit of grandiose aspiration. Science fiction is NOW, not THEN.

Nevertheless, Milton's *Paradise Lost*, Book II, with Satan crossing that "vast vacuity" between his world and ours, looks suspiciously like the pure quill.

Frontiers are by tradition ill defined. Happily, it is no difficult matter to identify the first true example of the genre.

Only in the late 1920s was the term "science fiction" used as a kind of generic trade mark. It was regarded as an improvement on the more ludicrous term "scientifiction." The mode itself was already in being, although this went unacknowledged for a time. The term was first applied to crudely constructed stories appearing in various American pulp magazines, of which *Amazing Stories* (1926 onwards) was the earliest. For more substantial British exercises in the same fields—many of an earlier date—the term "scientific romance" was sometimes used.

This somewhat parvenu feeling about science fiction has led its adherents to claim for it, in contradictory fashion, both amazing newness and incredible antiquity. Early potted histories of the genre liked to indulge their readers by cantering briskly back through Greek legends of flying gods like Hermes and satirical voyages to Moon and Sun undertaken by Lucian of Samosata in the second century AD.[3] Although science fiction can no more be said to have "begun" with Lucian than space flight "began" in Leonardo da Vinci's notebooks, this tired old litany is still chanted in various sequestered parts of the globe.[4]

On the long struggle upwards from Lucian to the celebrated date of 1926, the historians scoop in Thomas More, Rabelais, Cyrano de Bergerac, Jonathan Swift, and a whole clutch of eighteenth-century bishops. One of the more learned anthologists, in a Croatian science fiction anthology, enlists Dante and Shakespeare to the ranks[5], while the first chapter of Genesis has also been claimed, perhaps with more justification.

Trawls for illustrious ancestors are understandable, in critics as in impoverished families. But they lead to error, the first error being the error of spurious continuity—of perceiving a connection or influence where none exists. Forgetting that writers write with the flux of life going on about them, scholars rake through their books and pass over in a couple of pages the thirteen long centuries that lie between Lucian and Ariosto.[6]

The second error to which this ancestor search has led is the interpretation of science fiction as mainly a series of imaginary voyages to the Moon and other planets.

Interplanetary flight forms a noteworthy element in science fiction. In the 1950s, when space fever was high, it formed a major element. The rocketship became SF's trademark, and SF became "space fiction." All rocketeers were science-fiction readers, it is safe to say, in Germany as in the United States. The development and refinement of scientific imagining from Kepler on towards technological reality is a thrilling story in itself. This story has been documented by Marjorie Hope Nicolson.[7]

But the subject matter of SF is richly complex. It encompasses more than simply interplanetary flight. Fortunately, it is not necessary to leave this planet to qualify as a science-fiction writer. It is not necessary, either, to write specifically about technological developments. The imagery of technology and science is often employed for symbolic ends. All depends on the inclination of the individual author.

Science fiction is also diverse. Previous Lucian-to-Verne approaches to its diversity fail to grasp both its response to the world beyond the study window and to its sense of inwardness. Such mechanistic approaches became out of date with the entry of talented women writers into the field, exploiting in several cases the social aspects of SF.

As with all the arts, science fiction is more concerned than ever before with its own nature. The intention of this volume is not to banish science fiction's illustrious ancestors, who are as essential to it as cathedrals to a study of architecture, but to rescue them from a perspectiveless gloom.

The greatest successes of science fiction are those which deal with man in relation to his changing surroundings and abilities: what might loosely be called *environmental fiction*. With this in mind, we hope to show that the basic impulse of science fiction is as much evolutionary as technological. While thinking in these terms, it will be appropriate to regard Lucian and the other pilgrim fathers as relations of science-fiction writers, just as we regard the great apes as relations of man, to be allowed all due respect for primogeniture.

The evolutionary revolution and the Industrial Revolution occurred in the same period of time.

The quickening tempo of manufacture becomes more noticeable in Great Britain in the second half of the eighteenth century, at a time when populations were beginning to increase rapidly. This traditional incentive to industrial advance was coupled with the roster of inventions with which we are familiar from school: Hargreaves's spinning jenny, Cartwright's power loom, Watt's steam engine, and so on.

Industry was not alone in undergoing transformation. The American Declaration of Independence in 1776 and the French Declaration of the Rights of Man in 1789 were documents in man's revision of his attitude to his own kind. It is no coincidence that the abolition of slavery was a burning issue at this time. Or that Western man now began to alter his attitude towards his God.

It is from this changeable cultural climate that science fiction emerged—with a discreetly blasphemous nature it still retains, or did in its lean and hungry days before the seventies.

Speculations on evolution and natural selection were current at the end of the eighteenth century. The ancient Greeks had held enlightened views on these matters, Thales believing that all life originated in water, and Anaximenes that it came into being spontaneously from the primaeval slime. Later, in Christian Europe, the Bible defeated any such ideas, and a literal interpretation of Genesis generally held sway.

The debate on whether species were fixed or mutable was a long one. It gained force in the eighteenth century following the impact of Pacific exploration. The world of the South Seas—the first region of the globe to be opened up scientifically—provided new stimulus to old questions of how our planet, its animals, and its humans, had come about.

In the last decade of the century there appeared a remarkable foreshadowing of the theory of evolution, its arguments properly buttressed, its references up to date. Its author was Darwin—not Charles Darwin of the *Beagle*, but his grandfather, Erasmus Darwin. Erasmus Darwin (1731–1802) was a doctor by profession, a contemporary of Diderot and the Cyclopaedists, fired by their ideas. He was a witty and forceful talker with an enquiring mind. He leads us to Mary Shelley.

Many inventions stand to Erasmus Darwin's credit, such as new types of carriages and coal carts, a speaking machine, a mechanical ferry, rotary pumps, and horizontal windmills. He also seems to have invented—or at least proposed—a rocket motor powered by hydrogen and oxygen. His rough sketch shows the two gases stored in separate compartments and fed into a cylindrical combustion chamber with an exit nozzle at one end—a good approximation of the workings of a modern rocket, and formulated long before the ideas of the Russian rocket pioneer Tsiolkovsky were set to paper. The best discussion of this most interesting man and his inventions is by Desmond King-Hele.[8]

Darwin was a member of a distinguished group of men living and working in the English Midlands, which were then in the forefront of the world's manufacturing life. In 1776, Matthew Boulton took Dr. Johnson and Boswell on a tour of his famous Soho iron works, and said to Johnson (as quoted in Boswell's *Life of Johnson*), "I sell here, Sir, what all the world desires to have—POWER." As well as industry, literary and scientific societies prospered. A melancholy thought two centuries on, when the manufacturing life of this part of the world, where the Industrial Revolution grew up, now lies in ruins.

During this time, Erasmus Darwin had his portrait painted by Joseph Wright of Derby, whose paintings of scientific experiments are among the first of their kind. Of these, Wright's *An Experiment on a Bird in the Air Pump* is the most dramatic. Its group of figures is illuminated by the lamp on the experimenter's table. All is darkness around them. Most of the groups look on in rapt attention. A young girl weeps at the fate of the bird in its glass prison, struggling as the oxygen is exhausted. Behind the drama, the moon shines in at a casement.

Wright painted other scenes of industry, but *An Experiment* lingers in the mind. It is a testimony to the interest people then took in scientific experiment. Out of this exciting and inspiring intellectual environment was to come Frankenstein. One cannot help but wonder if Mary Shelley knew Wright's painting; it seems probable, since Wright's name was linked with that of Samuel Taylor Coleridge, a friend of Mary's father. Wright died in August 1797, the month and year in which Mary Shelley was born.[9]

The division between the arts and sciences had not then grown wide. Among his other capacities, Erasmus Darwin was a copious—and famous—versifier. In his long poems he laid out his findings on evolution and influenced the great poets of his day. His is the case of a once-gigantic, now-vanished reputation. Coleridge referred to him as "the first literary character of Europe, and the most original-minded man." By his grandson's day he was quite forgotten.

Erasmus's mighty work *Zoonomia* was published in two volumes in 1794 and 1796. It explains the system of sexual selection, with emphasis on primeval promiscuity, the search for food, and the need for protection in living things, and how these factors, interweaving with natural habitats, control the diversity of life in all its changing forms. Evolutionary processes need time as well as space for their stage management. Erasmus emphasizes the great age of the Earth. In this he contradicts the then-accepted view, established by Bishop James Ussher in the seventeenth century, that God performed the act of creation in the year 4004 BC, probably about tea-time—although the Scot, James Hutton, had declared in 1785, thrillingly, that the geological record revealed "no vestige of a beginning, no prospect of an end."

The philosophical movements of the nineteenth century, which were tinged with Darwinism, tended towards pessimism; philosophical men like Tennyson were all too aware of "Nature red in tooth and claw." Erasmus, in his heroic couplets, took a more serene view—an eighteenth-century view, one might say: equable, even Parnassian. It is easy to imagine that this century would have withstood the shock of evolutionary theory better than its successor.

> Shout round the globe, how Reproduction strives
> With vanquish'd Death—and Happiness survives;
> How Life increasing peoples every clime,
> And young renascent Nature conquers Time.

These lines come from the last canto of *The Temple of Nature*, posthumously published in 1803. Of course they strike us as slightly daft.* Erasmus concentrated on summing the whole course of evolution so far, from the almost invisible life of the seas to mankind and man's civilizations. In this poem of four cantos and some two thousand lines, he speaks of the way in which a mammal foetus relives the previous stage of evolution and of the survival of the fittest, as well as prophesying with remarkable accuracy many features of modern life—gigantic skyscraper cities, piped water, the age of the automobile, overpopulation, and fleets of nuclear submarines:

> Bid raised in air the ponderous structure stand,
> Or pour obedient rivers through the land;
> With crowds unnumbered crowd the living streets,
> Or people oceans with the triumphant fleets.

As we can see, Erasmus Darwin qualifies as a part-time science fiction writer! More securely than anyone before him, he has a grasp of future possibility.

His thrusts at church and state aroused his opponents and Darwin's voice was effectively silenced. Parodies of his verse in George Canning's *Anti-Jacobin*, entitled *The Loves of the Triangles*, mocked Darwin's ideas, laughing at his bold imaginative strokes. That electricity could ever have widespread practical application, that mankind could have evolved from lowly life forms, that the hills could be older than the

---

* Erasmus is deft as well as daft, for instance, in this couplet describing the marine organisms whose structures later formed chalk deposits:

Age after age expands the peopled plain
The Tenants perish but their cells remain

Bible claimed—those were sorts of madnesses that set readers of the *Anti-Jacobin* tittering. Canning recognized the subversive element in Darwin's thought and effectively brought low his reputation as a poet.

As for his reputation as scientific innovator—that also was overshadowed.

Once the famous grandson appeared luminous on the scene, eclipse was total. The reinstatement of this remarkable man (like the reinstatement of Mary Shelley) is recent.[10] King-Hele lists seventy-five subjects in which he was a pioneer.

One modern science fiction writer at least is interested in Erasmus Darwin. Charles Sheffield's *Erasmus Magister* (1982) paints a genial portrait of him as a kind of predecessor of Sherlock Holmes.

Most remarkably, Erasmus speculated on the origins of the universe. Before the eighteenth century closed, he framed the earliest intimations we have of the Big Bang hypothesis: "It may be objected, that if the stars had been projected from a Chaos by explosions, that they must have returned again into it from the known laws of gravitation; this however would not happen, if the whole of Chaos, like grains of gunpowder, was exploded at the same time, and dispersed through infinite space at once, or in quick succession, in every possible direction."

This in a footnote to Erasmus's *The Economy of Vegetation* (1791).[11] Before its long eclipse, Erasmus Darwin's thought illuminated those poets whose response to nature was closest to his own—the Romantics. Wordsworth and Coleridge owe him much; Shelley's debt is considerable, going far beyond echoes of similar lines. Shelley was a poet of science, a rebel, an atheist, an ardent lover of freedom and the west wind. No wonder he admired Erasmus, in whom also these qualities were strong.

As we shall see, there is another direction in which Darwin's influence on science fiction is both powerful and immediate.

We should recall here two novels published contemporaneously with the first volume of Erasmus Darwin's *Zoonomia*. William Godwin's *Caleb Williams* (regarded as the first psychological pursuit story), and Mrs. Radcliffe's *The Mysteries of Udolpho* (regarded as the high point of gothic) were both published in the year 1794.

Although Godwin and Erasmus never met, they had friends and sympathies in common, and were pilloried together as atheistical writers, most notably in the *Anti-Jacobin*. Godwin was a novelist and liberal philosopher whose reputation stood high among the poets and writers of his time. He married Mary Wollstonecraft, another contributor to the debate of the age, especially in her *Vindication of the Rights of Woman* (1772).

William Hazlitt reported that Coleridge "did not rate Godwin very high (this was caprice or prejudice, real or affected), but he had a great idea of Mrs. Wollstonecraft's powers of conversation." So had the Swiss painter, Henry Fuseli, who fell in love with her. After various misfortunes, Mary Wollstonecraft married Godwin and bore him a daughter, Mary.

This Mary grew up to write *Frankenstein* when still in her teens. Her novel is unique. But behind every unique work stand the predecessors to which it owes a cultural debt. In the case of *Frankenstein* we need to look at the gothic fashion from which it emerged.

Edmund Burke's essay on *The Sublime and the Beautiful* appeared in 1756. It became an arbiter of taste for many decades. Its influence lingers today. Burke distinguished between beauty, which is founded on pleasure and is placid, and the sublime, which inspires awe and terror and, with pain as its basis, disturbs the emotions. He speaks of "delightful horror, which is the most genuine effect and truest test of the sublime." If the perception reads strangely now, a welter of splatter movies has dulled our taste buds.

Art, as usual, copied art. The Ossianic poems were the first to fulfil Burke's specifications.* They were counterfeits by an ingenious Scot, James Macpherson, and immediately branded as counterfeit by Horace Walpole among others; but their enormous Celtic ghosts, giants, cliffs, storms, and buckets of blood thrilled many writers and artists, among them Fuseli, as well as much of the literate population of Europe.

The Ossian poems made their appearance from 1760 to 1763. In 1765 *The Castle of Otranto* was published pseudonymously. So popular was it that the author, Horace Walpole, admitted his identity in a preface to the second edition.

The Castle of Otranto is established as the earliest gothic novel. One commentator claims that the whole gothic revival began with a dream.[12]

---

* Perhaps the first painting to meet Burke's definition is George Stubbs's *White Horse Frightened by a Lion* (1770), a masterpiece containing beauty and sublimity. Stubbs was a capable scientist as well as a masterly animal painter.

On a June night in 1764, Walpole had a nightmare in which he saw a gigantic hand clad in armor, gripping the banister of a great staircase. When he woke, he began writing his novel.[13]

Walpole was an antiquarian. His most lively monument is not *Otranto* but Strawberry Hill, his residence, his own conception, built in gothic style, which is to say, in imitation of a medieval style. His dream was influenced by the *Prisons* of Piranesi[14]—another artist, like Wright or Stubbs, still in vogue today.

If *The Castle of Otranto* owes something to Piranesi, *Vathek* has more of Tiepolo in it. This single and singular novel by the eccentric William Beckford is full of magic and wit. Published in 1786, it nods to both Samuel Johnson's *Rasselas* and the *Arabian Nights*. Beckford's version of Strawberry Hill was the architecturally daring Fonthill Abbey (too daring—the tower collapsed after some years and the building was demolished).

Beckford wrote *Vathek* in French. Byron told Beckford's daughter, the Duchess of Hamilton, that *Vathek* was his gospel, and that he always carried a copy of the book with him. With its Faust-like theme, in which the calif Vathek sells himself to the powers of evil in exchange for the treasures of the pre-Adamite sultans, it had a natural appeal to what might be called the Byronic side of Byron. While *Vathek* is a much more enjoyable novel than Walpole's, both have exerted wide fascination—Beckford's not least on Oscar Wilde, whose *Picture of Dorian Gray* uses a similar theme and nods to Burke's dictum on the sublime.

The late eighteenth century was a time of botanical renaissance, brought about by the classification of plants by the Swede Linnaeus and, more especially, by the voyages to the South Seas of Sir Joseph Banks and Captain Cook (killed in Hawaii in 1779). Cook carried back to Europe not only fantastic landscapes and images, from the ice world of the Antarctic to the gigantic heads of Easter Island, but a treasury of plants: three thousand species, one thousand of them unknown to botany. The world was alive with news of itself.

These influences show in Erasmus Darwin's poems. In *The Loves of the Plants* (with its Fuseli decoration engraved by William Blake), he makes reference to the Antarctic and tells how

> Slow o'er the printed snows with silent walk
> Huge shaggy forms across the twilight stalk

a couplet that has left its imprint in that very gothic poem, Coleridge's
Rime of the Ancient Mariner, when the accursed ship is driven to the
Southern Pole:

> And through the drifts the snowy cliffs
> Did send a dismal sheen:
> Nor shapes of men nor beasts we ken—
> The ice was all between.

Today, Darwin's method of expressing exact technical detail in heroic
couplets and describing the sex life of plants in human terms appears
odd. We hardly expect Bentham and Hooker to talk like Pope's *Rape of
the Lock.* The loss is ours. Before Victorian times, art and science had
not come to the division that SF tries to bridge.

By the beginning of the nineteenth century, the gothic craze was
abating. It had produced its best-remembered work, including Matthew
"Monk" Lewis's *The Monk,* a novel overloaded with licentious monks,
romantic robbers, ghosts, and a bleeding nun, as well as episodes of
murder, torture, homosexuality, matricide, and incest. Even Lord Byron
was shocked. Ann Radcliffe's two most famous novels, *The Mysteries of
Udolpho* and *The Italian,* had appeared, as well as countless "blue
books," abridgements or imitations of gothic novels, selling very
cheaply and bearing cheap titles.[15] These were the sort of fictions made
fun of by Jane Austen in *NorthangerAbbey* and Peacock in *Nightmare
Abbey.* But fashion was everything; the poet Shelley himself wrote two
such novels, *Zastrozzi* and *St. Irryne,* while still at school.

Thomas Love Peacock (1785–1866) was no gothic novelist. However, he used the gothic *mise-en-scène,* and the very titles of his remarkable novels look back ironically to the fiction of his youth, from
Headlong Hall (1816) to *Gryll Grange,* published forty-four years later,
in 1860. Peacock's form of discussion novel, in which characters in remote country houses discouragingly discuss the world situation, and
anything else that enters their heads, while eating and drinking well,
provides a format for later writers such as Aldous Huxley.[16]

Mary Wollstonecraft Shelley read Peacock's *Melincourt,* published
two years before *Frankenstein.* The dangers of a critical method that
would explain everything in terms of influence and derivation are well
exemplified by Peacock's little-read novel. For the central character in

Melincourt is an orangutan called Sir Oran Haut-Ton, who does not speak but performs well on flute and French horn. Peacock was satirizing an early pioneer of anthropology, Lord Monboddo, who cherished a pet orangutan as an example of "the infantine state of our species." So is Sir Oran a symbol of the natural man, harking back to Rousseau? Is he a literary precursor of Frankenstein's monster? Is he a precursor of Poe's orangutan in "Murders in the Rue Morgue"? Is he, indeed, with his title and rolling acres, a precursor of Tarzan? We perhaps do better to turn back to gothic.

In the gothic mode, emphasis was placed on the distant and unearthly, while suspense entered literature for the first time—Mrs. Radcliffe was praised by Scott for her expertise in suspense. Nowadays, this quality in her work has worn thin, and what remains to attract in her best work is a dreamy sense of the exotic. Gothic's brooding landscapes, isolated castles, dismal old towns, and mysterious figures can still carry us into an entranced world from which horrid revelations start.

The revelations may prove a disappointment, as they do in *The Mysteries of Odolpho*. Then we rouse from our dreams to indigestion. We know that some Gothic-Romantic authors relied heavily on dreams for inspiration: Mrs. Radcliffe herself consumed indigestible food in order to induce dreams of terror, just as Fuseli ate raw meat toward the same end, in order to feed his voracious muse. Appropriately, Fuseli's most famous canvas is *The Nightmare*.

The methods of the gothic writers are those of many science-fiction and horror writers today. Stephen King is modern American Gothic, the Radcliffe of the Greyhound Bus. The horrid revelations will not lie down. It would be as absurd to suggest that most SF writers were serious propagandists for the cause of science as that the author of *Romano Castle: or, The Horrors of the Forest* was a serious critic of the evils of the Inquisition—however much both sides may have considered themselves in earnest.

Other planets make ideal settings for brooding landscapes, isolated castles, dismal towns, and mysterious alien figures[17]; often, indeed, the villains may be monks, exploiting a local population under the guise of religion.[18] The horrid revelations may be on an imposing scale: that mankind has been abroad in the universe long ago, but was beaten back to his home planet by a powerful adversary[19]; that Earth is merely a sort

of Botany Bay or dumping ground for the disposal of the vicious elements of the galaxy[20]; or that mankind is descended from rats which escaped from some interstellar vessel putting in at Earth.[21]

Again, for both Gothic and science-fiction writers, distance lent enchantment to the view, as the poet Campbell put it. If something un-
likely is going to happen, better to set it somewhere where the reader
cannot check the occurrence against his own experience.

For this reason, locations in Gothic novels lie in a distant and misty
past. Mrs. Radcliffe sets *The Mysteries of Udolpho* in the late sixteenth
century; his chateau commands views of a river, with fine trees (she always particularizes about trees, and many passages in her novels remind
us that this was the age of Gilpin's *Forest Scenery* and Repton's *Landscape Gardening*), and "the majestic Pyrenees, whose summits, veiled in
clouds, or exhibiting awful forms . . . were sometimes barren . . . and
sometimes frowned with forests of lofty pine." Mrs. Radcliffe is careful
with her locations; her imitators were often less precise.

So, with science-fiction novels distance lends enchantment. They
may locate themselves in distant futures on Earth, on one of the planets of the solar system, or anywhere in our galaxy, even a distant galaxy;
though enchantment is not in direct proportion to distance. Or they
may occupy a different sphere or another time-track entirely. We then
find ourselves cut off from our present, in an alternate universe.

There are several brilliant alternate universe novels. In Ward
Moore's *Bring the Jubilee*[22] the South won the American Civil War. In
Harry Harrison's *A Transatlantic Tunnel, Hurrah!*, George Washington
was shot and the American Revolution never happened. In Philip K.
Dick's *The Man in the High Castle*, the Axis powers won World War II.
In Keith Roberts's *Pavane*, Queen Elizabeth I was assassinated and En-
gland remained a backward Catholic country. In Kingsley Amis's *The
Alteration* (which wittily pays tribute to the two preceding titles), the
Reformation never happened. In all these novels, history (rather than
science) is used as incantation, according to a prescription dreamed up
by Walpole.

The Gothic novel was part of the great Romantic Movement. Its
vogue declined early in the nineteenth century. But terror, mystery, and
that delightful horror which Burke connected with the sublime—all of
them have remained popular with a great body of readers, and may be

discovered, sound of wind and limb, in science fiction to this day. Un-delightful horror is also in vogue, in movie and video particularly. Per-haps this taste set in with the decay of that calm eighteenth-century confidence in rationality expressed by Pope in the phrase "whatever is, is right." Shelley was born in 1792, and his is a different outlook with a vengeance!

> While yet a boy I sought for ghosts, and sped
> Through many a listening chamber, cave and ruin,
> And starlight wood, with fearful steps pursuing
> Hopes of high talk with the departed dead.[23]

This is the Gothic Shelley, always in quest of mystery.

The new age had a passion for the inexplicable, as we have in ours; its uncertainties were soon memorably enshrined in the pages of the novel written by Shelley's young second wife.

Frankenstein: or, The Modern Prometheus was published anonymously on 11 March 1818, in the same year as works by Shelley, Peacock, Scott, Hazlitt, Keats, and Byron. The Napoleonic Wars were over; *Savannah* crossed the Atlantic, the first steamship to do so; the early steam locomotives were chuffing along their metal tracks, Boulton's iron foundries were going full blast; the Lancashire cotton factories were lit by gas, and gas mains were being laid in London. Telford and McAdam were building roads and bridges, Galvani's followers and Humphry Davy were experimenting with electricity. "So much has been done," exclaimed the soul of Frankenstein, "more, far more, will I achieve!" (Chapter III)

As with Erasmus Darwin's reputation, the reputation of the modest author of *Frankenstein* has been too long in eclipse.

Mary Wollstonecraft Godwin was born in August 1797. Her intel-lectual and beautiful mother died ten days later, after an ague and a se-vere hemorrhage, leaving the impractical Godwin to care for the baby and for Fanny, Mary Wollstonecraft's three-year-old child from an ear-lier liaison.

Later, when Percy Bysshe Shelley took to calling at Godwin's house, he and Godwin became friends. Mary fell in love with Shelley and eloped with him to the Continent in 1814. In the following year

Mary[24] bore Shelley a son, who died. By then, her destiny was linked with the poet. Her eight brief years with Shelley, until his death by drowning in 1822, were the decisive ones in her life. Theirs remains one of the most fascinating marriages in literary history.

1816 marked a vital period in Mary's affairs. A son, William, was born in January. In May, Shelley and Mary, with Mary's half-sister, Claire Clairmont, left England for the second time, to stay in Switzerland, near Geneva. Here Mary began writing *Frankenstein,* before her nineteenth birthday. Shelley's first wife, Harriet, drowned herself in the Serpentine early in December, and Shelley and Mary were married before the end of that year.

Here is the portrait Trelawny paints of Mary: "The most striking feature in her face was her calm gray eyes; she was rather under the English standard of woman's height, very fair and light-haired, witty, social, and animated in the society of friends, though mournful in solitude."[25] This is a portrait of the first writer of science fiction; Mary had imbibed the philosophical ideas of Locke and the scientific ideas of Darwin, Humphry Davy, Joseph Priestley, and others.[26] She had read Condillac's *Treatise on the Sensations.* These helped shape her intellectual life and she set about applying her ideas to paper within a loose Gothic structure of suspense and pursuit.

Frankenstein was completed before Mary was twenty. She lived to write other novels, eventually supporting herself by writing. She never remarried, and died in 1851, the year of the Great Exhibition, aged fifty-three. She is buried in a churchyard in Bournemouth.[27]

Of her two sons and two daughters by Shelley, only Percy Florence survived beyond childhood. As Shelley put it in a poem to her:

> We are not happy, sweet! Our state
> Is strange and full of doubt and fear.

As if in response, Mary Shelley says that she wished her novel to "speak to the mysterious fears of our nature." This *Frankenstein* certainly does.

Mary Shelley's later novels should be listed. They are *Valperga* (1823), *The Last Man* (1826), *The Fortunes of Perkin Warbeck* (1830), *Lodore* (1835), and *Falkner* (1837); all were published anonymously.[28]

Her story "Matilda" remained unpublished until 1959.[29] Godwin, Mary's father, had greeted this manuscript with coldness and silence. It tells of motherless Matilda who is brought up by an aunt until, when she is sixteen, her father returns from abroad. All Matilda's emotions are lavished on him, and reciprocated—until she realizes that his love for her is physical as well as paternal. Overcome by horror, the father drowns himself in the sea. When a poet, Woodville, comes along offering love, Matilda cannot accept him. Neglecting herself, she contracts consumption, most romantic of nineteenth-century maladies, and dies.

Some commentators have seen in this piece of self-dramatization proof of Mary's incestuous feelings. More cautiously, her latest biographer says, "It is her father who incestuously desires Matilda, but the father in many ways resembles the forceful side of Shelley and his death by drowning and Matilda's nightmare pursuit in search of news of him find a parallel in Shelley's own death, a prognostication that Mary recognized in retrospect."[30]

The sea, the drowning, echo back and forth in Mary's writing. Both motifs emerge in a neglected story, "The Transformation,"[31] which throws light on the events of Frankenstein's wedding night.

A monstrous dwarf who is also a magician survives a shipwreck. Swimming to the Italian shore, the dwarf encounters Guido wandering along the beach. Guido was engaged to Juliet until his wicked behavior became too much for her. Guido and dwarf change bodies. The dwarf (as Guido) goes to Genoa, charms Juliet, and is accepted in marriage. Guido (as dwarf) discovers Juliet and his double whispering together. He springs from the shadows and puts his dagger to the real dwarf's throat.

Dwarf (as Guido) says, "Strike home! Destroy this body—you will still live."

The dwarf (as Guido) then draws a sword. Guido (as dwarf) throws himself on the blade, at the same time plunging a dagger into the other's side.

Guido revives, to find himself in his own body once more and the dwarf dead. Juliet tends him lovingly. But he has to live with the knowledge that it was the monstrous dwarf who won back Juliet's love and the creature she now reviles who was himself.

This doppelganger theme bears affinities with the Frankenstein-monster confusion; here as there, the misshapen partner has no name.

Both stories express the struggle Mary felt within herself between the loved and unloved side, the light and the dark. We understand that Shelley's death must have seemed to her like her own.

Readers and commentators alike are agreed that *Frankenstein* is Mary Shelley's great original novel. It is hardly surprising. *Frankenstein* is the one novel she wrote during Shelley's lifetime. As he in his poems was opening up new ground, she—wrapped in the aura of intellectual excitement that existed between them—also ventured into startling new territory.

Although Mary Shelley's reputation was long eclipsed by the fame of Byron and Shelley, the binary stars burning near her, *Frankenstein* was a success from the first.

One of the few joyous moments in her letters for 1823, when she returns to England from Italy, following Shelley's death, comes when she exclaims, "But lo and behold! I found myself famous!—*Frankenstein* had prodigious success as a drama and was about to be repeated for the twenty-third night at the English opera house."[32] The story of *Frankenstein: or, The Modern Prometheus* is familiar in outline, if distortedly, from film, stage, and TV versions. Victor Frankenstein assembles a body from various parts of fresh corpses and then endows it with life. He quickly rejects the new being, which disappears and becomes a threat to him and others. The novel is long and considerably more complex than brief synopsis suggests; it is stocked with political and philosophical observations that film versions ignore.

Frankenstein opens with letters from a Captain Walton to his married sister at home. Walton's ship is exploring in unfamiliar Arctic waters near the pole. Walton is a man with a love for the marvelous. Just as well, for he sights a monstrous being driving a sledge across the ice floes. Next day, the crew rescues a man from the ice. This proves to be Victor Frankenstein, a scientist of Geneva. He is close to death. Recovering from exhaustion, he tells his tale to Walton.

Frankenstein's narrative comprises the bulk of the book. At the end, we return to Walton's letters. His quest abandoned, Walton recounts the death of Frankenstein to his sister.

Contained within Frankenstein's narrative are six chapters in which his creation gives an account of its life, with emphasis on its education and its rejection by society because of its repellent aspect. Within the creature's account is a briefer story of injustice, the history of the De Laceys, beneath whose roof the creature finds shelter.

The novel contains few female characters, a departure from Gothic practice. Victor's bride to be, Elizabeth, remains distant and cold. The characters passionately seek knowledge; this quest means everything to Frankenstein and Walton; they are never disabused. Frankenstein, indeed, praises the voyage of discovery as an honorable and courageous undertaking even as the creature's hands are about to close around his throat. The constant litigation that takes place in the background represents another kind of quest for knowledge, often erroneous or perverted.

One of the attractions of the novel is that it is set, not in the shabby London Mary Shelley knew from childhood, but amid the spectacular alpine scenery she visited with Shelley. The puissance of the monster gains force by being associated with the elements presiding over the mountains, storm, snow, and desolation. Its first speech with its creator is on the glacier below Mont Blanc.[33]

What exactly is uniquely innovative about *Frankenstein?*

Interest has always centered on the creation of the nameless monster. This is the core of the novel, an experiment that goes wrong—a prescription to be repeated later, more sensationally, in *Amazing Stories* and elsewhere. Frankenstein's is the Faustian dream of unlimited power, but Frankenstein makes no pacts with the devil. "The devil" belongs to a relegated system of belief. Frankenstein's ambitions bear fruit only when he throws away his old reference books from a pre-scientific age and gets down to some research in the laboratory. This is now accepted practice, of course. But what is now accepted practice was, in 1818, a startling perception, a small revolution.

The novel dramatizes the difference between the old age and the new, between an age when things went by rote and one where everything was suddenly called into question.

Jiggery-pokery magic, of which Wells was to speak contemptuously, achieves nothing in this new age. Victor Frankenstein goes to the University of Ingolstadt and visits two professors. To the first, a man called Krempe, a professor of natural philosophy, he reveals how his search for knowledge led him to the works of Cornelius Agrippa, Paracelsus, and Albertus Magnus. Krempe scoffs at him: "These fancies, which you have so greedily imbibed, are a thousand years old."

This is a modern objection; antiquity is no longer the highest court to which one can appeal. "Ancient wisdom" is supplanted by modern experiment.

Frankenstein attends the second professor, Waldman, who lectures on chemistry. Waldman is even more scathing about ancient teachers who "promised impossibilities, and performed nothing." He speaks instead of the moderns, who use microscope and crucible, and converts Frankenstein to his way of thinking. Only when Frankenstein turns away from alchemy and the past, toward science and the future, is he rewarded with a horrible success.

In Wright of Derby's air pump, the white bird fluttered and died. Now something flutters and lives.

The "vital spark" is imparted to the composite body. Life is created without supernatural aid. Science has taken charge. A new understanding has emerged.

The Byron-Shelley circle understood themselves to be living in a new age. They felt themselves to be moderns. The study of gases was advanced; much was understood about the composition of the atmosphere; that lightning and electricity were one and the same was already clear—although that it was not a fluid was still so indefinite that Mary was able to use that misconception as a metaphor. Shelley had a microscope while at Oxford, and the study of morbid anatomy was well advanced. Mary lived in a thoroughly Newtonian world, in which natural explanations could be sought for natural phenomena. It is for this reason she sends Victor Frankenstein to Ingolstadt University; it was renowned in its time as a center for science. Mary knew more of the science of her time than has been generally granted. But Samuel Holmes Vasbinder's useful researches in this area should change this uninformed opinion.[34] Why, then, is so much time spent by Frankenstein with the alchemists, with Cornelius Agrippa and Paracelsus?

One practical answer is that Mary Shelley wished to make it plain that the old authorities who "promised impossibilities and performed nothing" had to go. She had to show that they were useless, outdated, and without merit in a modern age. Krempe's contempt is clear: "I little expected," he tells his student, "in this enlightened and scientific age, to find a disciple of Albertus Magnus and Paracelsus. My dear sir, you must begin your studies entirely anew."

Waldman summarizes the miracles the modern researchers have achieved. "They ascend into the heavens: they have discovered how the blood circulates, and the nature of the air that we breathe. They have acquired new and almost unlimited powers; they can command the thunders of heaven, mimic the earthquake, and even mock the invisible world with its shadows."

Thus Mary Shelley, like a practiced modern SF writer, prepares us beforehand for what is to follow. Of course she cannot show us how life is instilled in a dead body, any more than a modern writer could, but she can suspend our disbelief. The only problematic item in Waldman's listing of scientific wonders is "mocking the invisible world with its shadows."

This could be a reference, not to magic lanterns, or de Louther-bourg's Eidophusikon, or all the other devices relying on mechanics and optics that were popular at the time, but to the Spectre of Brocken. The Spectre of Brocken was just the sort of natural optical effect to attract the Shelleys and the Romantics. Like the Fata Morgana, the Spectre was a kind of mirage. It was seen in mountainous districts. One of the best accounts of it was given by M. Haue, who saw it in 1797, the year Mary was born. The sun rose at four one morning. At four-fifteen, Haue saw a human figure of monstrous size, apparently stand-ing on a nearby mountain. An innkeeper was called. The two men saw two monstrous figures, which mimicked their movements.[35] Though explicable in natural terms, such gigantic doppelganger figures created awe in all who beheld them. They too may have played a part in the creation of the monster.

As if to dispel any doubts about her aversion to "jiggery-pokery magic," Mary makes it plain that her central marvel shares the essen-tial quality of scientific experiment, rather than the hit-and-miss of leg-erdemain. She has Frankenstein create life a second time.

Frankenstein agrees to make a female companion for the monster, subject to certain conditions. When his work is almost finished, Frankenstein pauses, thinking of the "race of devils" that might be raised up by the union between his two creatures (a curious moment, this, for science fiction, looking back towards Caliban's snarl to Pros-pero in *The Tempest*—"I had peopled else the isle with Calibans!"— and forward to the monstrous legions of robots that were to tramp across the pages of the twentieth-century world). Victor destroys what he has begun, the monster discovers the breach of contract, utters his direst threat—"I shall be with you on your wedding-night"—and disappears.

The rest is a tale of flight and pursuit, punctuated by death and retribution, with everyone's hand turned against the wretched monster. This section contains much of Godwin's thinking, and of his novel, *Caleb Williams*, which, as its preface announced, was a review of "the modes of domestic and unrecorded despotism by which man becomes the destroyer of man."

The influence of Godwin and *Caleb Williams* is very strong. Frankenstein's friend, Clerval, is probably named after Mr. Clare, the one good man in *Caleb Williams*—as, in Mary Shelley's later novel, Lord Raymond is named after the Raymond, a kind of eighteenth-century Robin Hood, in her father's novel.

No celestial vengeance here. No devils, no retribution from God. Mankind is left alone, scheming to take over the vacant premises. Like *Caleb Williams*, *Frankenstein* becomes a story of implacable lay revenge, hatred, judicial blunder, pistols fired from open windows, a thwarted voyage of discovery, exhausting journeys without map or compass. There is nemesis but no promise of afterlife—unless it is the miserable hounded afterlife suffered by the monster.

Despite the powerful Godwin influence, Mary was her own woman. Her letters reveal an early preoccupation with politics.[36] They display, says her editor, an abiding belief in the freedom of the individual.

One enduring attraction of the book is its series of ambiguities, not all of which can have been the intention of an inexperienced novelist. We never see Frankenstein in his laboratory, throwing the fatal switch. That was the film. The book tells us only of the creature bending over his master. Again, in the pursuit, pursuer and pursued take turns. In particular, the language of the novel invites us to confuse the main roles. Perhaps we are meant to believe that the creature is Frankenstein's doppelganger, pursuing him to death. Which of them is "restored to animation"? "We . . . restored him to animation. . . . As soon as he showed signs of life we wrapped him up in blankets. I often feared that his suffering had deprived him of understanding . . . He is generally melancholy and despairing. . . ."

This is not the monster but Victor, before Victor tells his story to Walton. We have only his word for the story's accuracy, just as, finally, we have only the monster's promises, as he disappears into darkness and distance, that he will destroy himself. The outcome of all the trials (there are four in the book) are unreliable; are we then encouraged to trust our witnesses?

"I am the assassin of these most innocent creatures; they died by my machinations"; again not the monster but Victor is speaking of the deaths his creature caused. He seems unsure of the creature's actual physical existence (this uncertainty is here reinforced by his use of the term "assassin," which suggests hashish and an altered state of mind). There is a reason for the way the world has confused which is Frankenstein, which monster; the confusion seems to have been part of Mary's intention.

In 1831, a slightly revised edition of *Frankenstein* was published. The 1818 edition contains a Preface, the 1831 edition an Introduction. From these prefatory pieces, something of Mary's inspiration and intentions can be gathered.

In her Introduction to the 1831 edition Mary reveals that her story, like *The Castle of Otranto*, began with a dream, those signals from our inner selves. In her dream, she saw "the hideous phantasm of a man stretched out, and then, on the working of some powerful engine, show signs of life, and stir with an uneasy, half vital motion." It was science fiction itself that stirred.

The dream followed on late-night conversations with Shelley, Lord Byron, and John Polidori, Byron's doctor. Their talk was of vampires and the supernatural. Polidori supplied the company with some suitable reading material[37], Byron and Shelley also discussed Darwin, his thought and his experiments.[38] At Byron's suggestion, the four of them set about writing a ghost story apiece.

Mary's dream of a hideous phantasm stirring to life has the emotional coloration of a nightmare recorded in her journal a year earlier. In February 1815, she lost her first baby, born prematurely. On the fifteenth of March, she wrote: "Dream that my little baby came to life again; that it had only been cold, and that we rubbed it before the fire and it had lived."

From its very inception, the monster was a part of her.

In one of its aspects, *Frankenstein* is a diseased creation myth, prototype of many to come—an aspect we consider when we light upon *Dracula*.

Here we confront the more personal side of the novel. The struggle between Victor and his fiend is Oedipal in nature. Like Andre Gide's Oedipus, the fiend seems to himself to have "welled out of the unknown": "Who was I? What was I? Whence did I come?" it asks itself (Chapter XV). The muddying of generations and generation reflects the confusion Mary Shelley felt regarding her own involved family situation, surrounded by the half-sisters of both her mother's earlier and her father's later liaisons.

Some critics have read into the more macabre scenes of *Frankenstein* undertones of vampirism (a favorite with Lord Byron) and incest. "I shall be with you on your wedding night," cries the creature to Victor, who is in a sense its mother and father. Sexual tensions move throughout the book.

As she had to give birth alone, so—as she claims in her Introduction—Mary gave birth to her "hideous progeny" alone.

Through her own complexities Mary gained a deep understanding of Shelley, because their mutual passion was strong. One critic, Christopher Small, suggests that Frankenstein and Frankenstein's monster between them portray the two sides of the poet[39]—the side that was all sweetness and light, and the charnel side, the knowledgeable side and the irresponsible side.

The metaphorical quality of a good novel permits more than one interpretation. Small's interpretation does not rule out my own conviction that Mary's hurt and orphaned feelings are embodied in the unloved creature; it is because Mary felt herself monstrous that her monster has had such power for so long. Part of the continued appeal of her novel is the tragedy of the unwanted child.

The average first novel commonly relies for its material on personal experience. It is not to deny other interpretations to claim that Mary sees herself as the monster. As it does, she too tried to win her way into society. By running away with Shelley, she sought acceptance through love; but the move carried her further away from society; she became a wanderer, an exile, like Byron, like Shelley himself. Her mother's death in childbirth must have caused her to feel that she, like the monster, had been born from the dead. Behind the monster's eloquence lies Mary's grief.

But of course *mere* science fiction novels are not expected to contain autobiographical material!

In referring to *Frankenstein* as a diseased creation myth, I have in mind phrases in the novel with sexual connotations such as "my workshop of filthy creation," used by Frankenstein of his secret work. Mary's experience brought her to see life and death as closely intertwined. The phraseology employed to describe her dream, already quoted, is significant. She saw "the hideous phantasm of a man stretched out, and then, on the working of some powerful engine, show signs of life, and stir with an uneasy, half vital motion." The vigorous line suggests both a distorted image of her mother dying, in those final restless moments that often tantalizingly suggest recovery rather than its opposite, as well as the stirrings of sexual intercourse, particularly when we recall that "powerful engine" is a term serving in pornography as a synonym for penis.

Ellen Moers, writing on female gothic[40], disposes of the question of how a young girl like Mary could hit on such a horrifying idea (though the author was herself the first to raise it). Most female authors of the eighteenth and nineteenth centuries were spinsters and virgins, and in any case Victorian taboos operated against writing about childbirth. Mary experienced the fear, guilt, depression, and anxiety that often attend childbirth, particularly in situations such as hers, unwed, her consort a married man with children by another woman, and beset by debt in a foreign place. Only a woman, only Mary Shelley, could have written *Frankenstein*.

Great events were afoot between the publication of the first and second editions of *Frankenstein*. The first volume of Lyell's *Principles of Geology* had just appeared, drastically extending the age of the Earth. Mantell and others were grubbing gigantic fossil bones out of the ground, exhuming genera from the rocks as surely as Frankenstein's creature was patched together from various corpses. Already awakening was that great extension to our imaginative lives that we call the Age of Reptiles—those defunct monsters we have summoned back to vigorous existence.

The 1831 Introduction makes reference to galvanism and electricity. The preface to the first edition of 1818 is also instructive. Although

Mary had set herself to write a ghost story, according to Byron's decree, her intentions soon changed, she states expressly in the Preface, "I have not considered myself as merely weaving a series of supernatural terrors. "The Preface is an apologia, and Mary Shelley's chief witness for her defense, mentioned in her first sentence, is Erasmus Darwin.

Far from being supernatural in nature, the bestowal of new life to a corpse is to be regarded as "not of impossible occurrence."

The changes made to the novel between editions are also significant, and probably tell us something of Mary's sad emotional makeup. Different relationships are ascribed to Victor and his fiancée Elizabeth. In the first edition, Elizabeth is the daughter of his aunt. In the revision, she is brought into the family by adoption. In both versions, she is often referred to as "cousin." Mary's disastrous early years had bred confusion in her mind. The incestuous pattern of two children brought up under one roof almost as brother and sister and then falling in love recurs elsewhere.

In *The Last Man*, Mary's later scientific romance, it is Adrian and Evadne, both residing in Windsor. In a short story, "The Invisible Girl" (1833), it is Henry and Rosina: "They were playmates and companions in childhood, and lovers in after days."

Incest and necrophilia surface in the scene where Victor dismembers that hideous Eve, the female he is building for his macabre Adam. But incest was in fashion at the time, and not only as a reliable literary titillator: Byron and his dearest Augusta, his half-sister, provided living examples that must have interested Mary with her half-brothers and half-sisters in mind.

If Mary had read De Sade's novel *Justine*, as seems likely, she would find fathers raping and ruining their daughters[41], while in her husband's own verse-drama, *The Cenci*, the same theme holds court. Old Cenci rants over his daughter for all the world like one of the divine Marquis's heroes.

Algolagnia was certainly not absent from Mary's makeup. She wrote *Frankenstein* with her baby son William by her side; yet she makes the monster's first victim a little boy called William, Victor's younger brother. "I grasped his throat to silence him, and in a moment he lay dead at my feet. I gazed on my victim, and my heart swelled with exultation and hellish triumph." Which William was this, her father or her son? Her little William ("Willmouse") died in the summer of 1819.

Mary herself, in her Introduction to the 1831 edition, appears to invite a psychological interpretation of her story when she says "Invention . . . does not consist in creating out of a void, but out of chaos; the materials must, in the first place, be afforded: it can give form to dark, shapeless substances, but it cannot bring into being the substance itself."

This remark shows an acute understanding of literature, whatever else underlies it.

For every thousand people familiar with the tale of Frankenstein creating his monster from various cadaver spares and electrifying them into new life, only one will have read the novel. The cinema has helped enormously to disseminate the myth while destroying its significance.

Shortly after its original publication, *Frankenstein* was made into a play. Various versions were performed with great success until the 1930s. By that time, the cinema had moved in. There were short silent versions, but the monster began his true movie career in 1931, with James Whale's Universal picture *Frankenstein,* in which Boris Karloff played the monster. The dials in the castle laboratory have hardly stopped flickering since. The monster has spawned sons, daughters, ghosts, and houses; has taken on brides and created woman; has perforce shacked up with Dracula and Wolf Man; has enjoyed evil, horror, and revenge, and has even had the curse; on various occasions, it has met Abbott and Costello, the space monster, and the monster from Hell.

The Whale film borrowed much of its style from German Expressionism. The first Hammer Frankenstein, the 1957 *Curse of Frankenstein,* had sumptuous Victorian settings and a chilly Peter Cushing as Frankenstein. But all the films simplify. They allow only literal meanings.

They omit the social structure that greatly strengthens the novel, while giving it the leisurely pace movies must reject. In combining social criticism with new scientific ideas, Mary Shelley anticipates the methods of H. G. Wells—and of many who have followed in Wells's footsteps.

After *Frankenstein,* a pause. The idea of looking into the future was yet to be properly born in anything but a religious sense. Such writings about future developments as there were tended to be of a political or satirical nature, such as the anonymous pamphlet *One Thousand Eight Hundred and Twenty-Nine,* first published in 1819, which attacked the claims for Catholic emancipation and predicted the restoration of the Stuart kings in 1829.

An intuitive work, however, came from the poet who, next to P. B. Shelley, had been closest to Mary Shelley.

While *Frankenstein* was being written, Lord Byron was exiling himself from England forever. He took a house on the shores of Lake Geneva, the Villa Diodati (where John Milton had once stayed), during that cheerless summer of 1816. The Shelley entourage was nearby. It was then that Byron wrote his poem *Darkness*—the word again—a sort of grim evolutionary vision, the imagery of which, for our generation, carries promptings of nuclear winter. Like Mary's novel, *Darkness* too begins with a dream or at least a hypnoid fantasy.

> I had a dream which was not all a dream.
> The bright sun was extinguished, and the stars
> Did wander darkling in the eternal space
> Rayless, and pathless, and the icy earth
> Swung blind and blackening in the moonless air.

The Earth is in ruins, barbarism descends, whole populations starve. The last two men alive die of horror when they meet.[42]

The poem speaks of a deserted world, "treeless, manless, lifeless." That was the theme Mary Shelley was to explore in the best of her later novels, after both Byron and Shelley had died, one in Greece, one in Italy.

In Mary Shelley's lifetime, six of her novels and two travel journals were published. *The Last Man* (1826) appeared anonymously, as being "By the author of *Frankenstein.*" Like the earlier work, it carried on its title page a motto from *Paradise Lost,* this time the grim

> Let no man seek
> Henceforth to be foretold what shall befall
> Him or his children.

Novels at this period were not the major literary force they were later to become; the luminaries of the eighteen-forties were still below the horizon. It was a transitional period. For all its power, *The Last Man* strikes one as a rather transitional novel. Landscape forms a considerable part of it, used without the great allegorical power that landscape ("foreign parts") takes on in *Frankenstein*, reminding us how much prose fiction and travel literature, evolving together, are indebted to each other.[43] For all that, *The Last Man* can still hold our interest on more than literary-historical grounds.

It is the story of Lionel Verney, set towards the end of the twenty-first century. The king of England has abdicated, bowing to popular feeling. His son, Adrian, now known as the Earl of Windsor, befriends Verney and later becomes Lord Protector of England. Verney's father was a favourite of the king's but fell from favor, since then Verney has "wandered among the hills of civilised England as uncouth as a savage." He is converted to finer feelings by his friendship with Adrian.

Enter Lord Raymond, a youthful peer of genius and beauty. The date is A.D. 2073, but the Turks are still fording it over the Greeks; Raymond eventually becomes commander of the Greek army and besieges Constantinople.

This much, with many complications concerning the various sisters and mothers of the various parties, occupies the first third of the narrative. A modern reader hews his way through it by recalling that Mary was drawing portraits of people she knew, Shelley being Adrian, Byron Raymond, and Claire Clairmont Perdita, Verney's sister. Several of the infants are also identifiable. This cast is deployed in an England evolving peacefully from a monarchy into a republic—though all is swept away when plague arrives.

The *roman à clef* involvement is partly abandoned when Constantinople falls to its besiegers. They walk in unopposed, Raymond at their head. The defenders have died of plague: the city is empty.

With the introduction of the plague, the narrative gains pace, dire events and forebodings of worse flock one after the other.

What are we, the inhabitants of this globe, least among the many that people infinite space? Our minds embrace infinity; the visible mechanism of our being is subject to merest accident. (Volume 2, Chapter 5)

Raymond is killed by falling masonry, Perdita commits suicide by drowning. The plague spreads all over the world, so that "the vast cities of America, the fertile plains of Hindostan, the crowded abodes of the Chinese, are menaced with utter ruin."

Back in Windsor, Verney fears for his wife and children, although refugees from plague-stricken spots are allowed to find shelter within the castle walls; the parks are plowed up to provide food for everyone. Adrian is working for the general good in London, where plague has secured a footing. After helping him, Verney returns to Windsor, to find plague in the castle.

> Death, cruel and relentless, had entered these beloved walls . . . [Later] quiet prevailed in the Castle, whose inhabitants were hushed to repose. I was awake, and during the long hours of dead night, my busy thoughts worked in my brain like ten thousand mill-wheels, rapid, acute, untameable. All slept—all England slept; and from my window, commanding a wide prospect of the star-illumined country, I saw the land stretched out in placid rest. I was awake, alive, while the brother of death possessed my race. (Volume 2, Chapter 7)

Winter halts the advance of plague. Next summer brings renewed onslaughts, and England is invaded by hordes of Americans and Irish— an invasion force that Adrian quells with peaceful talk.

Adrian and Verney eventually lead the few English who survive from England to France. By then, one of Verney's sons is dead; his wife dies during a snowstorm.

Fifty survivors, their number dwindling, move southwards from Dijon. Mary Shelley leaves not a wither unwrung. "Images of destruction, pictures of despair, the procession of the last triumph of death, shall be drawn before thee," she warns her gentle reader.

Adrian and Verney, with two children, Clara and little Evelyn, reach Italy. Typhus claims Evelyn by Lake Como. The three survivors find nobody else alive. The country is desolate. They reach Venice, only to find it ruinous and slowly sinking under the lagoon.

Prompted by Adrian's wish to see Greece again, they set sail down the Adriatic. A storm rises, the boat sinks. They are plunged into the water—and eventually Verney flings himself ashore, alone. He is the last man alive.

Verney indulges in some bitter comparisons between his state and Robinson Crusoe's, after which he makes for the Eternal City (where

Shelley's ashes lie buried). Still he finds no living soul. In Rome, he gluts himself with Rome's treasures of the past, wandering in its art galleries and its libraries, until settling down to write his history. Our last glimpse of Verney is when he sets out with a dog for company to sail south through the Mediterranean, down the African coast, towards the odorous islands of the far Indian Ocean.

Surprisingly, the novel ends on a tranquil note. Instead of *Frankenstein's* final darkness and distance, distance here embraces the light, the glorious light of the south, the equator. The one survivor is another sort of Adam, more solitary than ever Frankenstein's creature was.

The name Verney is probably a tribute to Volney, the French count, Constantin Francois de Chasseboeuf, whose revolutionary book, *Les ruines, ou Méditations sur les révolutions des empires* (1791), describes the rise and fall of ancient civilizations and the prospects for a future in which tyranny will be abolished. Volney's book was known in English as *Ruins of Empires*. It is the book from which Frankenstein's creature learned "the science of letters."[44] It also formed the springboard for Shelley's ambitious poem, *Queen Mab*[45], in which Shelley (like Godwin before him) claims that

> Power, like a desolating pestilence
> Pollutes whate'er it touches

Volney may be responsible for that remarkable and contradictory preoccupation with ruins and ruin that haunts those who write of the future. Once Volney's philosophical superstructure is established, Mary Shelley's story takes on powerful suspense as we arrive at Constantinople. Some of the moralizing and rhapsodizing—Mary Shelley's prose has become fleshier since *Frankenstein*—may strike a modern reader as tedious, but there are moments of lurid truth, for instance in the dream in which Raymond's body becomes the pestilence itself.[46] Here to perfection is Burke's "delightful horror."

The gloom of *The Last Man* is also striking—and strikingly expressed. Here is Raymond speaking to Verney:

> You are of this world; I am not. You hold forth your hand; it is even as a part of yourself; and you do not yet divide the feeling of identity from the

mortal form that shapes forth Lionel. How then can you understand me? Earth is to me a tomb, the firmament a vault, shrouding mere corruption. Time is no more, for I have stepped within the threshold of eternity, each man I meet appears a corse, which will soon be deserted of its animating spark, on the eve of decay and corruption. (Volume 2, Chapter 2)

This obsession with corruption is alarming; the impulse behind *Frankenstein* has grown like a cancer, until revulsions that once applied to an exceptional case now condemn the whole human race. It is the race, rather than the individual, which is now hunted down to exile and extinction.

How are we to regard these two novels of Mary Shelley's? They are not merely subjective tales. *The Last Man is* not merely "a vast fantasy of entropy."[47] Nor can we pretend that it cannot be "placed in any existing category"[48], since many poems, tales, and paintings of the period devoted themselves to variations on the theme.[49] As has been pointed out elsewhere, *The Last Man* is in many of its aspects a transposition of reality, rather than fantasy.[50] Mary Shelley wrote of what was happening. Hers is a scientific romance.

Critics like chasing literary influences. Creative writers use the great world beyond books for their material. Entrenched behind this division, critics have hitherto failed to observe that a virtual plague was raging even as *The Last Man* was being written. When *Frankenstein* first appeared, in 1818 news was reaching England of a terrible epidemic in India. The inhabitants of Jessore, near Calcutta, had died or fled, spreading the contagion. In the spring of 1818, the epidemic broke forth again, more violently. Three years later, it crossed the Arabian Sea. The victims were so numerous their bodies were thrown into the waters. In Basra, 15,000 died in eighteen days. The disease was cholera—then regarded as untreatable.

By 1822 the infection had reached southern Russia. It had also spread eastward—Burma 1819—Siam 1820—then onwards, to the islands that now form Indonesia, as far as the Philippines. It slipped through the portals of China.

By 1830 the plague was in Moscow. It swept across Europe. The deaths became uncountable. The British watched uneasily as the plague approached their shores. Summer of 1831 was exceptionally fine and warm; then it was that cholera arrived in the North of England. Soon it infested London.

Almost as frightening as the pandemic itself was the civil disorder that accompanied its remorseless advance. Foreign doctors and the rich were often blamed. In Hungary, the homes of the nobility were stormed. Troops were called out in many cities.[51]

Mary Shelley, in *The Last Man*, was hardly doing more than issuing a symbolic representation, a psychic screening, of what was taking place in reality. In that, at least, she was setting an example to be followed by the swarming SF scribes of the twentieth century.

The last word on *Frankenstein* will never be said. It contains too many seemingly conflicting elements for that. A consideration of some of them concludes this chapter.

The outwardness of science and society is balanced in the novel by an inwardness that Mary's dream helped her to accommodate. This particular balance is perhaps one of *Frankenstein's* greatest merits: that its tale of exterior adventure and misfortune is accompanied by—encompassed by—psychological depth. Mary might have claimed for her drama what Shelley said in his Preface to *Prometheus Unbound*: "The imagery that I have employed will be found, in many instances, to have been drawn from the operations of the human mind, or from those external actions by which they are expressed."

Love, fear, the cruelty of parents and lovers—such familiar acquaintances are stirred up by the introduction of the central novelty.

Victor's lowly unique creature, outcast from human kind, takes a lofty view of itself and—in contrast with the almost dumb fiend to which the movies have accustomed us—is articulate regarding its sorrows.

Here we are given an educational prescription that looks both backward and forward—to a time when mankind does not judge merely by appearances.

Shelley read *Paradise Lost* aloud to Mary in 1816.

The monster likens himself to Adam in the poem—but how much less fortunate than Adam, for in this case the creator rushes away from "his odious handywork, horror-stricken." The creature's career has something in common with Adam's, with the vital exception of the missing Eve. He is first created, and then brought to full intellectual awareness of the world in which he lives—at which stage, "benevolence and generosity were ever present before me" (Chapter XV). He then undergoes his version of the Fall, when "the spirit of revenge enkindled in my heart" (Chapter XVI). Now the creature is frequently referred to as "the fiend." In many ways, it becomes less human, more a symbol of inhumanity. "I saw him," says Frankenstein, "descend the mountain with greater speed than the flight of an eagle, and quickly lost him among the undulations of the sea of ice" (Chapter XVII).

The fiend increasingly speaks of itself in Miltonic terms, saying of itself at last, over Victor's corpse, "the fallen angel becomes a malignant devil."

This change in the nature of the monster enables Mary Shelley to bring out two aspects of the struggle that are subordinate to the eschatological theme.

The first aspect is man's confrontation with himself, which the power of creation necessarily entails. The diseased creation myth prefigures Jekyll and Hyde, as Frankenstein struggles with his alter ego; their obsessive pursuit of one another makes sense only in metaphysical terms.

The second aspect is the disintegration of society that follows man's abrogation of power. One perversion of the natural order leads to another. *Frankenstein* is loaded with a sense of corruption, and "the fiend" moves about the world striking where it will, like a disease that, beginning naturally enough in a charnel house, can be isolated and sterilized only on a drifting ice floe.

The rejection of a just Heavenly Father, the concern with suffering, and the sexual obsessions have helped preserve *Frankenstein's* topicality. Not only does it foreshadow our fears about the two-edged triumphs of scientific progress; it is also the first novel to be powered by the evolutionary idea. God, however often called upon, is an absentee landlord. The lodgers have to fight things out between themselves.

Herein lies the force of the novel's subtitle. In Shelley's lyrical drama, *Prometheus Unbound*, mighty Jupiter has chained Prometheus to a rock. Prometheus suffers terrible torture, but is eventually freed when Jupiter is dethroned, to retire into obscurity.

What is mankind to seek, if not God? Answers to this modern conundrum include objectives like knowledge, power, and self-fulfillment. According to one's reading of the novel, Victor Frankenstein can be understood to seek all three.

The use of this modernized Faust theme is particularly suited to the first real novel of science fiction: Frankenstein's is *the* modern predicament, involving the post-Rousseauvian dichotomy between the individual and his society, as well as the encroachment of science on that society, and mankind's dual nature, whose inherited ape curiosity has brought him both success and misery. His great discovery apart, Frankenstein is an over-reacher and victim, staggering through a world where virtues are few (though the fiend *reads* of them). Instead of hope and forgiveness, there remain only the misunderstandings of men and the noxious half life of the monster. Knowledge brings no guarantee of happiness. For this critic's taste, the Frankenstein theme is more contemporary and more interesting than interstellar travel tales, since it takes us nearer to the enigma of man and thus of life; just as interstellar travel can yield more interest than such fantasy themes as telepathy.

Since the publication of *Billion Year Spree*, many scholars have been at work on *Frankenstein* from within and without the science fiction field. One of the most creative and ingenious is David Ketterer[52], though he seeks to deny that the novel is science fiction at all, on the grounds that it is much else beside. But so indeed is all good SF, which can live only on its appetite. Ketterer also implies that *Frankenstein* cannot be SF since SF was not a category in 1816. Nor, in 1816, did the word scientist exist: yet the world has adopted Frankenstein as the model of the irresponsible scientist.

Despite this, Ketterer's arguments regarding this extraordinary novel and the centrality of the quest for knowledge ("knowledge is what *Frankenstein* is all about") are stimulating and thought provoking. *Frankenstein* is also "all about" a parent/child relationship.

It is appropriate that "darkness and distance" should be the closing words of *Frankenstein* just as "darkness" is almost its first word, presented on the title page within the quotation from *Paradise Lost.* SF is often haunted by that same sense of corruption and loss.

Notes

1. H. G. Wells, Preface to *The Scientific Romances*, 1933.

2. Eric S. Rabkin, *Fantastic Worlds: Myths, Tales, and Stories*, 1979. Rabkin attempts to establish a continuum of the Fantastic, from realistic narratives that are minimally fantastic to thorough-going fantasies that are minimally realistic. Where this laudable scheme comes to grief, it seems, is in the elusiveness of the labels, rather than in the rigidity of Rabkin's structure.

3. Alex Eisenstein puts forward the story of Daedalus and Icarus, who flew too near the sun on homemade wings and perished as an early SF story. The sense in which Eisenstein is correct is immediately obvious. Here is hubris clobbered by nemesis. Nevertheless the story of Icarus is a legend and SF is not legend, however much it may aspire to that condition. SF consists of texts, those totems of a literate age. Icarus has no written text. Even today, his story is handed on semi-verbally, or through artistic interpretation. It is this, more than the impossibility of a man flying with artificial wings, I believe, which distinguishes the two cases.

4. Sequestered parts of the globe evidently include New York. There in December 1979, some years after the first publication of *Billion Year Spree*, Lester del Rey published *The World of Science Fiction 1926–1976*. Del Rey believes that SF is "precisely as old as the first recorded fiction. This is the *Epic of Gilgamesh*."

5. Darko Suvin, *Od Lukijana do Lunika*, Zagreb, 1965.

6. For instance, Roger Lancelyn Green, *Into Other Worlds*, 1957, and del Rey, *op. cit.*

7. Marjorie Hope Nicolson, *Voyages to the Moon*, New York, 1949.

8. *The Essential Writings of Erasmus Darwin*, chosen and edited with linking commentary by Desmond King-Hele, 1968. References to Darwin in relation to the exploration of the South Seas are contained in Bernard Smith, *European Vision and the South Pacific 1768–1850*, 1960.

9. Benedict Nicolson, *Joseph Wright of Derby: Painter of Light*, 1968. The Derby Art Gallery also produces an illustrated booklet, *Joseph Wright of Derby*, 1979.

10. See Desmond King-Hele, *Erasmus Darwin*, 1963; Donald M. Hassler, *Erasmus Darwin*, 1973; and Desmond King-Hele, *Doctor of Revolution*, 1977.

11. *Doctor of Revolution, op. cit.*, p. 215.

12. Alethea Hayter, *Opium and the Romantic Imagination*, 1968. "The whole Gothic Revival in English literature was in fact launched by a dream." Hayter goes on to illustrate a "general preoccupation with dreams in early nineteenth-century literature."

13. Horace Walpole, letter to the Reverend William Cole, Strawberry Hill, March 9, 1765. Explaining to Cole how he came to write *The Castle of Otranto*, he says, "Shall I even confess to you, what was the origin of this romance! I waked one morning, in the beginning of last June, from a dream, of which, all I could recover was, that I had thought myself in an ancient castle (a very natural dream for a head filled like mine with Gothic story), and that on the uppermost banister of a great staircase I saw a gigantic hand in armor. In the evening I sat down, and began to write, without knowing in the least what I intended to say or relate . . ."

14. Piranesi engraved his *Carceri* in Rome in 1745, heralding the whole Romantic movement or certainly its gloomier side. For the lighter side, one would have to turn to the etchings of another Italian, the Venetian G. B. Tiepolo, whose *Capricci* appeared at almost the same time as Prianesi's *Carceri*. In these pictures, mysterious figures talk or wait among mysterious ruins; in a later series, the *Scherzi di Fantasia*, the beautiful people are surrounded by magic and death, although they are still bathed in Tiepolo's glorious light.

15. For further details, consult, for instance, Margaret Dalziel, *Popular Fiction 100 Years Ago*, 1957.

16. Peacock's best novels remain very readable. *Gryll Grange*, published when the author was seventy-five, is a satire on progress in Victorian days, with the Reverend Dr. Opimian representing a churlish anti-scientific viewpoint sounding less strange in our time than it must have done in the 1860s: "The day would fail, if I should attempt to enumerate the evils that science has inflicted on makind. I almost think it is the ultimate destiny of science to exterminate the human race" (Chapter 19).

17. A fine example is Ursula Le Guin, *The Left Hand of Darkness*, 1969. The town of Suzlik, in David Brin, *The Practice Effect*, 1984, is a more recent example.

18. H. Beam Piper, "Temple Trouble," 1951.

19. H. B. Fyfe, "Protected Species," 1951.

20. A. E. van Vogt, "Asylum," 1942.

21. F. L. Wallace, "Big Ancestor," 1954.

22. Some while before Ward Moore's novel appeared, a volume was published called *If It Had Happened Otherwise*, edited by J. C. Squire, 1931 (published in the USA as *If: or History Rewritten*), which is full of alternative universes dreamed up by scholars and historians. One of the most interesting is Winston Churchill's "If Lee Had Not Won the Battle of Gettysburg."

23. Shelley, *Hymn to Intellectual Beauty*, Stanza 5.

24. A question in nomenclature arises with Mary Shelley, as with Erasmus Darwin. Since Charles Darwin has pre-empted the cognomen Darwin, his

grandfather is here Erasmus. Similarly, as P. B. Shelley has pre-empted Shelley, his second wife is here Mary.

25. Edward John Trellawny, *Recollections of the Last Days of Shelley and Byron*, 1858.

26. Samuel H. Vasbinder, *Scientific Attitudes in Mary Shelley's Frankenstein*, Ann Arbor, 1984.

27. The best biography is Jane Dunn, *Moon in Eclipse: A Life of Mary Shelley*, 1978. Other biographies include R. Glynn Grylls, *Mary Shelley: A Biography*, 1938; Eileen Bigland, *Mary Shelley*, 1959; and William A. Walling, *Mary Shelley*, New York, 1972.

28. Mary Shelley also contributed lives of "Eminent Literary and Scientific Men of Italy, Spain, and Portugal" and of "Eminent Literary and Scientific Men in France" to *The Cabinet Cyclopaedia* for 1835 and 1838 respectively.

29. Edited by Elizabeth Nitchie in *Studies in Philology*, Extra Series, no. 3, Chapel Hill, N.C., 1959.

30. Jane Dunn, *op. cit.*

31. "The Transformation" was published in one of the Keepsakes beloved by the early Victorians. It is collected with other pieces in *Tales and Stories by Mary Wollstonecraft Shelley*, edited by Richard Garnett, 1891.

32. Letter to Leigh Hunt, Spetember 9 1823, in Betty T. Bennett (ed). *The Letters of Mary Wollstonecraft Shelley*, Vol. I, Baltimore, 1980. The play was entitled *Presumption*, and opened on July 28. On August 18, another adaptation, entitled *Frankenstein: or, The Demon of Switzerland*, opened at another theatre.

33. How was it that Mary Shelley was astute enough to set her story on the Continent, and to have Victor go to the University of Ingolstadt, rather than setting it in the England she knew, and having Victor go to the University of Oxford (visited in Chapter XIX of the novel)? Could it be that there was a political attraction as well as a scenic one? Switzerland was newly formed and named only the year before the Shelleys visited it, following the Congress of Vienna. One historian (C. D. M. Ketelby: *A History of Modern Times from 1789*) speaks of a possible leader for the new entity, formed from the old Helvetic Republic, who "might be capable of welding into a whole the discordant parts". Here is a territorial and political analogy for the monster—sexually neutral, as Switzerland was designed to be constitutionally neutral.

34. Samuel Holmes Vasbinder, *op. cit.* The volume is also valuable for a summary of the conclusions of previous critics.

35. Description taken from Sir David Brewster, *Letters on Natural Magic, Addressed to Sir Walter Scott*, 1832.

36. *The Letters of Mary Wollstonecraft Shelley*, Vol. I, *op. cit.*

37. It would be interesting to see if Polidori supplied a copy of de Sade's Gothic fantasy *Justine*, published in 1791. There is a Justine in *Frankenstein*, wrongfully imprisoned, and "gazed on and execrated by thousands"—a very de Sade-like situation; though innocent, she perishes on the scaffold. Mario Praz indicates this parallel in *The Romantic Agony*, 1933. Curiously enough, de Sade's Justine perishes by lightning, the force that brings life to Frankenstein's creation in the James Whale film.

38. There is some discussion of this point by M. K. Joseph, in his edition of *Frankenstein*, published in the Oxford English Novels series, 1969. See also Maurice Hinde's long introduction to his edition of *Frankenstein*, 1985.

39. Christopher Small, *Ariel Like a Harpy: Shelley, Mary, and "Franken-stein"*, 1972.

40. Ellen Moers, "Female Gothic: The Monster's Mother," *The New York Review*, 21 March 1974, reprinted in *Literary Women*, 1976, and as "Female Gothic" in the excellent collection of essays, *The Endurance of Frankenstein*, edited by George Levine and V. C. Knoepflmacher, Los Angeles, 1979.

41. While in *Juliette*, Saint-Fond cries, *"Quelle jouissance! J'étais couvert de maledictions, d'imprécations, je parricidais, j'incestais, j'assassinais, je prostituais, je sodomisais!"*

42. The link between the "lost" summer of 1816 and Byron's poem is discussed in Antony Rudolf's pamphlet *Byron's Darkness: Lost Summer and Nuclear Winter*, Menard Press, 1984.

43. See Percy G. Adams, *Travel Literature and the Evolution of the Novel*, Lexington, Kentucky, 1983.

44. "The book from which Felix instructed Safie was Volney's *Ruins of Empires* . . . Through this work I obtained a cursory knowledge of history and a view of the several empires at present existing in the world; it gave me an insight into the manners, governments, and religions of the different nations of the earth . . . I heard of the discovery of the American hemisphere and wept with Safie over the hapless fate of its original inhabitants." The creature speaks. *Frankenstein*, Chapter XIII.

45. See for instance A. M. D. Hughes, *The Nascent Mind of Shelley*, Oxford, 1947.

46. This prodromic nightmare—presenting familiar objects out of context—is surrealist. Verney has found the beloved Lord Raymond dead in the ruins of plague-stricken Constantinople, and falls asleep: "I awoke from disturbed dreams. Methought I had been invited to Timon's last feast: I came with keen appetite, the covers were removed, hot water sent up its satisfying streams, while I fled before the anger of the host, who assumed the form of Raymond; while to my diseased fancy, the vessels hurled by him after me were surcharged

with a fetid vapour, and my friend's shape, altered by a thousand distortions, expanded into a gigantic phantom, bearing on its brow the sign of pestilence. The growing shadow rose and rose, filling and then seeming to endeavour to burst beyond the adamantine vault that bent over, sustaining and enclosing the world. The nightmare became torture; with a strong effort I threw off sleep, and recalled reason to her wonted functions" (*The Last Man*, Volume 2, Chapter 3).

Mary Shelley uses the same device just before Victor Frankenstein wakes to find his "miserable monster" has come to life. There again, the dream is of someone loved (in this case, his fiancée) transformed into a symbol of horror and disgust: "I slept, indeed, but I was disturbed by the wildest dreams. I thought I saw Elizabeth, in the bloom of health, walking in the streets of Ingolstadt. Delighted and surprised, I embraced her; but as I imprinted the first kiss on her lips, they became livid with the hue of death; her features appeared to change, and I thought that I held the corpse of my dead mother in my arms; a shroud enveloped her form, and I saw the grave-worms crawling in the folds of the flannel. I started from my sleep with horror; a cold dew covered my forehead, my teeth chattered, and every limb became convulsed" (*Frankenstein*, Chapter V). David Ketterer uses this passage to emphasize necrophile and incest themes in the novel.

47. Rosemary Jackson, *Fantasy: The Literature of Subversion*, New York, 1981.

48. Muriel Spark, *Child of Light*, 1951.

49. Examples are Byron's poem, *Darkness*, already mentioned; Thomas Campbell's poem, *The Last Man*; Jean-Baptiste Cousin de Grainville's *Le Dernier Homme* (1805); and John Martin's paintings *The Last Man* (watercolour, c. 1832; oil, 1849). The popularity of these works was international. For details of Byron's poem being translated into Russian, see Antony Rudolf, *op. cit.*

50. Introduction to *The Last Man*, by Brian Aldiss, 1985.

51. Norman Longmate, *King Cholera*, 1966.

52. David Ketterer, *Frankenstein's Creation: The Book, The Monster and Human Reality*, Victoria, Canada, 1979.

~

CHAPTER THIRTEEN

The Roots of Science Fiction

Robert Scholes

All fiction—every book even, fiction or not—takes us out of the world we normally inhabit. To enter a book is to live in another place. Out of the nature of this otherness and its relation to our life experiences come all our theories of interpretation and all our criteria of value. Previously, I argued the case for a particular relation between fiction and experience, expressed in temporal terms as "future-fiction." The polemical nature of my situation as advocate for a popular but critically deprecated form of fiction led me inevitably to make a case which is in certain respects too narrow for its subject. The laws of rhetoric force all radical advocates to choose between betraying their causes by an excess of conciliation or of hostility, and I understand those laws only too well. In compensation, I wish to be more tentative and speculative now, in describing the parameters of a fictional form that is both old and new, rooted in the past but distinctly modern, oriented to the future but not bounded by it.

It is customary in our empirically based Anglo-Saxon criticism to distinguish between two great schools of fiction according to the relationship between the fictional worlds they present and the world of human experience. Thus we have, since the eighteenth century, spoken of novels and romances, of realism and fantasy, and we have found the distinction useful enough at times, even though, because of our empirical bias, we have tended to value realism more highly than romance. It will be appropriate, then, at least as a beginning, to see the tradition that leads to modern science fiction as a special case of romance, for this tradition always insists upon a radical discontinuity between its world and the world of ordinary human experience. In its simplest and most ancient form this discontinuity is objectified as another world, a different place—Heaven, Hell, Eden, Fairyland, Utopia, the Moon, Atlantis, Lilliput. This radical dislocation between the world of romance and the world of experience has been exploited in different ways. One way, the most obvious, has been to suspend the laws of nature in order to give more power to the laws of narrative, which are themselves projections of the human psyche in the form of enacted wishes and fears. These pure enactments are at the root of all narrative structures, and are themselves the defining characteristics of all narrative forms, whether found in "realistic" or "fantastic" matrices. In the sublimative narratives of pure romance they are merely more obvious than elsewhere because less disguised by other interests and qualities. But there is another way to exploit the radical discontinuity between the world of romance and that of experience, and this way emphasizes cognition. The difference can be used to get more vigorous purchase on certain aspects of that very reality which has been set aside in order to generate a romantic cosmos. When romance returns deliberately to confront reality it produces the various forms of didactic romance or fabulation that we usually call allegory, satire, fable, parable, and so on—to indicate our recognition that reality is being addressed indirectly through a patently fictional device.

Fabulation, then, is fiction that offers us a world clearly and radically discontinuous from the one we know, yet returns to confront that known world in some cognitive way. Traditionally, it has been a favorite vehicle for religious thinkers, precisely because religions have insisted that there is more to the world than meets the eye, that the common-sense view of reality—"realism"—is incomplete and therefore false. Science, of course, has been telling us much the same thing for several hundred years. The world we see and hear and feel—"reality" itself—is a fiction of our senses, and dependent on their focal ability, as the simplest microscope will easily demonstrate. Thus it is not surprising that what we call "science" fiction should employ the same narrative vehicle as the religious fictions of our past. In a sense, they are fellow travelers. But there are also great differences between these kinds, of fiction, which must be investigated.

There are two varieties of fabulation or didactic romance, which corresponds roughly to the distinction between romances of religion and romances of science. We may call these two forms "dogmatic" and "speculative" fabulation, respectively. This distinction is neither complete nor invidious. It represents a tendency rather than delineating a type, but most didactic romances are clearly dominated by one tendency or the other. Even within the Christian tradition, we can recognize Dante's *Commedia* as a dogmatic fabulation and More's *Utopia* as a speculative one. Dante's work is greater by most accepted standards of comparison. But it works out of a closed, anti-speculative system of belief. A *Utopia* admits in its title that it is nowhere. A *Commedia*, human or divine, on the other hand, must fill the known cosmos. As opposed to dogmatic narrative, speculative fabulation is a creature of humanism, associated from its origins with attitudes and values that have shaped the growth of science itself. Swift detested the science of his time, which drove him to dogmatic posturing in Book III of *Gulliver*. But surely without the microscope and telescope Books I and II could not have been as they are. And Book IV is a speculation beyond all dogma. Since Dante, dogmatic fabulation has declined, though it always lurks in the worlds of satire. Since More, speculative fabulation has grown and developed. Born of humanism it has been fostered by science. But it has never flourished as it does at present—for reasons that it is now our business to explore.

As Claudio Guillen has taught us, literature may be usefully seen as aspiring toward system—as a collection of entities constantly rearranging themselves in search of an equilibrium never achieved. In the course of this process certain generic forms crystallize and persist or fade from existence, and among these forms some come into dominance at particular moments of history, only to yield their dominant position with the passage of time. In every age, as the Russian Formalists were fond of observing, certain generic forms are regarded as "canonical"— the accepted forms for the production of serious literature—and other forms are considered outside the pale, being either too esoteric ("coterie literature") or too humble ("popular literature"). But with the passage of time canonical forms become rigid, heavy, mannered, and lose their vital power. Even the dominant forms eventually give up their privileged position and move toward the edges of the literary canon. The reasons for this may be seen in purely formal terms—as the exhaustion of the expressive resources of the genre. Or they may be seen in broader cultural terms—as responses to social or conceptual developments outside the literary system itself. To my way of thinking, since fiction is a cognitive art it cannot be considered adequately in purely formal terms. Formal changes, to be understood, must be seen in the light of other changes in the human situation.

I propose, then, to examine a small—but important —part of the system of literature: the interaction of certain forms of fictional representation over a period of a few centuries, ending with the present time. And I further propose to see this interaction as an aspect of a larger movement of mind. My treatment will be extremely brief; the model I generate will be very sketchy. But in matters of this kind true persuasion is not to be achieved by the amassing of argumentative detail. I ask you simply to consider the fictional universe from the perspective of this model and then see if your old perspective can ever be comfortably assumed again. I will begin by raising a question seldom considered—perhaps because it is too large to admit of an answer. The question is, simply, "What makes a form dominant?" Admitting the phenomenon of dominance, why, for instance, should drama dominate the western countries of Europe for a hundred years from the late sixteenth through the seventeenth century? In general terms it has been argued, and I think convincingly, that drama was ideally suited to an era in which monolithic feudalism had lost its power over individual existence but bourgeois democracy had not yet come into being as a regulator of the power vacuum left behind by the crumbling feudal system. An age of princes (in the Machiavellian sense) made heroic drama conceivable as neither an earlier age of kings nor a later age of ministers ever could. The dramatic disposition of the age, with its incredible reversals of fortune, as seen, for instance, in the life of an Essex or a Ralegh, enabled a specific literary form to realize its maximum potential.

In the case of the novel, we find a form that came into dominance for parallel cultural reasons. The rise of the middle class did not "cause" the rise of the novel, but new concepts of the human situation enabled both of these phenomena to take place. In particular, a new grasp of history, as a process with its own dynamics resulting from the interaction of social and economic forces, generated a new concept of man as a creature struggling against these impersonal entities. And this struggle could hardly be represented on the stage in the same way as man's struggle with fortune or his own ambitious desires. It is not that plays dealing with socio-economic man could not be written. Writers from Steele to Ibsen struggled manfully to generate a rich social canvas on stage. But what the novel achieved easily and naturally, the drama could do only with great pains and clumsy inadequacy. The novel naturally came to be the literary form in which an age conscious of history as a shaping force could express itself most satisfyingly. The novel was the diachronic form of a diachronic age. In each volume of the great nineteenth-century realists we find the history of an individual against a background of the forces shaping his moment of history. And in the sequences of novels produced by writers like Balzac and Zola we can see whole eras taking human shape, becoming protagonists struggling in the grip of the large designs of History itself. For this, of course, was the age in which History acquired a capital H, becoming a substitute for God, with a Grand Purpose in Mind, which His angel the Time-Spirit sought to effect.

Let us narrow the focus, now, to the narrative forms of representation only, for dominance can be considered not only among the great generic kinds, and even among whole arts, but also within the boundaries of a single kind of literature. In the novel itself we can trace the rise and fall from dominance of sentimental fiction in the eighteenth century, of a more sociological and historical fiction in the nineteenth, and finally a more inward and psychological fiction in the early twentieth century. All of these forms have gone under the name of realism, and as an evolving tradition this realism preserved a dominant place among the forms of fiction from the time of Defoe and Marivaux until well into the present century. Other fictional forms have coexisted with the dominant realism—such as the gothic, which first emerged in the late eighteenth century to fill an emotive gap opened in the system by the move of social and sentimental forms away from situations of heroic intensity. And after Swift a speculative fabulation with satirical tendencies was kept alive by writers like Johnson in *Rasselas* and Carlyle in *Sartor Resartus*. But it is fair to say that this tradition lacked vigor and continuity—lacked generic certainty—until new conceptual developments put fictional speculation on an entirely different footing, changing the fabric of man's vision in ways that inevitably led to changes in his fiction.

This revolution in man's conception of himself was begun by Darwin's theory of evolution. It was continued by Einstein's theory of relativity. And it has been extended by developments in the study of human systems of perception, organization, and communication that range from the linguistic philosophy of Wittgenstein and the gestalt psychology of Kohler to the structural anthropology of Levi-Strauss and the cybernetics of Wiener. This century of cosmic rearrangement, crudely indicated here by this list of names and concepts, has led to new ways of understanding human time and space-time, as well as to a new sense of the relationship between human systems and the larger systems of the cosmos. In its broadest sense, this revolution, has replaced Historical Man with Structural Man.

Let us explore this great mental shift a bit. Darwin, and those who have continued his work, put human history in a frame of reference much grander than that of Historical Man. This stretched man's entire sense of time into a new shape and finally altered his familiar position in the cosmos. Early reactions to the evolutionary theory often tried to accommodate Darwinian evolutionary theory within the familiar dimensions of historical time, suggesting that some Superman lurked just around the evolutionary corner—in much the same way that people once believed the apocalypse to be scheduled for the very near future. But by expanding our sense of time the Darwinians reduced history to a moment and man to a bit player in a great unfinished narrative. The possibility of further evolution, with species more advanced than ourselves coming into being on this earth, displaced man from the final point of traditional cosmic teleology as effectively as Galileo had displaced man's planet from the center of the spatial cosmos. Thus Darwinian time, which has been continually extended with the discovery of new geological and archeological evidence, has had a profound effect on man's sense of himself and his possibilities. Historical time, then, is only a tiny fragment of human time, which is again a tiny fragment of geologic time, which is itself only a bit of cosmic time.

The theories of relativity have worked in a similar fashion to shake man out of his humanist perspective. By demonstrating that space and time are in a more intimate perspectival relation than we had known, Einstein too called history into question. When we think in terms of the cosmic distances and absolute velocities of the Einsteinian universe, not only do we lose our grasp on fundamental human concepts like "simultaneity" and "identity," we lose also our confidence in that common-sense apprehension of the world which replaced man's mythic consciousness as the novel replaced the epic in the hierarchy of narrative forms. And on the smaller scale of purely human studies in anthropology, psychology, and linguistics, ideas no less earthshaking have been developed. What does it do to our time sense to think of stone-age men living their timeless lives in the year 1974 in some remote jungle on our earth? And what does it do to our confidence in human progress when we see that though they lack all the things that our science and technology have given us, they live in a harmony with the cosmos that shames us, and know instinctively, it seems, lessons that we are painfully relearning by having to face the consequences of our ecological wantonness? At every turn we run into patterns of shaping forces that have gone unobserved by our instrumental approach to the world. We learn that men's visual perceptions are governed by mental leaps to whole configurations or "gestalts" rather than by patient accumulation of phenomenal details. We learn that we acquire language in similar quantum jumps of grammatical competence. And we know that our acquired languages in turn govern and shape our perceptions of this world. Finally, we have begun to perceive that our social systems and our linguistic systems share certain similarities of pattern, that even our most intimate forms of behavior are ordered by behavioral configurations beyond our perception and controlled through biological feedback systems that may be altered by the input of various drugs, hormones, and other biochemical messages.

In short, we are now so aware of the way that our lives are part of a patterned universe that we are free to speculate as never before. Where anything may be true—sometime, someplace—there can be no heresy. And where the patterns of the cosmos itself guide our thoughts so powerfully, so beautifully, we have nothing to fear but our own lack of courage. There are fields of force around us that even our finest instruments of thought and perception are only beginning to detect. The job of fiction is to play in these fields. And in the past few decades fiction has begun to do just this, to dream new dreams, confident that there is no gate of ivory, only a gate of horn, and that all dreams are true. It is fiction—verbal narrative— that must take the lead in such dreaming, because even the new representational media that have been spawned in this age cannot begin to match the speculative agility and imaginative freedom of words. The camera can capture only what is found in front of it or made for it, but language is as swift as thought itself and can reach beyond what is, or seems, to what may or may not be, with the speed of a synapse. Until the mind can speak in its own tongueless images, the word will be its fleetest and most delicate instrument of communication. It is not strange, then, that the modern revolution in human thought should find expression in a transformation of a form of fictional speculation that has been available for centuries. It took only a quantum jump in fictional evolution for speculative fabulation to become structural, and the mutation took place sometime early in this century.

What, then, is structural fabulation? I shall begin to explore specific instances of this modern fictional form in my next lecture, but here it will be appropriate to sketch the parameters of the form in a general way, as a preparation for that discussion. Considered generically, structural fabulation is simply a new mutation in the tradition of speculative fiction. It is the tradition of More, Bacon, and Swift, as modified by new input from the physical and human sciences. Considered as an aspect of the whole system of contemporary fiction, it has grown in proportion to the decline of other fictional forms. For instance, to the extent that the dominant realistic novel has abandoned the pleasures of narrative movement for the cares of psychological and social analysis, a gap in the system has developed which a number of lesser forms have sought to fill. All the forms of adventure fiction, from western, to detective, to spy, to costume—have come into being in response to the movement of "serious" fiction away from plot and the pleasures of fictional sublimation. Because many human beings experience a psychological need for narration—whether cultural or biological in origin— the literary system must include works which answer to that need. But when the dominant canonical form fails to satisfy such a basic drive, the system becomes unbalanced. The result is that readers resort secretly and guiltily to lesser forms for that narrative fix they cannot do without. And many feel nearly as guilty about it as we could hope to make any habitual offender against our official mores. The spectacle (reported by George Moore, as I recollect) of W. B. Yeats explaining with great embarrassment why he happened to be reading a detective story can stand as a paradigm of the guilt felt by intellectuals whose emotional needs drive them to lesser literary forms for pleasure. We do call people "addicts" if they seem inordinately fond of detective stories, or even of science fiction. But the metaphor of addiction is a dangerously misleading one. For this is emotional food, not a mind-bending narcotic, that we are considering.

Thus the vacuum left by the movement of "serious" fiction away from storytelling has been filled by "popular" forms with few pretensions to any virtues beyond those of narrative excitement. But the very emptiness of these forms, as they are usually managed, has left another gap, for forms which supply readers' needs for narration without starving their needs for intellection. The "letdown" experienced after finishing many detective stories or adventure tales comes from a sense of time wasted—time in which we have deliberately suspended not merely our sense of disbelief but also far too many of our normal cognitive processes. And this letdown grows to a genuine and appropriate feeling of guilt to the extent that we *do* become addicted and indulge in the reading of such stories beyond our normal need for diversion and sublimation. Even food should not be taken in abnormal quantities, especially if much of it is empty calories. We require a fiction that satisfies our cognitive and sublimative needs together, just as we want food that tastes good and provides some nourishment. We need suspense with intellectual consequences, in which questions are raised as well as solved, and in which our minds are expanded even while focused on the complications of a fictional plot.

These may be described as our general requirements—needs which have existed as long as man has been sufficiently civilized to respond to a form that combines sublimation and cognition. But we also have to consider here the special requirements of our own age—our need for fictions which provide a sublimation relevant to the specific conditions of being in which we find ourselves. The most satisfying fictional response to these needs takes the form of what may be called structural fabulation. In works of structural fabulation the tradition of speculative fiction is modified by an awareness of the nature of the universe as a system of systems, a structure of structures, and the insights of the past century of science are accepted as fictional points of departure. Yet structural fabulation is neither scientific in its methods nor a substitute for actual science. It is a fictional exploration of human situations made perceptible by the implications of recent science. Its favorite themes involve the impact of developments or revelations derived from the human or the physical sciences upon the people who must live with those revelations or developments.

In the previous era, historicist views of human culture led to a vision of man's future as guided by some plan beyond human comprehension, perhaps, in its totality, but solicitous of man and amenable to human cooperation. Thus great fictional narratives could be couched in terms of individual men and women seeking to align themselves with or struggle against the social forces through which history was working its will to achieve its idea. But now structuralism dominates our thought, with its view of human existence as a random happening in a world which is orderly in its laws but without plan or purpose. Thus man must learn to live within laws that have given him his being but offer him no purpose and promise him no triumph as a species. Man must make his own values, fitting his hopes and fears to a universe which has allowed him a place in its systematic working, but which cares only for the system itself and not for him. Man must create his future himself. History will not do it for him. And the steps he has already taken to modify the biosphere can be seen as limiting the future options of the human race. It is in this atmosphere that structural fabulation draws its breath, responding to these conditions of being, in the form of extrapolative narrative. The extrapolations may be bold and philosophical or cautious and sociological, but they must depart from what we know and consider what we have due cause to hope and fear. Like all speculative fabulations they will take their origin in some projected dislocation of our known existence, but their projections will be based on a contemporary apprehension of the biosphere as an ecosystem and the universe as a cosmosystem.

Obviously, not all works that are called "science fiction" meet this kind of standard. Many writers are so deficient in their understanding of the cosmic structure itself that they have no sense of the difference between purposeful discontinuity and a magical relaxation of the cosmic structure. And many others seek to present traditional romance as if it had some structural or speculative significance. But, if a writer fails to understand the discontinuity on which his work is based *as* a discontinuity *from* a contemporary view of what is true or natural, he is powerless to make that discontinuity function structurally for us. Thus any cognitive thrust in his work will be accidental and intermittent. And if a writer transports men to Mars merely to tell a cowboy story, he produces not structural fabulation but star dreck—harmless, perhaps, but an abuse of that economy of means that governs mature esthetic satisfaction. Or if he allows such a variety of magical events that his fictional world seems deficient in its own natural laws, his work will fail structurally and cognitively, too, though it may retain some sublimative force. But in the most admirable of structural fabulations, a radical discontinuity between the fictional world and our own provides both the means of narrative suspense and of speculation. In the perfect structural fabulation, idea and story are so wedded as to afford us simultaneously the greatest pleasures that fiction provides: sublimation and cognition.

Afterword

Some tying together of things may be in order, here, though I would hesitate to seek a "conclusion" to a study necessarily so open ended as this one. First, a review of terminology may be useful. And second, some discussion of problems raised by this terminology itself and the concepts it attempts to signify. I have at times accepted the traditional Anglo-Saxon distinction between romance and realism, and have at times rejected it. This needs some clarification. The distinction itself was made by an empirically oriented race in an age of developing empiricism. Thus, it must have some value, if only a historical one. The distinction was originally and has been traditionally invidious, with realism being the privileged form. This suited a materialistic and positivistic age, and the science of that age seemed to lend support to a realistic notion of the cosmos. But science has become increasingly removed from the world of common sense, increasingly imaginative and "unrealistic" in its search for the true structure of the cosmos, and this has ultimately strengthened the potential of didactic romance or fabulation as a form of cognitive fiction—thus striking at the roots of the very notion of "realism." That modern body of fictional works which we loosely designate "science fiction" either accepts or pretends to accept a cognitive responsibility to imagine what is not yet apparent or existent, and to examine this in some systematic way. The acceptance of this responsibility by a writer capable of measuring up to it leads to what I have called structural fabulation.

Seen in cultural terms, then, structural fabulation is a kind of narrative which is genuinely fictional but strongly-influenced by modern science. It is specifically romantic in that it breaks, consciously and deliberately, with what we know or accept to be the case. But it develops its arbitrary parameters with a rigor and consistency that imitates in its fictional way the rigor of scientific method. Seen in purely formal terms, structural fabulation is a development of a tradition of speculative fabulation that has a long history in Western culture. This tradition itself is rooted in the genre of didactic romance, and can be seen as a dialectical antithesis of dogmatic fabulation. This whole history can be seen in the diagram.

Perhaps the most crucial question or objection raised in the debates initiated by these lectures has involved the status of structural fabulation with respect to dogma. To some critics I have seemed to invoke a

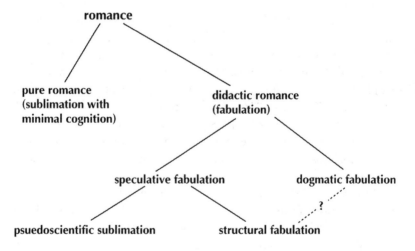

new orthodoxy and to preach a new dogma called structuralism, thus establishing for structural fabulation a kind of religious sanction based on science. There is a certain amount of truth in this charge, and I have acknowledged this by the dotted line with the question mark in the diagram. Can speculation be evaluated for truth-value and still be speculative? Can we ask for rigor without insisting on dogma? Can we expect the imagination to be regulated by something unimaginative without stifling creativity itself? Great questions—with social as well as literary implications. And I have no easy answers for them. I hope and believe these questions can be answered in the affirmative. Partly because our science itself must be speculative in order to continue. And even more because fabulation is not a science. It does not ask "What is?" It asks "What if?" And by doing so it forces us to think about what is and what may be. The surge of pleasure we get when we begin to read any new work of science fiction comes through the lift off from our land of Is into the land of May Be. But the final joy of structural fabulation, as Ursula Le Guin shows us so beautifully in her new book, *The Dispossessed,* comes not from the departure, nor even from the trip itself, but from the return. As an aging dogmatist once said:

> We shall not cease from exploration
> And the end of all our exploring
> Will be to arrive where we started
> And know the place for the first time.

~

CHAPTER FOURTEEN

Science Fiction and the Dimension of Myth

Alexei and Cory Panshin

The practice of mythmaking is so universal among mankind that it might be called a characteristic human activity. Mythmaking is the presentation in story and song, ceremony and drama, of accounts of the origin and destiny of things, cast in terms of encounters with transcendence in another world not our own.

The pattern of mythmaking is so much the same in all places and at all times that a contemporary student, Joseph Campbell, has analyzed many different examples of myth in his useful and suggestive book *The Hero with a Thousand Faces* and found "always the one, shapeshifting yet marvelously constant story."[1] Campbell calls this underlying structure "the monomyth," borrowing his term from a literary antecedent, James Joyce's massive dreamwork *Finnegans Wake*. Campbell writes: "The standard path of the mythological adventure of the hero is a magnification of the formula represented in the rites of passage: *separation—initiation—return:* which might be named the nuclear unit of the monomyth." And he summarizes the monomyth: "*A hero ventures forth from the world of common day into a region of supernatural wonder: fabulous forces are there encountered and a decisive victory is won: the hero comes back from this mysterious adventure with the power to bestow boons on his fellow men.*"[2]

The "region of supernatural wonder" which Campbell distinguishes from "the world of common day" is the dimension of myth, the realm of the creative imagination. This place has many names. As a name of convenience, let us call it the "World Beyond the Hill."

The World Beyond the Hill is the realm of infinite possibility. All things, known and unknown, are to be found in the World Beyond the Hill before they are to be found in our world. According to myth, the things of our world are "created" only when venturing heroes bring them back from the World Beyond the Hill as boons for their fellow men.

In myth, the World Beyond the Hill is close at hand—but distant. You cannot easily get to it. There are barriers and distances intervening, like the deadly deserts that surround and protect Oz. But this other world does have an essential connection with our own, so that with an effort of will, like the astral projection that carries John Carter to Mars, it is possible to make the transition.

We can catch a glimpse of the location and the paradoxical nature of the World Beyond the Hill in the broadest imaginings of science fiction. In Robert Heinlein's novella "Waldo" (*Astounding*, August 1942), a Pennsylvania hex doctor alerts the title character to the existence of "another, different, but accessible, world."[3] Waldo describes this world:

> Think of another continuum much like our own and superposed on it the way you might lay one sheet of paper on another. The two spaces aren't identical, but they are separated from each other by the smallest interval you can imagine—coextensive but not touching—usually. There is an absolute one-to-one, point-for-point correspondence, as I conceive it, between the two shapes, but they are not necessarily the same size or shape. . . . I think of it as about the size and shape of an ostrich egg, but nevertheless a whole universe, existing side by side with our own, from here to the farthest star.[4]

In some ways, the World Beyond the Hill is very like the world of common day. Everything that we know to exist here, exists there, "one-to-one, point-for-point." But the World Beyond the Hill is also marvelously different from anything we know. Things that are impossible here are possible there. The World Beyond the Hill contains wonders on end: magical abilities, fabulous creatures, strange beings, places that are alive. In the World Beyond the Hill all things are possible.

There is an indication of this in another classic science fiction story, Fredric Brown's *What Mad Universe* (*Startling*, September 1948).

In this story, the main character, a science fiction pulp magazine editor, is transported by the explosion of a failed moon rocket into another universe—which proves to be his image of the bizarre world that a callow science fiction fan might dream up. At the climax of the story, Mekky, a transcendent intelligence, tells the protagonist of the number of rooms that are to be found in the mansion of the World Beyond the Hill. Mekky says:

> Out of infinity, *all conceivable universes exist.* There is, for instance, a universe in which this exact scene is being repeated except that you—or the equivalent of you—are wearing brown shoes instead of black ones. There are an infinite number of permutations of that variation, such as one in which you have a slight scratch on your left forefinger and one in which you have purple horns. . . . And there are an infinite number of universes, of course, in which we don't exist at all—that is, no creatures similar to us exist at all. In which the human race doesn't exist at all. There are an infinite number of universes, for instance, in which flowers are the predominant form of life—or in which no form of life has ever developed or will develop. And infinite universes in which the states of existence are such that we would have no words or thoughts to describe them or to imagine them.[5]

Fascinating as these science-fiction descriptions are, they do not do complete justice to the World Beyond the Hill. A fuller and more complete portrait—the most suggestive that we know—is to be found in *The Mecca Revelations,* a great synthesis of ancient knowledge by Ibn Arabi, the thirteenth-century Sufi poet and writer. This book, so far untranslated in full into any Western language, was banned in Egypt as heretical as recently as 1979,[6] Ibn Arabi's description of the World Beyond the Hill—the mythic dimension—is cast as myth. He says that when God had created Adam as the origin and archetype of all humanity, there was a surplus of the leaven of the clay. From this, God created the palm tree. After the palm tree was created, there still remained a portion of the creative clay equivalent to sesame seed. "And it was in this remainder," Ibn Arabi says, "that God laid out an immense Earth." He writes:

> Since he arranged in it the Throne and what it contains, the Firmament, the Heavens and the Earths, the worlds underground, all the paradises

and hells this means that the whole of our universe is to be found there in that Earth in its entirety, and yet the whole of it together is like a ring lost in one of our deserts in comparison with the immensity of that Earth. And that same Earth has hidden in it so many marvels and strange things that their number cannot be counted and our intelligence remains dazed before them. . . . A multitude of things exist there which are rationally impossible, that is, a multitude of things about which reason has established decisive proof that they are incompatible with real being. And yet!—all these things do indeed exist in that Earth. . . . In the whole of all the universes that make up that Earth, God has especially created one universe in our image (a universe corresponding to each one of us). . . . In that Earth there are gardens, paradises, animals, minerals—God alone can know how many. Now, everything that is to be found on that Earth, absolutely everything, is alive and speaks, has a life analogous to that of every living being endowed with thought and speech.[7]

Behind the old and special language, aimed at a thirteenth-century Islamic audience, we can perceive that what is being described is the same Other World invoked by Heinlein and Brown, and more. Instead of being the size of an ostrich egg, as in Heinlein, the vast universes of the World Beyond the Hill are compressed into the size of a sesame seed. Notwithstanding this, our familiar universe, in its entirety, next to the World Beyond the Hill is like a ring lost in the desert. The World Beyond the Hill is so multiplex and infinite that it contains within itself a universe corresponding to each one of us and a multitude of things which are rationally impossible.

In the course of his chapter on the World Beyond the Hill, Ibn Arabi continues on to describe the penetration of the Earth of Sesame by human beings, and what they discover there. Again, the language is not of our own time. But the experience that is being described is clearly the same as Joseph Campbell's monomyth. Ibn Arabi says:

A marvelous race of forms and figures exist on that Earth, of an extraordinary nature. They keep watch over the entrances of the ways of approach lying above this world in which we are. . . . Whenever one of us is searching for the way of access to that Earth . . . the first condition to be fulfilled is the practice of mystical gnosis and withdrawal from the material body. Then he meets those Forms who stand and keep watch at the entrances to the ways of approach, God having especially assigned them to this task. One of them hastens towards the newcomer, clothes him in a robe suitable to his rank, takes him by the hand and walks with him over that Earth and they do in it as they will. He lingers to look at the divine works of art; every stone, every tree, every village, every single thing he comes across, he may speak with, if he wishes, as a man converses with a companion. Certainly they speak different languages, but this Earth has the gift, peculiar to it, conferring on whomsoever enters the ability to understand all the tongues that are spoken there. When he has attained his object and thinks of returning to his dwelling place, his companion goes with him and takes him back to the place at which he entered. There she says goodbye to him; she takes off the robe in which she had clothed him and departs from him. But by then he has gathered a mass of knowledge and indications and his knowledge of God has increased by something he had not previously envisioned. I do not think that understanding ever penetrates in depth with a speed compared to that with which it proceeds when it comes about in that Earth of which I am speaking.[8]

The sojourn in the World Beyond the Hill is more tranquil in Ibn Arabi than in Joseph Campbell. In Campbell's version of the monomyth, transcendence must be faced and conquered. A victory is won. In Ibn Arabi's account, the wayfarer meets transcendence in a less aggressive and more cooperative guise. But the result is the same. We can equate the creative boons brought back by Campbell's mythic freebooters with the not-previously-envisioned increase of knowledge gained in the World Beyond the Hill by Ibn Arabi's mystic travelers.

A fascinating account of a trip into the World Beyond the Hill—and how it might appear to an outside observer—is given by the contemporary anthropologist Peter Furst, who accompanied a group of Huichol Indians in Mexico on their sacred peyote hunt. Furst says that before they begin, the Huichols undergo a rite of purification which is intended to reverse "the pilgrim's passage through life to adulthood and return him or her symbolically to infancy and a state akin to that of spirit. The Huichols say: 'We have become new, we are clean, we are newly born.'"

Furst continues: "Having symbolically shed their adulthood and human identity the pilgrims can now truly assume the identity of spirits, for just as their leader is Tatewarí, the Fire God and First Shaman, so they become the ancestral deities who followed him on the primordial hunt for the Deer-Peyote. In fact, it is only where one has become spirit that one is able to 'cross over'—that is, pass safely through the dangerous passage, the gateway of Clashing Clouds that divides the ordinary from the nonordinary world. This is one of several Huichol versions of a near-universal theme in funerary, heroic, and shamanistic mythology."[9]

This near-universal theme, of course, is the monomythic passage into the region of supernatural wonder. And we may notice that the Huichol method of transition from this world to the World Beyond the Hill is exactly that stated by Ibn Arabi in the thirteenth century: "Whenever one of us is searching for the way of access to that Earth . . . the first condition to be fulfilled is the practice of mystical gnosis and withdrawal from the material body."

Once the Huichols have become spirit, they proceed to make the transition into the Other World under the eye of their anthropologist companions. Furst marvels:

> That this extraordinary symbolic passage is today located only a few yards from a heavily traveled highway on the outskirts of the city of Zacatecas seemed to matter not at all to the Huichols, who in any case acted throughout the sacred journey as though the twentieth century and all its technological wonders had never happened, even when they themselves were traveling by motor vehicle rather than on foot! Indeed, to us nothing illustrated more dramatically the time-out-of-life quality of the whole peyote experience than this ritual of passing through a perilous gateway that existed only in the emotions of the participants, but that was to them no less real for its physical invisibility.[10]

The novices in the party are blindfolded by the shaman leading the pilgrimage, amid weeping and joking, and then taken a few hundred yards to "the mystical divide, the threshold to the divine peyote country."[11] Furst continues:

> Visually, the passage through the Gateway of Clashing Clouds was undramatic. Ramon stepped forward, lifted the bow and, placing one end against the mouth while rhythmically beating the taut string with a composite wooden-tipped hunting arrow, walked straight ahead. He stopped once, gestured (to Kauyumarie, we were later told, to thank him

for holding the cloud gates back with his powerful antlers), and set out again at a more rapid pace, all the while beating his bow. The others followed close behind in single file. Some of the blindfolded neophytes held fearfully on to those in front, others made it by themselves.

There are two stages to the crossing of the critical threshold. The first is called Gateway to the Clouds; the second, Where the Clouds Open. They are only a few steps apart, but the emotional impact on the participants as they passed from one to the other was unmistakable. Once safely 'on the other side,' they knew they would travel through a series of ancestral stopping places to the sacred maternal water holes, where one asks for fertility and fecundity and from where the novices, their blindfolds removed, are allowed to have their first glimpse of the distant mountains of Wirikuta. Of course, one would search in vain on any official map for places that bear such names as Where the Clouds Open, the Vagina, Where Our Mothers Dwell, or even Wirikuta itself, either in Huichol or Spanish. Like other sacred spots on the peyote itinerary, these are landmarks only in the geography of the mind.

It was in the afternoon of the following day that we reached the sacred water holes of Our Mothers, the novices having remained blindfolded all the while. The physical setting again was hardly inspiring: an impoverished *mestizo* pueblo and beyond it a small cluster of obviously polluted springs surrounded by marsh—all that remained of a former lake long since gone dry. Cattle and a pig or two browsing amid the sacred water holes hardly helped inspire confidence in the physical—as opposed to spiritual—purity of the water the Huichols considered the very well spring of fertility and fecundity. On the peyote quest, however, it is not what we would consider the real world that matters but only the reality of the mind's eye. "It is beautiful here," say the Huichols, "because this is where Our Mothers dwell, this is the water of life."[12]

As this account so often reminds us, it is difficult if not impossible for those of us bound to the world of common day to perceive the realities of the World Beyond the Hill. The imperfections of our world veil and obscure the perfections that abound in the Other World. It puts one in mind of the traditional story of the would-be seeker who asks a mythic traveler to be shown something of the World Beyond the Hill. The venturer hands his inquirer an apple. The local person looks at it and protests, "This apple has a worm in it. Shouldn't an apple from the World Beyond the Hill be perfect?" And the traveler replies, "True, an apple from the World Beyond the Hill should be perfect. However, with your present state of mind, and seated as we are in this abode of corruption—this is as close to an apple from the World Beyond the Hill as you can get."[13] In the same way, polluted mud holes are as close as we, with our present state of mind and seated as we are in this abode of corruption, are ever going to get to the sparkling waters Where Our Mothers Dwell in the World Beyond the Hill.

But which place is more real? Perhaps because the World Beyond the Hill is the realm of infinite possibility and the source of all our creativity, Ibn Arabi, in a chapter title in *The Meccan Revelations*, calls it "The Earth of True Reality."[14] And it is not Ibn Arabi alone who considers the Other World to have a greater degree of reality than the world of common day. The character with the highest degree of knowledge in Heinlein's "Waldo," the Pennsylvania hex doctor, Grarnps Schneider, says, "We live in the Other World. . . . The mind—not the brain, but the mind—is in the Other World, and reaches this world through the body. That is one true way looking at it, though there are others."[15] Similarly, when the Huichol journey as spirits into the World Beyond the Hill, it is "the place of origin" that they seek.[16]

Let us look at one more short and provocative account of an excursion into the World Beyond the Hill and its result, from the viewpoint of the world of common day. This was written in the eighth century by the early British historian, the Venerable Bede, recounting the moment of inspiration of Caedmon, the first Christian poet in Britain. It has much in common with the testimony of science-fiction writers of today like A. E. van Vogt and Philip K. Dick, who have found inspiration for their stories in dreams.[17] Bede tells us that Caedmon was a cowherd. He was uneducated and knew no songs. When the harp was passed to him, he left the hall in humiliation, went to the stable and lay down to sleep:

> While he slept, someone stood by him in a dream, greeted him, calling him by name, saying to him, "Caedmon, sing me something."
>
> He replied, "I know not how to sing—that's the reason I left the feast. I'm here because I cannot sing."
>
> The one who spoke said: "No matter. You must sing to me."
>
> "Well," he answered, "what shall I sing?"
>
> The other responded: "Sing the beginning of created things."

At that, straight away Caedmon sang in praise of the Creator verses he had never heard.[18]

Again, what happens in this world, the world of common day, is dry and of no consequence to the worldly eye. Caedmon the cowherd goes out to sleep in the stable. He dreams. And when he awakens, he is suddenly and miraculously able to sing original verses to his fellows about the beginning of created things. This is his boon. We are not told what happens to Caedmon in the course of his dream, or what he sees—only a snatch of conversation. But we can recognize in the someone who greets him one of the transcendent Forms, described by Ibn Arabi, whose job it is to stand and keep watch at the entrances to the World Beyond the Hill and as newcomers.

One point that emerges from all these accounts and deserves special note is the high degree of reflectivity of the World Beyond the Hill. Since it contains within it everything that exists in this world, the Other World is able to serve as a perfect mirror of the persons who enter it and their cultures. What one has in mind in entering the World Beyond the Hill absolutely determines what one sees, what happens to one, and what one carries away again. Entered aggressively, the World Beyond the Hill responds with aggression. Boons must be wrested from it. Entered peaceably, the World Beyond the Hill offers robing maidens and strolling conversation.

The reflectivity of the World Beyond the Hill and the selectivity of those who enter it are alluded to in Ibn Arabi's depiction of the monomyth. This is what he means in saying that in the World Beyond the Hill there is a universe corresponding to each one of us.

There are further phrases in his description that suggest the selectivity and limitation of those who enter the World Beyond the Hill. The transcendent companion who waits at the entrance clothes him in a robe *suitable to his rank*. She walks with him over that Earth and they do in it *as they will*. Every single thing the newcomer encounters, he may speak with, *if he wishes*.

All this seems to indicate that what you see and do in the World Beyond the Hill is what you are prepared to see and do. There are an infinite number of places in the World Beyond the Hill. You, the mythic wayfarer, will enter those rooms and hold those conversations that are suitable to your nature and state of development, that are a mirror of you. The places that the Huichol choose to go in the Other World—like Where the Clouds Open and Where Our Mothers Dwell—are distinctly Huichol in character.

And the boons, the new knowledge brought back from the Other World, are also always in keeping with the culture and state of the traveler. As Ibn Arabi says, when the visitor has attained his object and gets the urge to return to his own dwelling place, he departs the World Beyond the Hill by the same door at which he entered. When Caedmon returns from his dream visit to the World Beyond the Hill to find himself waking in his bed of straw in the stable, the new gift that he has is the ability to sing to his fellow men of the beginning of created things—in seventh-century British Christian terms. Even Ibn Arabi's description of the limitless world of the imagination invokes palm trees, sesame seeds, deserts, gardens, paradises and hells, and other images appropriate to the understanding of a thirteenth-century Islamic audience.

The imaginative reflectivity of the World Beyond the Hill is recognized in both of the science-fiction stories we have used by way of example. And in the choices the protagonists each make out of the infinitude of options offered them, we can recognize the nature and limits of our own culture.

In Heinlein's "Waldo," the main character comes to the conclusion that he can imagine the World Beyond the Hill to be the way he wants it to be, impress his concept on his fellows, and the Other World will be that way. Heinlein writes: "The world varied according to the way one looked at it. In that case, thought Waldo, he knew how he wanted to look at it. He cast his vote for order and predictability!"[19] Waldo chooses to imagine the Other World as a repository of power and no more than that: "To its inhabitants, if any, it might seem to be hundreds of millions of light years around; to him it was an ostrich egg, turgid to bursting with power."[20] And Waldo draws on that power to heal his own physical weakness, and to become a tap dancer, surgeon, and popular personality.

At the conclusion of Fredric Brown's *What Mad Universe*, the science-fiction editor protagonist is given the opportunity to repeat the experience that first carried him into the World Beyond the Hill. He can travel to any variant universe that he is able to imagine. It is possible for him to go to a universe beyond description—if he is able to think of it. Or he can go to a universe where the style is brown shoes instead of black. The one he picks out of all infinitude is one that is exactly like the one he left except that he gets the girl, and that he owns his own chain of pulp magazines instead of working as an editor. Ah, such dreams!

From the viewpoint of the common day world, the mythmaking enterprise has two recognizable functions. In *Primitive Mythology*, the first book in *The Masks of God*, a four-volume study of myth, Joseph Campbell writes:

> Functioning as a "way," mythology and ritual conduce to a transformation of the individual, disengaging him from his local, historical conditions and leading him toward some kind of ineffable experience. Functioning as an "ethnic idea," on the ether hand, the image binds the individual to his family's system of historically conditioned sentiments, activities, and beliefs, as a functioning member of a sociological organism. This antinomy is fundamental to our subject, and every failure to recognize it leads not only to unnecessary argument, but also to a misunderstanding—one way or the other—of the force of the mythological symbol itself, which is, precisely, to render an experience of the ineffable through the local and concrete, and thus, paradoxically, to amplify the force and appeal of the local forms even while carrying the mind beyond them.[21]

The duality which Campbell describes is represented in the pilgrims of the Huichol peyote hunt. The ordinary Huichol seeks to find his life and to discover what it means to be Huichol. The *mora'akame* or shaman-like Ramon has a very different experience in mind.

Peter Furst writes: "A *mara'akome* embarks on the pilgrimage and the drug experience itself with a somewhat different set of expectations than the ordinary Huichol. He seeks to experience a catharsis that allows him to enter upon a personal encounter with Tatewarí and travel to 'the fifth level' to meet the supreme spirits at the ends of the world. And so he does. Ordinary Huichols also 'experience' the supernaturals, but they do so essentially through the medium of their shaman. In any event, I have met no one who was not convinced of this essential difference or who laid claim to the same kinds of exalted and illuminating confrontations with the Otherworld as the *mara'akame*."[22]

We can also see the two functions of mythmaking—the support and confirmation of culture on the one hand, and the venture beyond corruption and limitation on the other—in the hopeful intentions of Hugo Gernsback for his new magazine, *Amazing Stories*, in 1926. Gernsback, from his very first editorial, hoped that "scientifiction" stories would be an inspiration that would lead cold-blooded scientists to envision and bring into reality new wonders. And Gernsback also hoped that where this new form of myth did not inspire, it would at least teach and inform: "Not only do these amazing tales make tremendously interesting reading—they are also always instructive. They supply knowledge that we might not otherwise obtain—and they supply it in a very palatable form. For the best of these modern writers of scientifiction have the knack of imparting knowledge, and even inspiration, without once making us aware that we are being taught."[23]

In short, from the viewpoint of the common day world, myth exists to serve culture. Myth teaches us to be Roman, or Huichol, or twentieth-century American. It reinforces societal belief. It confirms. It tutors painlessly. And in those cases where the imaginative voyager travels far into the World Beyond the Hill to regions unknown to him, or to his people, or to anyone, he will still exit by the same door through which he entered. Whatever boon he returns with will be accepted as an increment to the culture.

But the viewpoint of the common day world is not the viewpoint of the World Beyond the Hill. From that standpoint—one of greater reality, we should remember—culture is not primary, but secondary. Culture is solidified imagination, the sum total of boons and gifts, inventions and inspirations brought back from the place of origin by countless dreamers. Culture is a Moses basket keeping us safe as we float in the great waters of infinite possibility. Culture is higher reality's way of keeping us from harm, as a baby's playpen defines an area of knownness and separates the child from more possibility than he can handle.

Myth then is the reality. It underlies culture, validates it, and gives it substance. Mythic imagination is the means of return to the World Beyond the Hill. Some humans return to the place of origin in order to discover how to repair and maintain their cultural ship. Others seek to add to it and alter it, and keep it on course.

Mythmaking is a constant, on-going, self-amending process. Myth—in our abode of corruption—does not exist outside the activity of mythmaking. There is no single, perfect, and final myth that all men should recognize and assent to. There is only the particular expression of myth in a certain time and a certain place for a certain audience.

If we are used to thinking of myth as given and final and perfect, it is because what we are most usually offered these days under the name of myth is not mythmaking as a present act, but the fossil remains of former mythmaking activity. Hawthorne's *The Wonder Book*, Bulfinch's *Mythology*, or Graves' *The Greek Myths* are not actual Greek myth in any meaningful sense—no more than a stone footprint or a coprolite are a dinosaur, particularly a dinosaur in its own proper context. Myth is for the moment fully valid and meaningful only for the instant, the surroundings and the persons for whom it is being made. After that, a husk.

As an indication of the ephemerality of mythmaking, we might look at the moment that Isaac Asimov has identified as the highpoint in his enjoyment of science fiction:

> It came in the month of August 1937, when I was spending the summer waiting for my junior year at Columbia to begin. In that month, the September 1937 issue of *Astounding Stories* arrived, and I remember the precise feelings that swept over me as I sat in the living room of our apartment and read the first installment of Edward E. Smith's new four-part serial, *Galactic Patrol*. Never, I think, did I enjoy any piece of writing more, any piece of any kind. Never did I savor every word so. Never did I feel so keen a sense of loss when I came to the end of the first installment and knew that I would have to wait a full month for the second. Never anything like it before. Never anything like it after.[24]

This is myth at the right time and place and with the right person. And, Asimov underlines the point we are making by writing further concerning *Galactic Patrol*: "Years later, I got a copy of the hardback version and sat down to relive past glories—but they weren't there. I found the book unreadable."[25]

Myth in practice is not neat, tidy, rational, and enduring. Myth is sloppy, contradictory, irrational, and ephemeral. It is of the moment and for a purpose. It will be superseded. If the purpose of myth and the human culture that depends on myth is to carry the human psyche out of the abode of corruption and limitation toward the higher realities of the World Beyond the Hill, then myth will always supersede itself until the final object is attained.

It is now possible for us to recognize that Hugo Gernsback's requirements for contributions to *Amazing Stories*, as enumerated in an early editorial, were nothing less than the requirements of all mythmaking in any culture at any time. Gernback wrote: "The formula in all cases is that first the story must be frankly amazing; second, it must contain a scientific background; third, it must possess originality."[26]

The amazing quality is, of course, transcendence, the evidence or proof of the World Beyond the Hill. The fabulous forces and forms, the stone and villages that speak, the spirit forces that hold back the cloud gates with their antlers, who speak to us in dreams, who recognize and robe us—all these are transcendent. They amaze us; they are higher than we are; they may be learned from.

What Gernsback calls "a scientific background" we may equate with the best knowledge of the culture. This will be different knowledges and sciences in different cultures. This best knowledge is the measure by which transcendence reveals itself. Transcendence, the infinite power of creativity, is always beyond the best knowledge of the culture. It leads best knowledge. The boons that are won from transcendence in the World Beyond the Hill answer the problems of the culture and are added to the science of the culture as new best knowledge.

Finally, the third quality, originality, is the evidence and demonstration that the mythmaker has ventured into the World Beyond the Hill, there contacted transcendence and returned from the place of origins with something never seen before in our world. Originality is the demonstration of authenticity. And it is also the means by which the mythic/cultural enterprise extends and amends itself.

Notes

1. Joseph Campbell, *The Hero with a Thousand Faces* (Cleveland: Meridian, 1956), p. 3.

2. Campbell, p. 30. Italics in original.

3. Robert A. Heinlein, "Waldo," in Heinlein, *Waldo and Magic, Inc.* (Garden City: Doubleday, 1951), p. 87. Since we wrote this essay, Robert Heinlein's *The Number of the Beast* has been published. It is a book with great relevance to the nature of the mythic dimension. We discuss some of the implications of Heinlein's book in "The Death of Science Fiction: A Dream," the new 30,000-word conclusion to the revised paperback edition of *SF in Dimension*.

4. Heinlein, pp. 91–92.

5. Fredric Brown, *What Mad Universe* (New York: Bantam, 1950), pp. 187, 188.

6. According to a story in *The New York Times*, 14 March 1979, entitled "Egyptians Furious About a Ban on 12-Century Mystic's Work."

7. Muhyiddin Ibn Arabi, "The Earth Which Was Created from What Remained of the Clay of Adam," in *Spiritual Body and Celestial Earth: From Mazdeon Iran to Shi'ite Iran* ed. Henry Corbin, Bollingen Series XCI:2 (Princeton, N.J.: Princeton, 1977), pp. 137, 138. This volume as a whole has great bearing on our subject, as does its companion volume, Henry Corbin, *Creative Imagination in the Sufism of Ibn Arabi*, Bollingen Series XCI: I (Princeton, N.J.: Princeton, 1969).

8. Corbin, pp. 139–40.

9. Peter T. Furst, *Hallucinogens and Culture* (San Francisco: Chandler & Sharp, 1976), pp. 116, 117.

10. Furst, p. 117.

11. Furst, p. 118.

12. Furst, pp. 118–19. We have reversed the original order of the first and second of these three paragraphs for narrative coherence.

13. Our version of this story is retold from Idries Shah, *The Sufis* (Garden City: Doubleday, 1964), pp. 63–64.

14. Corbin, p. 135. The full title of the relevant chapter of the original work, which is sometimes known as *The Book of the Spiritual Conquests of Mecca*, is "On the knowledge of the Earth which was created from what remained of the leaven of Adam's clay, and which is the Earth of True Reality, mentioning the strange things and marvels it contains."

15. Heinlein, p. 79.

16. Furst, p. 116.

17. For the influence of dreams on A. E. van Vogt and Philip K. Dick, see, A. E. van Vogt, *Reflections of A. E. von Vogt* (Lakemont, Ga.: Fictioneer, 1975), p. 78; and Philip K. Dick, "Man, Android and Machine," in *Science Fiction At Large*, ed. Peter (New York: Harper & Row, 1916), p. 196.

18. Bede, *Ecclesiastical History*. Our translation is based in part on the language of W. Scudder's translation, published by Everyman's Library, 1910, as

quoted in Campbell, *The Masks of God: Creative Mythology* (New York: Viking, 1968), in part on our own rendering of the Anglo-Saxon as found in James R. Hulbert, *An Anglo-Saxon Reader. Revised and Enlarged* (New York: Holt, Rinehart and W 1935), p. 9.

19. Heinlein, p. 102.

20. Heinlein, p. 103.

21. Joseph Campbell, *The Masks of God: Primitive Mythology* (New York: Viking), p. 462.

22. Furst, p. 131.

23. Hugo Gernsback, "A New Sort of Magazine," *Amazing Stories* (April 1926), p. 3.

24. Isaac Asimov, *Before the Golden* Age (Garden City: Doubleday, 1974), p. 910.

25. Asimov, p. 947.

26. Hugo Gernsback, "Editorially Speaking," *Amazing Stories*, Sept. 1926, p. 483.

PART FOUR

EXCAVATION

The preceding section, "Derivation," and the final section, "Anticipation," might well have been combined with this one in a single section that would provide the sweep of science-fiction history from its origins to the present and beyond, but we have pursued a different rationale.

Histories of science fiction are available elsewhere. The purpose of this volume is to deal with the ways in which science fiction has been envisioned, interpreted, re-envisioned, and re-interpreted. In this anthology, the actual events of science fiction history are seen obliquely, through the lenses of critics' arguments about the characteristics, classification, or development of the genre. Students seeking a history of the genre may find them in James Gunn's *Alternate Worlds* (or his six-volume anthology *The Road to Science Fiction*), Lester Del Rey's *World of Science Fiction*, Brian Aldiss' *Trillion Year Spree*, Edward James's *Science Fiction in the Twentieth Century*, or John Clute's *Encyclopedia of Science Fiction*.

In "Some Notes Toward the True and Terrible," and "Wrong Rabbit," Barry Malzberg turns his skeptical, at times satirical, but always insightful and interesting, vision on what he sees as the decline and fall of John W. Campbell's editorship of *Astounding Stories/Astounding Science Fiction/Analog*. His focus, however, is not so much on Campbell as it is on the historicizing of science fiction, although the figure of the most influential editor in science fiction provides a powerful backdrop for Malzberg's musings. In "Some Notes Toward the True and Terrible," Malzberg posits the existence of an unwritten and unwritable history of science fiction that explains how the genre came to be the genre that it is, including how a number of alternate genres were shut down by the insular and parochial nature of science fiction's architects, a concept that will be explored again in James Kelly's "Slipstream." He also posits a general tendency of editors, as they age, to buy more and more from fewer and fewer individuals, creating periods of arthritic rigidity when the magazines or publishing houses they work for are insensitive to the dominant currents in the genre. "Wrong Rabbit," is a scathing critique of historians' tendency to generalize about the periods of science fiction's development. His particular focus is the belief that science fiction of the forties was all optimistic, but he reminds us that the genre has always been characterized by diversity, even when it was controlled by a relatively small number of individuals.

It may be a symptom of our age that more new books of science-fiction criticism are being produced than ever before, and one of the effects of this is that most of the seminal works of science-fiction criticism, many of them excerpted in this anthology, are out of print, crowded off the shelf by new perspectives on the genre. While many of these new texts are valuable, it is nonetheless a shame that books like Colin Greenland's *The Entropy Exhibition* are unavailable to many scholars of the genre. In this second chapter from his book, "The 'Field' and the 'Wave': The History of *New Worlds*," Greenland explores the manner in which the magazine fell into the hands of the idealistic genius Michael Moorcock, and how Moorcock forged it into the voice of a truly new genre. Although there are many caveats to the myth of the New Wave, and some may point to other inflexion points in the history of the genre, it is against the New Wave that all other movements from within the genre or without are judged, and Greenland's book is the best analysis of the New Wave ever written. Serious students of this period in science fiction are strongly encouraged to seek out Greenland's book.

David Hartwell and Kathryn Cramer in "Space Opera Redefined," come the closest of any of these selections to giving students an actual history. Their article, however, is not a history of "space opera," the way that this particular subgenre grew and changed, but, rather, a history of the concept of space opera, the manner in which this contested term arose and transformed from a precise, derogatory description into a more generalized and positive catch-all. Hartwell and Cramer also point out that the new definition is inherently two-fold. First, it is a marketing term, used to describe SF designed to be popular entertainment, and, second, it has become more recently a chosen descriptor for the newest wave of cutting-edge SF adventure, most of which belongs to what has been called the British Renaissance.

CHAPTER FIFTEEN

∿

Some Notes toward the True and the Terrible

Barry N. Malzberg

I first made reference to the true and terrible unwritten history of science fiction in a review of James Gunn's *Alternate Worlds: The Illustrated History of Science Fiction* in 1975, but did not begin to develop the
concept until I spoke at the University of California at Berkeley in
1978. Standing at the podium, shaking with fever, ampicillin, dread,
and wonder that any stranger would pay $3.75 cash on the barrelhead
to listen to me,* I said that the history of science fiction must, by definition, exist truly in the interstices, that by definition the field could
be explained only by material which would be by turns libelous, private, intuitive, or paranoid and that even the most rigorous and lucid
of scholarly works could deal only with symptomatic representations of
the great underside of the field.

Surely I must have been anticipating that May the publication, a
year and a half later, of the dense, scholarly and invaluable *Encyclopedia of Science Fiction*, edited by Peter Nicholls (the best reference work
on our field that has appeared to date), because the Nicholls work
manages through one intricate, brilliantly cross-referenced and almost

---

* There were actually about forty such misguided souls in the audience, added to about 150
who had registered for a ten-session course called "The Writers Speak." Or mumble. Or
drink. But never simultaneously if you want to be invited back.

impishly accurate volume to make clear to insiders and outsiders alike practically everything about science fiction that they would need to know to get through doctoral orals except for two factors: (a) How it got this way and (b) why it has its peculiar and binding effect upon a readership, a larger proportion of which are emotionally involved with the literature than the readers of any other genre.

The *Encyclopedia* reminds me of the one-line criticism of Shaw's plays: that a literate alien could, from them alone, deduce everything about humanity except that it possessed genitals. Nicholls and his staff make everything about science fiction comprehensible except the existence of a 700,000-word trade paperback about it which can expect to sell eventually well over a million copies. Try that in quality lit, mystery, or romance. The Gothic Encyclopedia? *The Illustrated History of Literary Writing? Barlow's Book of Flannery O'Connor?*

The true unwritten history is where the answers lie and the unwritten history cannot—by definition, be pointed out laboriously—be composed. In a spirit of scholarship and sacrifice, however, I would like to offer a few notes, leads as it were toward what it would contain and with what it would have to deal. Perhaps by the end of the twenty-first century when all of us now reading, writing, and propitiating the category are all safely dead and with the evolution of low-feed, multiplex stereophonic video-tape cassette recall, the abolition of the written, that is to say, the true unwritten history might be retrieved.

To the unborn and penitent, hence, a few suggestions:

(1) "Modern" science fiction, generally dated as having begun in late 1937 with the ascent of Campbell, was a literature centered around a compact group of people. It was no Bloomsbury but there could have been no more than fifty core figures who did 90 percent of the writing and the editing. All of them knew one another, most knew one another well, lived together, married one another, collaborated, bought each others' material, married each other's wives, and so on. For a field that was conceptually based upon expansion, the smashing of barriers, the far-reaching and so on, science fiction was amazingly insular. One could fairly speculate that this insularity and parochialism were the understandable attempts of frightened human beings faced with *terra incognita* to hold on to one another and to make their personal lives as limited and interconnected as possible. It could be speculated further that this

parochialism shut off an entire alternative science fiction. (Alexei Pan-shin has intimated this possibility but not this particular set of reasons.) Who is to know what writers and manuscripts *not* connected in any way to the Central Fifty languished in slush piles or in stamped, self-addressed envelopes? Science fiction simply was not for them; it was being cooked up in offices and bars and bedrooms and apartment houses; people would stream from Central to write it all up in their own way and send it back in (and then write up next month's issue taking up the stuff already laid down in print), but the field was based on personal access and very few writers and stories were getting into the magazines without personal acquaintance with other writers and with the editors. The first thing that Damon Knight did in the forties as a science fiction writer *manque* was to accept Fred Pohl's invitation to come out from Oregon to Brooklyn and live with the Futurian Club; the young Asimov was introduced to present contributors by Campbell before Asimov had sold a word; Malcolm Jameson, pensioned off by the Navy for medical reasons, began to write science fiction (and became, briefly, an *Astounding* regular in the mid-1940s) at the urgings of his old friend and fellow Navy officer Robert A. Heinlein.

(2) One of the clear symptoms of editorial decline (this ties, in a way, to the point above but only by suggestion; hear me out) is the increasing proportion of material in a magazine or book line written by a decreasing number of contributors; venery, laziness, exhaustion or friendship seem to make almost any long-term editorship vulnerable to this condition. (I am not saying that science fiction in this case is any different than any other genre.) The *Astounding* of the late 1950s had narrowed to four or five regular contributors in between whom a few asteroids squeezed the short stories: Silverberg, Anvil, Garrett, Janifer/ Harris, and Reynolds must have accounted for 70 percent of the magazine's contents in the period 1958 to 1962. Over at *Galaxy* Fred Pohl, Robert Sheckley, and Philip M. Klass must have contributed more than half the contents in the last three years of Horace Gold's editorship (1957–1960). This is not to dispute that this core group might have overtaken the magazines simply because they were the best, at least in terms of meeting the editorial vision (and there is no disputing that the *Galaxy* group at least includes three of the finest writers of science fiction thus far), but the consequences of such narrowing are obvious; the

medium becomes insular and ambitious potential contributors become discouraged. There is, needless to say, a fine line an editor must tread between gathering the best writers he can and encouraging them . . . and buying from friends and familiars, but there is such a line of clear demarcation: Campbell in the early forties was on one side of it and in the late fifties on the other, and the quality of work and its persistence today (little of the late fifties *Astounding* is now reprinted) constitute judgement.

(3) The clearest signal of Campbell's loosened grip and influence on the field from 1960 (the time at which his obsessive pursuit of pseudo-scientific chicanery became his editorial obsession rather than weakness) is to compile a list of those writers who arose to prominence in that decade who never published in his magazine. Once for my amusement a long time ago (in the last couple of years of his life for I hoped that he would see it) I did so and published it in *Science Fiction Review*. Here is a partial (I am sure to miss someone) list of science fiction writers who did *not* appear in *Analog* from the issue of January 1960 until the last issue assembled by Campbell dated December 1971:

J. G. Ballard, Brian W. Aldiss, Ursula K. Le Guin, Samuel R. Delany, Joanna Russ, Larry Niven, Michael Moorcock, R. A. Lafferty, George Alec Effinger, Gardner R. Dozois, A. J. Budrys, Terry Carr, Kate Wilhelm, George Zebrowski, Norman Kagan, Theodore Sturgeon, Philip K. Dick, Pamela Sargent, Robert Sheckley, Roger Zelazny.

Silverberg *almost* makes the list; his last story was in the February 1960 issue (sold, of course, in the fifties). Tiptree's first story and one other appeared in *Analog*; Niven's first piece, published at last in 1972, was apparently Campbell's last purchase.

And yet. And yet when I heard of Campbell's sudden death on July 11, 1971, and informed Larry Janifer. I trembled at Janifer's response and knew that it was so: "The field has lost its conscience, its center, the man for whom we were all writing. Now there's no one to get mad at us any more."

~

CHAPTER SIXTEEN

Wrong Rabbit

Barry N. Malzberg

And here is A. J. Budrys, who should know better, in a fairly recent (May 1979) issue of *Fantasy and Science Fiction*, discussing 1940s science fiction: "Modern science fiction as you know[*] was marked by a verve we do not often see these days, fueled by a pervading technological optimism and a set of ethical assumptions slightly to the right of the John Birch credo. Might was not only right, it was moral . . . technological action—exploring the physical possibilities and applying deft means of conveying maximum comfort to the maximum number of individuals—offers the best hope . . ."

It may do all of that—in the world which technology has bequeathed *only* technological action can accomplish change—but Budrys is wrong about the science fiction of Campbell's first decade, and before shibboleth passes all the way into law and the forties *ASF* is forever characterized as being packed by the Happy Engineer, I would like to, as the man said to the committee, try to set the record straight.

The Happy Engineer is one of the great uninvestigated myths of contemporary science fiction. (Another is that *Astounding/Analog* was/is devoted to stories whose background is "hard science" requiring "heavy tech," but that is next Sunday's text.) The truth, as any fresh

---

[*] Say *what*, Boss?

confrontation of the material would certainly make clear, is that the forties *ASF* is filled with darkness, that the majority of its most successful and reprinted stories dealt with the bleakest implications of technology and that "modern" science fiction (defined by Budrys as that which originated with Campbell's editorship of *Astounding* given him in October 1937) rather than being a problem-solving literature was a literature of despair.

Only in the fifties as Campbell's vision locked and dystopia was encouraged by Horace Cold and Anthony Boucher did *Astounding* begin indeed to invite in the Happy Engineer: the complexities of Heinlein became the reflexive optimism of G. Harry Stine, Christopher Anvil, Eric Frank Russell (some of the time) and the somewhat more ambivalent optimism of Gordon R. Dickson, Poul Anderson, or Randall Garrett. It would not be difficult to argue that this represented a drift from the *periphery* of the forties *ASF:* the *Venus Equilateral* stories of George O. Smith, say, or the *Bullard* series of Malcolm Jameson.

But consider the text entire. The Kuttners from the outset of their career were publishing stories of complexity and pessimism: "Mimsy Were the Borogoves" and "Shock" and "What You Need" and "When the Bough Breaks"* and the (superficially humorous) "Gallagher" series in which a drunken inventor's drunken inventions went crazy. "Jesting Pilot" and "Private Eye" and "The Prisoner in the Skull" were grim and desperate visions of the (failed) efforts to maintain autonomy and compassion in the shining, uncontrollable future. Heinlein's "Universe" is one of the grimmest visions in the history of the field; a centuries-long starflight gone astray, a civilization of the descendants of the original crew stripped of memory and reduced to barbarism.

Asimov's "Nightfall," not the best but certainly the best-known story Campbell ever published, describes the collapse of a civilization into anarchy and madness; L. Ron Hubbard's *Final Blackout,* a freehand template of World War II cast into an ambiguous future, depicts—as does Heinlein's *Sixth Column*—the use of the machineries of destruction to destroy linear cultural evolution. Heinlein's "By His Bootstraps" is a solipsistic nightmare cast as a time paradox story in which the protagonist cannot escape the simple and repeated loop of his life (and has

---

* this giggler was about infanticide.

for friendship only versions of himself). Van Vogt's work, from his first story "Black Destroyer" (a murderous alien loose on a spaceship kills most of the crew; the alien is in terrible emotional distress), put vision after horrid vision of the future into *ASF*, paranoid reaction toward militancy ("The Weapon Shops" series), the hopelessness of human evolution ("The Seesaw"), the collapse of causality (*The World/The Players of Null-A*).

In the wake of Hiroshima, Campbell published a series of apocalyptic stories (Kuttner's *Tomorrow and Tomorrow & The Fairy Chessmen*, Chan Davis's "The Nightmare," Sturgeon's "Thunder and Roses") and postapocalyptic speculations (Russell's "Metamorphosite," Kuttner's "Fury") in such profusion that at the world science fiction convention of 1947, at which he was guest of honor, he begged for the fans' indulgence at the profusion of despair, claiming that he could only publish what the writers were delivering . . . but he was sending out pleas to cease and desist. (The writers got the message, finally, and fled to Gold and Boucher as soon as they opened shop.)

It could be said that by making good on this pledge, shutting down certain themes and approaches rather than (as before) encouraging the writers to get the best version of their ideas, Campbell was taking the first steps in the decline of his editorship and that the fifties *Astounding* can be seen as the product of a man who, having faced the abyss, had decided that he wanted no part of it. Through the fifties the other major editors accommodated the underside . . . but it must be noted that Godwin's "The Cold Equations," the best-known *ASF* story of the fifties, as "Nightfall" was the best-known of the forties, was a stunning and despairing enactment (a little girl stows away in a one-man rocket that does not have sufficient fuel to carry her and is jettisoned) of the limitations of technology, the implacability of the universal condition.

Seeing "modern" science fiction as cheerful and brave, upstanding and problem-solving—and Budrys is only the best of the critics to have taken this line; only John Clute seems to have disdained it thus far—makes for easy history of course: the primitive twenties, wondrous and colorful thirties, systematized and optimistic forties, quiet and despairing fifties, fragmented and chaotic sixties, expressionless seventies . . . and history, as has been noted, is an inherently comforting study, demonstrating, if nothing else, a retrospective order to what was chaotic. A proof that, at least, we got through.

But the price we are paying for this misapprehension is too high. It makes us consider science fiction as one thing when from the very beginning it surely was another.

Which makes us the inheritors of what we can never know, adopted children, scurrying obsessively through the closed or closing files of headquarters, seeking evidence that even if retrieved will be meaningless.

∽

CHAPTER SEVENTEEN

The "Field" and the "Wave":
The History of *New Worlds*

Colin Greenland

Perhaps the most characteristic volume of *New Worlds* writings did not appear as an issue of the magazine, but as an anthology edited by one of Moorcock's co-editors and regular contributors, Langdon Jones. Under the title *The New SF*[1] he collected pieces from almost all the principal writers—Moorcock himself, Brian Aldiss, James Sallis, Charles Platt, Michael Butterworth, John Sladek and Thomas Disch—and from other associates—Giles Gordon, Maxim Jakubowski and Pamela Zoline—with poetry by George MacBeth and D. M. Thomas, and an interview presenting J. G. Ballard at his most emphatic and enigmatic.

In his preface to the anthology Moorcock declared: "If proof were needed of the contention that much of the very best modern literature is emerging from the SF field, this book should supply that proof."[2] The notion of an "SF field" and a modern literature "emerging from it" is central to my analysis. Hilary Bailey's precise and witty survey of the "field," "this mysterious stretch of land, property no doubt of some worried farmer with many sons,"[3] demonstrates how uneven and populous it is, and how inadequate any generalizations about it must be. It is a task for the theoretical critic to say what science fiction should, and for the encyclopedist to say what it does, encompass. I shall do neither. As more critics turn their attention to it, the problem of defining science fiction is becoming more difficult, not less. I shall not attempt to contribute to the solution, since one of the few things the *New Worlds* writers shared was their impatience with the limitations of genre fiction. Their own fiction was intended to defy categorization, and I shall follow that as far as possible. I may even end up contributing to the problem; though when I speak of "the *New Worlds* writers," I am not instituting a new category, only stating that they all contributed to the magazine and so may temporarily be considered together. Similarly, the term "New Wave," which is as misleading as most critical labels, signifies only that the writers *were* considered together, as a collective movement sharply distinct from and hostile to what they saw as the old order. This collectivity the writers themselves affirmed in editorials and in public. Though they now disclaim any artistic unanimity, they were associated at the time, and much, I think, may be critically induced from that association, however unstable it proved.

So injustice is about to be done all round. I shall refer sweepingly to "traditional science fiction," and more often to "SF," the initials unexpanded as a reminder of their uncertain provenance. Many better read than I will probably take issue with my assertions and disagree with how I present "the tradition," especially since I shall be looking at it over my shoulder and in contrast to the achievements of Moorcock and his dissenters. Attracted by the imaginative potential of SF and inspired by its best, they felt strongly that it was encumbered by its worst and struck out accordingly. They saw no reason why SF should be segregated from the rest of fiction, and resented editors, writers and readers who seemed to be in conspiracy to keep it insulated, governed only by low standards hardly changed for forty years.

SF is popular fiction. Its public image as a trivial, sub-literary pastime was a product of the specialist SF magazines and their cultivation of a coterie audience. Magazines bring writer and reader closer than any other form of publishing. Serialization can permit readers" reactions to influence a story during composition, and they will almost certainly have an effect on what revisions the author makes before publishing it as a complete novel. From month to month (or quarter to quarter), the magazine relies directly on audience approval for survival. An editor will often court readers by appealing to them not as isolated individuals engaged in the private act of reading, but as participants in a larger group, a society of like-minded people, to which the magazine is the en-trée. Some of these groups actually exist. Of these, the SF enthusiasts are surely the most organized, vociferous and demanding. They have a nationalistic (though anarchic) conception of themselves as "fandom," with hierarchical degrees of greater or lesser loyalty; they converse in their own jargon; when not gathering at "SF cons" they gossip inde-fatigably about writers, and about each other, in "fanzines"; they judge authors fiercely and possessively, idolizing favorites and heaping scorn on the rejected. No editor can ever remain in doubt as to their feelings about his policies. However, those feelings are those of an elite, and tend to be conservative. The period when specialist magazines domi-nated SF publishing is over, but fandom has survived the transition to paperbacks, intact.

New Worlds was itself created within this close collaboration. In the late 1930s the Science-Fiction Association, a group of fervent fans, keen writers and readers, met in London pubs and teashops to plot, if not the future of mankind, then fictional versions of that future. Their fanzine, Novae Terrae, was a typical cyclostyled newsheet, but E. J. Carnell, the Association's treasurer, had plans and material to develop it into a magazine of fiction and discussion, a British alternative to the American magazines that they all read and to which some of them had sold stories. After the war he was given the opportunity to do so. His magazine, now called New Worlds, was issued by Pendulum Publica-tions in July 1946. The economic uncertainty of the period brought about the collapse of Pendulum in the following year, but not before three issues of New Worlds had been produced and the old Association had swollen from an itinerant board meeting to a vast informal con-gregation that occupied the White Horse Tavern in Fetter Lane every Thursday evening. Carnell acquired the title and in 1948 he and five others set up Nova Publications Ltd to publish and distribute the mag-azine themselves.

NW was not the first British SF magazine, but it was the first to be "home-grown" in this way, from the very capital of British fandom. The six directors met formally in the private bar of the White Horse while the fans and pilgrims overflowed the saloon. NW survived where oth-ers failed: Tales of Wonder, for example, and Fantasy, both edited by Walter Gillings, had already folded when he became a co-founder of

Nova. *NW* came to be respected in America too. Nova Publications were taken over by a larger firm and brought out a sister magazine, *Science Fantasy*, which Carnell also edited. The company acquired a third title, *Science Fiction Adventures*, an American magazine which was dying in 1958; revived, it ran for another five years in England.

Nevertheless, the Americans still dominated the market in the early 1960s (with *Amazing, Analog, Fantastic, Galaxy,* and *Fantasy and Science Fiction*), while Nova was running into difficulties. The parent company, faced with declining sales and dim prospects, decided to discontinue the remaining two magazines. Carnell's last issue of *NW*, no. 141 for March 1964, gave the results of a statistical survey of 350 readers. Limited though this sample was, it showed a fall in demand for specialist SF magazines of any nationality, and a corresponding rise in paperback purchasing. Import restrictions imposed in wartime had been lifted in 1958, causing a flood of cheap commercial fiction from America. Sales of *NW* had begun to fall off in 1959, and had never recovered.

The correspondence columns of *NW*, no. 141 included a letter from Michael Moorcock, a young fan whom Carnell had published in both his magazines. Moorcock deplored their demise; he was an adventurous writer, impatient of timid editors, who knew that Carnell, though essentially conservative, could be persuaded to print experimental work that the American SF magazines would not entertain and that did not conform to the specifications of magazines like *Argosy*, or *Playboy*. Together with J. G. Ballard, another unconventional author similarly frustrated, Moorcock put together a crummy issue of an ideal magazine, in a large format on good quality paper, intended to bridge the widening gap between experimental art and the general public. As well as popularizing the work of artists already established in more exclusive circles (such as William Burroughs and Eduardo Paolozzi), it would offer an outlet for the different and the new by authors yet unrecognized (such as Michael Moorcock and J.G. Ballard); moreover, "it would attempt a cross-fertilization of popular SF, science and the work of the literary and artistic avant garde."[4]

For the moment their idealism was only wishful thinking, stimulated by the death sentence on *New Worlds* and *Science Fantasy*. But just before his last issues appeared Carnell had written to Brian Aldiss telling him that "Nova has sold the two magazines to . . . Roberts and Vinter

Ltd who plan to continue them immediately."[5] David Warburton of
Roberts and Vinter saw in the magazines some potential for publishing
imaginative fiction of a higher standard than the American magazines
maintained. This was a policy that Carnell had always tried to pursue,
and the company asked him to continue as editor; but, as he told Aldiss, "After a whole weekend of mulling things over, I turned down their
offer and have recommended a 'certain person' to them as editor. He
sees them today." This was Michael Moorcock, whose name Carnell
had advanced without his knowledge, though with sympathy for his aspirations and faith in his editorial experience—as well he might, since
Moorcock had begun with a magazine devoted to the fantasies of Edgar
Rice Burroughs, at the age of seventeen. Also interested in the Nova
magazines was Kyril Bonfiglioli, a novelist and bookseller, and Warburton decided to give them one each. Moorcock explains,[6]

> Many people expected me to opt for the editorship of *Science Fantasy*,
> since most of my work had previously appeared in that magazine, but in
> fact I was interested in broadening the possibilities of the SF idiom and
> *New Worlds*, being a much more open title, seemed the best place to do it.

He had to shelve his ideal *NW* because of financial restrictions, so
issue 142 for May and June 1964, Moorcock's first, came out in Compact Books as a cheaply produced paperback on familiar pulp paper. Its
editorial announced that, however familiar the format, the contents of
NW would be altogether new, "a kind of SF which is unconventional
in every sense."[7] "A *popular* literary renaissance," declared Moorcock,
"is around the corner. Together, we can accelerate that renaissance."
The new Renaissance Man would be William Burroughs—"his work is
the SF we've all been waiting for"—whom J. G. Ballard champions in
the same issue as the "true genius and first mythographer of the mid-
twentieth century."[8] The excitement and exaggeration aside, Moorcock proved himself as practical an editor as Carnell had hoped. Aware
that too swift a transformation would alienate the habitual buyers of
NW before it could build up a new readership, Moorcock changed the
contents of the magazine much more slowly than he pretended to.
Alongside Ballard's fiction and his own, "taboo-breaking" stories by
Langdon Jones and Hilary Bailey, and novelties by John Hamilton and

David Rome, Moorcock continued to include plenty of traditional SF. In his first year on *NW* he published perfectly commonplace work by P. F. Woods, Donald Malcolm, Sydney J. Bounds, E. C. Tubb—even Arthur C. Clarke. The correspondence columns began to fill with altercation over the new versus the old. The unfamiliar fiction did not seem to have any corporate identity or even many common factors, but it was quickly lumped together under the label that now seems to be attached to surprising developments in any popular art, a label that may be useful historically but otherwise only compounds confusion: the "New Wave" Advocates (led by the eclectic American anthologist Judith Merril) and opponents began to convene.

There were many who completely misinterpreted Moorcock's policies. Carnell, editing his new series of anthologies, *New Writings in SF,* understood nothing of what was going on back at the old homestead. After three issues of Moorcock's editorship, Carnell wrote to Aldiss: "The new *NW* . . . is degenerating into an imitation of *Nebula*—in fact, I think the salvation of my old magazines lies solely with Bonfiglioli and S-F."[9] But Bonfiglioli had none of Moorcock's vision or skill. He lost circulation by changing his title from *Science Fantasy* to *SF Impulse* at a time when distributors were reluctant to handle new promotions. In 1966 he resigned the ailing magazine to J. G. Ballard, who took only a few days to realize he didn't want it after all. The amiable Harry Harrison caught it, knocked it back into a more traditional shape, and kept it alive until the end of the year when Thorpe and Porter, distributors for Roberts and Vinter, went bankrupt, owing £20,000. Cutting back, Roberts and Vinter decided to amputate SF, the less profitable end of their range.

In fact Moorcock had improved the sales of *NW* and was just getting into his stride. Brian Aldiss, who had been hesitant over Moorcock's reorganization at first, but was now convinced that he had "worked . . . wonders with the magazine,"[10] began to look for someone to buy it from Roberts and Vinter. Aldiss, never having suffered from the disrepute that writing SF could often earn, had more influence in the republic of letters than Moorcock, who in any case had personal and principled disagreements with the literary establishment. He sought help from Kingsley Amis, Charles Osborne of the *London Magazine,* and Douglas Hill of Pan Books. In addition he approached a number of writers and critics to gather support for an application to the Arts Council for a grant for *NW*: "a wild idea, but everything must be tried."[11] Kenneth Allsop, Anthony Burgess, Edmund Crispin, Roy Fuller, Marghanita Laski, and J. B. Priestley all replied in favor, and on 11 January 1967 Aldiss wrote to Ken Slater and Doreen Parker of the British Science Fiction Association:

> I seem to have saved the day with New Worlds. I was up in London yesterday, met David Warburton, and we went round to the Arts Council. We had a brief discussion there, but it appears the Council has already made up its mind to move on our behalf ... and ... provide financial help for a year. . . . Although there is a 95% certainty we shall get the grant, this won't be confirmed yet awhile.

Moorcock, who had not been altogether in agreement with the application and had never expected it to be approved, found himself in receipt of a guaranteed £150 per issue. It was not enough to finance a whole magazine, but the award and the prestige it brought persuaded Warburton to continue his involvement. He entered partnership with Moorcock to produce *NW* themselves, though Panther and Fontana had already expressed interest in it. In the meantime a couple of bridging issues (nos. 171 and 172) had been assembled from shelved material and special donations (including stories by Aldiss and Ballard that had proved too radical for other publishers), and personally guaranteed against loss by Aldiss and Warburton. With Charles Platt, responsible for the design, layout and later much of the editing of *NW*, Moorcock looked over the dummy magazine he and Ballard had originally compiled, and Warburton agreed to print it in that format. There was an unexpected delay in the certification of the grant—on 17 May Aldiss wrote to Judith Merril, "The damned thing is still not official"—but in July 1967 *NW*, no. 173 came out as a large magazine, on glossy paper, with a cover that reproduced a picture by M. C. Escher. This was a clean break with the traditional SF "pulps"; in neither form nor content did it now bear any resemblance to the magazine Carnell had left three years earlier, though its progress was to be no less uneven. Merril, writing to Moorcock in October 1967, was already referring to "*New Worlds'* current difficulties." While Moorcock was in America in November

Warburton decided that the sales had not been good enough to sustain his interest. To Moorcock[12]

> it seemed yet again that *New Worlds* was to fold. . . . David Warburton
> had decided to end his involvement with the magazine and had gone to
> Scotland, leaving me a note to tell me that the magazine was now mine
> to do with as I pleased

and, of course, solely his financial responsibility. Unexpectedly Sylvester Stein of Stonehart Publications offered rescue; his firm had scant experience of dealing with fiction, much less the radical and *avant-garde,* but Stein had a liking for *NW.*

Before long there was trouble of a different kind. Norman Spinrad's *Bug Jack Barron,* an aggressive and tumultuous story of media and political corruption in a near future America, was serialized for most of 1968. It was intended to disturb, and did. A member of Parliament dubbed Spinrad a degenerate and asked the Minister of Arts why taxpayers' money was being spent on an obscene publication. W. H. Smith and John Menzies refused to stock it, thus effectively crushing its circulation and consigning it to commercial obscurity. Stonehart began to regret their agreement. Moorcock had lost heavily by investing his own money in pay for contributors; contributors were not paid, and began to queue up; there were difficulties with the Arts Council grant; Stonehart delayed paying the printers; the printers refused to deliver; the press, enticed by bans and accusations of obscenity, gave *NW* some inaccurate and unwelcome publicity; the distributors grew nervous, secretly withheld stocks and pulped back numbers; the staff were to be seen selling copies on the street.

Despite all, the quality and aspirations of the magazine were upheld. In October 1968 Moorcock took over complete responsibility and published it himself. Since his energies were stretched between this and writing commercial fantasy to finance it, the magazine came to depend heavily on the commitment of everyone involved, each issue being assembled communally. The Arts Council seemed about to withdraw but renewed their grant; but in April 1970 Moorcock and Platt found they could stand the strain no longer. No. 200 was the last of the series; Moorcock made up a special farewell issue, containing an index, for subscribers only, and it seemed that this time *NW* really was dead.

In autumn 1971, however, the first *New Worlds Quarterly* came out from Sphere Books. Moorcock, determined that *NW* should continue, but avoid the troubles that had beset the magazine's publication, thought the answer was to return to paperback editions distributed and controlled as ordinary books (much as Carnell's *New Writings in SF* were). It was an excellent opportunity to relax a little and to reprint some material from previous issues that few people had had the chance to read, but the *Quarterly* never achieved the immediacy and vigor of the monthlies, and after only a year had contracted their endemic irregularity of appearance. A letter to Moorcock from the publishers mentions a contract for volumes 7 to 11,[13] but another breakdown intervened. Moorcock gave up editorial involvement again, handing no. 7 to Charles Platt and Hilary Bailey, "experienced editors who have not become, as, frankly, I feel I have become, jaded!"[14] A disagreement with Sphere resulted in a change to Corgi Books for nos 9 and 10, and then a long silence. In 1976 Moorcock wrote, "Plans are afoot to publish *NW* again in large size, probably through Quartet. Format will be reminiscent of the old *NW* under my editorship but even more lavish. Hilary Bailey will edit."[15] Two years later, in spring 1978, an envelope of xeroxed sheets calling itself *New Worlds*, no. 212 was distributed to a small number of interested parties. Once again, Moorcock was responsible. Most of the material featured, by regular contributors, had first been printed in *Frendz* magazine.[16] A flyer for the next issue announced, "There will be no conventional narrative fiction in *New Worlds* and little conventional criticism. The majority of the material will have a strong visual flavour." This last series was irregular and short lived. Moorcock edited two issues, David Britton a third and Charles Platt a fourth. The principle was that editorial continuity and conformity of design and schedule are unnecessary impositions: the material should dictate the magazine, not vice versa. Sales were hardly encouraging; plans for a fifth issue by Phil Meadley were not carried out; personal disagreements became divisive. Now Moorcock warns, "If ever I start to talk about doing another issue, that's the time to send for the ambulance."

The divorce between *NW* and the genre SF magazines was inevitable rather than intentional. When Moorcock's original bid to develop SF on its own terms met with misunderstanding and vehement resistance, he rejected those terms and committed the magazine to a broader range of imaginative fiction which might still acknowledge SF, but only as a point of departure.[17]

> We were surprised by the lack of response from old guard SF fans, who we had assumed were as hungry for real imagination as we had been. Naively, we had honestly expected that these readers would be more open to new kinds of writing. It took me some years to learn that a certain kind of SF fan is about the most conservative reader of all!

The ventures that Moorcock proposed threatened the denizens of fandom. What the outsider may perceive as the limitations of genre the fan feels as the security of city walls. Commercial genres exist by exclusion, have specific functions, satisfy particular tastes. Some less parochial enthusiasts would be happy to open the gates and encourage visitors to enjoy the peculiar virtues of the region, its climate, geography, flora and fauna—the critical benevolence of C.S. Lewis and Kingsley Amis, for example. Others want to keep the walls closed, prize the esoteric delights of belonging to a clique, and relish exchanging conspiratorial grins while the outsider stands baffled—the nationalist zeal of Sam Moskowitz and Donald A. Wollheim. Moorcock's program amounted to knocking down the walls and trading local resources with countries far and wide. It met with much disapproval. Begun in a spirit of benign optimism, it was pursued determinedly, even aggressively. Editorial manifestos pounded a party line, belying the fact that the party hardly knew where to draw one. Today it was a return to the values of H. G. Wells; tomorrow an advance to the innovations of William Burroughs; next month a sidestep to embrace Mervyn Peake. Meanwhile reviewers sniped at the sacred colossi: Heinlein, Asimov, Blish. *NW* broke the pulp taboos, kindling controversy, to challenge the reader's assumptions and stretch the limits of his acceptance. Nowhere was there more scandal, or more success, than in the areas of psychology and sexuality, two topics of much popular interest and excitement in the 1960s, and two respects in which science fiction, with its chaste and cardboard characters, was famous for its deficiency.

Notes

1. *The New SF: An Original Anthology of Modern Speculative Fiction*, ed. Langdon Jones (London: Hutchinson, 1969).

2. Michael Moorcock, Preface, ibid, p. 7.

3. Hilary Baily, "Some Corner of a Funny Field," *Foundation: The Review of Science Fiction*, no. 13 (May 1978), pp. 78–83.

4. Moorcock, "New Worlds: A Personal History," *Foundation*, no. 15 (January 1979), pp. 5–18.

5. E. J. Carnell, letter to Brian Aldiss, 25 February 1964.

6. Moorcock, "New Worlds—Jerry Cornelius" *Sojan* (Manchester: Savoy, 1977), p. 144.

7. Moorcock, editorial: "A New Literature for the Space Age," *NW*, no. 142 (May–June 1964), pp. 2–3 (author's italics).

8. J. G. Ballard, "Myth Maker of the 20 Century," *NW*, no. 142 (May–June 1964), pp. 121–27.

9. Carnell, letter to Aldiss, 19 October 1964.

10. Aldiss, letter to Lee Harding, 22 February 1967.

11. Aldiss, letter to Harry Harrison, 26 February 1967.

12. Moorcock, "A Personal History," op. cit., pp. 13-14.

13. 14 November 1973.

14. Moorcock, Introduction, *NWQ*, no. 7 (Autumn 1974), p. 9. Hilary Bailey, a writer and critic, was Moorcock's wife at the time.

15. Moorcock, Letter to Charlie Brown, 29 February 1976.

16. *Frendz* (23 June 1971).

17. Moorcock, "A Personal History," op. cit., p. 11.

~

CHAPTER EIGHTEEN

Space Opera Redefined

David G. Hartwell and Kathryn Cramer

For the past twenty years (1982–2002), the Hugo Award for best novel has generally been given to space opera—from David Brin, C. J. Cherryh, and Orson Scott Card to Lois Bujold, Dan Simmons, and Vernor Vinge. (The shorter fiction awards have been distributed much more widely over the range of SF and fantasy styles and possibilities.) One might go so far as to say that the Hugo Award for best novel has always gone primarily to space opera, as currently defined, though many of the earlier winners, up to the end of the 1970s, would have been mortally offended to have their books so-labeled. Space opera used to be a pejorative locution designating not a subgenre or mode at all, but the worst form of formulaic hackwork: really bad SF.

A lot of people don't remember this and that distorts our understanding of both our present and our past in SF. Perfectly intelligent but ignorant people are writing revisionist history, inventing an elaborate age of space opera based on wholesale redefinitions of the term made up in the sixties and seventies to justify literary political agendas. To say it flatly, before the mid-1970s, no one in the history of science fiction ever consciously and intentionally set out to write something called "space opera" (except Jack Vance, who accepted the assignment from Berkley Books in the late 1960s to write a novel to fit the title, *Space*

Opera—at the same time Philip K. Dick got the assignment to write a book called *The Zap Gun*. These were editorial jokes to be shared with the fans).

On the other hand, there are a number of examples of works from the late 1940s on published as intentional parodies of space opera, that in effect apply the term to works either fairly or unfairly for humorous effect, often poking fun at the big names of the past. This, too, is literary politics. Nevertheless, there is now a real body of work that gets nominated for awards and often wins them, that is authentically and consciously written as space opera. Much of it is on one cutting edge or another of SF in the last two decades—and there are a number of cutting edges.

Here is the origin and description of the term from the early dictionary of SF, the *Fancyclopedia II* (1959):

> "Space Opera" ([coined by Wilson] Tucker) A hack science-fiction story, a dressed-up western; so called by analogy with "horse opera" for Western bangbangshootemup movies and "soap opera" for radio and video yellow-drama. [To here, the entire entry from Fancyclopedia, 1944]. Of course, some space operas are more crass about their nature than others; early *Captain Video* TVcasts were a hybrid of original space scenes and footage from old Western movies (purporting to represent a Spy Ray checking up on the Captain's Earthly agents). Terry Carr once unearthed a publication *genommen Space Western Comics*, in which a character named Spurs Jackson adventured in a futuristic Western setting with his "space vigilantes," and the old prewar *Planet Comics* intermittently ran a strip about the Fifth Martian Lancers and their struggles with rebel tribesmen.

What Bob Tucker actually said in his fanzine in 1941 was:

> In these hectic days of phrase-coining, we offer one. Westerns are called "horse operas," the morning housewife tear-jerkers are called "soap operas," For the hacky, grinding, stinking, outworn space-ship yarn, or world-saving for that matter, we offer "space opera."

We emphasize that this original definition applied to all bad SF hackwork. It did not refer to good space stories in *Astounding*, or to Doc Smith and Edmund Hamilton, leading lights of the field, but to the subliterate hackwork appearing in, say, *Amazing*, in those days and never reprinted or praised today. It did not confine itself to the future, or off-Earth settings, or refer to any "good old days." Those twists of the term were introduced much later.

"Space opera" was still a negative term in the 1950s. An ad on the back cover of the early issues of *Galaxy* (then an ambitious new magazine) bore the headline, "You'll never find this in Galaxy . . . ," that gave a stereotypical example of space opera for the time. When the term appeared in review columns in the '50s, I recall someone, perhaps even Damon Knight, referring to Hamilton's hackwork series, *Captain Future*, as an example of space opera, while distinguishing it from his better work. And I recall Knight praising Leigh Brackett. There was no sense of "space opera" meaning anything other than "hacky, grinding, stinking, outworn" SF stories of any kind. Still, as the fifties ended, the term became associated specifically with space stories and its meaning began to be contaminated with fondness for outworn, clunky, old-fashioned SF, guilty pleasures.

We don't know the first time anyone used the term in reference to Doc Smith, but by the 1960s it was so used, though not universally. That was the first real signpost of a shift in meaning to give space opera an air of nostalgic approval.

The next signpost was the New Wave project in England. Pushing for a revolution, Michael Moorcock and J. G. Ballard in the early 1960s used their prestige and polemical gifts to condemn most SF of prior decades. They declared space fiction over with, and the fiction of the near future, inner space, and the human mind the only true contemporary SF. In the process they conflated all SF adventure in distant futures or distant in space with space opera and said it was all bad, all literary history, and no longer a living part of SF. Their associates in the later '60s and early '70s, including Harry Harrison (in the parodies *Bill, The Galactic Hero*, and *Star Smashers of the Galaxy Rangers*), M. John Harrison (in the Besterian deconstruction *The Centauri Device*), and Brian Aldiss in his two-volume anthology, *Space Opera* and *Galactic Empires*, enforced these ideas by example.

When Aldiss edited *Space Opera* in 1974, he was approaching the height of his reputation both as a writer and as a literary critic (and was also editing with Harry Harrison a prestigious *SF: The Year's Best anthology* series). In his introduction, he pronounced space opera dead, except as a hothouse cultivation: Essentially space opera was born in the pulp magazines, flourished there, and died there. It is still being written, but in the main by authors who owe their inspiration and impetus to the pulps.

He presented space opera as a guilty pleasure for readers of good, serious SF: This is not a serious anthology. Both volumes burst with voluptuous vacuum. They have been put together to amuse.

Aldiss also said, "The term is both vague and inspired, and must have been coined [here Aldiss is being especially coy] with both affection and some scorn. . . . Its parameters are marked by a few mighty concepts standing like watch-towers along a lonely frontier. What goes on between them is essentially simple—a tale of love or hate, triumph or defeat—because it is the watch-towers that matter. We are already familiar with some of them: the question of reality, the limitations of knowledge, exile, the sheer immensity of the universe, the endlessness of time."

In effect, this elaborate description is a wholesale redefinition of "space opera" as the good old stuff.

It used to be possible before about 1973 for SF critics to distinguish space opera (from the 1920 to the 1970s) from popular SF adventure (as written by, for instance, Poul Anderson or Henry Kuttner, and sometimes called "planetary romances"). The SF adventures of Edgar Rice Burroughs and later, Leigh Brackett, were fast paced, colorful, heroic, and (at least in Brackett's case) well written, for all their pulp clichés. They were not considered mere hackwork, although a taste for Burroughs, say, was often considered a guilty pleasure. It is still the working definition for some SF people.

The redefinition of "space opera" collapsed all adventure forms into merely varieties of space opera and they are since then usually indistinguishable in SF discussions—as are the aforementioned works of Edward E. Smith, once an early model of good, hard SF adventure. Doc Smith got published in *Astounding*, even in the Campbell Golden Age years, and Robert A. Heinlein respected, and praised, Smith's works. But Smith's now the poster child of early space opera. And the days of SF before the 1950s are often referred to as the days of space opera, and that's at least a partial triumph for the new wave.

And now for the next signpost. Leigh Brackett, by the mid1970s, was one of the respected elder writers of SF: in the middle and late

1970s, Del Rey Books reissued nearly all her early tales, calling them space opera as a contemporary term of praise!

Here's how that happened: Lester Del Rey had set out to bring SF back to its roots as non-literary, or even anti-literary, entertainment, to specifically reject the incursions of Modernism into SF after what he declared the pretension and excesses and failed experiments of the New Wave. Lester and his wife Judy Lynn accepted the new wave conflation of SF Adventure and Space Opera and used the terms synonymously— both in Judy's marketing for Del Rey books and in Lester's review columns in *Analog*—as terms of approbation.

I often heard them speak about space opera in public without realizing, until years later, the effect it was having: to finally and entirely reverse the polarity of space opera. Back then I thought they were just crass marketeers. At the time, while Gardner Dozois and Terry Carr and Charlie Brown and I and a bunch of others sat around at Worldcon dead dog parties in the late 1970s joking about the Del Rey's passionate, lowest-common-denominator, anti-literary, SF populism, "space opera" was becoming a term of approbation denoting the best kind of contemporary and past SF as just the type of SF Aldiss had described as dead.

Lester even went to the extreme of denying that any writer could set out to write SF as art. This of course flew in the face of both the Knight/Merril/Sturgeon axis in the USA, and of the New Worlds crew in the United Kingdom. Moorcock, Ballard, Aldiss, and the rest, all believed that SF could be good art and that good writers could aspire to art through SF—if they discarded the traditions of space opera.

It took nearly ten years to accomplish the redefinition, but by the early years of the 1980s the Del Reys' efforts succeeded in altering the perceived meaning of "space opera." Their model by the end of the 1970s at Del Rey became *Star Wars* (the book, and the film) and its sequels. And in the end Del Rey Books attached Brackett's considerable prestige and authority to the *Star Wars* project when Brackett, also an accomplished screen writer, did the script for *The Empire Strikes Back*. The Del Rey novelization of the film has both her name on it as well as the novelizer's. And so in the popular mind, within a few years, *Star Wars* was conflated with *Star Trek* fiction to contour the new image of "space opera": by the mid-1980s "space opera" was a code term in U.S. marketing circles for bestselling popular SF entertainment.

Here's the big irony: the Del Reys were conservative, and were shooting for a restoration of past virtues, and instead hit the future. What they did was to allow the postmodern conflation of marketing and art, the inclusion of media in the artistic project of SF, and to permit the mixing of all levels and kinds of art in individual works. They established the artistic environment for works they would never have considered publishing or supporting. They set the stage for postmodern space opera.

Many readers and writers and nearly all media fans that entered SF after 1975 have never understood the origin of space opera as a pejorative and some may be surprised to learn of it. Thus the term "space opera" reentered the serious discourse on contemporary SF in the 1980s with a completely altered meaning: henceforth, "space opera" meant, and still generally means, colorful, dramatic, large-scale science fiction adventure, competently and sometimes beautifully written, usually focused on a sympathetic, heroic central character, and plot action [this bit is what separates it from other literary postmodernisms] and usually set in the relatively distant future and in space or on other worlds, characteristically optimistic in tone. What is centrally important is that this permits a writer to embark on a science-fiction project that is ambitious in both commercial and literary terms.

The new traditions, of contemporary space opera come only partly from the Del Rey marketing and philosophical changes, though they start there. Good writers immediately began in the 1980s to trace their own roots back to space opera classics of the past. The most ambitious parts of contemporary space opera now derive from such models as Brackett's *The Sword of Rhiannon*, and Charles Harness's "The Rose," Jack Vance's *The Dying Earth*, the *Norstrilia* stories of Cordwainer Smith, Samuel R. Delany's *Nova*, Larry Niven and Jerry Pournelle's *The Mote In God's Eye*, Michael Moorcock's *Dancers at the End of Time* series, Norman Spinrad's *Riding The Torch* and *The Void-Captain's Tale*, C.J. Cherryh's *Downbelow Station*, Gene Wolfe's four volume *The Book of the New Sun*, and particularly its sequel, *The Urth of the New Sun*, Orson Scott Card's *Ender's Game*, et. seq., David Brin's *Uplift* series, Melissa Scott's *Five Twelfths of Heaven*, Mike Resnick's *Santiago*, Lois McMaster Bujold's Miles Vorkosigian series, Colin Greenland's *Take Back Plenty*, et. seq., and Iain M. Bank's *Consider Phlebas*, and the succeeding novels in his *Culture* series. Together such works formed not one cutting edge but many, a constellation of models (once the definitional barriers were removed so they might all be considered as part of a space opera tradition) for ambitious younger writers by the end of the 1980s, an exciting decade for space opera indeed.

Because Banks's novels were bestsellers in England, spectacularly and unexpectedly successful, Banks, in spite of his relatively small impact in the United States, was the foremost model in the United Kingdom as the 1990s began. Paul Kincaid, in an essay on 1990s SF, *The New Optimism*, called him the most influential writer in Britain today, and said: His huge commercial success (bigger than any genre writer except for Terry Pratchett), has spawned a host of successors, from those opportunistically likened to him in publishing blurbs to those who have genuinely been inspired by his approach, his vigorous literary style or his view of the future."

There is no one thing that is *the* new space opera though, no matter how the Brits would like to think so, and claim it. There are a number of dissimilar yet important and ambitious individual writers in the SF world, all of them sometimes stretching genre boundaries, including Dan Simmons, John Varley, David Brin, Iain Banks, Catherine Asaro, Orson Scott Card, John Clute, Peter Hamilton, Lois McMaster Bujold, M John Harrison, Donald M. Kingsbury, David Weber, Ken MacLeod, Alastair Reynolds, Mike Resnick, C. J. Cherryh, and many others. All of them have made a valid claim to be writing ambitious space opera (some of the time), and all of them are or have been popular and influential. Since the reversal of polarity of the term "space opera" in the 1970s was a covert literary battle, not a public argument and discussion, the nature of space opera boundaries has been fluid and imprecise, constantly updated by new examples—hey, look at *Startide Rising*; look at *Ender's Game*, look at *Santiago*; look at *Use of Weapons*; look at *Hyperion*; look at *Appleseed*. The new space opera of the past twenty years is arguably the literary cutting edge of SF now.

In closing, we note that the majority of websites devoted to space opera today are media fan sites, and with deadpan sincerity they generally trace the origins of film and TV space opera back to *Captain Video*. The authors of *Fancyclopedia* may be laughing.

PART FIVE

INFATUATION

One characteristic of science fiction is its large and interactive fandom. What is fandom and why does science fiction have it, while other genres, originating in parallel during the pulp era, developed fandoms much later, if at all? Several scholars in this anthology maintain that people read science fiction differently than they read other types of literature, and the answer to two difficult questions—why fandom? And why different reading protocols?—may emerge from a consideration of a genre and its readers. The selections in this section explore in detail the challenges and pleasures of this particular type of reading.

The first chapter from David Hartwell's *Age of Wonders*, "The Golden Age of Science Fiction Is Twelve," is directed, primarily, at nonreaders of science fiction, which makes it the ideal starting place for persons unacquainted with the genre, although, as Hartwell points out, one would probably have to have been frozen in a cave or lost in outer space for at least half a century to remain ignorant of it. Hartwell's tone is light, like Malzberg's, but it would be a mistake to overlook its seriousness. Hartwell, who earned a Ph.D. in literature before he created a distinguished career as editor and anthologist, and thus is an example of the phenomenon he records, puts many of the elements of the science fiction phenomenon into context with one another in ways that other critics have alluded to, but not undertaken, and for this reason, among others, Hartwell's section is useful here. Hartwell addresses the connections between the fans of science fiction, the publishers, and the writers, as well as their interactions with the various media forms in which the genre appears. He asks us to examine our own science fiction experience and come to a better understanding of the way each of us subjectively creates our own referent for the term.

Samuel Delany's theories of the reading conventions of science fiction are among the most important tools for any modern student of the genre. Both his selections in this anthology address the issue to some degree, but "Some Presumptuous Approaches to Science Fiction" takes a number of interesting approaches to the study. In this essay, Delany's conversational style is crucial, for its characteristic digressiveness allows him to build an almost hyper-textual analysis not only of the differences between readers of science fiction and those of "mundane" literature, but of the entire linguistic and cultural context which causes people to ask the "baroque unanswerables that plague an SF writer's life."

James Gunn's essay, "Touchstones," is also almost hypertextual, although in a very different way from Delany's. While "Some Presumptuous Approaches" explores the ways that science fiction readers and writers approach the text from both sides, "Touchstones" comes entirely from the direction of the reader, seeking the source of pleasure that science fiction provides, what Sam Moskowitz and Damon Knight (and Hartwell after them) termed "wonder." Gunn shows how the joy of science fiction comes from the individual moments in which the created world of the text stands out sharply in our mind against the mundane world in which we live, coincidentally, the very moments that Delany shows to be incomprehensible to readers unversed in the genre's particular idiom. Unlike Hartwell's book, this essay is directed at longtime readers of science fiction, and newer readers are encouraged to revisit it at a later date.

⁓

CHAPTER NINETEEN

The Golden Age of
Science Fiction Is Twelve

David Hartwell

Immersed in science fiction. Bathing in it, drowning in it; for the ado-lescent who leans this way it can be better than sex. More accessible, more compelling. And the outsider can only wonder, What's the matter with him? What is he into, what's the attraction, why is it so intense?

Grown men and women, sixty years old, twenty-five years old, sit around and talk about "the golden age of science fiction," remembering when every story in every magazine was a masterwork of daring, origi-nal thought. Some say the golden age was circa 1928; some say 1939; some favor 1953, or 1970. The arguments rage till the small of the morning, and nothing is ever resolved.

Because the real golden age of science fiction is twelve.

This is a book about the science-fiction field and that body of con-temporary writing known as science fiction, or SF. Over the years there have been a number of books on the writing the field has produced, its artwork and illustration, histories, memoirs, even a book devoted to the amateur publications of the fans. But no general attempt to describe both the literature and the specific subculture out of which the litera-ture flows has ever been presented to the world at large. Donald A. Wollheim, in *The Universe Makers*, and Lester del Rey, in *The World of Science Fiction 1926–1976*, come closer than any others and you might try them, though both are dated.

For one thing, the world at large, especially all who do not read and do not wish to read SF, couldn't have cared less. "Everyone" knows that science fiction is not serious literature and that since the word "science" occurs in the name you wouldn't be interested or able to understand if you did try to read it—so why try?

Despite the fact that twelve-year-olds who read it understand it perfectly, and that millions of readers over the years have found it great fun (it *is* supposed to be fun), the majority of educated readers in the English-speaking world spurn SF without reading it or knowing anymore about it than what "everyone" knows. Well, this book is not an attempt to convert anyone (although later on I do recommend some SF for people who have not read in the field before). What I do intend is to offer a book that informs you about an amusing and significant phenomenon that reaches into every home and family in the country and influences the way we all see the world around us.

This is an outsider's guidebook and road map through the world of science fiction, pointing out the historical monuments, backyard follies, highways, and back streets of the SF community—a tour of main events and sideshows, and a running commentary on why the SF world is the way it is. I hope it will be particularly useful for the casually curious, the neophyte reader, and of course the person who knows people in SF and wonders why they are that way. Is your child threatened by this strange stuff, or by the companionship of lovers of science fiction? Does SF rot the mind and ruin the character? Just how wild and crazy are those SF people and what do they really do, where do they come from, why do they stay in the SF world? This tour, if successful, should take you not only through the nooks and crannies of the SF world, but into some unsuspected aspects of the everyday world as well.

Written science fiction, like cooking, mathematics, or rock 'n' roll, is a whole bunch of things that some people can understand or do and some not. We all know people who love cooking, math, or rock (perhaps all three), and others who can hardly boil water, add two plus two, or distinguish music from noise. Your present tour guide stopped trying to convert people to instant appreciation of science fiction years ago when he finally understood that most new readers have to go through a process of SF education and familiarization before they can love it. Just because someone can read does not mean that he necessarily can read SF, just as the ability to write Arabic numerals and add and subtract doesn't mean you necessarily can or want to perform long division.

So I have set out to describe science fiction without assuming that you have read any or would even know what to do if you were faced with the text of an SF story. I will discuss as clearly as possible all the barriers you might have against understanding SF and all the barriers that SF has erected to keep from being understood by outsiders—for like the world of the circus and the carny, the SF world only wants insiders behind the scenes. And more, the SF world does not want an audience (such as the "mass audience") who won't take the time to learn the rules and conventions of the game.

SF is special within its community, which has built complex fortifications and groundworks surrounding its treasures; and for most people, the rewards of reading SF or being an SF-type person are worthless or pernicious or even a bit scary. To one who is comfortable and has adjusted to the compromises of our culture, being or becoming something of an outsider has no advantages.

Wait for a moment though, before you make up your mind that you don't really have to become acquainted with what is going on in this other reality. The underground world of SF interpenetrates with your daily world so thoroughly in so many ways that finding out what those relatively few people who live the SF world are like may let you understand a lot more about how your own world operates. Besides, as Thomas Pynchon so amusingly posited in his eccentric novella, *The Crying of Lot 49*, if you begin to look beneath the surface of everyday life, almost everyone is involved in some sort of underground or underground activity. This kind of activity is so much a part of what everyone does (without ever seeing the big picture) that if you pull back and look at it all, the real world seems very different. That is, in one very real sense, what this book is about.

When you spot a science fiction devotee on a bus, in a library, or on lunch break in the cafeteria, she or he is identifiable only by a display of some kind: She is reading a flashy paperback that says "Science Fiction" on the cover; he is wearing a "*Star Trek* Lives!" T-shirt over his bathing trunks at the beach; she is quietly asking the bookseller if there is a copy of *Women of Wonder* in the store; he is arguing loudly with a friend that *Star Wars* is much better than *Close Encounters* (which is not truly SF) while munching a sandwich and sipping Coke.

Otherwise, there are no reliable outward signs, unless you happen to stop over at a hotel or motel anywhere in the United States where one of the at least weekly science fiction conventions is being held—after one look, you switch accommodations, because the whole place is filled with people in costumes, bacchanalian howls, teenagers in capes with swords, normally dressed adults wearing garish name tags that identify them as Gork or Kalinga Joe or Conan or David G. Hartwell or Beardsley Trunion. Your immediate perception of this social situation is either "Feh!" or "Let me back off and view these weirdos from a safe distance, say, at the end of tomorrow's newscast!"

The science-fiction person, you see, always lives in the SF world, but under cover of normality most of the time—except while attending a gathering of like minds such as the SF conventions given in understated flashes above. The science-fiction reader may be your attorney, your dentist, your children's schoolteacher, the film projectionist at your local theater, your wife or husband or child, happily living in two worlds at once, the real world of science fiction and the dubious reality of everyday life.

If you have lived with or worked with a science-fiction person you will have noticed how intensely she seems to be involved in science fiction, how much she reads it, watches it, recommends to those around her that they try it, because it is her special kind of fun. And if you examine her behavior in everyday life, you may well notice an impatience with the way things are, an ironic, sometimes sarcastic attitude toward everyday things (particularly imposed tasks of a wearisome nature), a desire for change. This complex of attitudes is closely congruent to the complex of attitudes found in the normal human teenager.

In fact, a majority of all science-fiction readers are under the age of twenty-one. The question is not how they got that way but why it should surprise anyone that they are. Teenagers are not fully integrated into the tedium of adult life and tend to view such everyday life with healthy suspicion. Quite logical. The science-fiction reader preserves this attitude as long in life as his association with science fiction continues, more often these days into full maturity. It makes him act strangely sometimes. But mostly he feeds his head with more science fiction and continues to get the job done, whatever it is.

Nearly a thousand readers of *Locus*, the newspaper of the science-fiction field (a semiprofessional monthly published by California fan Charles N. Brown), responded a couple of years ago to a survey, which indicated that the median age of *Locus* readers is twenty-two but that the initial involvement in science fiction of almost every respondent happened between the ages of ten and fourteen. This lends a great deal of substance to the tradition in the science-fiction world that active involvement starts early and lasts at least until the early twenties. Science fiction is an addiction (or habit) so reasonable in any teenager who can read (and many who can't very well, in this age of *Star Trek* and *Star Wars*) that it is superficially a curiosity that it doesn't always last. But it doesn't, and most of us do end up well-adjusted, more or less, resigned to life as it is known to be beyond 1984.

The science-fiction drug is available everywhere to kids, in super-hero comics, on TV, in the movies, in books and magazines. It is impossible to avoid exposure, to avoid the least hint of excitement at Marvel Comics superheroes and *Star Trek* reruns and *Star Wars*, impossible not to become habituated even before kindergarten to the language, clichés, basic concepts of science fiction. Children's culture in the contemporary U.S. is a supersaturated SF environment. By the time a kid can read comic books and attend a movie unaccompanied by an adult, his mind is a fertile environment for the harder stuff. Even the cardboard monsters of TV reruns feed the excitement. The science-fiction habit is established early.

In some cases, accompanied by the hosannas of proud parents, a kid focuses his excitement on the science part and goes on to construct winning exhibits in school science fairs, obtain scholarships, and support proud parents in their old age with his honorable gains as a career corporate technologist. Most often, a kid freezes at the gosh-wow TV/comics/movies stage and carries an infatuation with fantastic and absurd adventure into later life. But sometimes, usually by the age of twelve, a kid progresses to reading science fiction in paperback, in magazines, book club editions—wherever he can find it, because written SF offers more concentrated excitement. This is the beginning of addiction; he buys, borrows, even steals all the science fiction he can get his hands on and reads omnivorously for months or even years, sometimes until the end of high school years, sometimes a book or more a day. But the classic symptom is intense immersion in written SF for at least six months around age twelve.

Publishers adore this phenomenon, akin to the addiction to mystery and detective fiction that flourished in the decades prior to the mid-1960s. One major publisher of SF had been heard to remark that his books are supported by twelve-year-olds of all ages. Every professional writer, editor, and publisher in the science-fiction field knows that the structure of science-fiction publishing is founded on the large teenage audience, which guarantees a minimally acceptable market for almost every book or magazine published—it requires extreme ignorance and professional incompetence, determination akin to constipating oneself by an act of will, to be unsuccessful when selling science fiction to the omnivorous teenage audience.

What happens to science-fiction omnivores? Well, obviously, most of them discover the compulsive excitement of the opposite (or same) sex, and stop reading much of anything for pleasure, most of them permanently. However, once you have been an omnivore, your life has been permanently altered, if only in minor ways. Years later, you may experience an irrational desire to watch *Battlestar Galactica* on TV, even though you know it's dumb stuff. You tend not to forbid your kids or kid your friends if they want a little toke of science fiction from time to time. A news report on solar energy possibilities in the near future doesn't seem like total balderdash, just, perhaps, a bit optimistic in the short run. A front-page newspaper article on the U.S. space probe to Jupiter doesn't read like Sanskrit or form associations with guff like spirit-rapping. Surprise! Your life has been altered and you didn't even notice.

Discovering sex (or competitive sports or evangelical Christianity or demon rum) is not always a total diversion, though. You can, of course, read with one hand. And there are further activities open to the fan in the omnivorous stage: Hundreds, often thousands, of fans gather at conventions every weekend throughout Western civilization (the World Science Fiction Convention of 1979 was in Brighton, England; the 1985 Worldcon will be in Australia) to act strangely together. To a teenage omnivore, such a weekend of license to be maladjusted in the company of and in harmony with the covertly alienated of all ages can be golden. No one much notices how you dress or act as long as you do not injure yourself or others.

Swords and capes (ah! Romance!) are particularly favored among the fat and pimply population, male and female. One wag counted seventy-two Princess Leias at the World SF Convention of 1978 in Phoenix! *Star Trek* costumes still abound in the mid-1980s. Or you can hang out in your everyday slacks and jacket or jeans and T-shirt with like minds. And right there among the crowd are all the big-name professionals, from Asimov to Zelazny, by tradition and in fact approachable for conversation and frivolity. Just being there makes you a potentially permanent member of the SF family.

It's a clique, you see. Just like the ones you are cut out of in the local junior high or whatever, only now you are automatically a member until you do something beyond the pale. You might be so shy as to be tongue-tied for your first ten conventions; still, if you walk into a room party you can sit on the floor and listen to Isaac Asimov sing Gilbert and Sullivan—and join in if you like. And go home and tell your friends that you spent time with Asimov last weekend. Just so you don't feel lonely in the arid stretches between conventions you can afford to attend, there are approximately 4,000 fan magazines produced by individuals and written by themselves and/or other fans to keep you in communication with the SF world day to day.

As you might have gathered, the great family aspect of SF is, in the long run, only for the most ardent—maybe 10,000 active fans in the U.S. at any time. Most often, fans mature socially enough to adjust to their home environment and just read the stuff off and on, attending, perhaps, a World Convention every year or two to keep contact with a few friends. This is the chronic stage of addiction, following the active omnivore phase. And *this* stage can last for life.

If you grew up in isolation from movies, TV, and comics and have never read a work of science fiction (or if you tried one once, and found it dumb, incomprehensible or both), you might ask, at this point, why the fuss? The answer is that even if you have kept yourself in pristine separation from the material, you are interacting daily with people who have progressed to at least a stage-one involvement in science fiction and who have altered your environment because of it.

Science fiction as written and published during the last twenty years is so diverse in every aspect that no reader except at the height of the omnivorous stage can expect to be attracted to all of it. And more science fiction has been published in the 1970s and 1980s than ever before: twenty or thirty new paperbacks every month, several magazines, even a number of hardbounds—too much even for the most dedicated omnivore to read. The quality of the individual book or story varies from advanced literary craftsmanship to hack trash, from precise and intellectual visions of the future to ignorant swordsmen hacking their way through to beautiful damsels (less than one-quarter clad) across an absurd environment. There are enough varieties of science fiction and fantasy to confuse anybody.

If you look at a wide spectrum of covers in your local SF paperback section, you begin to notice a lot of categories of science fiction. How do the advanced omnivores and chronics select what to read? By this very process: As in any other kind of book, you can tell the importance of the author of a science fiction book by the size of the author's name on the cover. Another reliable gauge to importance, or at least popularity, is how many copies of an individual title by an author the store has and how many of the author's titles are on the shelf.

But popularity and importance aside, how do you identify whether this is the kind of SF you are looking for? By the complex symbology of the cover. Not always, of course, because the paperback industry (never mind hardcover publishers, who tend to be indeterminate) is guilty of lack of confidence, or ignorance, leading to mispackaging fairly regularly—but in the huge majority of cases, science fiction is quite precisely marketed and packaged.

The images on science fiction covers range from futuristic mechanical devices (which connote a story heavily into SF ideas, or perhaps just science fictional clichés) to covers featuring humans against a futuristic setting, with or without machines (which connote adventure SF) to covers with humans carrying swords or other anachronistic weapons (which connote fantasy or fantastic adventure against a cardboard or cliched SF background) to hypermuscled males carrying big swords and adorned with clinging hyperzaftig females, both scant-clad against a threateningly monstrous background (which connote sword-&-sorcery or heroic-fantasy adventures, with perhaps some SF elements) to covers representing several varieties of pure fantasy (from rich romantic flowery quests to freaky supernatural horror). Every SF omnivore has sampled all the varieties of SF, from Lovecraftian supernatural horror to the swashbuckling adventure tales of Poul Anderson to the technical and literary conundrums of Samuel R. Delany. Chronic readers usually center their interests in one limited area and read everything packaged to their taste.

The net effect is that there is a rather large number of SF audiences with focused interests, all of which interlock and overlap to form the inchoate SF reading audience. Most individual books reach their targeted audience and prosper from overlap into other related audiences. Occasionally, an SF work satisfies several of these overlapping audiences at once (for example, *Dune* by Frank Herbert) and reaches what the publishing industry calls the mass audience (truly humongous numbers of readers)—and then extends for a decade or more in sales into the audience that consists of normal people who decide to try the stuff and have heard three or four big names (like Robert A. Heinlein's *Stranger in a Strange Land,* which paid most of the light bills in the period 1961 to 1984 for its publisher and allows Mr. and Mrs. Heinlein to visit opera festivals in Europe on whim).

The situation is exceedingly complex. Some say that the whole SF audience (the market) is composed of teenagers, for all practical purposes, and turns over almost completely every three to five years. This theory, the omnivore theory, eliminates all chronic readers from consideration. It has the virtue of practicality from the publishing point of view, though it means you can recycle individual books endlessly and can publish practically anything, no matter how crippled, and reach a basic, dependable, supposedly profitable (though small) audience.

The combined, or omnivore/chronic theory, which is the unarticulated basis behind most SF publishing, would sound something like a classier version of the omnivore theory—keep the good books in print for omnivores who pass into the chronic state and for the non-SF reader who wishes to sample the field through books or authors he has heard of, and scatter the rest of your publishing program among the three spectra (fantasy/ science fantasy/science fiction) in hopes of discovering chronic sellers—works that everyone who reads SF must sooner or later hear about and read. At its best, this philosophy (if we may so dignify a marketing strategy) leads to the publishing of soaring works of the speculative imagination—but mostly it leads to carefully marketed crap. But even that is okay. Both omnivores and chronics are patient and have long memories; they are willing to wade through a fair amount of swamp to find islands of rationality and the real thing—wonderful SF.

It's a kind of quixotic quest, you see, admirable in its way. The SF reader is willing to keep trying, reading through rather large numbers of half-cooked ideas, clichés, and cardboard characters and settings in search of the truly original and exciting and good. How many of us outside the SF field could be so determined? The SF reader has fun along the way that is not often visible to outsiders.

The SF reader sneers at fake SF, artificially produced film tie-in novels and stories, most SF films, most TV SF. This he calls sci-fi (or "skiffy")—junk no right-thinking omnivore or chronic should read, watch, or support. But with beatific inconsistency he will pursue his own quest—through endless hours of *Space: 1999*, *Battlestar Galactica*, *Mork and Mindy*, *My Favorite Martian*, and some truly horrendous paperbacks and magazines—in search of something as good as he remembers finding during his initial omnivore excitement. This quest through the rubble is not without its rewards.

Consider: The aforementioned conventions are broken down into discrete areas of programming and many conventions have a general or even quite limited theme. Aside from the World Science Fiction Convention, which is a general gathering of the clans, there is a World Fantasy Convention, numerous Star Trek conventions, a pulp-magazine convention (Pulpcon), Ambercon (devoted to the Amber novels of Roger Zelazny), an SF film convention, numerous "relaxicons" (at which there is no programming—chronics and omnivores gather to party with like minds for a weekend), and literally dozens of localized conventions, ranging from hundreds to thousands of attendees: Pghlange (Pittsburgh); Boskone (Boston); Lunacon (New York City); Westercon (West Coast); V-con (Vancouver); Kubla Khan Klave (Nashville); Philcon (Philadelphia); Balticon (Baltimore); Disclave (Washington, D.C.). The list is extensive, each with a guest of honor, films, panels, speeches, a roomful of booksellers, an art show, and many special events (often including a masquerade), and parties (pretty dependably twenty-four hours a day). Aside from general saturnalia, these conventions build audiences for name authors (guests of honor and other featured guests) and reflect audience fascination with discrete kinds of SF.

The World Science Fiction Convention, a six-day bash, has nearly five twenty-four-hour days of programming. Iguanacon (Worldcon '78), named after a favorite fan animal (Tennessee Williams, *Night of the Iguana*: "Women are fine, Sheep are divine, but the Iguana is el numero uno."), had attendees who came specifically for the Edgar Rice Burroughs Dum-Dum (famed great ape party); feminists and those interested in women writers came for the several Women in Science Fiction events; film fans came for the twenty-four-hour-a-day film programs (a bargain); Georgette Heyer fans came for the Regency Dress Tea (yes, at a science fiction convention); some came to see and hear their favorite big-name authors—heroic fantasy readers to see Fritz Leiber and L. Sprague de Camp, Darkover fans to see Marion Zimmer Bradley, Amber fans to see Roger Zelazny; L-5 fans came to proselytize for space industrial colonies.

Of the almost five thousand attendees, a variety of audiences were represented, often recognizable from the individual package. Aside from the general run of jeaned teenagers and suited publishing types, the *Star Trek* fans often wore costumes from the show (or at least Spock ears), the regency fans dressed regency, the heroic fantasy fans sported swords and capes, the medieval fans and Society for Creative Anachronism members dressed in a variety of medieval costumes, the women rapped in the special "womenspace" room (the year before there was a "happy gays are here again" party), Princess Leia costumes abounded, and David Gerrold, well-known *Star Trek* author, handed out David Gerrold fan club cards and buttons. These people filled more than four hotels. Each reader discovers his or her special fun at conventions. Sponsoring similar events, Constellation, the 1984 Worldcon in Baltimore, had about six thousand attendees.

Omnivores tend to form preferences early on in their reading spree, and chronics are usually fixed for life. This is a quick rundown of the main possibilities an omnivore might fix on: classic fantasy (ghost stories, legends, tales); supernatural horror (two categories: classic—from Le Fanu, Blackwood, and Machen to Stephen King and *Rosemary's Baby*; and Lovecraftian, the school of H. P. Lovecraft and his followers); Tolkienesque fantasy (in the manner of *Lord of the Rings*—carefully constructed fantasy worlds as the setting for a heroic quest); heroic fantasy (barely repressed sex fantasy in which a muscular, sword-bearing male beats monsters, magicians, racial inferiors, and effete snobs by brute force, then services every willing woman in sight—and they are all willing); Burroughsian science fantasy (adventure on another planet or thinly rationalized SF setting in which fantasy and anachronism—sword fighting among the stars—are essentials); space opera (the Western in space); hard science fiction (the SF idea is the center of attention, usually involving chemistry or physics or astronomy); soft science fiction (two alternate types: one in which the character is more important than the SF idea; the other focusing on any science other than physics or chemistry); experimental science fiction (stylistically, that is); fine writing science fiction (may include a work from any of the above categories, hard though that may be to accept); single author (reads all published stories of H. P. Lovecraft, his nonfiction, the five volumes of collected letters, the volumes of posthumous collaborations, all pastiches, and so on. Archetypal fan behavior). You can begin to see the enormous variety available.

The most significant development of the last decade for the future of SF is that by about the mid-1960s, enough "fine writing" had been done in the SF field so that a chronic might fixate on that aspect of SF without running out of reading matter before running out of patience. There has always been excellent writing in the SF field, but now there is an actual audience looking for it—before the 1960s, literate prose was fine when it was found, but was generally irrelevant to the SF omnivores and most chronics.

The increased volume of the fine-writing category has had its effect on outsiders' evaluation of the medium. In the Seventies the academic appraisal of SF moved from "It's trash" to "It's interesting trash" to "Some of it is important and worth attention, even study." Oh, sigh. Already there are dissertations written by Ph.D.s on science fiction. But SF is alive and still growing, not literary history, and most of the Ph.D. work is a waste of good dissertation paper because many advanced omnivores have read more SF than almost all of the Ph.D.s, and, given the categories presented above, no one has yet been able to define SF well enough so that non-SF readers can figure it out. SF readers know it when they see it, what is real and what is sci-fi (which have come to denote, among the chronics, what is probably admissible as SF but is extremely bad—able to fool some of the people some of the time).

SF people know, for instance, that Superman is real SF. In his book *Seekers of Tomorrow*, Sam Moskowitz tells the story of the teenage fans associated with the creation of the character and its early publication in Action Comics in 1938—and if the first generation of science-fiction people had produced nothing more than Superman and Buck Rogers, the effect of science fiction on American culture still would have been profound. Because to the science-fiction devotee, SF is naturally carried over into every area of everyday life. She tends to solve problems at work with science-fictional solutions or by using the creative methodology learned through reading SF. He tends to see visions of alternative futures that can be influenced by right actions in the present. She tends to be good at extrapolating trends, and especially good at puncturing the inflated predictions of others by pointing out complexities and alternatives. He tends to be optimistic about ecology through technology, has no fear of machines, and tends to be a loner. The science-fiction person never agrees with anybody else in conversation just to be friendly. Ideas are too important to be betrayed. Science-fiction people, among their own kind, are almost always contentious—after all, a favorite activity is to point to an unlabeled work that may be considered SF and argue about whether or not it is, really, SF.

For the science-fiction person, SF is what holds the world together. It is important, exciting, and gives the science-fiction person a basis for feeling superior to the rest of humanity, those who don't *know*. The early fans, the generation of the Thirties, many of whom (Forrest J. Ackerman, Bradbury, Asimov, Frederik Pohl, Donald A. Wollheim, and a host of others) are among the major writers, publishers, and editors today, evolved a theory to justify the superiority of science-fiction people, then a persecuted, mainly teenage, minority. At the Third Annual World Science Fiction Convention in Denver in 1941, Robert A. Heinlein—then, as now, the most respected author in the field—gave a speech intended to define the science-fiction field for its readers and authors. The theme of the speech was change, and it examined the concept and problem of "future shock" nearly thirty years before Alvin Toffler wrote his famous book.

"I think," said Heinlein, "that science fiction, even the corniest of it, even the most outlandish of it, no matter how badly it's written, has a distinct therapeutic value because *all* of it has as its primary postulate that the world does change." He then went on to tell the fascinated audience, in this speech that is legendary even after four decades, that he believed them to be way above average in intelligence and sensitivity—a special group:

> Science fiction fans differ from most of the rest of the race by thinking in terms of racial magnitude—not even centuries but thousands of years. . . . Most human beings, *and those who laugh at us for reading science fiction*, time-bind, make their plans, make their predictions, only within the limits of their immediate personal affairs. . . . In fact, most people, as compared with science fiction fans, have no conception whatsoever of the fact that the culture they live in does change; that it can change.

We can only imagine the impact of such a coherent articulation of alienation and superiority on a bunch of mostly late-adolescent men at the end of the Great Depression. *Though the inferior mass of humanity laughs at us, we are the ones who know, we are the wave of the future, the next evolutionary step in the human race.* If only our pimples would clear up, we could get on with changing the world. Fans *are* Slans! (*Slan*, a novel by A. E. Van Vogt serialized in *Astounding Science Fiction*, about a superior race living in secret among normal humans, was an instant classic in 1941.)

Adults ignore lousy technique when they are being deceived (in literature or elsewhere) if the deception supports the view of reality they have chosen to embrace. Adults stand to lose their sense of security if they don't cling to everyday reality. Teenagers (and the other groups of people described above) have no sense of security as a rule. They are searching for something—change, a future—and unconvincing, mundane reality does not satisfy. Oddly, then, the assumptions made in a science-fiction story, which are transparently assumptions and which the young social-reject of any age can share as an intellectual exercise, are more acceptable to him than the everyday assumptions made in a "serious" work of fiction about real (mundane adult) life in which he cannot or does not wish to participate.

Thus the science-fiction novel or story is generally aimed at the person who has not embraced a particular set of assumptions about the way things are—this helps to explain both SF's appeal to the young and its seeming shallowness to most "mature" readers. Science fiction is shallow in its presentation of adult human relations (most often the sole concern of most other literature), but it is profound in the opportunities it offers the reader to question his most basic assumptions, even if you have to ignore lousy technique a lot of the time to participate in the illusion. This last is easy for the omnivore and chronic reader—in fact, the minute you overcome the suspension of disbelief problem, admittedly much easier in the early teenage years than in later life, you tend to enter your omnivore stage. Make no mistake—you don't lose your critical ability or literary education when you begin to read science fiction. You just have to learn the trick of putting *all* your preconceptions aside every time you sit down to read. Hah! You were right, this is just another piece of hack work. But the next one, or the story after that may be the real thing, innovative, well written, surprising, exciting.

Throughout the past decade, there has been a growing number of adults who have discovered science fiction as a tool without discovering the thing itself. There are now many new uses for SF in the mundane world: It can be used to combat future shock, to teach religion, political science, physics and astronomy, to promote ecology, to support the U.S. space program, to provide an index to pop cultural attitudes toward science, and to advance academic careers and make profits for publishers, film producers, even toy makers. But the business of science fiction is to provide escape from the mundane world, to get at what is real by denying all of the assumptions that enforce quotidian reality for the duration of the work.

This is reflected in what really goes on at science-fiction conventions. Beneath the surface frivolity, cliquishness, costumery, beneath the libertarian or just plain licentious anarchism of the all-night carousing, beyond the author worship, the serious panel discussions, and the family of hail-fellow-fan-well-met, the true core of being a science-fiction person is that the convention is abnormal and alienated from daily life. Not just separated in time and space—different! There is no parallel more apt than the underground movements of the last two hundred years in Western civilization: the Romantics in England, Baudelaire and his circle in France, the Modernists, the Beats. (Note to literary historians: This would make an interesting study.) The difference is that to an outsider, it just looks like fun and games, since these people go home after a convention go back to work, school, house-wifery, unemployment, mundane reality, or so it seems.

While they are spending time in the science-fiction world, though, things are really different. How different? Let's circle around this for a moment. For instance, you can almost certainly talk to people there who, in normal life, are removed from you by taboos or social barriers. No matter how obnoxious you are, people will talk to you unless you insult them directly, and the chances are excellent that you can find one or more people willing to engage in serious, extended, knowledge-able conversation about some of the things that interest you most whether it is the stock market or macramé, clothing design or conser-vative politics, science or literature or rock 'n' roll. Science-fiction peo-ple tend not to be well rounded but rather multiple specialists; the only thing that holds them and the whole SF world together is science fic-tion. Actually you spend a minority of your time at a convention talk-ing about science fiction, but the reality of science fiction underlies the whole experience and is its basis. For the duration of the science fiction experience, you agree to set aside the assumptions and preconceptions that rule your ordinary behavior and to live free. A science-fiction con-vention, like a work of science fiction, is an escape into an alternate possibility that you can test, when it is over, against mundane reality. Even the bad ones provide this context.

Harlan Ellison, writer and science-fiction personality, has spoken of his first encounter with science fiction as a kid in a dentist's office, where he discovered a copy of a science-fiction magazine. On the cover, Captain Future was battling Krag the robot for possession of a scantily clad woman; the picture filled his young mind with awe, wonder, and excitement. His life was changed. He wanted more. The reason science fiction creates such chronic addicts as Harlan Ellison is that once you admit the possibility that reality is not as solid and fixed as it used to seem, you feel the need for repeated doses of science fictional reality.

Of course, sometimes what you discover in the science-fiction field that attracts you is *not* the thing itself but one of its associates. A chronic reader may actually read almost entirely classical fantasy and Lovecraftian supernatural horror, or a writer such as Fritz Leiber may spend a career writing in every variety of fantasy and science fiction, and yet always be "in the field." There is an interesting investigation to be done someday on why the classical fantasy, a main tradition of Western literature for several millennia, is now part of the science-fiction field. In the latter half of the twentieth century, with certain best-selling exceptions, fantasy is produced by writers of science fiction and fantasy, edited by editors of science fiction, illustrated by SF and fantasy artists, read by omnivore fantasy and SF addicts who support the market. Fantasy is not SF but is part of the phenomenon that confronts us.

Since the 1930s, science fiction has been an umbrella under which any kind of estrangement from mundane reality is welcome (though some works, such as the John Norman "Gor" series and the sado-masochistic sex fantasies in a Burroughsian SF setting are admitted but generally despised and generally believed to sell mostly to an audience outside any other SF audience). To present the broad, general context of the SF field, let us consider in more detail the main areas and relationships as they have evolved over the past several decades.

The general question of fantasy has been dealt with frequently, from Freud's well-known essay on the uncanny through recent structuralist works such as Todorov's *The Fantastic*, and is not central to our concern with science fiction. Several things need to be said, however, about fantasy literature before we move on to varieties of science fiction. Fantasy, through its close association with science fiction since the 1920s in America, has developed a complex interaction with science fiction that has changed much of what is written as fantasy today.

H. P. Lovecraft, the greatest writer of supernatural horror of the century, a literary theoretician, and mentor, through correspondence and personal contact, to Frank Belknap Long, Robert E. Howard, Robert Bloch, Fritz Leiber, Clark Ashton Smith, August Derleth, Donald and Howard Wandrei, and a number of others, was an agnostic, a rationalist, and a believer in science. His work was published both in *Weird Tales*, the great fantasy magazine between the Twenties and the early Fifties, and in *Astounding Stories*, the great science fiction magazine of its day. Almost all his acolytes followed the same pattern of commercial and literary ties to both areas.

In 1939, after the greatest SF editor of modern times, John W. Campbell, took the helm at *Astounding*, he proceeded to found the second great fantasy magazine, *Unknown*, encouraging all his newly discovered writing talents—Heinlein, Sturgeon, L. Sprague de Camp, L. Ron Hubbard, Anthony Boucher, Alfred Bester, H. L. Gold, Frederic Brown, Eric Frank Russell, as well as Henry Kuttner, Jack Williamson, C. L. Moore, and Fritz Leiber—to create a new kind of fantasy, with modern settings and contemporary atmosphere, as highly rationalized and consistent as the science fiction he wanted them to write for *Astounding.* Through Lovecraft and Campbell a strong link was forged not only commercially but also aesthetically between fantasy and science fiction. Today, and for the last two decades, the most distinguished and consistently brilliant publication in the field has been the *Magazine of Fantasy and Science Fiction,* required reading for all who wish to discover the field at its best and broadest, though it has never been the most popular magazine in the field, always surpassed in circulation by more focused magazines.

After Lovecraft and Campbell, the third towering figure in fantasy so far in the twentieth century is J. R. R. Tolkien, whose *Lord of the Rings* trilogy is both a classic of contemporary literature and an example of the dominant position of the science-fiction field as stated above. Tolkien's works, although literary hardcovers at first, were popularized in paperback through SF publishers and have spawned an entire marketing substructure to support works of world-building fantasy in the Tolkien tradition. More books appear every month featuring the quest of a single heroic figure across a detailed and rationalized fantasy world, accompanied by a group of major and minor fantasy characters and ending in a confrontation between Good and Evil, in which Good always wins.

The fourth towering figure is not one person, but is a posthumous collaboration between the artist Frank Frazetta, formerly a comic illustrator, and the author Robert E. Howard, pulp fantasy adventure hack who committed suicide in 1936 the day his mother died and who created a number of fantastic heroes, the best known of which is Conan the Barbarian. Howard's works had been mostly out of print since his death, except for several small press editions and a few paperbacks, until the early 1960s. Then L. Sprague de Camp obtained the rights from Howard's estate to arrange and anthologize the whole Conan series for the first time in paperback, and to write additions and sequels himself and with others. Through a stroke of genius, comic-strip artist Frazetta was hired to illustrate the paperback covers, which seized the imagination of the audience enough to sell in the millions of copies, established the Howard name, and made Frazetta wealthy and famous. Howard now has nearly fifty books in print in the third decade following his death, and a sword-swinging barbarian hero brutishly adventuring across a fantasy/historic landscape (inside a book with a cover by Frazetta or an imitation) is the principal reading focus of a large number of chronic SF readers. This category, which was formerly called sword-and-sorcery fiction, is now referred to more accurately as heroic fantasy. If Mickey Spillane wrote SF, it would be heroic fantasy. In fact, a hundred years from now SF may have acquired Spillane's works under this rubric.

There are only two areas of fantasy that have not been annexed under the SF umbrella, perhaps because these two areas have never fallen into popular disrepute: Arthurian romances and the occult horror bestseller. There are indications that these two areas may remain separate and independent—both types tend to be written by authors who have no desire to associate themselves and their works with low-class, nonliterary, low-paying (until recently) stuff.

The only science in all the areas of fantasy is either strawman science (which cannot cope) or black science (used by the evil sorcerer). Amoral science is a recent addition to some heroic fantasy (especially noticeable in the works of Michael Moorcock), as is the idea of magic as a scientific discipline (a contribution of the Campbell era). And I can generalize without fear of contradiction by saying that except in a tiny minority of cases, technology is associated with evil in fantasy literature. So it is particularly curious that the element of estrangement from everyday reality has come to yoke by itself the two separates, fantasy and science fiction, even though SF was invented to exclude "mere" fantasy. This complex of seeming contradiction will be investigated in more depth shortly. For the moment we will move on to a consideration of the subdivisions of the center of the field, science fiction.

Hugo Gernsback, who invented modern science fiction in April 1926, knew what he meant by "scientifiction" (as he named it) and assumed it would be evident to others: all that work Wells and Verne and Poe wrote ("charming romance intermingled with scientific fact and prophetic vision," as Gernsback says in the editorial in the first issue of the first magazine, *Amazing Stories*). In addition to this confusion,

Gernsback, an eccentric immigrant and technological visionary, was tone deaf to the English language, printing barely literate stories about new inventions and the promise of a wondrous technological future cheek by jowl with H. G. Wells, Poe, Edgar Rice Burroughs (!), and a growing number of professional pulp writers who wanted to break into the new market. The new thing was amorphous, formed and reformed over the decades by major editors and writers, and all the chronic readers, into the diversity that is science fiction today.

It is a source of both amusement and frustration to SF people that public consciousness of science fiction has almost never penetrated beyond the first decade of the field's development. Sure, *Star Wars* is wonderful, but in precisely the same way and at the same level of consciousness and sophistication that SF from the late 1920s and early 1930s was: fast, almost plotless stories of zipping through the ether in spaceships, meeting aliens, using futuristic devices, and fighting the bad guys (and winning).

By now it should be obvious that we are dealing not with a limited thing but with a whole reality. More than an alternate literary form or an alternate lifestyle, science fiction is coequal reality, informing the lives of thousands and affecting the lives of millions, a fact of life more intimate than inflation, whose influence is so all-pervasive that it is traceable daily in every home, through the artifacts and ideas that represent all possible futures and all possible change.

CHAPTER TWENTY

~

Some Presumptuous Approaches to Science Fiction

Samuel R. Delany

"Do you think science fiction should be taken seriously as literature?" Over the past handful of years, I've found—what with teaching various SF courses at various universities and giving talks on science fiction to both formal and informal groups—that this question threatens to oust, "Where do SF writers get their ideas?" from the number-one position on the list of baroque unanswerables that plague an SF writer's life.

What makes such questions so difficult is that they presume a set of conditions that any accurate answer could not possibly fulfill. For example, the question, "Where do SF writers get their ideas?" presumes that there is a place, or a number of places, where ideas exist quite apart from writers, and that the writers can go there to obtain them. The question has the same grammatical/logical form as, "Where do restaurant chefs get their steaks?" But there is no answer of the grammatical/ logical form, "From the better West Side meat packing plants below 14th Street," that can answer it. And an answer in that form is what the question demands.

If, however, we change the form of the question from, "Where do SF writers get their ideas?" to, "By what process do science-fictional ideas come up in SF writers' minds?" then the answer is fairly simple:

By and large, SF writers get their ideas through having quirky and imaginative responses to the everyday, the ordinary, and the humdrum.

An example? My friend Luise is driving down the thruway, and I'm sitting beside her, reading a magazine. At one point I glance out the window just as three billboards go by. But I return to my magazine even before they've passed. Five minutes later, again I look up . . . as two more billboards pass. But I go right back to my magazine. Another five minutes, and again I look up . . . to see still *another* billboard! Now during the time I was actually reading, there may or may not have been other billboards beside the road. I know this perfectly well. Still, over a 10-minute period, every time I happened to look up I saw some. Suddenly I think: Suppose the whole side of the road were filled with billboards—along its entire length! Suppose both sides of the road were walled in by advertisements. . . ! And if I had happened to be Frederik Pohl or C. M. Kornbluth, I would have stored that idea away for my 1952 SF novel *The Space Merchants*, where you can still find it doing impressive duty (among myriad other ideas) today. In general, science-fictional ideas generate when a combination of chance and the ordinary suggests some *distortion* of the current and ordinary that can conceivably be rationalized as a future projection. Now for what it's worth, I suspect that for every fifty such ideas occurring to an SF writer, 49 are discarded as trivial or silly. And once several, or several hundred, good ideas are collected, putting them together into a story is another game entirely. But like most habits of thought, this one comes more easily with practice. Also, I think it's safe to say that, in general, this is probably not the way that writers of present-day mundane fiction get their ideas, or that writers of drama get their ideas, or that writers of historical fiction get their ideas, or that writers of poetry get their ideas—unless the idea gotten happens to be a specifically science-fictional one.

Try to recall this the next time Jean-Luc Godard's "science fiction" film *Alphaville* comes on television. The visuals in the film are all from the ordinary, everyday world: elevated trains moving at night above a Paris suburb, men in identical business suits, fluorescent-lit halls in office buildings after hours, window fans turning behind their wire grills. The voiceover on top of it, however, is all about spaceships moving through intergalactic night, supertrained inhuman spies, superscientific institutions, and monstrous futuristic machines. In short, the visuals are composed *not* of science-fictional ideas, but rather of the current and ordinary things that inspire science-fictional ideas, whereas the dialogue (and action) are about the science-fictional ideas these ordinary things might inspire. The film is about nothing *but* the way SF writers (or filmmakers) get their ideas!

This should explain something I've been saying (and writing) for over 10 years now: Science fiction is not about the future; it uses the future as a narrative convention to present significant distortions of the present. And both the significance of the distortion and the appropriateness of the convention lie precisely in that what we know of present science does not *deny* the possibility of these distortions eventually coming to pass. Science fiction is about the current world—the given world shared by writer and reader. But it is not a metaphor for the given world, nor does the catch-all term metonymy exhaust the relation between the given and science fiction's distortions of the given. Science fiction poises in a tense, dialogic, agonistic relation to the given, but there is very little critical vocabulary currently to deal with this relationship of contestatory difference the SF figure establishes, maintains, expects, exploits, subverts, and even—occasionally, temporarily—grandly destroys.

Science fiction is about the contemporary world; and the possibility of its futuristic distortions gives its side of the dialogue its initial force. Sympathetic critics of science fiction run aground, however, when they try to show that the significance of science fiction lies in the much more limited area of things that will probably come to pass, should come to pass, or must not come to pass.[1] This mistake Julia Kristeva has called, in another context, the "positive trap."

But what of our initial question:

"Should science fiction be taken seriously as literature?"

What's presumed here?

First, there is the presumption that the way literature is traditionally taken seriously is a good thing and has grown up historically as an accumulation of right knowledge in an appropriate response to the innate worthiness of the literary text.[2] This means that what's really being asked here is this: Is science fiction, like literature, innately of value? Second is the much vaguer and more general presumption that science fiction and mundane fiction work along the same general lines to produce their respective plays of meaning, so that they might be considered in the same way productively.

The first presumption, that the way literature is traditionally taken seriously is a good thing, has been under a general, if somewhat halfhearted, attack since the spread of public education from the middle of the nineteenth century on; but the attack has been for primarily pedagogic reasons. The general exhortation of the pedagogue to "know what the text means," along with the varied repertoire of interpretive techniques by which this accomplished, have been neither effective nor popular with the run of students, despite the efforts of the best-intentioned teachers. More recently, in the literary studies falling under the double-named debate "poststructuralism/semiotics," the attack has been renewed on a theoretical level that leaves the pedagogic reasons standing at the gate.

Following the critical and philosophical studies of Jacques Derrida, it is evident that practically any text, if read carefully enough, generates both denotations and connotations that contradict each other, that subvert each other, that interfere with each other in such a way that the very concept of "knowing what the text means" begins to fall apart—becomes "highly problematic," in comparative literature jargon. Unpacking these multiple and contradictory denotations and connotations from a text and then undoing the distinctions between them in some informal way is called, in the same jargon, "deconstructing" the text.

Although today one hears a great deal about "structuralism," "semiotics," and "deconstruction," the truth is that critics who actually explore textual plays of meaning from this point of view are rather rare. To do it in any truly productive way takes much skill, tremendous acuity, endless patience, and great critical inventiveness. And none of these virtues are particularly rampant in the run of university English departments. Despite the new disciplines, most English departments go on doing what they have been doing all along: teaching the standard repertoire of ways to know what the text means, whether it can be done (in theoretical terms) or not.

Which brings us to our second presumption: that the SF narrative works on more or less the same lines as the mundane narrative, so that they might both be dealt with profitably by the same interpretive repertoire.

The play of meanings, contradictory or otherwise, that makes up the SF text is organized in a way radically different from that of the mundane text.

I've discussed the nature of the unique organization of meanings in the SF text in some of the essays in my collection *The Jewel-Hinged Jaw* and, on a much more technical level, in my book *The American Shore*, in which I have taken a sixteen-page SF story, "Angouleme," by Thomas M. Disch, and examined the way we read it as an SF story from beginning to end. When we read science fiction carefully, we can see that practically any rhetorical figure operates differently in an SF text from the way the same, or similar, figure would operate in a text of mundane fiction. Catalogues, exaggerations, historical references, descriptions of the beautiful, parodic figures, psychological speculations, even the literal meanings of various sentences and phrases are all read differently in science fiction from the way they are read in mundane fiction. The details *do* take a book to explain. But the general lines along which the differences are organized are easy enough to see.

The writer of mundane fiction tells a story set against a more or less vividly evoked section of the given world. I say "given world" rather than "real world" because the world of the most naturalistic piece of mundane fiction is a highly conventionalized affair; and these conventions, when one studies them, turn out to have far more to do with other works of fiction than with anything "real." The SF writer, however, *creates* a world—which is harmonized with (or contrasted with, or played off against) both the story's characters *and* the given world in a much freer way. Certainly this way follows its conventions too; still, rather than simply recognize which part of the given world the mundane writer is highlighting in a particular mundane story, the reader of the SF story must create a new world that operates by new laws for each new SF story read. The various verbal devices SF writers use to lay out, sketch in, and color their alternate worlds, as well as the verbal constructs that direct the play between the world and the story, constitute the major distinctions between the SF and the mundane text, altering the reading of the various rhetorical figures that appear in both texts and generating the different rhetorical figures for each kind of text.

Universities are filled with people who simply won't read science fiction. These folks suffer from nothing worse than snobbism, and their affliction doesn't really interest me. But there are many people, both in and out of universities, who honestly *can't* read science fiction—which is to say they have picked up a few SF stories and tried to read them, only to find that much of the text, to them, simply didn't make sense. Frequently, these are very sophisticated readers of literary texts, too.

Several times now I have had opportunities to read some SF texts with such readers, to read an SF text slowly, phrase by phrase, sentence by sentence, checking on what has been responded to and what has not been. When you read an SF text this way with such readers, it becomes clear that their difficulty is almost entirely in their inability to create the alternate world that gives the story's incidents all their sense. Although these readers have no trouble imagining a Balzac provincial printing office, a Dickens boarding school, or an Austen sitting room, they are absolutely stymied by, say, the contemporary SF writer's, most ordinary "monopole magnet mining operations in the outer asteroid belt of Delta Cygni."

But the failure is not so much a failure of the imaginative faculties as it is a failure to respond, word by word, to the text. Let's examine that failure with this particular textual fragment.

Monopole Magnet

First of all, most of the readers I worked with had no idea what monopole magnets might be. Monopole magnets happen not to exist, at least as far as we know. All magnets that we have ever discovered or created on Earth are dipoles: they have two poles, a "north" and a "south." If you put like poles together, they push each other apart. If you put unlike poles together, they draw one another. And this is true of *every* magnet known. For this reason, the very mention of "monopole magnets" means that in *this* universe a completely new kind of magnet has been discovered; this suggests, in turn, that there may be a whole new branch of electromagnetic technology at work (any electric motor, electric generator, or transformer is an example of current electromagnetic technology), which has reorganized things in the world, or worlds, of this SF text's universe.

Monopole Magnet Mining Operations

I had one reader who, besides not knowing what monopole magnets might be, assumed that, whatever they were, the mining was done *with* these magnets rather than for these magnets (i.e., according to the schema of *strip mining operations* or *pellet mining operations*), even though a phrase like *gold mining operations* or even *uranium mining operations* would not have created such confusion. Needless to say, this reader would be perfectly lost in any further mentions of the goings-on in these mines.

Monopole Magnet Mining Operations in the Outer Asteroid Belt

Another reader, already as confused as the others over monopole magnet mining, thought an asteroid belt was "a ring of stones around a world." Well, if you substitute *sun* for *world*, you might describe it that way. But when I questioned this reader further, I discovered that the mental picture the reader had was that the stones "were not very big, maybe a few feet or so across" and that they were "packed together" so that they were only "a few feet or a few inches apart." For this reader, the mines were "probably tunnels that went from stone to stone. . . . Maybe the stones are even inside the tunnels. . . ?" And what about the word *outer*? Over half of these readers thought *outer* meant that the mining took place on the outside of this wall of stones, rather than inside it. And *Delta Cygni*? Maybe that was "an area of space" or "a planet."

Patiently and repeatedly I had to explain to these readers (several of whom, incidentally, had published books or articles on various literary subjects) that the asteroid belt in our own solar system is "a ring of stones" that circles the sun at a distance greater than our Earth's orbit; and that, although a few of the stones are as large as a mile or even hundreds of miles in diameter, most are much smaller: pea-sized or dust-sized. I also had to reiterate that even the dust-sized ones are miles apart, and the pea-sized or larger ones, hundreds or even thousands of miles apart. ("But then how do they build mine tunnels from one to another?") They had to be told that Delta Cygni is a star—a sun—in the constellation Cygnus the Swan, and that it was the fourth star named. ("How do you know it was *the fourth* one. . . ?" "Because *delta is* the fourth letter of the Greek alphabet and there's an astronomical naming convention that says. . . . ") Nor was it a matter of simply saying these things once. They had to be repeated and questioned and repeated again. ("What do you mean, 'a sun?'") They had to be told that "outer asteroid belt" was the writer's shorthand way of first reminding you that our sun has only one asteroid belt while suggesting that Delta Cygni might be a star with *two* asteroid belts, one farther out than the other. ("Well, how much farther out?" "There's no way to be sure, of course, but one can make a safe guess that it would be many millions of miles." "Many *millions* of miles?") They had to be told that it was in this outer asteroid belt, rather than in the inner one, that these mining operations were going on. ("But how does the writer *know* there are two? How do you know?") These readers were all capable of negotiating the nineteenth-century novel, whether it was written by a Russian count on a family estate outside Moscow; or a tubercular parson's daughter living with her sisters on the edge of an English moor; or an ex-printer in Paris who, having penned nothing but potboilers till age 30, had decided to try his hand at something more ambitious.

Yet for these same readers a sentence like *The stars are suns, many with planets like our own* does not call up a clear, concrete visualization, laid out to the proper scale, of the planetary, stellar, and galactic organization of the universe. Rather, it is a muzzy and confusing statement associated with the vast and impossible complexities of "all that scientific stuff" they have tried to avoid all their lives.

In the 19th century Sir Arthur Conan Doyle, whose "Dr. Challenger" stories are some of the clearest examples of proto-science fiction, was surprisingly aware of the problem. He talked about it in, oddly enough, one of his Sherlock Holmes tales.

In one Holmes story (the same one, incidentally, in which we learn that Holmes takes cocaine) Dr. Watson is astonished to learn that his friend Holmes, who can infer so much from cat hairs, heel prints, and plaster scratchings, does not know that the Earth moves around the sun—that he is ignorant, in Dr. Watson's words, "of the entire Copernican theory of the solar system."

Holmes explains (however disingenuous that explanation sounds today) that, while cat hairs, heel prints, and so on, affect his current life and livelihood, it makes absolutely no difference to him whether the Earth moves around the sun or the sun moves around the Earth. Therefore he doesn't have to know such facts; and what's more, even though

Dr. Watson has informed him of the truth of the matter, he intends to forget it as quickly as he can. If Holmes is right about himself, we can say with fair certainty that he would be as lost in the monopole magnet mining operations of that outer asteroid belt as any of our nineteenth-century novel readers—although one is equally sure that Watson (just as Doyle was a born SF writer) would probably have been a born SF fan—had he ever read any of his creator's proto-SF stories.

But the inability to visualize scenes on the astronomical level does not exhaust the "imaginative failure" of these readers. These readers, who are perfectly comfortable following the social analysis of a Balzac or an Austen, or even a Durkheim, Marx, or Weber, are at sea when they come across a description of a character who, on going to the drugstore to purchase a package of depilatory pads, ". . . inserted his credit card in the purchasing slot; his bill was transmitted to the city accounting house to be stored against the accumulated credit from his primary and secondary jobs."

To the SF reader, such a sentence implies a whole reorganization of society along lines of credit, commerce, computerization, and labor patterns. Certainly from a single sentence no one could be expected to come up with all the details of that reorganization; but by the same token, one should be able to see at least a shadow of its general outline. And that shadow should provide the little science-fictional *frisson* that is the pleasure of the plurality of the SF vision. The readers I worked with, however, responded to such a sentence: "But why didn't he pay for it with the money in his pocket?" and were very surprised when I told them the character probably carried no money. ("But how do you *know*. . . ?") Such readers, used to the given world of mundane fiction, tend to lay the *fabulata* of science fiction over that given world—and come up with confusion. They do not yet know that these *fabulata* replace, displace, and reorganize the elements of that given world into new worlds. The hints, the suggestions, the throwaways, and even, sometimes, the broadest strokes by which the skillful SF writer suggests the alternate world do not come together for them in any coherent vision, but only blur, confuse, and generally muddy the vision of the given world they are used to.

Reading SF texts with these readers, I was able to bring them to a point of understanding—for the particular texts we read. But the feeling that they were better prepared to read more SF texts was about equally mixed with the feeling that the real complexities of science fiction were even more daunting than they had dreamed till now.

One reason for the pedagogic problems literature has been having for the last century and a half is a simple phenomenon anyone who has ever traveled in another country must understand: Once one knows a language, it is almost impossible to imagine someone else's not knowing it. No matter what indications a person gives they understand us not at all, on some deep level there remains in us the insistent suspicion that they're only fooling—or are lazy, or malicious. The conventions of poetry or drama or mundane fiction—or science fiction—are in themselves separate languages. Once you learn one of these languages and are comfortable with the texts employing it, it is very hard to conceive of someone else's not knowing this language, especially when the texts are written in English, presumably *the* language you both speak. Like most languages, the SF language is best learned early and by exposure. Some of my adult readers found it a bit deflating however, to realize that their twelve-year-olds were frequently at home in both the monopole magnet mines and the computerized credit economy in ways that their parents were not.

At this point, however, it is time to return to our initial question: "Should science fiction be taken seriously as literature?"

By now we should be able to see that we are really presuming two questions with opposite answers.

First is the question, *Should science fiction be taken seriously?*

For me, the answer is an unequivocal, *yes.* It is a fascinating language phenomenon, and its intricate differences from traditional "literary" language sustain its interest.

Second is the question, *Does science fiction work in the same way as other, literary categories of writing?* Here the answer is *no.* Science fiction works differently from other written categories, particularly those categories traditionally called literary. It works the same way only in that, like all categories of writing, it has its specific conventions, unique focuses, areas of interest and excellence, as well as its own particular ways of making sense out of language. To ignore any of these constitutes a major misreading—an obliviousness to the play of meanings that makes up the SF text.

Notes

1. One could make a somewhat fanciful argument that science fiction has grown up to compensate for the fact that, unlike ancient Greek and Sanskrit, modern Western (and Oriental) languages no longer have an optative mood, *optative* being the Greek grammatical term for the verb mood of a whole tense system from which we get the modern term *options*—which, as critic Ihab Hassan has suggested, is what science fiction is all about.

2. The French scholar Michel Foucault has suggested that most current critical interpretive methods are simply based on habits of thought left over from the verification procedures once applied to writings suspected of having been authored by saints and thus suspected of being Holy Writ.

CHAPTER TWENTY-ONE

~

Touchstones

James Gunn

The notion of touchstones in science fiction induces in me a sense of wonder, since I have come to believe, as I said in a recent article, "Toward a Definition of Science Fiction," that we respond intuitively to a story and then read it, or misread it, as science fiction or fantasy or traditional fiction or whatever. But what is it we respond to? Whatever it is, we recognize "the right stuff" when we encounter it.

Touchstones imply the same kind of process at work. I would like to suggest, however, that touchstones in science fiction are not the same kind of touchstones that Matthew Arnold described. Sublimity has little to do with it. "Sense of wonder" is closer. But I would like to propose that a true touchstone in science fiction (I leave fantasy to others) should contain, or even better epitomize, the element of discontinuity that makes the work science fiction. Science-fiction touchstones should bring the reader up short, cause a re-evaluation of older ideas or an adjustment to new conditions, make the reader think.

Let me cite two stories of Isaac Asimov's that have been much praised, that he likes very much, and that I called "uncharacteristic" in my book about Asimov's work. They are "The Ugly Little Boy" and "The Bicentennial Man." "The Ugly Little Boy" ends with a touching moment when the Neanderthal boy, being sent back to his own time, calls the stern Miss Fellowes "mother."

"Yes. Yes. It's all right. And I won't leave you any more and nothing will hurt you. I'll be with you to care for you always. Call me Mother, so I can hear you."

In "The Bicentennial Man," Andrew the robot has given up those attributes of the machine that make him superior to humanity, including eternal life, in order to be declared human and, at the end:

With mankind watching, the World President said, "Fifty years ago, you were declared a Sesquicentennial Robot, Andrew." After a pause, and in a more solemn tone, he said, "Today we declare you a Bicentennial Man, Mr. Martin."

Not too long after that Andrew "dies," his last thought of his first little human mistress.

The difficulty with identifying these passages as touchstones, effective though they may be in context, is that their effectiveness is not science-fiction effectiveness. Let me give some examples from other works before I move on to better examples from Asimov, who may be a touchstone in his own right. One may, that is, have different attitudes toward the quality and effectiveness of Asimov's science fiction, but one should recognize that it has the right stuff, that Asimov is dead center in the tradition. In *The Road to Science Fiction #3* I called "The Cold Equations" a touchstone story because it separates science-fiction readers from non-SF readers. Unless the reader (students, in my case) understands that Marilyn Lee Cross's *ignorance* is what kills her one has not read the story properly and has not yet learned to read science fiction. The touchstone passage is not the final line, "I didn't do anything to die for. . . .," but an earlier explanatory passage:

The men of the frontier had long ago learned the bitter futility of cursing the forces that would destroy them for the forces were blind and deaf; the futility of looking to the heavens for mercy, for the stars of the galaxy swung in their long, long sweep of two hundred million years, as inexorably controlled as they by the laws that knew neither hatred nor compassion.

I have, of course, favorite final lines that offer the science-fiction quality of re-evaluation or of continuing the story in new ways. Let me offer a handful of them without explanation and let curious readers look them up if they wish:

"I am the master." "Farewell to the Master," Harry Bates.

"Sam woke up." *Fury*, Lawrence O'Donnell (Henry Kuttner and C. L. Moore).

"The house was dynamited six days later, part of the futile attempt to halt the relentless spread of the Blue Death." "Vintage Season," Lawrence O'Donnell.

"The car turned off the shining avenue, taking him back to the quiet splendor of his home. His futile hands clenched and relaxed again, folded on his knees. There was nothing left to do." "With Folded Hands," Jack Williamson.

"'They would turn me back into a dog,'" said Towser.

"'And me,'" said Fowler, "'back into a man.'" "Desertion," Clifford Simak.

"Overhead, without any fuss, the stars were going out." "The Nine Billion Names of God," Arthur C. Clarke.

"And you fall through." "Sundance," Robert Silverberg.

"And Petersen lay down to die amid their victory." "Founding Father," Isaac Asimov.

I could go on like this for pages. I could devote as many pages to great opening touchstones, beginning with Alfred Bester's beginning to "Fondly Fahrenheit":

He doesn't know which of us I am these days, but they know one truth. You must own nothing but yourself. You must make your own life, live your own life and die your own death . . . or else you will die another's.

But I should get on to other examples not necessarily confined to final (or opening) lines. I remember that moment in Robert A. Heinlein's "Universe" when Hugh sees the stars for the first time:

Faithfully reproduced, shining as steady and serene from the walls of the stellarium as did their originals from the black deeps of space, the mirrored stars looked down on him. Light after jeweled light, scattered in careless bountiful splendor across the simulacrum sky, the countless suns lay before him—before him, over him, under him, behind him, in every direction from him. He hung alone in the center of the stellar universe.

This passage deals, like "The Cold Equations," with the realization
of humanity's relationship with the universe. If we call science fiction, broadly, a literature of change, of ideas, of anticipation, or of
the human species, perhaps this touchstone belongs to the literature
of ideas.

Another kind of touchstone is more concerned with the human
species. In Heinlein's *Have Spacesuit—Will Travel* a teenager must convince a Council of Three Galaxies that humanity has a right to live:

> "It's not a defense, you don't *want* a defense. All right, take away our
> star—you will if you can and I guess you can. Go ahead! We'll *make* a
> star! Then, someday, we'll come back and hunt you down—all of you!"
>
> Nobody bawled me out. I suddenly felt like a kid who has made a hor-
> rible mistake at a party and doesn't know how to cover it up. But I meant
> it. Oh, I didn't think we could *do* it. Not yet. But we'd try. "Die trying"
> is the proudest human thing.

Theodore Sturgeon also was concerned with the species in "Thunder
and Roses":

> He looked down through the darkness for his hands. No planet, no uni-
> verse, is greater to a man than his own ego, his own observing self. These
> hands were the hands of all history, and like the hands of all men, they
> could by their small acts make human history or end it. Whether this
> power of hands was that of a billion hands, or whether it came to a fo-
> cus in these two—this was suddenly unimportant to the eternities which
> now enfolded him.

John Campbell defines the human species in "Twilight" with an action
that, as in Asimov's "Founding Father," turns a human tragedy into a
kind of triumph:

> So I brought another machine to life, and set it a task which, in time to
> come, it will perform.
>
> I ordered it to make a machine which would have what man had lost.
> A curious machine.

Arthur C. Clarke provides another such experience at the end of "Rescue Party," where the "lords of the universe" have caught up with a fleet

of chemically powered rockets far beyond Pluto carrying humanity away from the exploding Sun.

> "You know," he said to Rugon, "I feel rather afraid of these people. Suppose they don't like our little Federation?" He waved once more towards the star-clouds that lay massed across the screen, glowing with the light of their countless suns.
>
> "Something tells me they'll be very determined people," he added. "We had better be polite to them. After all, we only outnumber them about a thousand million to one."
>
> Rugon laughed at his captain's little joke.
>
> Twenty years afterward, the remark didn't seem so funny.

From Clarke's *Childhood's End*, rather than Carol McGuirk's touchstone, I would choose Karellen's defiant musings after humanity's inhuman children had destroyed the Earth in the process of joining the Overmind:

> For all their achievements, thought Karellen, for all their mastery of the physical universe, his people were no better than a tribe that had passed its whole existence upon some flat and dusty plain. Far off were the mountains, where power and beauty dwelt, where the thunder sported above the glaciers, and the air was clear and keen. There the sun still walked, transfiguring the peaks with glory, when all the land below was wrapped in darkness. And they could only watch and wonder; they could never scale those heights.
>
> Yet, Karellen knew, they would hold fast until the end: they would wait without despair whatever destiny was theirs. They would serve the Overmind because they had no choice, but even in that service they would not lose their souls.

There is that wonderful moment of re-evaluation in A. E. van Vogt's *The World of Null-A* when Gilbert Gosseyn calls for the lie detector to verify his statement of identity, and it replies, "No, you are not Gilbert Gosseyn. . . ." And the shock (I think it came at the end of the first installment in *Astounding*) when:

> The unbearable part was that he clung to consciousness. He could feel the unrelenting fire and the bullets searching through his writhing body.

The blows and the flame tore at his vital organs, at his legs, his heart, and his lungs even after he had stopped moving. . . .

Somewhere along there, death came.

Only in science fiction could the hero be killed with three-fourths of the book yet to come.

Another group of touchstones belongs to the literature of change. Frederik Pohl has always been good at the shock of recognition that occurs when the familiar changes into something new and revealing, as in *The Space Merchants*:

"Speaking for myself, I've done well. My summer place looks right over one of the largest parks on Long Island. I haven't tasted any protein but new meat for years, and when I go out for a spin I pedal a Cadillac."

Another example is from "The Midas Plague":

With a steel-tipped finger, it pointed to the door marked GROUP THERAPY.

Someday, Morey vowed to himself as he nodded and complied, he would be in a position to afford a private analyst of his own. . . .

There were eleven of them: four Freudians, two Reichians, two Jungians, a Gestalter, a shock therapist and the elderly and rather quiet Sullivanite.

A final Pohlstone, to coin a phrase, comes from "Day Million":

Balls, you say, it looks crazy to me. And you—with your after-shave lotion and your little red car, pushing papers across a desk all day and chasing tail all night—tell me, just how the hell do you think you would look to Tiglath-Pileser, say, or Attila the Hun.

Let me conclude with some examples from the author I described earlier as a touchstone in his own right, Isaac Asimov. One of Asimov's favorite stories is "The Last Question," which consists of a question asked repeatedly of a steadily improving computer until it is finally answered by AC in hyperspace after all humanity has merged with it, matter and energy had run down, and space and time had ended: How may entropy be reversed?

The consciousness of AC encompassed all of what had once been a Universe and brooded over what was now Chaos. Step by step, it must be done

And AC said, "LET THERE BE LIGHT!"

And there was light—

That reminds me of another, oft quoted passage from a short-short story by Frederic Brown, titled, coincidentally, "Answer":

He turned to face the machine. "Is there a God?"

. . . The mighty voice answered without hesitation, without the clicking of a single relay.

"Yes, *now* there is a God."

I've begun to think that one difference between science-fiction writers and writers of traditional fiction, including many who were grouped as the New Wave, is their attitude toward human nature. The writer of traditional fiction believes that human nature is unchangeable; the science-fiction writer believes that if conditions change, people will change, too.

I like to compare E. M. Forster's "The Machine Stops" with John W. Campbell's "Twilight." Both are about the decline and eventual destruction of the human species, but "The Machine Stops" blames human corruptibility; "Twilight," the choices that people made as they conquered their environment. They also differ in their attitudes toward machines: "The Machine Stops" says that the basic quality of machines is that they break down; "Twilight," that like the Bicentennial Man, the basic quality of machines is that they don't break down, wear out, or stop.

Asimov wrote in an essay somewhere that philosophers through the ages have written against the evils of slavery and have not freed a slave, but the Industrial Revolution freed all the slaves, as a side effect, by making slavery uneconomic. His two earliest Robot Novels, *The Caves of Steel* and *The Naked Sun*, are mainly about the ways in which changed environments will change people.

On a crowded Earth robots are hated and feared because they might take human jobs; on a sparsely inhabited Solaria, where robots outnumber people, the people take robots for granted. On Earth, the cities have grown up and roofed themselves over with caves of steel, and the people have responded by developing agoraphobia. On Solaria people live so far apart that they can scarcely bear to come into the same room with another person.

The theme of the novels is that although people are shaped by their environments, they can liberate themselves from their fears and prejudices. Elijah Baley, for instance, must cope with his distrust of the robot R. Daneel Olivaw; the process of the novel brings him to the point where he can think about Daneel:

Whatever the creature was, he was strong and faithful, animated by no selfishness. What more could you ask of any friend? Baley needed a friend and he was in no mood to cavil at the fact that a gear replaced a blood vessel in this particular one.

And at the end, "Baley, suddenly smiling, took R. Daneel's elbow, and they walked out the door, arm in arm."

On Solaria Baley must face the agoraphobia that has been produced in him by his life within the caves of steel, and he does so in a series of effective scenes. Once having arrived on Solaria, he tricks the robot driver into opening the top and exposing him to Solaria's naked sun:

Blue, green, air, noise, motion—and over it all, beating down, furiously, relentlessly, frighteningly, was the white light that came from a ball in the sky.

But perhaps most effective, and most revealing as a touchstone, is the conquering of claustrophobic fears by a native of Solaria, the beautiful young Gladia. In 1956 I received a postcard from Asimov in which he chortled that he had just written a pornographic scene that the postmaster general couldn't touch (those were the days when postmasters censored what could be sent through the mail). On the rare occasions when Solarians meet they are fully clothed, even wearing gloves, but in a final scene Gladia is alone with Baley, who has cleared her of the murder of her husband.

"May I touch you? I'll never see you again, Elijah."
"If you want to."

Step by step, she came closer, her eyes glowing, yet looking apprehensive, too. She stopped three feet away, then slowly, as though in a trance, she began to remove the glove on her right hand.

Baley started a restraining gesture. "Don't be foolish, Gladia."

"I'm not afraid," said Gladia.

Her hand was bare. It trembled as she extended it.

And so did Baley's as he took her hand in his. They remained so for one moment, her hand a shy thing, frightened as it rested in his. He opened his hand and hers escaped, darted suddenly and without warning toward his face until her fingertips rested feather-light upon his cheek for the barest moment.

Can a touch be a touchstone? Why not? Where but in the literature of change, the literature of discontinuity, could a passage as innocent as this carry so great a weight of meaning? Here the twin philosophical sources of science fiction meet: people can be changed by changing the conditions under which they live, and people, if they are strong enough and sufficiently motivated, can break their environmental chains and choose what they wish to do or what they wish to be.

PART SIX

ANTICIPATION

Where is science fiction going now that the millennium mark has turned over, and we have bypassed many of the most significant science-fictional dates: 1984, 2000, 2001? The latter is most striking, of course, because of the disparity between the actual 2001 and the future envisioned by Clarke and Kubrick in 1968, which at the time seemed so realistic, so much within our grasp. It has become a commonplace that we live in a science-fictional world, and this cannot help but impact the nature of science fiction we produce. The essays in this section all grapple with the shape of things to come.

Michael Swanwick's "User's Guide to the Postmoderns" sets the stage for the genre as it exists today. This essay looks at the rise of the '80s generation of writers and their fragmentation into two camps, the "cyberpunks" and the "humanists." The cyberpunks are writers of data-packed, breakneck stories set in highly technological futures, while the humanists are writers of elegant, thoroughly researched character-oriented stories, just as likely to be set in the past as the future. This essay reads like Swanwick's fiction: fast-paced but thoughtful, serious but almost self-satirical, with deft characterization of all the players.

Many of the characters in Swanwick's essay reappear in Judith Berman's "Science Fiction without the Future," which won the Science

Fiction Research Association's "Pioneer" award for the best scholarly article of the year. Berman assesses the current state of the genre and finds it lacking. Her detailed study of the fiction in the pre-millennial issues of *Asimov's Science Fiction* (with a less detailed consideration of *Fantasy and Science Fiction* over the same period), shows a genre that must fail to appeal to upcoming generations of readers because it is deeply steeped in nostalgia for its past. Some may argue against her assessments of any given story, but as a whole her essay presents a strong case for the decline of the genre, not as a simple indictment, but as a call to action.

"Slipstream" by James Patrick Kelly might serve as an answer to Berman's call. Published originally as two articles in Berman's magazine under the microscope, *Asimov's Science Fiction*, the two have been edited into a single piece for publication here. While the idea of "slipstream" or "cross-genre" writing is not new, Kelly examines the wave of incoming writers who practice this style. Kelly looks at the ramifications that the move to slipstream writing might have on the genre itself, and he looks at the new venues in which these writers are showing themselves and honing their craft, which is especially crucial, since the rise of new innovations in science fiction have often been accompanied by the rise of new venues or the reinvention of old ones: *Amazing Stories* in 1926, *Astounding Science Fiction* in 1937, *Galaxy* and *Fantasy and Science Fiction* in 1949 and 1950, and the re-envisioned *New Worlds* in 1964. Kelly's essay serves as a marker of hope that the genre, far from turning in on itself through nostalgia, may instead be launching a new cycle. Like the New Wave, it may enrich without transforming, and while many slipstream writers, like the most characteristic New Wave writers, have their greatest success the more their work leaves science fiction behind, there has been an accompanying resurgence from within the genre. Sometimes called the British Renaissance, it is a re-imagination of the space opera, and Hartwell and Cramer touch on it in their essay in this anthology.

~

CHAPTER TWENTY-TWO

A User's Guide
to the Postmoderns

Michael Swanwick

Including the Battle for the Future, Unbridled Ambition, the Fate of the Children in the Starship, the Cyberpunk-Humanist Wars, Blood Under the Banquet Tables, Metaphors Run Amok, and the Destruction of Atlantis!

It's been said that every generation creates its own horde of invading barbarians in its young. This is certainly the case in the radioactive hothouse of science fiction, where new literary generations arise once every five or so years to challenge the establishment with a new vision of how the stuff ought to be written. A careful scholar could trace these waves from Hugo Gernsback's original gang of engineer-savants onward, but a simple demonstration proof can begin in the mid-1960s, when Samuel Delany, Thomas Disch, R. A. Lafferty, Norman Spinrad, and Roger Zelazny ushered in the New Wave. In the early seventies, it was Ursula K. Le Guin, Barry Malzberg, Joanna Russ, James Tiptree, Jr., and Gene Wolfe. In the *mid*-seventies, it was Gregory Benford, Jack Dann, Gardner Dozois, Michael Bishop, Joe Haldeman, John Varley, and . . . but more of them later. The significant point being that from the very beginning these changeovers have been accomplished with a certain amount of grumbling, screaming, firing off of guns and fisticuffs in the hallways. It was either traditional, or a law of nature. No one was sure which.

The most extreme example of generational conflict came, of course, in the 1960s, when the controversy over the new wave escalated to near-violence. On one side were the new writers entering the field who were not willing to abide its traditional restrictions (no graphic sex, a plain, "naturalistic" prose style, emphasis on idea to the exclusion of character) and on the other side their predecessors, suddenly labeled Old Wave, who objected to the new influences tainting their literary water hole (graphic sex, "experimental" prose, emphasis on mood or character to the exclusion of idea). Even today, when the positions of each side can be calmly discussed and evaluated—not here!—it is hard to understand why the debate got as acrimonious as it did, with each side vociferously denying the right of the other to even exist. Though Freud might have made some shrewd guesses.

In the 1980s, a new generation came into science fiction. This time, however, the army marched into the Eternal City and found it undefended. The lion gates were open; there were no archers on the walls. The citizenry turned out to throw to flowers, and petty officials proffered the key to the city. The barbarians were dumbfounded. They'd spent years assembling their arms, perfecting their tactics, honing their skills, and they were spoiling for battle. They had to fight *some*one.

They looked at one another.

The generation I want to talk about hasn't been named yet. In this essay I'll call them the postmoderns, because it's a nonjudgmental term, and because it fairly reflects their unspoken belief that all science fiction leading up to and culminating in their generation is—let's face it—dead. All the postmoderns are talented, ambitious writers, steeped in the lore and history of the field, and the controversies of previous generations are old news to them, settled long ago and to their complete satisfaction. It's only natural that they would want to seize control of the future of science fiction, to plot its directions and aims and goals—this is exactly what all previous generations demanded and, more or less, got. But there are truths that can only be discovered in the heat of argument, and as writers they all knew that you can't generate excitement without conflict. A revolution is no good without an active opposition.

Fortunately, there was a natural division within the postmodern ranks.

The first group, the humanists, produce literate, often consciously literary fiction, focusing on human characters who are generally seen as frail and fallible, and using the genre to explore large philosophical questions, sometimes religious in nature. A short list of names would have to include Connie Willis, Kim Stanley Robinson, John Kessel, Scott Russell Sanders, Carter Scholz, and James Patrick Kelly.

The other group has been tagged the cyberpunks (a story in itself; see the postscript for details and controversy). Their fiction is stereotypically characterized by a fully-realized high-tech future, "crammed" prose, punk attitudes including antagonism to authority, and bright inventive details. They would have to include William Gibson, Bruce Sterling, Lewis Shiner, Greg Bear, possibly Rudy Rucker, and sometimes Pat Cadigan.

Several streams of influence came together to form the cyberpunk thing. In the early seventies a group formed up that came to be known as the outlaw fantasists—Howard Waldrop, Steve Utley, Jake Saunders, Tom Reamy, a few others. They wrote truly strange fantasies marked by eclectic themes and outrageous ideas. Waldrop, for example, has written fantasies about dodoes, phlogiston, tractor pulls, telekinetic sumo wrestlers, and in one unforgettable flight of lunacy ("God's Hooks") had Izaak Walton and John Bunyan fishing in the Slough of Despond. *Nothing* seemed out of bounds to them, though, oddly enough, they rarely created high-tech futures. Since many of the outlaws lived in Texas, it was only natural that they should get together now and then, and the Turkey City Writers' Workshops brought in a wave of new young writers. Some, like Leigh Kennedy, became outlaw fantasists in their own right (witness her excellent and disturbing "Her Furry Face"). Others, like Shiner and Sterling, kept this wild sense of freedom, but mutated into something new.

The second major component is a kind of love-hate relationship with "hot tech," and here the track runs in and out of genre, from the high trash of A. E. Van Vogt and Charles Harness, through the 1950s future portrayed in *Popular Science* and *Popular Mechanics* (later satirized by Gibson in "The Gernsback Continuum"), the scat rhythms of Alfred Bester, corporate propaganda such as the 1964 World's Fair dioramas, the street-loner stance of Harlan Ellison, Japanese commercial art, the punk attitudes of John Shirley*, and the societal backlash against the sixties' antitechnological Arcadianism. Stir in strong doses of early Delany and Zelazny, a few out-of-genre writers, some Varley, a dollop of Stapledon, and you have the primal soup from which this new life form arose.

The humanists, on the other hand, have an easier, more immediate line of descent. They are the legitimate children of science fiction's "lost generation"—those post-New Wave writers of the seventies who have never been adequately celebrated or even examined collectively, and whom Tom Disch, in an article most of them found offensive, tagged "The Labor Day Group." This band would have to include George R.R. Martin, Ed Bryant, Vonda McIntyre, Joe Haldeman, Jack Dann, Elizabeth Lynn, Michael Bishop, Gardner Dozois, Greg Benford, and Joan Vinge. What they shared was a primary loyalty to science fiction and a belief that there is no argument between art and their chosen genre—that science fiction need not be written in oblique, metafictional *New York Review of Books* approved modes to be—really and truly—literature. (These writers are all still producing and in many cases turning out their best work to date, but the cutting edge of change has moved beyond them. In biological terms, they have donated their genetic material, and are now superfluous to our argument.)

To this direct influence the humanists bring a strong interest in outside literature, the high art "mainstream" stuff that outrages many of the pulp traditionalists (a group which, strange to say, includes several of the cyberpunks). John Kessel won a Nebula for "Another Orphan," a story which presupposes a certain familiarity with Melville's *Moby Dick*. Kim Stanley Robinson quoted Jean Paul Sartre—approvingly!— in "Green Mars." Is there anything better calculated to make the propeller beanie crowd gnash their teeth in outrage? I doubt it. I also doubt that this new generation is any more literate or better read than their progenitors. But where Martin, Bryant, *et al.* were too cagey (and perhaps too weary of the endless meaninglessness of the New Wave wars)

---

* I've listed Shirley as a literary ancestor where others would include him as a cyberpunk proper because he made his mark on the field years before any of the writers discussed here. His footprints are all over the cyberpunks' turf. It could be said that he serves as their John the Baptist figure.

to breathe their extrageneric influences aloud, the humanists stride forward with the fearless tread of angels.

What the postmoderns on both sides of the divide share in common is a confidence that borders on arrogance. They may like and even praise selected older writers (though they prefer 'em dead or obscure), but mostly they feel their predecessors are irrelevant, for good or for ill. "I hesitate to say it," Kessel is quoted in an interview in *Fantasy Review*, "but many of the works we call the best the field has to offer just do not measure up to the best of English and American fiction of the last couple of hundred years. Melville, Nabokov, Flannery O'Connor, Jane Austen, Faulkner, Conrad—these authors are a lot better, by almost any standard, than Herbert, Heinlein, Asimov, Zelazny and others." The science fiction writers mentioned would probably be surprised that anyone felt this statement needed to be made. And yet, you can tell, Kessel deplores the situation. "If we want to make it in the big leagues," he continues, "we've got to face big league pitching." Listen carefully and you can hear under his mild words the implicit brag that science fiction *can* make it in the big leagues, that it *can* face down Faulkner's spitball or Nabokov's sinker, and in his use of the first person plural, he reserves for himself a place in the batting lineup. This kind of ambition is alien to none of the postmoderns. They are all (and let's not lose sight of this fact) aiming high. They want to make it in the majors, and small fry like Heinlein, Asimov, and Clarke, are simply not the competition.

Commenting on this very phenomenon, James Patrick Kelly wrote of his fellow postmoderns, "It's ambition that makes them take the time to write killer short stories when they know that in practically the same amount of time and with less psychic effort they could cop a quick 10K for novelizing episodes of 'The Misfits of Science.' It's ambition that supports them as they stagger out of libraries laden with armloads of books that haven't been taken out since 1962. They're determined to stand out in this overcrowded field and they're willing to do the extra work." Which brings up another interesting topic, the curious mingling of respect and disdain with which the postmoderns approach their audience. They are willing to do that extra month's research it takes to establish that below-decks layout of a Spanish galleon or how Mozart actually spelled his middle name, for a story whose proceeds are not going to cover that month's food bill, because they know their readers care. And if their readers don't care, they can just go pound sand.

When the postmoderns entered the field, science fiction was in an uncharacteristically self-effacing state. As Sterling later put it, "SF was drifting without a rudder, at the mercy of every commercial breeze. New Wave had nothing to tell me. I'd grown up on it, and it was yellow and crisp around the edges, like an atticful of *New Worlds*." Nobody was fighting for the leading edge of SF. There was scattered chest-thumping and self-promotion, to be sure, but no organized cabals plotting the Overthrow and Destruction of Everything Sacred. The best writers were silent: The Old Wavers and New Wavers had by and large bludgeoned each other into critical quiescence. The Labor Day Group was either lying fallow (several of their best had written very little in recent years) or working on large, serious books that they hoped would break them either out of the genre or into major critical acclaim. (George R.R. Martin's *Fevre Dream* and Michael Bishop's *No Enemy But Time* are works of this period.) The guards were absent from their posts and the security systems had been shorted out. The starship's control room was vacant. Soft lights flickered, and the instrument panels hummed gently to themselves, waiting for somebody's guiding hand.

It was 1980. The children pushed open the door and stood blinking, a little bit afraid, in the sudden light.

As the postmoderns began their careers, they engaged in a frenzy of influence swapping and alliance forming. Here the cyberpunks stole an early march, forming themselves into as tight a clique as the field had seen since the Futurians, while the humanists were still gosh-wowing at the mere fact of being allowed to play with the Big Kids at all. Later, the pseudonymous Vincent Omniaveritas would launch his single-sheet Xeroxed fanzine *Cheap Truth*, the *de facto* propaganda organ of the cyberpunk movement. Aggressively uncopyrighted and mailed free to whomever Vincent thought should read it, it was to prove remarkably influential. (Its opening words, "As American SF lies in a reptilian torpor, its small, squishy cousin, Fantasy, creeps gecko-like across the bookstands," both put the challenge to the status quo, and demonstrated Vince's talent for invective. When he raises his arms to call down anathema upon the unworthy, toads fall from the sky.) In the meantime, both the protocyberpunks and the humanists-to-be were meeting, workshopping, and, in furies of creativity, hammering together the prose machines with which to take the asylum by storm.

But artistic satisfaction is not enough if your ambitions aspire to the reformation and redirection of all science fiction. Influence is not achieved without recognition and even popularity, and a way of keeping score was needed. The best-of-the-year anthologies were too easy, and the Hugos, which largely depend on pre-existing popularity, were too hard. Much of the cyberpunk-humanist wars would be slugged out in the Nebula Award banquets of the next few years.

While our aspirant writers are busy producing the stories they hope will reshape the future, let's take a quick look at two of them, both humanists:

In some ways Connie Willis is the most subversive of the lot, refusing to give in to the bohemian conventions of the field, even to her defiantly normal appearance (shortly after she won two Nebulas in a single year, there was a tempest-in-a-teapot controversy over whether a Nebula winner should be *allowed* to wear Peter Pan collars). Interviewed in *Mile High Futures*, she admitted to attending church, and said that she got some of her best ideas from adult Sunday School classes. In a field that is still defending Galileo from Urban VIII, and producing thinly disguised attacks on the Spanish Inquisition, this is heresy of the first magnitude. She also started out by writing for the women's confession magazines, and is not only unashamed of the experience, but claims to have learned useful skills from it.

Willis' prose is notable for her use of characterization by plotting and the sparsity of physical description. This gives a Willis story a unique and recognizable look and is in its own right an interesting technique. Also notable is that no two of her stories are alike. Willis is deliberately stretching her range, from the traditional realism of "Fire Watch" through such fairytale retellings as "The Father of the Bride" and the screwball comedy of "Blued Moon." It will be a long time, if ever, before she lets herself be restricted to a single type of story.

John Kessel is tall and quiet, with a large, dark mustache and an oxymoronic smile that manages to be both shy and confident at the same time. He has a Ph.D. from the University of Kansas and is an assistant professor of English at North Carolina State University. This, he has said, gives him the freedom to write whatever he likes, even in defiance of popular tastes, since he needn't rely on his writing to keep him alive. Despite a baccalaureate in both English and physics, his work is almost exclusively fantasy. It is, however, a fantasy that is not interested so much in the fantastic as in the human reactions to it. In "The Lecturer," for example, a teacher becomes interested in a strange living statue that stands on campus engaged in an endless (and perfectly dull) lecture, and finds that nobody—even, ultimately, himself—wants to face up to the fact that this is simply *not natural*. The statue is never explained.

Kessel's output, while influential, is not large, and much of it has been written in collaboration with James Patrick Kelly. The bulk of their collaborations were conceived as parts of a whole and make up their novel, *Freedom Beach*.

The mere existence of Willis and Kessel was enough to annoy cyberpunk sensibilities. The fact that they were writing strong stories in competition for the same limited number of awards, limited niches in *Omni* (which offers a word rate that a writer could almost live on, if they only bought more stories)* and the same limited amount of popular and critical attention, made them a menace.

The humanists may not have been as well organized, but the first blood went to them. In 1982 they won the first Nebulas. John Kessel took Novella with "Another Orphan," and Connie Willis took both Novelet and Short Story for "Fire Watch" and "A Letter From the Clearys." A little later "Fire Watch" also won a Hugo. It was a clean sweep for the humanists. (Novel went to Michael Bishop, but since neither faction had anything up in that category, this was irrelevant.) Worse, "Fire Watch" beat out "Burning Chrome" by Gibson and "Swarm" by Sterling. What made this all but unbearable is that these latter were not just good stories, but major works that were seen in many quarters as instant classics, and the cyberpunks were not likely to be writing better soon. They had gone into the fray with their best, and they had lost.

---

* Here too, the cyberpunks got in their groundwork early, finding a warm welcome in *Omni*'s pages. For a time, in fact, fiction editor Ellen Datlow was known, for her support of the group in general and her discovery of William Gibson in particular, as "the queen of punk SF."

Vincent Omniaveritas cranked the *Cheap Truth* propaganda machine up high. Demanding across-the-board reforms, he snarled: "It is little wonder that rock videos, like Napoleon, have pulled SF's crown from the gutter and placed it on their own head. Movement, excitement, color, reckless visionary drive: you will find these in abundance in the work of video directors and bands raised from birth on SF. Consequently they are producing not only excellent SF but SF often better than that in the written media." And, getting down to cases, Sue Denim wrote, "This year's Nebula ballot looked like a list of stuff that Mom and Dad said it was okay to read." Not long after, reviewing the Dozois Best of the Year anthology from Bluejay Books (in which Dozois singled out the "'80s generation" for praise, and listed its members), Omniaveritas wrote, "If these heirs-designate were dropped into a strong magnetic field, Gibson, Shiner, Sterling, Cadigan, and Bear would immediately drift to one pole . . Robinson, Kessel, Kelly, Murphy, and Willis would take the other." This was the moment of schism. Sides had been chosen, names dropped, and the battle could commence.

This hotted-up phase of the campaign lasted for the next few years. But before leaving 1982, let's take a quick look at two more postmoderns, both cyberpunks this time.

Bill Gibson bears a striking resemblance to Elvis Costello, but is much taller; like Costello, he is seen by his supporters as working right at the artistic edge, a position they deem virtuous in and of itself. As of 1982, his already formidable reputation was based on exactly two stories, "Burning Chrome," and "Johnny Mnemonic," both published in *Omni*. (He'd written a few other stories, mostly minor, but they brought him little attention—though no opprobrium either.) Sooner or later he would have to write a novel, and there was a certain tension to the question of whether he could carry the magic over into the greater and more demanding length.

Gibson's work is quintessential cyberpunk, with the hottest of technological futures, fast action, tight construction, and a disdain for all that is slow and boring. He has been acclaimed as a new breed of hard science fictioneer, a laurel he gracefully declined in an interview for *Interzone*: "I think that a number of reviewers have mistaken my sense of realism, of the *commercial surfaces* of characters' lives for some deep and genuine attempt to understand technology. I'm as fascinated—well, a bit more so, actually—by what motivates someone to go out and buy a pair of Calvin Klein jeans as I am by the workings of a surgical laser. Which is not to say that I am blind to the beauty and importance (or the poetry) of surgical lasers . . ." In all the excitement it would be easy to overlook the fact that he's an exacting craftsman and stylist on the small scale—line by line—as well as the large, a writer who can join two phrases seamlessly and with a swipe of the chamois make them glitter darkly. He was universally seen as the cyberpunks' big threat, their Babe Ruth, the Moses who was going to lead them out of the literary wastes and into the promised land of New and Better Science Fiction.

Bruce Sterling has already, in his short career, had three literary incarnations. First as a promising, largely ignored young writer (his first novel, *Involution Ocean*, a Harlan Ellison Discovery Series book, was . . . well, promising and largely ignored). Following *The Artificial Kid*, a now-rare hardcover in which he broke through into (and possibly invented) cyberpunk, he emerged as the suddenly hot writer of the Shapers/Mechanists Fictions stories, which combined pulp sensibilities and plotting, Stapledonian perspective, and cyberpunk incandescence. "Swarm" was a Factions story, and one of the best of them. After the publication of *Schismatrix*, his culminative Factions novel, in 1985, he moved into a third stage as a slick and quirky literary stylist, in stories (such as "Telliamed," "The Greening of Brunei," and "Dinner in Audoghast") which retain the color and excitement of cyberpunk, but move beyond it into something new. In his chameleonic incarnations, this shamanistic skin-shedding trick makes him by far the most interesting postmodern to watch, just to see what surprises come next.

It was 1983. The battle lines were drawn. And a surprising new ally presented himself. Greg Bear, who had been laboring in the promising-and-largely-ignored vineyards for several years, suddenly found his voice, and published two stories ("Hardfought" and "Blood Music") which in their bright inventiveness, bold daring, and cheerful pessimism were—there was no getting around it—cyberpunk. Working in perfect isolation from the faction, Bear had independently invented the cyberpunks' style, and they loved him for it. He was welcomed to the ranks with open arms.

At the same time, the cyberpunks saw a new threat shaping up, a writer who seemed to them the most talented and menacing of all the humanists, Kim Stanley Robinson.

Kim Stanley Robinson has the cold glitter of a gunslinger to him, the kind of contained look that makes rivals nervous. To see him and Gibson talking together, even in photographs, is to be struck that there is much that these two are *not* saying to each other, that there are killer truths hiding just beneath the skin. Robinson combined high literary sensibilities (I've heard an editor who missed signing him up try to shrug him off as obviously being a mainstream art writer who didn't yet realize he was just passing through SF on the way to bigger things) with a strong, lucid prose style. He'd already gotten critical attention with stories ("At the North Pole of Pluto," "Exploring Fossil Canyon," and "Venice Drowned," for example) that combined topnotch writing and traditional science-fiction themes pushed that little bit further. In 1983 he published "Black Air," a novella about a young boy dragooned into the Spanish Armada. It was about suffering and mercy, the writing was so good you could taste the North Atlantic, the underlying mysticism all worked, and to the cyberpunks it was infuriating. "It's so nice to read a straightforward historical story, just like that Frank G. Slaughter used to write," Sue Denim hissed in *Cheap Truth*, "and it's just too bad he had to tack on that fantasy mumbo jumbo at the end just so he could sell it."

"Black Air" won the World Fantasy Award for 1983, and once again the humanists had stolen a march on the cyberpunks. Another major award had fallen to the enemy. That same year Bear left the Nebula ceremonies with two awards, for "Blood Music" and "Hardfought," and while this was a moral victory and an encouraging sign that the Right Stuff might yet win through, it was not enough. Bear was only an honorary cyberpunk; he had earned a place in the ranks through sheer merit, much as he had earned his Nebulas. He was not part of the cabal that had labored late into the dark night of obscurity, shivering in unheated garages to create cyberpunk and make it work. The victory they wanted so bad they could taste it, their vindication, could not be obtained that easily.

1984, and the trenches were manned. Terry Carr was editing the revitalized Ace Specials line for Susan Allison at the Berkley Publishing

Group, and he shrewdly managed to line up many of the most promising new writers. The lineup of the first five books contained the conflict in miniature. It led off with Kim Stanley Robinson's *The Wild Shore*, followed by Lucius Shepard's *Green Eyes*, William Gibson's *Neuromancer*, Carter Scholz's and Glenn Harcourt's *Palimpsests*, and Howard Waldrop's *Them Bones*. These books got a lot of serious attention, most of it favorable, and there was much year's end discussion of the New Generation of writers, and where they might lead SF.

(Carter Scholz, who has not been discussed previous to this, belongs firmly in the humanist camp. He is the most defiantly intellectual of the lot, and this has to a certain degree slowed down his career. And yet works like his screamingly funny "The Nine Billion Names of God"—knowledgable readers will realize that the joke begins with the title—show that he is out there on the literary intellectual outposts not through ignorance or inability but by choice.)

Robinson was first out of the gate. In *The Magazine of Fantasy and Science Fiction*, Algis Budrys wrote, "Kim Stanley Robinson . . . is an uncommonly gifted writer. But he is also an uncommon sort of writer for our whereabouts, and therefore it's notable to me that Terry Carr and Ace, in re-instituting the Ace Special series, waited until they had his novel to begin the series with. They literally did that—there are other books in the Special inventory, from other new and promising writers, that waited for Robinson to deliver *The Wild Shore*."[*] The novel itself fulfilled John W. Campbell's dream of a literature as it might be written by somebody in the future in which the story is set (though it's doubtful what JWC would have made of this *particular* fulfillment). It is a classical *Bildungsroman*, a gentle, almost introspective exploration of a boy's growth to manhood and the beginnings of wisdom, within an enigmatic post-Collapse America. It defies and plays against the expectations of the genre adventure novel, even including within itself a parody of the book it could have been. (There is an unforgettable and telling moment during a public reading of this supposedly non-fiction work, when the adults can no longer hold in their laughter, and fall to

---

[*] In fact, Budrys was mistaken about this, according to Kim Stanley Robinson. Robinson notes that his novel was not originally supposed to lead off the line, but was hastily shoved forward when the scheduled lead novel was not received in time.

the ground, howling, great tears of mirth rolling down their cheeks, while the children glare at them angrily.) It was received with critical and popular acclaim.

When the dust settled, the cyberpunks realized that this was their showdown at last. William Gibson was marching slowly down Main Street, gun at thigh, to face down Kim Stanley Robinson. It was *Neuromancer* against *The Wild Shore*. Cyberpunk versus humanist. It was High Noon.

To read *Cheap Truth* from this period, it's fairly obvious that the cyberpunks expected another defeat. It wasn't just that Budrys and Ace had already crowned Robinson king. *Neuromancer* was simply too good, too far ahead of its time. It was destined to be defeated by the purblind provincialism of the field.

Tensions ran high. "The 1985 Nebula Awards will be handed out on May 4," Sue Denim wrote, "fifteen years to the day from the shootings at Kent State University in Ohio. Once again the armed might of conservatism faces the radical vision of a new generation, this time across the distance of a ballot," and she vowed, "Political oppression breeds revolution. For every Heinlein that smites a Gibson, thousands more will rise in his place."

If for no other reason than to preserve dramatic pacing and properly draw out suspense, it's best we pause here to look quickly at several other writers who play significant roles in our narrative. In the humanist camp, we have yet to introduce James Patrick Kelly, whose work has been largely overshadowed by that of his collaborator, John Kessel. It would be a mistake to overlook him. A quiet man who has been known to wear three-piece suits to science fiction conventions, Kelly has an exceptionally lucid prose style, employing what Kessel calls "the kind of skill that hides skill." This is not only a tough style to attain but a brutal one to have mastered, since it leaves the writer with not a florid adjective to hide behind. He has written some first-rate hardcore humanist stories (notably, "The Empty World," which is about an encounter with Emily Brontë) and is also getting attention for his trilogy of stories, "Solstice," "Rat," and "The Prisoner of Chillon." Of which, more soon.

Scott Russell Sanders makes no strong distinctions between his genre and mainstream writings. In his words, "I write what I feel like writing, in whatever form or mode seems appropriate, and then agents and editors have to worry about how to publish and market it." This is the voice of a generation; none of the postmoderns are overconcerned about writing to expectations. However, where others feel this freedom in principle, he puts it into practice writing everything from *Wonders Hidden* (a "historical" about Audubon) through the science fictional *Terrarium*, into the non-fiction *Stone Country* (with photographer Jeffrey A. Wolin, a study of Indiana limestone and the men who cut it, in history and lore). In his SF story "Ascension," the husband of the mayor of a small town suffering from mass insomnia retreats into a surplus space suit, there to sleep and await his symbolic transcendence. (And what, one wonders, would John W. Campbell have made of *that?*)

On the cyberpunk side, Rudy Rucker, the third of their Big Guns, strays farther from consensus reality than any of the other postmoderns, producing work strongly reminiscent of what Henry Kuttner once published under the name of Lewis Padgett. A mathematician by training (he has written popular books on the subject), he pulls off admirably zany excesses with great nonchalance. His novels in particular (*Clear White Light*, *Master of Time and Space*, and *Software* leap to mind) have earned him an enthusiastic following. Comparing his text to that of his cohort, one has to sadly conclude that he is *sui generis*, no cyberpunk at all, but rather a one-man subgenre all by himself. However, the cyberpunks love him for his daring, excess, and clear-eyed craziness, and have claimed him as one of their own.

Lewis Shiner has thus far rested in the shadow of the Big Three—his first novel, *Frontera*, in an almost allegorical juxtaposition, landed on the Nebula ballot opposite Gibson—but he was a strong writer to begin with, and shows constant growth. Lately he seems to be coming more and more into his own voice with such stories as "Till Human Voices Wake Us," the well-received "The War at Home," and his crisp, unforgiving look at working-class failure, "Jeff Beck." If you strip away the fantastic element from his work (he likes dealing with outré belief systems, such as those of Aleister Crowley or current particle physics), what remains is a particularly vivid brand of realism. Finally, it has been charged that Pat Cadigan, while a fine writer, is no cyberpunk at all (she has also been called "the Dorothy Parker of science fiction," but that's another can of terms entirely, and one we won't open.) And while stories like "Roadside Rescue" (which is, if anything, Outlaw Fantasy) support this contention, her Pathosfinder stories and the hard-edged grittiness of "Rock On" and "Pretty Boy Crossover" put her firmly—if only occasionally—among the cyberpunks. When she veers into fantasy, however, she often displays the keenest, and occasionally meanest, sense of humor of any of the postmoderns, excepting only Rucker.

Which brings us back to the 1984 Nebulas, and William Gibson's climactic showdown. His weapon was a novel that "eroticizes computers the way that Bruce Springsteen eroticizes cars" (here I'm quoting his publisher's publicity sheet), and he didn't expect it to find a large audience. But Nebula Fever strikes where it will, and as the date approached, his followers had their secret hopes. Adrenaline flowed, nerves stretched the breaking point, palms grew sweaty and . . .

Neuromancer took everything with embarrassing ease. It not only won the Nebula for best novel, but the Philip K. Dick award for best paperback original, and the Hugo award as well. At the same time, it was garnering overwhelmingly positive reviews both in and out of genre, in everything from *Amazing* to the *Whole Earth Review*. Even the *New York Times* gave it a rave, though it waited over a year to do so, and then (in their recommended Christmas reading list) got the plot wrong. It was an unprecedented triumph for a first novel, the kind that every writer dreams of yet dares not hope for. And Gibson got it all.

This success threw the ranks into disarray. The cyberpunks were left all alone in the middle of the battlefield, enemy in full retreat, the spoils before them, the acknowledged New Direction of SF all theirs, and they were barely winded. Without warning, they were victorious.

It was just too damned easy.

The fight hadn't been as much fun as they'd expected. And the result? Virtue *rewarded*? It was as if they'd found themselves suddenly transported into the middle of a Christian allegory; the fact that one of their number had been cast as the Pilgrim, made it no more palatable. In *Cheap Truth*, Candace Barragus proceeded to trash Gibson, writing "There is little true anger in *Neuromancer* or in punk rock. The rest is posturing, and finally rings hollow . . . If SF is to give us new lands, it will have to try harder than this. *Neuromancer* has little thought in it— surely the old corporate-run future, with Japanese electro-dominance, can't be counted on as a new idea?—but much attention to the cosmetics of a time only slightly beyond our own." But while Ms. Barragus (who, to judge by prose styles, is probably not Gibson himself, though that is an attractive possibility) spelled out several valid (but irrelevant) flaws in the novel, nobody rose to the bait. It seemed they had not an enemy in the world. Victory was complete.

In the aftermath, everybody was left feeling vaguely dissatisfied. A new generation of cyberpunks—identifiable by their prose, but nobody that anybody had ever *met*—was coming up. The cyberpunks had created a subgenre that was easy to imitate, and they couldn't help but wonder if somehow they shouldn't have aimed higher. It was around this time that Sterling said resignedly, "I don't worry much about the future of razor's edge Techno-punk. It will be bowdlerized and parodied and reduced to a formula, just as all other SF has been." Revolutions cannot survive this kind of total success, and at this point, whether they knew it or not (and most of them did not) cyberpunk as a movement was dead.

But if the factions were no more, the postmoderns remained. Everybody shifted literary position a little. Nobody, after all, was really *happy* with their labels. By now the cyberpunks had a rep as flash stylists but weak on character, and the humanists were deemed good with people, but a trifle lacking in idea content. Both judgments were unfair, but they still left everyone wondering what to do next, and full of energy. Across the ranks, there was movement, as people stretched their literary muscles. James Patrick Kelly made an abrupt stylistic veer into the flash and pyrotechnic display of his "Cyberpunk Trilogy" (the aforementioned, "Solstice," "Rat," and "The Prisoner of Chillon") and, three-piece suit or not, they were *good*. Lewis Shiner moved more and more into a lean, sinewy prose style that owed little to cyberpunk proper. Kim Stanley Robinson, whose *The Wild Shore* and *Icehenge* had both been received enthusiastically by critics and readers alike, moved on to new works (and also, temporarily, to Switzerland for reasons unrelated to science fiction). John Kessel and Bruce Sterling decided to collaborate on a story. Pat Cadigan put out a final issue of her highly-regarded fanzine, *Shayol*, and went merrily on her way with her own idiosyncratic mix of fantasy and SF. Out of a clear blue sky, Rudy Rucker wrote *The Meaning of Life*, which under its ornamentation is a gently self-satirical look at growing up in the sixties. Sterling put his Factions stories behind him, and revealed himself as a master stylist. Many of his new works are an attempt to explore the impact of science in a way free of the technolatry characteristic of current utopian and distopian SF. A belated *rapprochement* was in the works. New alliances were forming, and new constellations of writers, and they were all casting about for a new challenge. Something bigger this time.

But in the midst of all this carnage and triumph, art and defeat, something significant happened. Another postmodern popped up. Lucius Shepard, whose Ace Special novel *Green Eyes* (a weird combination of biochemistry and voodoo) had been largely ignored at first, suddenly blossomed. In 1983, he had published his first story, "Solitario's Eyes." Now in 1984 he produced what seemed an endless stream of excellent stories, including the darkly savage "Salvador." By year's end, he had three stories on the Nebula ballot, and while he did not win *then*, everybody knew it was just a matter of time.

Shepard is another damned tall writer—to stand in conversation with him, Gibson, and Kessel, is to guarantee a stiff neck the next morning. He wears a silver skull in one ear, and has a possibly romantic past about which everyone seems to know something, but not much. He almost certainly *has* traveled extensively about the world, to judge by the convincing quality of his varied and exotic settings. He has also met genuine lowlife—a type that SF writers often tackle, and usually miss—again by testimony of such stories as "Black Coral" and "A Traveler's Tale." Often he writes from a Third World perspective, something very few Americans dare even attempt.

What is significant to our account is that Shepard belongs in neither cyberpunk nor humanist camps. His fiction has the mean edge of the cyberpunks, and the human angle of the humanists, and yet lacks the hot tech ambiance of the one, and the defiant literariness of the other. Still, Shepard intuitively belongs with the postmoderns. So, rather than try to shoehorn him into either badly-fitting label, let's just see him as symptomatic of the new surge of writers coming up from obscurity. The ground is bubbling underfoot, and new talent is climbing into the sunshine. The cutting edge is about to move on. Some who have it now will lose it, and others will keep it. Reputations will grow and dwindle. Some will almost but never quite make it. Others will linger in the shadows for years before bursting out to dazzle us all. The mighty shall be humbled, and the humble exalted. All Biblical prophesies shall be fulfilled. In short, it will be a time much like any other for science fiction.

Looking back over what I've written, I regret all the significant writers I've had to leave out in the interest of simplification. No discussion of our literary time and place would be complete, for example, without mention of the Bay Area group of Philip K. Dick disciples that includes Tim Powers, K.W. Jeter, and the infinitely strange James Blaylock. I've also neglected the gang of Space Cadets—the ones Omniaveritas calls "Reagan Youth"—who have accreted about the twin nuclei of Jim Baen and Jerry Pournelle. I've skipped over all the lone wolf writers for lack of a convenient niche (where does one place Jack McDevitt, Nancy Kress, Pat Murphy, Tim Sullivan, or Gregory Frost, to name just five?). Finally, and I regret this most but it was done out of ignorance rather than malice, I haven't said a word about the writers (R.A. McAvoy, John Crowley, Patricia McKillip, Michael Shea, Jane Yolen, Robin Mckinley, and of course, Tanith Lee) currently at work to shape the new fantasy. To all of them, and you, I apologize.

Ah, but for a dazzling instant there, it was possible to see it all: To choose up sides, name names and list lists. The lines of literary influence were exposed for all to see, bright as lasers across the literary map, running from Texas to British Columbia, from New Hampshire to North Carolina, with nexuses in Denver, in Austin, in Kansas City, in Philadelphia even, and for that single bright instant before the continents shifted, the future was laid out sparkling and clean, the roads were clear, and the gateways into brave new words of fiction swung wide. All of Atlantis was prosperous and at peace.

It was a terrific time to be alive and young and writing stories so good that they made the competition slam fists into walls and throw typewriters through closed windows in blind fits of jealous rage.

CHAPTER TWENTY-THREE

~

Science Fiction without the Future

Judith Berman

At conventions and parties and in private conversation, I've been hearing for years now about the declining subscription base of the major sf print magazines, and the failure of both the magazines and original booklength sf to attract younger readers. For years I, like many, took this solely as evidence of the decline of reading as a leisure activity and the increasingly short attention spans of the young. The birth of my own child has given me a fresh perspective.

I am now sure that my 16-month-old son, who already shows an alarming interest in print, will be a reader. But will he be an sf reader? In my own childhood, I happily consumed Golden Age science fiction written before I was born. When I try to imagine what today's sf will look like to my son, I am afraid not only that little of it will be of interest, but also that the fault lies in the science fiction itself.

Recent issues of *Asimov's* provide an illustration. *Asimov's*—arguably the most influential sf magazine—garners major awards year after year, supplying the Hugo ballot in 2000, for example, with 11 out of the 16 nominated stories and all three short fiction winners. *Asimov's* editor Gardner Dozois has himself won twelve of the last thirteen Hugos handed out for best editor. If; as has often been said, short fiction is the place where sf's speculative tools are honed and its new visions first emerge, Asimov's should be a reliable barometer of the state of current sf.

Among the contents of the issue with the cover date of my son's birth, October-November 1999, we find the following stories by some of the field's top authors:

Connie Willis's "The Winds of Marble Arch," a novella about aging and the fear of growing old, as represented by winds blowing through the London Underground.

Mike Resnick's "Hothouse Flowers," on a future where the very old are not allowed to die but are kept on life support as vegetables for decades (not so different from the present!).

Michael Swanwick's "Riding the Giganotosaur," about an old man dying of cancer who is rich enough to have his brain transplanted into a giganotosaur back in the Cretaceous.

Dozois's "A Knight of Ghosts and Shadows." It's about an old man, close to death and possibly delusional, who has lived into a world of disorienting social and technological change.

Kim Stanley Robinson's "A Martian Romance," about a newly frozen Mars and two very old people close to death, who are sad about the death of Blue Mars and their own approaching ends.

Robert Silverberg's column on the autographs of Golden Age greats he possesses in his book collection.

Jack Williamson, living Golden Age great, column that looks back over his life and career.

Nelson Bond, another writer of the same generation, with "Proof of the Pudding," a joke short-short.

The Williamson retrospective, taken by itself, is free of nostalgia. Swanwick's old man turns exuberant in his dinosaur body. Willis's couple is rescued at the last minute by the wind of hope, and yes, the two young people in Robinson's story aren't sad because they are at the start of their lives and have hope for the future.

But as a group the stories are full of nostalgia, regret, fear of aging and death, fear of the future in general, and the experience of change as disorienting and bad. These stories aren't about dystopias. They are about individuals trying to cope with what the present has inexorably and dislocatingly become. Not that this is a bad topic or that good and moving stories can't be written about it. And, in fairness, Willis and Robinson offer at least the notion of hope and adaptation to change. What gives me pause is how recurrent and pervasive the fears are, and the way they are presented within a frame of nostalgia for the Golden Age past of sf.

A poem in the issue by Bruce Boston, "Another Short Horror Story," suggests a more specific reading of these stories: that what's really being expressed is fear of the present. Boston's poem concerns the loneliness of the last man on earth who hasn't jacked into the neural net. Embedded in the poem is the notion that the Internet will drive unmediated authenticity into oblivion, that the net connects people only by alienating them from their essential humanity. (This fear echoes the traditional media's reporting on any crime in which the Internet figures ever-so-peripherally: "Victim met murderer in chat room, police say." How often, in contrast, do you see headlines such as "Victim talked with murderer on telephone"? Anxiety about computers and the Internet is to a significant degree generational—for those of us who met computers relatively early in life, computers *are* just an appliance like the telephone.)

Boston's poem, and the Golden Age nostalgia that frames the issue, point toward a particular fact of the sociology of science fiction. Baby boomers—the cohort for whom Golden Age authors evoke fond recollections of childhood—currently dominate sf production and consumption. This supersized slice of the demographic pie has exerted hegemony over the pace and direction of cultural change for decades, but the Age of the Internet and the New Economy have, it seems to me, begun to dethrone them in favor of the twenty- and thirtysomethings who are as comfortable in the seething, mutating cultural ferment of the web as fish are in the sea. The Internet is perhaps the best symbol—of everything disquieting to boomers (and their elders) about the present, including the generational divide with respect to technology. This divide is the subject of the old joke about the eight-year-old being the one who programs the family VCR. Part of what the joke expresses is the fear that members of the younger generation, at ease with all new technology, are growing up strangers to their parents.

I would argue that these *Asimov's* stories are about, or are strongly shaped by, the anxieties experienced by many boomers at a particular historical moment in which they no longer feel in control either of society at large or of their own lives. Dozois' musty antihero might stand as a proxy for these anxieties: an old man who was famous for having in his youth suggested that society slow the pace of technological change, but whose manifesto on the topic failed to have the desired effect.

Golden Age sf: hope for the future of technology. Millennial sf: fear of the present, fear of technology? If this is what's happened, no wonder younger readers aren't drawn into the field. The changes that frighten older people—*they don't perceive as change*. How much more archaic will babyboom anxieties seem to my son's generation?

Yet boomer writers and boomer-specific themes can't take the entire rap for declining magazine readership. Surely fearfulness is not the dominant reaction of all boomers to change, nor do I imagine that the stories I have cited are the sole response of their authors to millennial unease. And even if both these things were so, examination of a subsequent year-plus of *Asimov's*—the issues leading up to the start of the twenty-first century—shows that the overwhelming majority of the stories avert their gaze to some degree from both present and future. As the age of most of the authors is unknown to me, I have to suppose that an anxious, backward-looking perspective is distributed well beyond the baby boom generation.

Fully one-third of the stories in these issues are set in the past, or are set in the present but entirely concerned with the past. There are stories of time travel to the Cretaceous, the Silurian, to eighteenth-century Amsterdam, eighteenth-century Leipzig, fourteenth-century France, and 1920s California (Swanwick 10–11/99, Utley 10–11/00, Baker 7/00, Purdom 5/00, Garcia y Robertson 8/00, Baker 12/00). In only two time-travel stories does a future hero come back to the "present" (Baker 1/00, Turtledove 12/99), and nowhere do we have a hero traveling to the future.

There are stories about nineteenth-century author Stephen Crane, the 1912 Scott expedition to the South Pole, the bombing of Tokyo during World War II, British aviators during World War II, the death of the last mammoth in a 1940 fire, and God and the Devil deal-making over the fate of JFK (Wilber 6/00, Yolen and Harris 5/00, Parks 12/00, MacLeod 12/99, Baxter 1/00, Baker 3/00), among others.

Where the history is of another timestream, there are no Dickian alternate presents to be found. The stories are concerned with alternate *past* history: Theodore Roosevelt chasing Jack the Ripper; a Civil War Jason and Medea pursuing hidden gold; a present-day hero playing god in pre-Columbian Mesoamerica (Resnick 12/00, W. J. Williams 10-11/99, Reed 5/00). Of special interest here is Greg Egan's "Oracle," in which fictional versions of Alan Turing and C. S. Lewis debate whether unbridled technological change, especially advances in computation and the development of artificial intelligence, is good or evil (7/00).

Two of these backward-looking stories gaze toward the field's own past: one visits Cthulhu-worshipping trailer trash (Friesner 2/00); the other follows the alternate-universe adventures of Isaac Asimov and Robert Heinlein during, again, World War II (Gunn, Duncan, Murphy, and Swanwick 4/00).

This leaves roughly two-thirds of the stories that are set in the present or future. But of these, some contain very few if any essential speculative elements (e.g., Rusch 1/00, Palwick 5/00). The most notable in terms of the present discussion is Cory Doctorow's "At Lightspeed Slowing," a story of a techie so overstimulated by modern life that he has rejected the present to seek mental and emotional refuge in a primitive commune in Costa Rica (4/00). Here also belongs John Alfred Taylor's literal talking-head tale, "Calamity of So Long Life," another that examines the fears of someone old, disabled, and helpless (5/00).

A number of stories ostensibly take place in the future, but bristle with anachronisms that are often nostalgic or ironically retro: we have safaris, chess tournaments, pioneer homesteads, or the old European class system (albeit upside-down) on distant planets (Resnick 12/99, Neube 8/00, de Noux 2/00, Le Guin 2/00). In Rick Wilber's "To Leuchars," we are even told that the setting for the novella, a colony world's first settlement, was intentionally built to look like a centuries-old Scottish city (9/00).

On future Earths we have Spanish-style bullfighting and Cretan bull-dancers; a small circus touring rural Vietnam; and expats and communards in a future version of 1920s Paris (Abraham, Roessner Walker, and W. J. Williams 10–11/00; Shepard 8/00; Doctorow and Skeet 12/00). Or retro imagery dominates a fictional present: a nineteenth-century balloon transports a hero from contemporary New York; a man drills to the hollow center of the earth (Cowan 1/00; Bond 10–11/99).

A surprisingly large proportion of the future landscapes in these *Asimov's* issues are pastoral or primitive, whether found on Earth (Kress 6/00, Swanwick 3/00, Doctorow 4/00, Sarafin 2/00, Tilton 9/00) or an alien planet (Arnason 10–11/00, Nordley 2/00, L. Williams 10–11/00, de Noux 2/00, Resnick 12/99, Robinson 10–11/99). We even have pastoral virtuality (Daniel 10–11/99). And when aliens come to Earth, they nearly always appear in small-town, rural, or downright primitive settings, whether in the past (Sullivan 7/ 00), near-present (Abraham 12/99, Pieczynski 1/00, Reed 7/00), or future (Pendleton 7/00). In only one case do they show up in a suburban setting—though one which the *protagonist* sees as hick and small-town (Fintushel 12/99).

Any of these pastoral landscapes would seem unremarkable by itself. It's the frequency with which such environments appear especially in contrast with the relative scarcity of urban and suburban settings. This is a decidedly nostalgic trend given the present-day worldwide reality of burgeoning population and metastasizing sprawl. Curiously, only one of the fantasy stories not set in Earth's own historical past has a primitive setting (Martin 12/00). The few others untold largely in contemporary urban or suburban landscapes (Willis 10–11/99, Fintushel 3/00, Stableford 4/00).

Some of the stories with retro elements or pastoral settings do nevertheless address contemporary issues in a speculative fashion. We have, for example, Daniel Abraham's small-town aliens who play the role of unwelcome immigrant group (12/99), or the pattern-crunching digital espionage practiced by the hero of Cory Doctorow and Michael Skeet's retro Paris story (12/00). Egan's Turing-and-Lewis debate, though set in an alternate postwar England, nevertheless appears to embrace the still-unfolding wonders of the future (7/00).

Of the future stories without overt retro or pastoral elements, one group takes place on or near the starships of a far-future interstellar human diaspora. Interestingly, with the exception of Richard Wadholm's "Green Tea," a piece dealing with a catastrophic industrial accident (10–11/99), these almost uniformly have an old-fashioned flavor, concerned as they are with themes and issues belonging to previous eras. The motif of dyadic warring superpowers, for example (in Reynolds 5/00, Baxter 10–11/00, Niven 10–11/00), arises out of the Cold War, not out of this present age of balkanization and brutal local genocides. The conflict between communalism and individuation, another Cold War theme, is also found here (Baxter 9/00, Nordley 2/00; note also Baxter 4/00). Absent from these distant futures are types of conflict more in tune with the current *Zeitgeist*—for example the fragmentation of local communities, the burgeoning of ethnic and cultural diversity, and ideological and religious retrenchment in the face of these trends.

The future stories that remain grapple with current issues or have, a contemporary flavor (e.g., Reynolds 12/99, Marusek 3/00, Kress 6/00, Reed 8/00, Langford 9/00, Kelly 6/00, MacAuley 7/00, and Purdom 10–11/00). (Wadholm's story, 10–11/99, mentioned above, probably belongs in this group.) These, what I would term "real futures," make up only a quarter of the total sample—one or two stories out of the 86 in the sample are nearly impossible to categorize so the figure is not exact.

And even here the fiction is not all as forward-gazing as it might appear. Most of these "real futures" exhibit anxiety, even dread, with respect to technology and its consequences (e.g., Barton 1/00, Duchamp 2/00, Purdom 3/00, Rusch 3/00, Sheffield 3/00 and 6/00, MacLeod 6/00, Kress 8/00, Stableford 8/00, Taylor 9/00, Arnason 10–11/00, Bell 12/00). That leaves us with no more than a handful of the stories in the sample that *look forward to the future* in both senses of the phrase.

With so many writers apparently uneasy about the state of the world, I would expect plenty of mordant commentary on our entanglement in the wheels of the runaway technological locomotive. But almost none of the stories in these 13 *Asimov's* issues—not even those set in a "real future"—offer a genuine *critique* of technology, of its use by and its impact upon humanity. David Marusek's biting "VTV," about new extremes of media manipulation, is a standout exception (3/00). Critique requires that its author gaze unflinchingly at present and future, ugly and perverse as those might appear. What we have instead here is a pervasive techno-anxiety that for the most part looks away from the source of its fears.

I don't mean to convey here that I'm advocating that all sf must explore serious social issues, or that sf mags aren't the better for a periodic romp in medieval France or the brain of a rutting giganotosaurus. When the stories are well done, I read all the subgenres of sf I've mentioned—e.g., time travel, alternate history, far-future interstellar adventure—with pleasure. Nor should this argument be taken as a judgment on the quality of any individual story, which is generally high. Moreover, I'm guilty myself of writing some of the types of stories I've cited. My problem is not with individual stories but with trends.

I would further like to stress that I don't mean to be picking on *Asimov's* to the exclusion of any other print magazine. On the contrary, my assumption here is that Dozois buys the best fiction he sees, and as *Asimov's* editor, he sees a great deal of the best that is written. These, it seems, are the types of stories that are being written.

For comparative purposes, my friend and colleague Christopher East has supplied some figures for *Fantasy Science Fiction*, the field's other short-fiction standard bearer. *F&SF* publishes a much higher ratio of fantasy to sf: in the year 2000 the proportion of fantasy stories was around 50 percent, compared with 10 percent in *Asimov's*. Of the 42 percent of *F&SF* devoted to science fiction, a little fewer than half the stories, or around 20 percent of the total, were set at least ostensibly in the future. A smaller number belongs in what I'm calling the "real future" category: about 31 percent of the sf stories, but only 13 percent of the total. (These figures are derived from year-2000 *F&SF* issues, excluding March and May.)

All together, then, "real future" science fiction appears in one in four stories in *Asimov's* and fewer than one in seven in *F&SF*. I have to believe the numbers for book-length sf fall more or less in the same range. We have a field that is increasingly fearful of the present, looking ever more wistfully toward the past. Meanwhile the thoughtful future dealing with fresh themes is becoming rare—even endangered.

Three stories from the premillennial issues of *Asimov's*, each fine in its own right, seem to illuminate the state of the field with particular clarity. The first is Jim Cowan's, bearing the suitably old-fashioned title "The True Story of Professor Trabuc and His Remarkable Voyages Aboard the *Sonde-Ballon De La Mentalité*" (1/00). This is the tale of two old men, weary with their present lives, who together explore the infinite Mindscape in a "device that might have been discovered by a nineteenth century French physicist, but wasn't." The vehicle in which they travel through the country of all things imaginable is a rough canvas helium gasbag attached to a wooden boat, accessorized with wooden propeller, handblown lightbulbs, and open-top batteries of sloshing, fuming acid.

Cowen's *sonde-ballon* seems emblematic of millennial sf: in a trend presaged by steampunk, the archaic and the antique are replacing the techno-futuristic as the source of the very coolest things. Our more primitive past—in this case industrial and polluting rather than pastoral—has become, in Levi-Strauss's words, good to think.

One suspects this phenomenon is connected to the fashion for new furniture with "distressed" finishes, and the practice of naming subdivisions after the pastoral landscapes they have replaced—Pine Woods, Mill Creek, Sunny Meadows. Things that are genuinely old are disappearing from everyday American experience. This loss of roots is part of the millennial alienation of many Americans, who feel adrift in a sea of images and information devoid of meaning. The primitive certainties of the past, represented by the *sonde-ballon,* might seem to be the only vehicle sufficiently authentic to navigate the millennial Mindscape. But where sf writers are concerned, I would wish for greater sophistication—for *purposive* exploration of all this devotion to the past, as well as of the anxiety generated by the present. Science fiction can't just follow those elements in the larger culture that feel soothed by contemplation of simpler times.

The second story, already mentioned, is Dozois' elegiac "A Knight of Ghosts and Shadows" (10–11/99), about an old man born in the 1980s who has "outlived most of his world":

> The society into which he'd been born no longer existed; it was as dead as the Victorian age, relegated to antique shops and dusty photo albums and dustier memories, the source of quaint old photos and quainter old videos . . . and here he still was somehow . . . in THE FUTURE. . . . [N]othing had turned out the way he'd thought it would be.

The future in which he now finds himself is presented less as an interrelated whole than as a bundle of sf tropes, most shown to the reader as the old man walks a future Philadelphia: a World War III nuclear Armageddon; orbitally based AIs who revolt from and then rule their human former masters; ghostly time travelers who come back from the future to view a critical historical moment; the promise, at least, of starships and human colonies on distant worlds; genetically engineered supermen; quasi-living city-enclaves; machines slaved to distant intelligences; magical nanotech substances; people lost in virtual realities.

While Dozois's old man seems to sum up the millennial dislocation of today's older generations, the landscape through which he moves could stand for millennial sf in general, a city built to its limits by earlier generations of writers. At the turn of the century, we who live in this city have been doing precious little new development, and that seems cosmetic: a new awning on the AI building, a little sandblasting applied to the sooty bricks of the colony-ship high-rise. Time-traveling paleontologists visit the Silurian rather than the Cretaceous. The post-holocaust survival tale takes place in rural Alaska rather than the continental west.

The third story, James Patrick Kelly's "Feel the Zaz," is set in a near-future Earth, and is one of the few in this sample to deal with mass media and the Internet. It's also one of the few that feels as if it genuinely belongs to the future from the standpoint of 2001. It's about a media production company struggling to expand its market beyond its current demographic of aging boomers. The company's stock-in-trade, however, is nostalgia: virtual representations of dead twentieth-century celebrities. It's difficult for me now not to read "Zaz" as wish fulfillment about sf: if only we can pump enough blood back into the stale tropes from the past, Kelly seems to be arguing, we can rescue sf from oblivion. If only we can sufficiently spruce up our aging sf city, a new population will rush in to party along its now-deserted streets.

But I would argue that in fact we need to let go of our field's equivalents to Judy Garland and Cary Grant and find new stars to celebrate, new ideas to explore. We need to find vehicles that could never have been thought of before now to travel the twenty-first-century Mindscape. The survival and renewal of sf depend on the degree to which we can annex new territory to our city, or tear down and rebuild that city for our own ends, for the new uses of the present age.

Because if the past succeeds in crowding the future out of sf, the entire field will die. By this I do not mean to invoke some academic definitional debate over whether you can still have what we are used to calling "science fiction" without the future. I'm talking about original print science fiction in the inclusive sense: about its increasing unattractiveness to younger generations of readers and its declining relevance to the culture at large—its failure to attract not just the young, but any readers who don't share its current anxieties.

It's not just the fiction that the past has invaded. SF writers and fans seem increasingly gripped by the iron hand of the past. I find it striking that at cons writers and fans are always talking about the history of the field, and the great practitioners of the past. The fact that *Asimov's* begins each issue with Silverberg's column, which is practically dedicated to Golden Age nostalgia, fits in perfectly with the discourse of the field as a whole. Convention panels gripe endlessly about the bad new days and look back fondly toward the good old ones. Convention discussions often devolve into exchanges of trivia about Golden Age writers who have been transmogrified from being merely a part of sf's historical canon into cult figures.

If sf is truly a vital, evolving field, why should readers under thirty know or care who Robert Heinlein is? I think it's sometimes forgotten that *Stranger in a Strange Land,* for example, predates the Vietnam War—and how close and relevant is that for anyone under forty today? Did boomers in the 1960s need to know the canon of Depression-Era blues in order to groove to the Rolling Stones?

The phenomenon of sf nostalgia is particularly odd in comparison with, say, the social sciences. In anthropology—my own field—few people know or care about the history of the discipline. The big annual conferences might have a handful out of hundreds of sessions that are devoted to history. Many graduate programs don't even have a course requirement for history of anthropology. Instead of historical awareness, people stumble over their own feet to jump on every new theoretical bandwagon. This seems very American to me. In the America I grew up with, what's new is always better than what's old. This assumption is annoying and highly regrettable at times, but it is an important component of American creativity.

Too much nostalgia poisons vitality and creativity in any field. But sf should be especially allergic to nostalgia. Science fiction's most important contribution to the culture, it seems to me, is not to predict the future but to imagine it. To help us get our minds around the headlong-into-the-future-without-brakes nature of current times. To ponder how to remain/be/become human amidst the profound technological and cultural change that's under no one's control. Dozois's main character raised that question in the past of his story, but the story itself does not address it.

How to be human is a universal problem in any time and space. It's not the same issue as quarreling with the present. Quarreling with the present is the territory of the Luddites, and William Morris inveighing against industrialization, and the origins of today's pastoral, pseudo-medieval genre fantasies. Quarreling with the present is a hair's-breadth from being *reactionary*. Are we going to use the great speculative toolbox of sf to deimagine the present? Is sf becoming anti-sf?

We can't imagine the future if we can't even look at the present. To connect with a wider, growing, more youthful audience, sf has to grapple with millennial horrors and alienation, with the rootlessness and ferment and absurdity, and, yes, with the millennial fear of the future, in ways other than to say, "I wish things weren't like this. I liked it better in the past." Without a vital link to the ever-changing *Zeitgeist*, sf will become a closed system where recycling subject matter and theme is all that's possible. And science fiction right now seems to be not only losing its connection to *and its interest in* the *Zeitgeist*, but becoming antagonistic to it. *Of course* that brings with it declining relevance to anyone outside the narrowing circle.

~

CHAPTER TWENTY-FOUR

Slipstream

James Patrick Kelly

Canned Worms

Slipstream is the name given by some to a type of writing that crosses the genre boundaries in and out of science fiction and that seems to be growing in popularity, but before we can consider slipstream we have to consider something more basic: genre.

What is genre? Mssrs. Merriam and Webster have this to say: "a category of artistic, musical, or literary composition characterized by a particular style, form, or content." This is, alas, a not very useful definition, especially when applied to SF. For it is possible to imagine stories that have no science fictional content, but are written in a science fictional style or that mimic the forms of science fiction. Slipstream, for example. But SF is all about content, no?

There is a wonderful site created by Turkish fan Neyir Cenk Gökçe, "Definitions of Science Fiction," which offers fifty-two (count 'em!) different and sometimes conflicting attempts to characterize our genre. Here are three pretty good ones:

"SF is a controlled way to think and dream about the future. An integration of the mood and attitude of science (the objective universe) with the fears and hopes that spring from the unconscious. Anything that turns you and your social context, the social you, inside out.

Nightmares and visions, always outlined by the barely possible." Gregory Benford.

"Science Fiction is the branch of literature that deals with the effects of change on people in the real world as it can be projected into the past, the future, or to distant places." James Gunn.

"A science fiction story is a story built around human beings, with a human problem and a human solution, which would not have happened at all without its scientific content." Theodore Sturgeon.

Contracts

Science. Change. The Future. We can all point to reams of SF that address these issues. But then there are many stories that "feel" like SF but probably aren't, under most of the fifty-two definitions. Alternate history is yet another example of fiction that seems related to our genre but doesn't feature SF content.

In thinking about what science fiction might be, it helps to distinguish between the genre as art and the genre as a commercial product. The writer's intentions and those of the publisher are by no means the same. When I sit down to start a new project, I'm not immediately concerned with whether I am going to be writing SF, fantasy, slipstream, mainstream, or whatever. I'm just trying to write a Jim Kelly story. As I shape the piece, however, it often becomes clear what genre I've wandered into. But even if it's not clear, I might nevertheless send the manuscript to Gardner and Sheila to see if they'll publish it in their SF magazine. If they do, does that then decide my story's genre?

Sure.

Well, maybe.

Actually not. Longtime subscribers may recall that *Asimov's Science Fiction* once had a letters column, presided over by the indefatigable Isaac Asimov himself. From time to time irate readers would write to ask what certain stories (some perpetrated by me) were doing in their favorite SF magazine, when said stories had little or no discernible fantastic element. Isaac always rose to the writers' defense and proclaimed his confidence in the judgment of the editors. But I understand why those letters got written. It was because the stories didn't fulfill the genre contract.

That contract is a set of promises that a genre implicitly makes its readers. For example, readers buy magazines with certain expectations. You would be understandably chagrined if *all* the stories in *Asimov's Science Fiction* were about people solving crimes. You want detection, plunk down your $3.99 for *Alfred Hitchcock's Mystery Magazine*. Gardner and Sheila might slip an occasional story in that doesn't strictly adhere to the genre contract, but this is *Asimov's Science Fiction*, by god, and it's SF you're going to get. However, the marketing of *Asimov's* as an SF magazine does not always address the genre intentions of the writers herein.

Another component of our peculiar genre is what Samuel R. Delany has called the *protocols* by which readers interpret context. You read the stories in *Asimov's* differently than you do those in *Hitchcock's*. Impossible things can be commonplaces, moral certitudes can be discredited—the very sentences themselves can take on strange, new meanings. On the most basic level, consider some of the jargon we toss off so blithely. Hive-mind. FTL. Wetware. AI. Nano. Hyperspace. VR. Cyborg.

Namely

In a previous installment I commended a raft of new writers to your attention. One thing that struck me as I took stock of the next generation was how often they practice their craft in the slipstream. Now you should understand that many writers who might arguably fit into this literary movement reject the term *slipstream*. In the *Encyclopedia of Science Fiction*, John Clute refers to it as fabulation. Some writers prefer to call what they do cross-genre or interstitial fiction, while others bristle at the notion that anyone is trying to label them at all. But it may well be too late to stick another name on slipstream, since the critical term has been around for some fourteen years now and people seem to have a general idea of what kind of writing it points at.

It was in July 1989 that Bruce Sterling coined the term in his Cat Scan column in the late great zine *SF Eye*. Here's the big moment: "It is a contemporary kind of writing which has set its face against consensus reality. It is fantastic, surreal sometimes, speculative on occasion, but not rigorously so. It does not aim to provoke a 'sense of wonder' or to systematically extrapolate in the manner of classic science fiction.

Instead, this is a kind of writing that simply makes you feel very strange; the way that living in the late twentieth century makes you feel, if you are a person of certain sensibility. We could call this kind of fiction Novels of Postmodern Sensibility, but that looks pretty bad on a category rack, and requires an acronym besides; so for the sake of convenience and argument, we will call these books 'slipstream.'" While I think Bruce's provisional definition holds up pretty well, most of his inductees into the slipstream club were folks whom we in the genre might actually think of as mainstream, for instance Kathy Acker, Isabel Allende, Martin Amis, Margaret Atwood, and Paul Auster. And those were just Bruce's "A's"!

Our Stream

While I certainly acknowledge that there are many mainstream writers whose work "simply makes you feel very strange," I am going to take a parochial approach here. Why? Well, I've taught Clarion, the science fiction writers' workshop at Michigan State University, six times now. I've also taught at Odyssey, the other six-week genre workshop, held in Manchester, New Hampshire, and Viable Paradise, a one-week intensive that takes place on Martha's Vineyard. I've taken a good hard look at the people who are going to be writing your favorite stories of 2013 and what I've noticed is that more and more of them are modeling themselves after Karen Joy Fowler and Jonathan Lethem as opposed to . . . say, Greg Egan and Bruce Sterling. Don't get me wrong; I admire all four of these writers; I say we should pitch as large a literary tent as we can. But there's something going on here that's worth paying attention to. So for now, I'm more interested in tracking the folks who start out from our tradition in their journey across genres than I am in mainstream writers who stop in to mess with our tropes. And I've invited two of the sharpest minds in science fiction, writer Jeff VanderMeer and critic Rich Horton, along as guides.

So what is slipstream, Rich? "Most commonly defined, I think, as fiction that crosses genre boundaries (lots of people seem to prefer 'cross-genre' as a term). However, I'm not sure that's very satisfying: is *The Caves of Steel* slipstream because it crosses genre boundaries between SF and mystery? So, thinking about it, I decided that to me slipstream stories feel a bit like magical realism. The key is—they are un-explained. 'Real' fantasy or SF has these elements embedded in the background so that they make sense—in slipstream they are just there. In a sense, SF tries to make the strange familiar—by showing SFnal elements in a context that helps us understand them. Slipstream tries to make the familiar strange—by taking a familiar context and disturbing it with SFnal/ fantastical intrusions."

Jeff is uneasy with definitions. "I prefer, like Ellen Datlow, to call it 'cross-genre.' Today, we have literally many dozens of writers in both mainstream and genre who are working from these influences and creating new forms of cross-pollination. The problem with talking about cross-genre is that it's not a single movement—it's a bunch of individual writers pursuing individual visions that tend to simply share some of the same diverse influences. So it's difficult to pin down and say 'this is what it is and what it isn't.' That's what is exciting to me about it—that it is difficult to categorize. In a sense, that means it's a complex, organic creature."

Top Two

Perhaps *the* place to begin looking for slipstream on the Web is *Fantastic Metropolis*. I will admit to being surprised by the quality of the writing FM offers—both fiction and non-fiction—since it's not a paying site. Everything you see here is donated. Clearly some of our best practitioners have decided that this is a site worth supporting, in part because it advocates so eloquently for the importance of taking genre in new directions. There is a wealth of fiction here, some original, but mostly reprints from the likes of China Miéville, Carol Emshwiller, L. Timmel Duchamp, Paul Di Filippo, and Kelly Link, to name but a handful. And as good as the stories are, the critical essays and interviews are equally accomplished, with work from Michael Moorcock, David Langford, James Sallis, and Jeffrey Ford.

Here is new writer Alan DeNiro struggling to define the relationship of cross-genre writing to the established genres in his original essay published in FM, "The Dream of The Unified Field." "The genre's new shape might be less of a centralized state and more of a Hanseatic League, a confederation or constellation of different styles, techniques, and even audiences. This is not quite as scary as it sounds, it's a different but more realistic model for the way the field is already going. The larger magazines will have the central place at the head of the table, but there will be a lot more activity at the side tables—or better yet, in the kitchen amongst the help. There may not be a Next Wave, implying a stable shore, a body of water, and a singular undertow. There might be lots of little waves."

While not explicitly in the slipstream, *Strange Horizons* has published most of the up-and-coming writers who experiment with genre. As editor-in-chief Mary Anne Mohanraj wrote in "Avoiding the Potholes: Adventures in Genre-Crossing," I think at *Strange Horizons*, our editors often choose material that lives in the borderlands between specific and other genres. And while it can be tricky navigating these roads, in the long run, I think that border-crossing enriches literature." While in his wonderful "Where Does Genre Come From?" Senior Fiction Editor Jed Hartman wrote, "By a loose definition of slipstream, probably the majority of the fiction that we at *Strange Horizons* publish could be labeled that way, but calling us a slipstream magazine would probably give the wrong idea. . . . We in the *Strange Horizons* fiction department are definitely interested in slipstream, but we do generally require that stories we publish have a fairly clear speculative element."

Some of the writers to watch who have appeared recently in *SH* are Aynjel Kaye, Benjamin Rosenbaum, Jenn Reese, Jay Lake, Tim Pratt, and Timons Esaias.

Slippage

In her essay "An Introduction to Interstitial Arts," Delia Sherman imagines a continent called Literature filled with countries called Mystery and Romance and Thrillers and Regional fiction. She writes, "Historical fiction, Literary Realism, African-American fiction, and Regional fiction have formed an alliance, Mainstream Literature, which allows them to pass freely over one another's borders." Other countries, including Fantasy and SF, are isolated. She argues that certain writers whose work we might be tempted to call slipstream are, in fact, interstitial, that is, they prowl the borders between these literary countries. This is a useful conceit because it keeps the slipstream from becoming a genre unto itself. Interstitial writers sign no genre contract—or rather, the contract is that rules will be broken and genre expectations thwarted.

You can find Sherman's essay on the website for Interstitial Arts, the site of a group calling themselves Artists Without Borders. Many of these folks have strong ties to SF and might well be considered slipstream writers. However they claim that not only do they cross borders between science fiction and other genres, as slipstream traditionally does, but they cross genres that have nothing to do with SF. Terri Windling lays out the Interstitial Arts agenda: "We're not seeking to create a new category of fiction, but to establish a better way of reading border-crossing texts. In fact, we're not seeking to create a new movement at all, but to recognize a movement that already exists."

That is a telling point. Slipstream may be hot but is it new? Haven't SF artists been crossing boundaries for some time? The theory of interstitial arts and its subset, slipstream, is that these forms inhabit the territory between our genre and various other genres. But the best minds of our genre can't agree on what SF is, and without a coherent definition, how does a writer know when she's crossed a boundary?

Consider Carol Emshwiller who has just, as I write this, won her first Nebula, for her story "Creature." Her work is brilliant and idiosyncratic and much of it is undeniably slipstream. Carol started selling stories in the 1950s. Here's Carol on her writing process: "Whenever I sit down to write too consciously (and I do sometimes) it ends up with no resonance. It looks and feels planned. When I do that it has no . . . what? Underwear? Underside? This is why Kafka is my favorite writer. Kafka's stories aren't about what they're about. I like them for what they don't say. Sometimes Stephen King stories sound like Kafka stories but they're only about the stories you see. They're only about their surface . . . about what happens. Kafka's stories are not about their stories."

How about Jonathan Carroll whose first novel, *The Land of Laughs*, was published twenty-four years ago? He writes: "Over the years my work has been described as Fantasy, horror, SciFi, mainstream, slipstream, Rap, House, and Cha Cha Cha. In the end who cares what it is is as long as it is worth reading? Categories often, sadly, keep people from experiencing things that would enrich their lives."

Then there's Karen Joy Fowler, who has been delighting readers since the mid-eighties. Although her recent story, "What I Didn't See" touched off a firestorm among some of the self-appointed guardians of genre purity, it's of a piece with most of her earlier work. Karen's stories are complex and deep; even her subtext has subtext. As she writes, "I can not reduce my themes to a single sentence. They are not messages but constellations of issues and questions. It takes the whole story. If I could say what I wanted to say in a sentence, I would do so and save us all a lot of time."

It's true, though, that we've seen a flurry of new genre crossings in the last few years. Besides online zines like *FM*, *SH*, and the promising *Singularity*, three print sources stand out: the *Leviathan* anthologies, edited by Jeff VanderMeer and Forrest Aguirre, the *Polyphony* anthologies edited by Deborah Layne and Jay Lake, and *Lady Churchill's Rosebud Wristlet*, edited by Gavin J. Grant.

A frequent contributor to *Lady Churchill's* is Kelly Link, who last year won the Nebula for her novelette "Louise's Ghost." Kelly talks about her struggles with genre: "I'll start out thinking 'I'll write a ghost story' or 'I'll write a detective story.' Then I'll begin and think, 'I can't do this. I can't put this together.' So I'll write around the ghost story, vaguely sort of a ghost story, but not really. I'll know when it's not the story I meant to write, but if people ask me questions like, 'What exactly happened here?' my brain will shut down and I'll say, 'I don't know!'"

Exit

I asked both Jeff and Rich whether slipstream might be the next big thing in our genre, or is it perhaps a successor species to SF? Rich wrote, "I hope not the latter—I don't want to lose 'old-fashioned SF.' But I do think that slipstream techniques can help describe a world that [is?] SF-nal around us—a world that is changing fast enough and that is multicultural enough, that everyday life can seem strange in a 'slipstream' fashion."

Jeff agrees, "I certainly don't want it to replace SF. I love SF, too. The problem, the friction or opposition, comes from some of the more traditional genre gatekeepers either being too slow to incorporate these new kinds of writings or totally resistant to doing so—which makes those of us who practice them put more energy into just opening up new ways to find an audience. This energy is perceived as in opposition to traditional genre, even though it really isn't. My fear, again, is that if this is the wave of the future and genre doesn't allow it access, it will turn somewhere else, like the mainstream, and we'll lose energy that would otherwise help create further mutation within genre."

My take? First a confession. I learned everything I know about writing across genre from these three muses of slipstream: Carol Emshwiller, Karen Joy Fowler, and Kelly Link. I've had the honor of workshopping with all three. I've listened to them react to critiques of their own work and learned from the way they unpack other people's stories, especially my own. And over the years, because I admire what they do, I've tried to do it myself. To hell with the anxiety of influence—I can point to specific stories of mine that are in dialogue with the work of each of these fine writers. The thing is, I know what it feels like when I'm writing science fiction and fantasy; I understand what it takes to build the worlds and complicate the plots. But when I write slipstream, I find myself adopting different strategies, shifting my expectations. I don't understand everything; the writing *feels* different. Strange. I suppose that's not very useful description, but there it is. So on a personal level, I can say that *my* slipstream has its own techniques, its own possibilities and its own rewards. It is close to SF, but it is not the same as it. But as it accretes more talented writers, slipstream is pulling SF in its direction. Where will both of these kinds of writing end up?

In his provocative 1998 essay, "The Squandered Promise of Science Fiction," sometime slipstreamer Jonathan Lethem proposed an alternate history of our genre. "In 1973 Thomas Pynchon's *Gravity's Rainbow* was awarded the Nebula, the highest honor available to the field once known as 'science fiction'—a term now mostly forgotten." In our reality, Arthur C. Clarke won for *Rendezvous with Rama*. Jonathan's essay was a thought experiment about what would have happened if SF merged with the mainstream. He argued that it might be better for all concerned if there were no genres, if Delia Sherman's continent of Literature had no boundaries. In such a literary utopia there would be no SF or slipstream or mainstream. We'd all be just one big happy family.

Yeah, right. That'll happen just about the time that a robot becomes Pope.

Bibliography

Sources

Amis, Kingsley. *New Maps of Hell: A Survey of Science Fiction*. New York: Harcourt, 1960.

Bailey, James O. *Pilgrims Through Space and Time: Trends and Patterns in Scientific and Utopian Fiction*. New York: Argus Books, 1947.

Berman, Judith. "Science Fiction without the Future." *New York Review of Science Fiction*. No. 153 (May 2001): 1, 6–8.

Bretnor, Reginald. *Modern Science Fiction: Its Meaning and Its Future*. New York: Coward-McCann, 1953.

Clareson, Thomas D, ed. *SF: The Other Side of Realism*. Bowling Green, Ohio: Bowling Green U Popular P, 1971.

Delany, S. R. *Starboard Wine: More Notes on the Language of Science Fiction*. Hastings-on-Hudson, N.Y.: Dragon, 1984.

Kelly, James Patrick. "Genre." *Asimov's Science Fiction*. February 2004: 10, 12–14.

———. "Slipstream." *Asimov's Science Fiction* December 2003: 10–13.

Ketterer, David. *New Worlds for Old: The Apocalyptic Imagination, Science Fiction, and American Literature* Bloomington and London: Indiana University Press, 1974.

Knight, Damon F., ed. *In Search of Wonder: Essays on Modern Science Fiction*. Chicago, Ill.: Advent: Publishers, 1956.

Le Guin, U. K., and Susan Wood, eds. *The Language of the Night: Essays on Fantasy and Science Fiction*. New York: Putnam, 1979.

Scholes, Robert. *Structural Fabulation: An Essay on the Fiction of the Future*. Notre Dame: University of Notre Dame Press, 1975.

Suvin, Darko. *Metamorphoses of Science Fiction: On the Poetics and History of a Literary Genre*. New Haven, Conn.: Yale University Press, 1979.

Wolfe, Gary K. *Critical Terms for Science Fiction and Fantasy: A Glossary and Guide to Scholarship*. Westport, Conn.: Greenwood, 1986.

Online Materials

Science Fiction and Fantasy Research Database, ed. by Hal W. Hall. June 2000–. College Station, Tex.: Cushing Library, Texas A&M University. http://library.tamu.edu/cushing/sffrd

Additional Reading

Ahrens, John, and Fred D. Miller, Jr. "Beyond the Green Slime: A Philosophical Prescription for Science Fiction." *Philosophy in Context* 11 (1981): 1–10.

Altov, Genrikh. "Levels of Narrative Ideas: Colors on the SF Palette." *Science-Fiction Studies* 5 (1978):157–63.

Amann, W. F. "The Pseudoscientific Spirit in the Treatment of Literature." *Journal of Higher Education* 24 (1953):195–97.

Angenot, Marc. "The Absent Paradigm: An Introduction to the Semiotics of Science Fiction." *Science-Fiction Studies* 6 (1979):9–19.

Asimov, Isaac. "What Makes Good Science Fiction?" *Asimov on Science Fiction*. Garden City, N.Y.: Doubleday, 1981. pp. 269–74.

Bailey, K. V. "Cyber and Some Other Metaphors." *Vector* (BSFA) No. 159: 10–13. February/March 1991.

Balsamo, Anne. "Signal to Noise: On the Meaning of Cyberpunk Subculture." Wolf, Milton T. and Mallett, Daryl F., eds. *Imaginative Futures: Proceedings of the 1993 Science Fiction Research Association Conference*. San Bernardino, CA: Jacob's Ladder Books, 1995. pp. 217–228.

Barr, Marleen S. "Biological Wishful Thinking: Strange Bedfellows and Phallic Fallacies." Barr, Marleen S., ed. *Alien to Femininity*. Westport, Conn.: Greenwood, 1987. pp. 103–24.

———. *Feminist Fabulation: Space/Postmodern Fiction*. Iowa City, Iowa: University of Iowa Press, 1993.

Barron, Neil. *Anatomy of Wonder: Science Fiction*. New York: Bowker, 1976.

Bartter, Martha A. "Normative Fiction." Davies, Philip J., ed. *Science Fiction, Social Conflict, and War*. Manchester: Manchester University Press, 1990. pp. 169–85.

Baudrillard, Jean. "Simulacres et Science–fiction." Baudrillard, Jean. *Simulacres et Simulation*. Paris: Galilee, 1981. pp. 179–88.

Becker, Allienne R., ed. *Visions of the Fantastic: Selected Essays from the Fifteenth International Conference of the Fantastic in the Arts*. Westport, Conn.: Greenwood, 1996.

Beghtol, Clare. *The Classification of Fiction: The Development of a System Based on Theoretical Principles*. Metuchen, N.J.: Scarecrow, 1994.

Benford, Gregory. "SF, Rhetoric, and Realities." *Science Fiction Review* 1(1990): 32–34.

———. "Style, Substance and Other Illusions." *Australian Science Fiction Review* 4(5) Summer 1989: 15–19.

Benison, Jonathan. "Jean Baudrillard on the Current State of SF." *Foundation* 32 (1984): 25–42.

———. "SF and Postmodern Fiction." Pagetti, Carlo, ed. *Cronache del Futuro: Atti del Convegno su Fantascienze e Immaginario Scientifico nel Romazo Inglese Contemporaneo Torino, Gaggio 1990*. s.l.: Adriatica Editrice, 1992. Vol. 1, pp. 19–34.

Bester, Alfred. "A Diatribe against Science Fiction." Bester, Alfred. *Alfred Bester Redemolished*. New York: Ibooks, 2001. pp. 400–404.

Biederman, Marcia. "Genre Writing: It's Entertaining, But Is It Art?" *Poets and Writers Magazine* 20 January/February 1992: 21–25.

Biggle, Lloyd, Jr. "The Morasses of Academe Revisited." *Analog* 98 September 1978: 146–63.

Birkin, Lawrence. "The Blind Spot in Science Fiction: A Reconsideration." *Extrapolation* 37(2): 139–50.

Blackford, Russell. "Skiffy and Mimesis: or Critics in Costume." *Australian Science Fiction Review* 4 Summer 1989: 26–30.

Bogstad, Janice. "SF as Surrealism: Imagination & the Unconscious." *Janus* No. 12/13 Summer/Autumn 1978: 31–33.

Booker, M. Keith. *Dystopian Literature: A Theory and Research Guide*. Westport, Conn.: Greenwood Press, 1994.

Boon, Kevin A. "Epistemeology of Science Fiction." *Journal of the Fantastic in the Arts* 11(2001): 359–74.

Bourbon, Brett. "Is Science Fiction a Who or a What?" *Extrapolation* 40(1999): 189–99.

Brandis, Evgeni and Vladimir Dmitrevskiy. "The Future, Its Promoters and False Prophets." *Magazine of Fantasy and Science Fiction* 29 October 1965: 62–80.

356 ⌣ Bibliography

—. "In the Land of Science Fiction." *Soviet Literature* 5 (1968): 145–50. 1968.

Briggs, Peter. *The Span of Mainstream and Science Fiction: A Critical Study of a New Literary Genre.* Jefferson, N.C.: McFarland, 2002.

Brin, David. "Waging War with Reality." Slusser, George E. and Rabkin, Eric S., eds. *Styles of Creation: Aesthetic Technique and the Creation of Fictional Worlds.* Athens: University of Georgia Press, 1992. pp. 24–29.

Broderick, Damien. *Reading by Starlight: Postmodern Science Fiction.* London and New York: Routledge, 1995.

—. "Reading SF as a Mega–Text." *New York Review of Science Fiction.* No. 47 July 1992: 1, 8–11.

Brooke–Rose, Christine. *Rhetoric on the Unreal.* Cambridge: Cambridge University Press, 1981.

Buckley, Kathryn. "How Do We Evaluate a Work of Science Fiction." *Foundation* 1 March 1972: 13–20.

Budrys, Algis. "Literatures of Milieux." *Missouri Review* 7(2) 1984: 49–63.

—. *Non–Literary Influences on Science Fiction.* Polk City, IA: Drumm, 1983.

Caillois, R. "Science fiction." *Diogenes* No. 89 Spring 1975: 87–105.

Card, O. S. "Where Is the Cutting Edge of Science Fiction." *Science Fiction Review* 15 November 1986: 8–13.

Cioffi, Frank. *Formula Fiction? An Anatomy of American Science Fiction, 1930–1940.* Westport, Conn.: Greenwood, 1982.

Cogell, E. C. "Hopeful Art or An Artful Hope?: Darko Suvin's Aesthetics for Science Fiction." *Essays in Arts and Sciences* 9(1980): 235–46.

Conklin, Groff. "What Is Good Science Fiction?" *Library Journal* 83(1958): 1256–58.

Conquest, Robert. "Science Fiction and Literature." *The Critical Quarterly* 5(1963): 355–67.

Cooke, Brett. "Sociobiology, Science Fiction and the Future." *Foundation* No. 60 Spring 1994: 42–51.

Cox, Arthur J. "The Anatomy of Science Fiction." *Inside* No. 2: 40–48.

Daniel, Jerry L. "The Taste of the Pineapple: A Basis for Literary Criticism." Edwards, Bruce L., ed. *The Taste of the Pineapple.* Bowling Green, Ohio: Popular Press, 1988. pp. 9–27.

Day, Martin S. "Imaginary vs. Imaginative Literature." *English in Texas* 1 (1965): 75–83.

De Vos, Luk. "Science Fiction as Trivial Literature: Some Methodological Considerations." *Comparative Literature Studies* 14(1977): 4–19.

Del Rey, Lester. *The World of Science Fiction.* New York: Ballantine/Del Rey, 1979.

Delaney, Samuel R. "Critical Methods: Speculative Fiction." Delaney, Samuel R., ed. *Quark: A Quarterly of Speculative Fiction*. New York: Paperback Library, 1970.

Delany, S. R. "Some Reflections on SF Criticism." *Science–Fiction Studies* 8 (1981): 233–39.

———. *The Jewel–Hinged Jaw: Notes on the Language of Science Fiction*. Elizabethtown, New York: Dragon Press, 1977.

———. "Modernism, Postmodernism, Science Fiction." *New York Review of Science Fiction* No. 24 August 1990: 1, 8–9.

Dirda, Michael. "The Genre Ghetto." *Nation* 234 May 22, 1982: 635–36.

Disch, T. M. "Science Fiction vs. Literature: The Prosecution's Case." *Patchin Review* 2 September 1981: 18–23.

———. *The Dreams Our Stuff is Made of: How Science Fiction Conquered the World*. New York: Free Press, 1998.

Dollerup, Cay, ed. *Scandinavian Views on ScienceFiction*. Copenhagen: Department of English, University of Copenhagen, 1978.

Edquist, Andrew. "Science Fiction Should Serve the People." *Cor Serpentis* No. 3 May 1972: 4–10.

Eizykman, Boris. "On Science Fiction." *Science–Fiction Studies* 2(1975): 164–66.

Feeley, Gregory. "The Hole in a Hole: A Theory of Science Fiction and Fantasy." *Bulletin of the Science Fiction and Fantasy Writers of America* No. 157 Spring 2003: 4–10.

Fekete, John. "Stimulations of Simulations: Five Theses on Science Fiction and Marxism." *Science Fiction Studies* 15(1988) 312–24.

Garnett, Rhys/Ellis, R. J. ed. *Science Fiction Roots and Branches: Contemporary Critical Approaches*. New York: St. Martin's, 1990.

Gilmore, Chris. "Why Is Science Fiction?" *Interzone* No. 62 August 1992: 48–49.

Grant, Richard. "Profession of Science Fiction, 41: Git Along, Little Robot." *Foundation* No. 47 Winter 1989/1990: 55–66.

Grant, Richard. "The Exile's Paradigm." *Science Fiction Eye* 2 February 1990: 41–51.

Green, T. M. "What Rough Beast?" *Thrust* 20 Spring/Summer 1984: 20–21, 32.

Griffiths, John. *Three Tomorrows: American, British, and Soviet Science Fiction*. London: Macmillan, 1980.

Gunn, James. "The View From Outside: Form and Content." *Fantasy Newsletter* 5 June 1982: 15–16.

———. "Science Fiction Scholarship Revisited." *Foundation* No. 60 Spring 1994: 5–9.

———. "The Plot-Forms of Science Fiction, Part 1." *Dynamic Science Fiction* 1 October 1953: 44–53.

———. "The Plot-Forms of Science Fiction, Part 2." *Dynamic Science Fiction* 1 January 1954: 37–48.

———. "The Worldview of Science Fiction." *Extrapolation* 36(1995): 91–95.

Handy, William J. "Science, Literature, and Modern Criticism." *Texas Quarterly* 1(1958): 147–153.

Haschak, Paul G. *Utopian/Dystopian Literature: A Bibliography of Literary Criticism* Metuchen, N.J.: Scarecrow, 1994.

Heinlein, Robert A. "Science Fiction: Its Nature, Faults and Virtues." Davenport, B., ed. *Science Fiction Novel*. Chicago: Advent, 1964. pp. 17–63.

Hillegas, M. R. "The Literary Background to Science Fiction." Parrinder, Patrick, ed. *Science Fiction: A Critical Guide*. New York: Longman, 1979. pp. 2–17.

Hollinger, Veronica. "Contemporary Trends in Science Fiction Criticism, 1980–1999." *Science Fiction Studies*. 26(1999): 232–62.

———. *Future Presence: Intersections of Science Fiction and Postmodernism*. Ph.D. Dissertation, Concordia University, 1994.

Hougron, Alexandre. *Science–Fiction et societe*. Paris: Presses Universitaires de France, 2000.

James, Edward. "Before the Novum: The Prehistory of Science Fiction Criticism." Parrinder, Patrick, ed. *Learning From Other Worlds: Estrangement, Cognition and the Politics of Science Fiction and Utopia*. Liverpool: Liverpool University Press, 2000. pp. 19–36.

Jones, Gwyneth. *Deconstructing the Starships: Science, Fiction and Reality*. Liverpool: Liverpool University Press, 1999.

Kaplan, Cora. "Feminist Criticism Twenty Years On." Carr, Helen, ed. *From My Guy to Sci Fi*. London: Pandora, 1989. pp. 15–23.

Keim, Heinrich. *New Wave: die Avantgarde der modernen anglo-amerikanischen Science Fiction*. Meitingen: Corian, 1983.

Keller, Lech. *Stanislaw Lem's Theory of Science Fiction Literature*. Clayton, Vic.: Monash University, Polish Studies, 1997.

Kellett, Edward R., Jr. *Social Criticism in Science Fiction*. Bachelor's Thesis, Massachusetts Institute of Technology, 1966.

Knight, Damon F., ed. *In Search of Wonder: Essays on Modern Science Fiction*. 2nd ed., revised and enlarged. Chicago, Ill.: Advent: Publishers, 1967.

———. *In Search of Wonder: Essays on Modern Science Fiction*. 3rd ed., enlarged and extended. Chicago, Ill.: Advent: Publishers, 1996.

Larson, D. M. "Thematic Structure and Conventions in Science Fiction." *The Spinx: A Magazine of Literature and Society* 4(1981): 38–47.

Lem, Stanislaw. *Microworlds*. San Diego: Harcourt, 1984.

Lerner, Fred. "Modern Science Fiction and Its Reception by the American Literary and Educational Communities, 1926–1970." Ph.D. Dissertation, Columbia, 1981.

Letson, Russell. "Contributions to the Critical Dialogue: As an Academic Sees It." Sanders, Joe, ed. *Science Fiction Fandom*. Westport, Conn.: Greenwood, 1994. pp. 229–34.

Light, Alison. "Putting on the Style: Feminist Criticism in the 1990s." Carr, Helen, ed. *From My Guy to Sci Fi*. London: Pandora, 1989. pp. 24–35.

Lindauer, Paul K. "Science Fiction: Myth–Making for a New Millennium." Master's thesis, Midwestern State University, 1998.

Lowentrout, Peter M. "Metamorphoses of Darko Suvin: Final Synthesis or Dogged Antithesis?" *Foundation* 42 (1988): 37–45.

Maglin, Arthur. "Science fiction in the age of transition." *Radical America* 3.4 (1969): 4–11.

Maitland, Sara. "Futures in Feminist Fiction." Carr, Helen, ed. *From My Guy to Sci Fi*. London: Pandora, 1989. pp. 193–203.

McClintock, M. W. "Some preliminaries to the criticism of science fiction." *Extrapolation* 15(1973): 17–24.

McKnight, Ed. "Theory and Beyond: Reader-Response Theory and Science Fiction." *SFRA Review* No. 247: 13–17. July/August 2000.

Michalson, Karen. "Mapping the Mainstream: Surveying the Boundaries between Fantasy and Realism." *Riverside Quarterly* 8 (1991) [No. 32]: 244–48.

Monleón, José B. *A Specter Is Haunting Europe: A Sociohistorical Approach to the Fantastic*. Princeton: Princeton University Press, 1990.

Moorcock, Michael. *Wizardry and Wild Romance: A Study of Epic Fantasy*. London: Gollancz, 1987.

Moylan, Thomas P. "Science Fiction since 1980: Utopia, Dystopia, Cyberpunk, and Beyond." *Chung Wai Literary Quarterly* 22(12): May 1994.

Ohlin, Peter. "The Dilemma of SF Film Criticism." *Science-Fiction Studies* 1 (1974): 287–90.

Panshin, Alexei. "A New Paradigm (I)." *Fantastic Stories*. 20(6) August 1971: 110–13.

———. "A New paradigm (II)." *Fantastic Stories* 21(1) October 1971: 120–26.

Panshin, Alexei and Cory. *SF in Dimension: A Book of Explorations*. Chicago: Advent, 1976.

———. *The World beyond the Hill: Science Fiction and the Quest for Transcendence*. Los Angeles: Tarcher, 1989.

Parrinder, Patrick. "Revisiting Suvin's Poetics of Science Fiction." Parrinder, Patrick, ed. *Learning From Other Worlds: Estrangement, Cognition and the Politics of Science Fiction and Utopia.* Liverpool: Liverpool University Press, 2000. pp. 36–50.

———. ed. *Learning From Other Worlds: Estrangement, Cognition, and the Politics of Science Fiction and Utopia.* Liverpool: Liverpool University Press, 1999.

Puschmann-Nalenz, Barbara. *Science Fiction and Postmodern Fiction: A Genre Study* New York: Peter Lang, 1992. (Trans. of *Science Fiction und Ihre Grenzberieche.*)

Renault, Gregory. "Science Fiction as Cognitive Estrangement: Darko Suvin and the Marxist Critique of Mass Culture." *Discourse* No. 2 Summer 1980: 112–41.

Roberts, Robin. "It's Still Science Fiction: Strategies of Feminist Science Fiction Criticism." *Extrapolation* 36(1995): 184–97.

Rottensteiner, Franz. "Aesthetic Theory of Science Fiction." *Australian Science Fiction Review* No. 15 April 1968: 3–12.

Ruddick, Nicholas, ed. *State of the Fantastic: Studies in the Theory and Practice of Fantastic Literature and Film.* Westport, Conn.: Greenwood, 1992.

Russ, Joanna. *To Write Like a Woman: Essays in Feminism and Science Fiction.* Bloomington: Indiana University Press, 1995.

———. "Toward an Aesthetic of Science Fiction." *Science-Fiction Studies* 2(1975): 112–19. Also in: Hartwell, David G. and Milton T. Wolf, eds. *Visions of Wonder: The Science Fiction Research Association Anthology.* New York: Tor, 1996.

Samuelson, David N. "Necessary Constraints: Samuel R. Delany on Science Fiction." *Foundation* No. 60 (1994): 21–41. Also in: *Review of Contemporary Fiction* 16(3): 165–169. Fall 1996. Also in: Sallis, James, ed. *Ash of Stars: On the Writings of Samuel R. Delany.* Jackson: University Press of Mississippi, 1996.

Sanders, Joe S. "Queer Theory and Beyond." *SFRA Review* No. 246 May/June 2000: 3–6.

Silvester, Niko. "The More Things Change: Science Fiction Literature and the New Narrative." *Strange Horizons* November 25, 2002.

Singh, Kirpal. "Science Fiction and the Plight of the Literary Critic." *Science Fiction: A Review of Speculative Literature* 4(3): 106–109.

Slusser, George E. and Eric S. Rabkin, ed. *Mindscapes: The Geographies of Imagined Worlds* Carbondale: Southern Illinois University Press, 1989.

Smith, Kevin. Towards a Critical Standard *Vector* October 1980: 4–6.

———. "Towards a Critical Standard (II)." *Vector* December 1980: 15–16.

———. "Towards a Critical Standard (III)." *Vector* Apr. 1981: 4–5, 29.

———. "Toward a Critical Standard (IV)." *Vector* June 1981: 5–7.

Sparks, E. K. "New Wave." Cowart, David, ed. *Twentieth-Century American Science Fiction Writers*. Detroit: Gale, 1981. v. 2, pp. 225–35.

Stockwell, Peter.*The Poetics of Science Fiction*. New York: Longman, 2000.

Stratton, Susan. "Theory and Beyond: Ecocriticism." *SFRA Review* No. 249: 2–6.

Suvin, Darko. "Cognition and estrangement: an approach to SF poetics." *Foundation* 2 (1972): 6–16.

———. "On the Poetics of the Science Fiction Genre." *College English*. 34(1972): 372–82.

———. "The State of the art in science fiction theory: determining and defining the genre." *Science-Fiction Studies*. 6 (1979): 32–45.

———. "With Sober, Estranged Eyes." Parrinder, Patrick, ed. *Learning from Other Worlds: Estrangement, Cognition and the Politics of Science Fiction and Utopia*. Liverpool: Liverpool University Press, 2000.

Taylor, Angus. "The Two Perspectives (Sociological Paradigm of SF vs. Literary Paradigm of SF)." *Seldon's Plan* 6 (1974): 15–17.

Tymn, Marshall. "Science Fiction: A Brief History of Criticism." *American Studies International* 23(1985): 41–66.

Watt, Donald. "New Worlds through Old Tools: Some Traditional Critical Tools for Science Fiction." *Essays in Arts and Sciences* 9 (1980): 131–37.

Westfahl, Gary. "Academic Criticism of Science Fiction: What It Is, What It Should Be." *Monad* No. 2 March 1992: 75–96.

———. "In Research of Wonder: The Future of Science Fiction Criticism." Wolf, Milton T. and Mallett, Daryl F., eds. *Imaginative Futures: Proceedings of the 1993 Science Fiction Research Association Conference*. San Bernardino, Calif.: Jacob's Ladder Books, 1995.

———. "The Undiscovered Country: The Finished and Unfinished Business of Science Fiction Research and Criticism." *Foundation* 60 (1994): 84–94.

Williams, Charles E. "Fantasy Theme Analysis: Theory vs. Practice." *Rhetoric Society Quarterly* 17 (1987): 11–20.

Wilson, Colin. *Existentially Speaking: Essays on the Philosophy of Literature*. San Bernardino, Calif.: Borgo Press, 1989.

Wishnia, Kenneth. "Science Fiction and Magic Realism: Two Openings, Same Space." *Foundation* 59 (1993): 29–41.

Wolfe, G. K. *Known and the Unknown: The Iconography of Science Fiction*. Kent, Ohio: Kent State University Press, 1979.

Index

~

About the Contributors

Brian Aldiss's writings have become more and more diverse, with his autobiography, *Twinkling of an Eye*; his elegy for his wife, *When the Feast Is Finished*; his utopia written with Roger Penrose, *White Mars*; his poetry; his plays; and now, a possible opera based on his forthcoming novel, *Jocasta*, and entitled *Oedipus on Mars*. His surreal novel, *Affairs at Hampden Ferrers,* was published in February 2004, and two other novels are in the pipeline. Aldiss is also known as an actor and lively speaker. He celebrates his eightieth birthday in 2005. Aldiss has written over 350 short stories. For such an independent-minded writer, he enjoys moderate success, critical acclaim, and an affectionate audience in Europe. He has won most of the important awards in the science fiction field and was recently made a Doctor of Literature. He is also Grand Master of Science Fiction. At the IAFA Conference of the Fantastic, Aldiss is Permanent Special Guest.

Judith Berman is an anthropologist and science-fiction writer whose scholarly output has focused on the oral literature, ethnohistory, and history of ethnographic research among the indigenous peoples of the north Pacific coast. Her short fiction has appeared in *Asimov's, Interzone, Realms of Fantasy, Black Gate,* and the anthology *Vision Quests,* and Ace Books is publishing her first novel, *The Bear's Daughter*. "Science Fiction without the Future" received the Science Fiction Research Association's 2002 Pioneer Award for best critical essay. Judith blogs at futurismic.com, and she lives and works in Philadelphia.

Matthew Candelaria is working on his Ph.D. at the University of Kansas. He has published articles on topics ranging from paramagnetic spectroscopy to science fiction to Edmund Spenser's *The Faerie Queen*. He won the 2003 Golden Quill Award from the L. Ron Hubbard's Writers of the Future Contest for his novelette "Trust Is a Child." His current projects are a novel and his dissertation, a study of verminous animals in literature.

Kathryn Cramer (www.kathryncramer.com) is a writer and anthologist, website designer and housewife, presently doing suburban renewal, and co-editing *Year's Best Fantasy*, *Year's Best SF*, and a forthcoming Space Opera anthology. She won a World Fantasy Award for best anthology for *The Architecture of Fear* co-edited with Peter Pautz; she was nominated for a World Fantasy Award for her anthology *Walls of Fear*. She co-edited several anthologies of Christmas and fantasy stories with David G. Hartwell and now does the annual Year's Best Fantasy with him. The huge anthology of hard science fiction, *The Ascent of Wonder*, was also co-edited with David G. Hartwell. She is on the editorial board of *The New York Review of Science Fiction*, of which she is also the art director (and for which she has been nominated for the Hugo Award seven or more times). Her dark fantasy hypertext *In Small and Large Pieces* was published by Eastgate Systems, Inc. She lives in Pleasantville, New York.

Samuel R. Delany was born and raised in Harlem, New York. His first novel, *The Jewels of Aptor* (1962), was published when he was just 19 years of age. His first major award (the Nebula) was won for *Babel-17*, a novel reflecting his interest in semiotics. Delany is considered to be a "high brow" science-fiction author, one of the true intellectuals in the field. In fact, Delany is a professor of English, having served in that position at numerous universities, most recently at Temple University. He has written his memoirs in *The Motion of Light in Water: Sex and Science Fiction Writing in the East Village*, which won the Hugo Award for nonfiction in 1989.

Colin Greenland was born in Dover, Kent, in 1954, and educated at Pembroke College, Oxford. His doctorate thesis on "new wave" science fiction, published in 1983 as *The Entropy Exhibition*, was honored in 1985 with the University of California's Eaton Award for SF Criticism. Since then he has become one of Britain's best-loved authors of science fiction and fantasy. His work has been translated into a dozen languages and won several prizes, including the Arthur C. Clarke Award.

James Gunn, emeritus professor of English at the University of Kansas, has divided his literary career between writing and writing about science fiction, evidenced by his presidency of the Science Fiction Writers of America and of the Science Fiction Research Association. He has published 100 short stories and forty books, including a dozen and a half novels and half a dozen collections, and has edited a dozen anthologies. He has won numerous awards, including the Hugo, the Pilgrim Award, and the Eaton Award. His classic novels *The Listeners* and *The Immortals* have just been reprinted. Next to be published is his new novel *Gift from the Stars*.

David G. Hartwell (www.davidghartwell.com) is a senior editor of Tor/Forge Books. He is the proprietor of Dragon Press, publisher and bookseller, which publishes *The New York Review of Science Fiction*; and the president of David G. Hartwell, Inc., a consulting editorial firm. He is the author of *Age of Wonders* and the editor of many anthologies, including *The Dark Descent*; *Masterpieces of Fantasy and Enchantment*; *The World Treasury of Science Fiction, Northern Stars, The Ascent of Wonder* (co-edited with Kathryn Cramer), and a number of Christmas anthologies, among others. Recently he co-edited his eighth annual paperback volume of *Year's Best SF*, and co-edited the new *Year's Best Fantasy*. John Updike, reviewing *The World Treasury of Science Fiction* in

372 ~ About the Contributors

The New Yorker, characterized him as a "loving expert." Currently he is revising the history of SF, working on four anthologies and attending lots of cons. He has won the Eaton Award, the World Fantasy Award, the Science Fiction Chronicle Poll, and has been nominated for the Hugo Award twenty-eight times to date. He also has theories about fashion in clothing, especially men's neckties. A lot more info is available at his website, always badly in need of updating.

James Patrick Kelly was born in Mineola, New York, in 1951. He is the author of four novels and over fifty stories, in addition to poetry, plays, and essays. He has won two Hugo awards and numerous times been a finalist for the Nebula. He has been a resident of New Hampshire since 1975 and aspires someday to become a native. He currently lives in Nottingham, New Hampshire, with his wife Pamela D. Kelly. He has too many hobbies.

Paul Kincaid is a prolific commentator on science fiction, primarily British, with a number of single-author chapbook studies of British authors such as Keith Roberts and Bob Shaw. His first collection of essays and reviews, *What It Is We Do When We Read Science Fiction*, was published in 2004 by Borgo Press. He is also a writer of fiction, both professional and fanfic. He is an administrator for both the Arthur C. Clarke Award and the GUFF fund.

Ursula K. Le Guin writes in various modes including realistic fiction, science fiction, fantasy, books for children and young adults, screenplays, essays, and poems. As of 2003 she has published nineteen novels, over a hundred short stories (collected in eleven volumes), twelve books for children, two collections of essays, five volumes of poetry, and four of translation. Among the honors her writing has received are a National Book Award, five Hugo Awards, five Nebula Awards, the Howard Vursell Award, the PEN/Malamud Award for Short Fiction, etc.

Barry Malzberg knows a great deal about science fiction, as a reader, writer, editor, and student of the genre. He exploded into science fiction in 1967, under the pseudonym K. M. O'Donnell, and since then he has published around 400 stories, seventy-four novels, and eleven collections of short stories and essays, the majority of which have been in science fiction, but also include some pornographic, mystery, and mainstream works as well. His novel *Beyond Apollo* (1972) won the first John W. Campbell award for the best novel of the year, and he continues to produce fiction and has garnered many Hugo and Nebula Award nominations, despite his semi-retirement only ten years after his first story appeared.

Alexei and Cory Panshin have been writing about the nature of science fiction since the 1960s. Their conceptual history of SF, *The World Beyond the Hill*, received a Hugo Award from the 48th World Science Fiction Convention in 1990. Alexei is also a prize-winning fiction writer, winner of the Nebula Award for his novel, *Rite of Passage*. Their website at http://www.panshin.com includes song lyrics, tales of the Old Space Ranger, the complete text of Alexei's *Heinlein in Dimension*, and an account of the first telling of *Alice's Adventures in Wonderland*.

Robert Scholes is currently a professor at Brown University, where he has taught courses on modernism, modern literature, art, opera, and thought. Though he retired from full-time teaching in 1999, he continues to direct dissertations and theses, and teaches courses and delivers lectures as a visiting professor all around the world. His most recent books are *The Crafty Reader* (2001) and *The Rise and Fall of English* (1998).

Darko Suvin was a professor of English and Comparative Literature at McGill University in Montreal until he retired. He is also an author of *Russian Science Fiction in 1956–1974*, and other works. He serves *FEM-SPEC* as a contributing editor and a noted author. His books include the ground breaking *Metamorphoses of Science Fiction* (1979), *Victorian Science Fiction in the UK: The Discourses of Knowledge and Power* (1983), and *To Brecht and Beyond* (1984). For several years he also edited *Science-Fiction Studies*. He currently resides in Lucca, Italy

Michael Swanwick is a prolific, varied, and successful writer with works ranging from fantasy to hard science fiction. His fiction has been honored with the Hugo, Nebula, Theodore Sturgeon, and World Fantasy Awards, and has been translated and published throughout the world. His novels include *Jack Faust*, *The Iron Dragon's Daughter*, and the Nebula-Award-winning *Stations of the Tide*. Swanwick lives in Philadelphia with his wife, Marianne Porter.

Gary K. Wolfe, professor of humanities and English and past dean of University College at Roosevelt University in Chicago, is the author of six books and hundreds of essays and reviews on topics ranging from popular culture and science fiction to literary research and adult education. Currently he is a contributing editor and reviewer for *Locus* magazine. His most recent book is *Harlan Ellison: The Edge of Forever*, co-authored with Ellen R. Weil. Among the awards that Wolfe has received are the Distinguished Scholarship Award from the International Association for the Fantastic in the Arts, the Pilgrim Award from the Science Fiction Research Association, the Eaton Award for the year's best critical work on science fiction from the Lloyd J. Eaton Conference, and the James Friend Memorial Award for literary criticism from the Friends of Literature.

DATE DUE